D0710667

Making Vancouver*

Making Vancouver explores social relationships in Vancouver from 1863 to 1913. Up to the crash of 1913, the city was a dynamic centre. Rapid growth, easy access to resources, a narrow industrial base, and the influence of ethnicity and race softened the thrust towards class division inherent in capitalism. Vancouver stands apart from many other North American cities of the period in the degree to which it retained elements of its frontier past. Despite its separation into groups ranked by wealth, education, and influence, society remained open and fluid. Shaughnessy Heights lumber barons, Mount Pleasant tradespeople, and East End labourers were all part of a complex society and displayed sharp differences in attitudes and behaviour that cannot all be attributed to class.

If class does not by itself explain the differences, though, what does? Identities reflected a host of influences, of which the economic system was only one. Equally important was European migrants' quest for status, a process of social definition based on mutual regard or prestige that structured relationships in a hierarchical manner from the very outset of settlement on Burrard Inlet. The anglophone majority, whose members considered themselves 'citizens,' were divided from the 'immigrants,' transients, and poor, whom they categorized as 'outsiders,' by a social boundary that is revealed as much more fundamental than the separation of labour from capital.

This work both confirms and challenges our understanding of Vancouver's early history. Class tensions still emerge as a central feature of city life, and racism still divides Vancouverites from one another. But conventional wisdom also gives way to new understanding when status is recognized as an important but overlooked aspect of urban experience.

Robert A.J. McDonald teaches in the Department of History at the University of British Columbia. With Jean Barman, he co-edited *Vancouver Past: Essays in Social History* (UBC Press).

Robert A.J. McDonald

Making Vancouver

Class, Status, and Social Boundaries, 1863–1913

UBC PRESS / VANCOUVER

© UBC Press 1996

All rights reserved. No part of this publication may be reproduced, stored in a retrieval system, or transmitted, in any form or by any means, without prior written permission of the publisher.

Printed in Canada on acid-free paper ∞

ISBN 0-7748-0555-2

Canadian Cataloguing in Publication Data

McDonald, Robert A.J., 1944-
    Making Vancouver

    Includes bibliographical references and index.
    ISBN 0-7748-0555-2

    1. Vancouver (B.C.) – Social conditions. 2. Vancouver (B.C.) – History. 3. Elite (Social sciences) – British Columbia – Vancouver. I. Title.

FC3847.394.M32 1996   971.1′33   C95-911150-6
F1089.5.V22M32 1996

This book has been published with the help of a grant from the Social Science Federation of Canada, using funds provided by the Social Sciences and Humanities Research Council of Canada. Funding has also been provided by the University of British Columbia's K.D. Srivastava Fund.

UBC Press gratefully acknowledges the ongoing support to its publishing program from the Canada Council, the Province of British Columbia Cultural Services Branch, and the Department of Communications of the Government of Canada.

Set in Galliard by George Vaitkunas
Printed and bound in Canada by Friesens
Copy-editor: Camilla Jenkins
Proofreader: Gail Copeland
Indexer: Annette Lorek
Designer: George Vaitkunas

UBC Press
University of British Columbia
6344 Memorial Road
Vancouver, BC V6T 1Z2
(604) 822-3259
Fax: 1-800-668-0821
E-mail: orders@ubcpress.ubc.ca

To my parents

Contents

Maps and Photographs

Acknowledgments

WRITING A BOOK is a solitary enterprise, yet completion is seldom achieved without the support and encouragement of friends, family, and colleagues. A project that has been 'in progress' as long as this one creates especially large debts of gratitude. Acknowledgment of the people who most directly supported my research and writing seems, at best, a barely adequate way to say thank you.

Three individuals deserve special mention. Margaret Prang's helpful suggestions and enduring patience were indispensable to the successful completion of my dissertation. More than anyone else Keith Ralston showed me that regional history did not have to be parochial and that British Columbia offered a field of inquiry both exciting and intellectually nourishing. He has served as a mentor and friend through the life of this project, and could tell more stories about its history than any of us would care to hear. Jean Barman has also given far more support than a friend can reasonably expect, encouraging me to believe that I had something to say, cajoling me to get on with my writing, and reading the many drafts of text that emerged when I did. Conversations with Keith and Jean substantially influenced the organization and argument of this book.

Several other colleagues and friends offered thoughtful and encouraging comments on the manuscript. Alan Tully and Louise Robert read the work in its entirety, and Roderick Barman, Fran Gundry, Irene Howard, Tina Loo, Elizabeth Mancke, Tim Stanley, and Jim Winter did so in part. Tina Loo provided references to several important theoretical works and tried to make a middle-aged empiricist more theoretically informed. Readers for the Social Science Federation presented thorough and helpful evaluations. Jocelyn Smith edited the entire work, smoothing away the rough edges of my prose. Vicky McAuley typed a grant application that saved a project.

Some debts stretch further back into the past. Such is the case with helpful comments on my earlier publications by Norbert MacDonald, Jeremy Mouat, Logan Hovis, Sharon Meen, Jill Wade, and Peter Ward. Colleagues and staff in the UBC Department of History supported the project with practical help and unstinting encouragement. Sharon Meen 'drove home' to me the advantages of writing in the active rather than passive voice.

Over the years I have received the generous assistance of many other individuals and organizations. Anne Yandle, George Brandak, and Frances Woodward at UBC's Special Collections Division provided a wonderful environment for the study of British Columbia history. Sue Baptie and the staff at the City of Vancouver Archives generously offered their professional assistance and a place to work at 'the back table.' In the early stages of my research I spent many months in Victoria reading newspapers in the basement of the Legislative Library and examining files piled high in the far corner of the Registrar of Companies Office. The British Columbia Archives and Records Service (then the Provincial Archives) similarly offered helpful assistance on many occasions. Brenda Dickau, Elizabeth Lees, Towser Jones, and Karen Peplow lightened the burden of research by exploring the lives of Vancouver's social elite, recording and coding the 1881 and 1891 censuses, and unravelling the mysteries of the Matthews Collection. Virginia Green of the UBC Arts Computing Centre always treated my uninformed questions with tolerance and respect; I appreciate her assistance very much. Jeremy Wilson provided similar guidance back in the days when computing meant punch cards and prehistoric machines. Eric Leinberger crafted the maps that grace this study, and George Vaitkunas created its attractive design. Jean Wilson of UBC Press provided wise counsel in guiding the manuscript through review, and Camilla Jenkins edited the book with impressive and sometimes daunting rigour. I am indebted as well to the Social Sciences and Humanities Research Council of Canada for their generous support of my work.

Chapter 1 of this text is based on an earlier article, 'Lumber Society on the Industrial Frontier: Burrard Inlet, 1863-1886,' which appeared in *Labour/Le Travail* 33 (Spring 1994):69-96.

Finally, to my many friends and family I say thank you for your support and your faith that the 'book' would, eventually, be finished. I dedicate it to my parents Elsie and Lorne McDonald, who, regretfully, did not live to see the happy day.

Introduction

FOR CENTURIES the waters of Burrard Inlet on the north-west coast of North America and the shores surrounding it were the territory of Native people. Gulf of Georgia Salish people came in the early summer each year – Squamish from the north and Musqueam from the south – to harvest the bounty of resources that Burrard Inlet and False Creek offered. Europeans first appeared in 1792, but Burrard Inlet's isolated location kept White traders at bay for another sixty years. The Fraser River to the south provided a much more useful passageway into the continental interior.

Borrowed time came to an end in the late 1850s. A rush for gold brought thousands of European men to the alluvial sands of the Fraser canyon. More Europeans in the region meant greater demand for food and greater interest in new sources of natural wealth, such as timber. Both increased the presence of Europeans on Burrard Inlet. Majestic stands of Douglas firs proved especially enticing to White intruders, who in 1863 opened a water driven sawmill on the Inlet's north shore. A Native labour force settled permanently in the area and a second mill started production, this time on the south side. Burrard Inlet had entered the industrial age. The high-pitched scream of metal cutting wood ricocheted across the Inlet as an ethnically diverse labour force of loggers, millhands, longshoremen, hotelkeepers, and shop owners went about the business of extracting wealth from the dense rainforest of British Columbia's lower coast.

Twenty years of gradual change ended in the mid-1880s when the Canadian Pacific Railway announced plans to terminate its transcontinental line at Coal Harbour, near the entrance to Burrard Inlet. The area's population exploded, transforming the village of Granville into the city of

Vancouver. By the turn of the century Vancouver had become British Columbia's largest urban centre, and within another decade the fourth largest in Canada. The traditional influence of sawmilling persisted, and lumber remained a principal source of wealth for the city's expanding business community. But Vancouver had become something more, a metropolitan centre that provided trade, shipping, and management services to coastal and inland parts of the province. Sophistication also permeated social life. A vast array of voluntary associations emerged, many emulating the practices of Vancouver's big city counterparts in London, New York, Chicago, Montreal, and other eastern centres. With Aboriginal people now a negligible presence and an Asian minority cast to the social and geographic margins, Vancouver had become by the First World War an English-speaking European city much like Toronto and Seattle, far different from Burrard Inlet's culturally and racially diverse lumber communities of days gone by.

Yet Vancouver stands apart from many other North American cities of the period in the degree to which it retained elements of its 'frontier' past. Despite its separation into groups ranked by wealth, education, and influence – a process of social differentiation that began in the 1870s but accelerated with the coming of the railway – Vancouver society remained open and fluid. Hugh Keenleyside, a child of those years, described the city as 'effervescent with optimism.'[1] During the several years leading up to 1913, easy access to resources and cheap capital created in British Columbia an economic boom that depended heavily upon speculation in urban and rural land, mineral claims, and timber limits. As a consequence of directing this investment, Vancouver remained a boom town. Its conservative bankers, railway managers, and lawyers from well-established eastern families were offset by the seemingly endless number of timber brokers, real estate agents, and job-seeking construction workers who crowded into the city. In other words, despite a population of more than 150,000 people by 1913, Vancouver and its burgeoning suburbs retained the qualities of a young community, a place where population and institutions had not yet stabilized and expectations of material betterment remained high.

My interest in exploring the urbanization of Burrard Inlet was stimulated in the early 1970s by exciting new work in urban history. Placing the city at the centre of historical inquiry, urban history promised to lead studies of the past away from their traditional emphasis on political elites and national themes, and to focus instead on average people in local settings. The most original work in the field harnessed the information-processing capacity of the computer to the task of discerning the social and economic characteristics of whole communities.[2] Census tracts, church records, tax assessment rolls, and street directories provided important sources of information that, with the aid of new research techniques, promised to bring to light the lives of ordinary people.

Inspired by the promise of urban history, I set out to explore the social impact of rapid population growth in Vancouver. Unfortunately, the rich variety of quantifiable sources available to Michael Katz and others who examined mid-nineteenth-century communities were not to be found for turn-of-the-century Vancouver. Only a fraction of the tax rolls for the period were available; the city's religious pluralism and the spotty nature of church records did not provide the documentary foundation for a systematic analysis of Vancouver's social structure; and the nominal census for the years 1881, 1891, and 1901 became accessible to researchers only much later, during the life of the project.[3] To overcome these limitations, I created my own database of economic and social information on leading businessmen[4] in Vancouver. I then explored this database in a doctoral dissertation for the period before the First World War.[5] My goal was to apply to Vancouver – of necessity in a sharply truncated form – the structural approach to historical inquiry that characterized the 'new urban history.'

The results were not entirely satisfactory. Analysis of one elite group did not itself provide much insight into the process by which the many groups that constituted Vancouver society related to one another as part of the urban whole. More significantly, by the late 1970s critics had begun to question the new history's exaggerated emphasis on abstract economic and social structures and to call for greater attention to the human side of urban life. As Michael Frisch suggested in reference to the United States, American scholarship was falling short precisely where European literature was strong: 'in finding an analytic way to discuss individual and group agency; in relating structural analysis to consciousness; in exploring class and other collective experience as central dimensions of social life and change; [and] in understanding culture ... in terms of political and economic processes.'[6] Canadian urban history was equally vulnerable to such criticism. At the same time, my own thinking about what I felt to be significant in the transformation of Vancouver from 'milltown to metropolis' had become clearer: the relationship between different parts of a society to one another, entailing elements of both cohesion and conflict, must be central to any social history of urbanization.[7] Yet this broader picture of social organization was often missing from the new literature on North American cities.[8]

Regional perspectives also influenced my approach. Historians and sociologists have tended to see class or race as the principal sources of organization among British Columbia's non-Aboriginal people. Labour historians argued for some time that British Columbia was different from other Canadian provinces, its working people historically more militant and radical than their counterparts to the east. In the early 1970s Martin Robin, a political scientist, broadened the scope of this thesis in a two-volume survey of British Columbia's political development. Throughout its history, Robin wrote, British Columbia had experienced high levels of class polarization. In a region dominated by resource-extractive industries, the need for large pools of both capital and wage labour in the forest, fishing, and mining industries and the relatively limited significance of family farms primarily determined the structure of social organization and politics; heavily capitalized corporations and a heavily unionized labour force resulted. This made economic function a powerful source of social and political identity in 'the company province.' Peter Ward subsequently challenged the notion that class provided the frame around which British Columbia society had been constructed, arguing that a closer examination of the province's social structure would show instead that the 'boundaries separating one race from another have been much more rigid and less porous than any historical division based upon consciousness of class.'[9] Nonetheless, histories of labour relations, industrial communities, and racism continue to be written from a Marxist perspective, with interpretations that place class at the centre of their analyses becoming more sophisticated and nuanced.[10]

The problem with the 'class versus race' approach to understanding the structure of British Columbia society is that it emphasizes one interpretive perspective at the expense of the other. Recent work on the subject of social boundaries, especially by feminist theorists, underlines the need for historians to move away from single-category forms of social analysis and to build into their research strategies the capacity to explore complexity. In *The Gender of Breadwinners* Joy Parr calls for categories of analysis that are flexible enough to reveal the 'wholeness of consciousness and experience,' and urges Canadian historians to admit the possibility that 'social identities are simultaneously formed from a multiplicity of elements.'[11] David Cannadine has made a similar case for Britain, urging British historians to explore more fully 'the variety of associations in people's lives,' a variety, he argues, that 'gave rise to many fluctuating and sometimes contradictory senses of identity and patterns of behaviour.'[12] Marianna Valverde's examination of the movement for moral reform in English Canada in the late nineteenth and early twentieth centuries emphasizes the multidimensional nature of discourses on moral purity; 'race, gender, and sexuality are best understood not as secondary, adjectival features of class subjects,' she concludes, 'but rather as relatively autonomous categories that can be constructed and experienced as more basic than class.'[13] Carol Smart, a feminist legal theorist, writes that above all, we must question 'the master theory approach' that attempts 'to account for everything in relation to one mode of explanation.'[14]

Collectively these observations suggest that the most important question is not whether class divided Vancouver society more profoundly than race, but rather how best to think about social relationships and social boundaries in the first place. To explore what class or race meant to the people of Vancouver requires a structure of analysis that places these single forms of identity within the context of others, and that moves away from the 'master theory approach' to historical inquiry.

To explore analytically the 'contested nature' of identities in early Vancouver, I chose to examine the impact of urbanization on relationships of class and status. Given British Columbia's historiographical emphasis on class, I determined first to test for Vancouver – the province's central place and largest city – the prevailing wisdom that people's lives were structured significantly, and perhaps primarily, by capitalist relations of production.

In defining class I drew on both Marxist and Weberian traditions of analysis. From the former I took the notion that capitalism inherently divides society between those who own the means of production and those who do not, and thus have to sell their labour. Wage labour, sold as a commodity in the marketplace, characterizes the system. Such a model reflects in theory the inherent tendency of industrial societies to divide into two fundamental groups. But few Marxists would agree that such a simple two-class model describes the complexity of class relations as they exist in practice. Consequently, the following study adopts a three-class model. The upper class is defined as those individuals and families who owned the means of production (such as land and capital), or whose interests, aspirations, and skills (including top managers and some professionals) led them to identify with the owners and serve as their agents. Small businessmen, lower-level managers, and professionals not closely tied to the upper class are identified as the middle class. Among its members were real estate agents, contractors, commercial travellers, shopkeepers, school teachers, and clergymen. People who worked for wages, whether white-collar office employees and store clerks or blue-collar machinists and street labourers, are defined as the lower, or working, class.[15]

These classes were far from homogeneous, however. Each is divided internally by what German sociologist Max Weber called 'market situation.' Weber argued that aggregates of individuals who shared a similar capacity to 'dispose of goods or skills for the sake of income' constituted a class.[16] Critics have correctly noted that as a basis for understanding the class system, this theory is deeply flawed, suggesting as it does the possibility of an endless number of market-oriented classes and undervaluing the relationship of classes to the structure of the economy.[17] For this study, classes are therefore defined in structural rather than market terms, as noted above. But Weber's analysis does underline the fact that differential possession of income, job authority, and education could divide people from one another within classes. These differences were reinforced, according to Weberian theory, by the inclination of groups sharing a similar market situation to maximize rewards for themselves 'by restricting access to resources and opportunities to a limited circle of eligibles.'[18] Ethnicity, race, skill, and gender were possible sources of eligibility within circles of privilege. This blending of Marxist and Weberian approaches to defining class reflects a trend among analysts to see the two not as rival models of social organization – Marx being 'especially concerned with power and ... conflict,' Weber with 'values and lifestyle' – but as complementary ways of understanding society.[19]

Writing a half-century after Karl Marx, Weber accepted Marx's notion of the inherently conflictual nature of relations between capital and labour in modern, industrial societies. Yet he rejected Marx's theory of history, which predicted fundamental social change when one mode of production gave way to another. He also challenged the Marxist view that class was 'the single most important division around which social groups organize and contend for political power.'[20] As American sociologist Val Burris recently observed, Weber believed that 'the importance of class divisions is historically variable and contingent. Class relations coexist with other forms of oppression and other bases of association that are independent of class and potentially no less important for the organization of particular societies or the transition between types of societies.'[21] Given that capitalist societies in the industrial era were intrinsically class societies,[22] the questions of what class meant to people in their everyday experience and how class identities related to other identities are open to historical inquiry.

While accepting the importance of class identities, Weber emphasized forms of group structure such as prestige, religion, ethnicity, and family that originated outside the economic order.[23] Crucial to all was the notion of status. As interpreted by American sociologist Seymour Martin Lipset, Weber took the concept of 'status' to mean 'the positive or negative estimation of honour, or prestige, received by individuals or positions. Thus it involves the felt perceptions of people. Those in a similar status position tend to see themselves as located in a comparable position on the social hierarchy.'[24] Claims to social esteem are founded upon lifestyle, formal education, heredity, or occupation. E. Digby Baltzell, whose book *Philadelphia Gentlemen* is a classic study of an American status group, argues that people in status groups 'treat each other as social equals, encouraging the intermarriage of their children, joining the same clubs and associations, and participating together in such formal activities as visiting, dances, dinners, and receptions.'[25] Typically, social discrimination also characterizes circles of social equals, with insiders defining themselves through the rejection of outsiders.[26] Ethnic associations are excellent examples of status at work, linking people who share a common cultural identity while excluding others who do not.[27] The construction of racial categories that define in moral terms the physical characteristics of people also exemplifies what Weberians refer to as social, or 'exclusionary,' closure: 'the attempt by one group to secure for itself a privileged position at the expense of some other group through a process of subordination.'[28] The concept of status in this text is drawn from the work of Weber, and from scholars influenced by him.

A comment by one of Canada's leading social critics, James S. Woodsworth, hints at the importance of status as a source of social identity in early Vancouver. After working on city docks as a longshoreman in the winter of 1918-19, Woodsworth was struck by the powerful thrust among

Vancouver people to develop social hierarchies. 'So much of our time seems to be spent in distinguishing ourselves from our brethren,' he lamented. 'Wealth, social position, academic titles, dress – all are used to set one above [the other].'[29] For a socialist who believed in the ideal of social equality, this tendency for people to construct identities based on hierarchical relationships was troubling. Woodsworth was pointing not to class in the Marxist sense but to a more subtle and dynamic form of ranking to which sociologists have given the name social status.

One last point about method should be noted. In lieu of more comprehensive sources of data on the city's social structure, I chose to create collective biographies of four leadership groups: top businessmen, families who defined themselves as social leaders (or 'Society'), civic politicians, and activists in the Vancouver Trades and Labor Council (VTLC). These I employ as a technique for understanding the process of social organization. The first group, leading businessmen, was identified and researched at the initial stage of the project. I studied leading businessmen for two different periods (1890-3 and 1910-13) and sorted each group internally into 'leaders' and 'subleaders.'[30] I later added the other three groups to facilitate my exploration of the relationship between class and status. This relationship occurred as follows. Leading businessmen were part of, but not the whole of, the upper class. Society members belonged to both the upper and the middle class but stood at the top of the status system. Civic politicians resided in the middle of both class and status hierarchies. VTLC executive members belonged to the working class but were also of 'middling' status. These biographies of various groups of leaders are conceptualized not as substitutes for, but as aids in the study of, Vancouver's class and status structures. In a manner synonymous with the concept of 'leaders,' the word 'elite' also appears occasionally to refer to groups of people who held positions 'at the summits of key social structures.'[31]

The language I employ when describing occupational groups is often gender specific. This is deliberate. In the period being studied, leading entrepreneurs, top managers, skilled artisans, and coastal fishers were almost always men, and the words I use to describe them – businessmen, tradesmen, fishermen – are intended to convey the gendered nature of their work. When I am discussing occupations that included women as well as men, or when I am referring to people in a general rather than in an historical sense, I have tried to employ language that is inclusive.

Finally, while informed by theoretical influences, this book takes as its guiding premise the notion that 'groups and boundaries are made and unmade in history, not in theory,' and that only through concrete analyses of people's lived experiences can the contingent, contested, and changing nature of identities in times past be uncovered.[32] It is organized both chronologically and thematically. It starts with the early years when settlement on Burrard Inlet centred around two lumber mills, and explores periods of elite dominance of city institutions and then of growing social and political conflict following the arrival of the railway. It examines the heightening of class tensions at the turn of the century, charts economic growth during the boom years before the war, and concludes with three chapters on the tripartite status hierarchy that emerged in concert with that of class. It ends in 1913, when depression inaugurated a quarter-century of uncertain urban growth and the hardening of class boundaries into more sharply etched lines of demarcation.

The study both confirms and challenges our understanding of Vancouver's early history. Class tensions still emerge as a central feature of city life, and racism still divides Vancouverites from one another. But conventional wisdom also gives way to new understanding when status is recognized as an important but overlooked aspect of urban experience. Canadian historians who specialize in the study of class relations tend to focus on the lives of wage-earning people, to the exclusion of the middle and upper classes. This examination of the whole of Vancouver society suggests, however, that class identities were most keenly felt at the summit of the social structure, where social status reinforced economic position to create a coherent, powerful, and self-conscious upper class. By contrast, the identities of middle- and working-class residents were more complex. Vancouverites who, by virtue of their relationship to the economic structure, belonged to different classes also formed a broad 'middling' group that thought of itself as respectable. In other words, social status and class identities coincided less fully across the broad middle of Vancouver society than they did at the top.

Three factors are crucial in explaining why Vancouver's middle class and upper working class formed a social *status* group – here termed 'middling' – that crossed class lines: the city's stage of development (relatively new), its economic conditions (generally prosperous, at times to the point of excess), and its ethnic identity (the upper, middle, and working classes

were all primarily of British birth or background, thus constituting a dominant ethnic group). Especially during the prewar boom, high wages, low
land costs, and the widespread optimism of the age made status mobility
seem possible to many Vancouverites. A scramble for the symbols of social
status ensued. This condition temporarily undermined awareness of class
interests and gave greater meaning to aspirations and experiences that
'respectable' people of the middle and working classes shared.

An exploration of status relationships is especially revealing when
analysis shifts from the upper and middle reaches of the social structure to
people at the bottom. Here status analysis retrieves from obscurity the
manner in which Vancouver's British majority, regardless of class, successfully defined themselves as respectable citizens[33] and the single men, the
'immigrants,' and the poor as not respectable, as non-citizens, as 'outsiders.'
This approach leaves unexplored the outsiders' sense of themselves but
tells much about the structure of dominance and meaning of marginality
for the city as a whole. In particular, an exploration of Vancouver's status
hierarchy suggests that the division between citizens and non-citizens constituted a boundary more definitive than the one separating capital from
labour and more complicated than the one dividing Asians from Whites.

Making
Vancouver

Crowded between Forest and Shore

From the mid- to late nineteenth century, the small population of settlers in British Columbia formed isolated and discrete communities. A number of factors made local distinctiveness the outstanding characteristic of community life on British Columbia's settlement frontier. Among them were the character of the several resource-extractive economies upon which society was founded; ethnic diversity, ranging from the prevailing Britishness of society at the region's political and administrative centre in Victoria to the social mixing of Aboriginal and European peoples on the resource periphery; the transient and disproportionately masculine nature of populations in non-agricultural areas of settlement; and the generally new and incomplete quality of institutional life outside of the region's two principal urban centres, Victoria and New Westminster.

The future city of Vancouver would emerge from one such local society, the settlements that congealed around two sawmills on Burrard Inlet over a twenty-year period from the mid-1860s to mid-1880s. What little has been written about the social organization of industrial capitalism along North America's northwest coast has focused on coal mining and, to a lesser extent, salmon canning; the social history of lumbering, by contrast, has not been much told by British Columbia historians.[1]

This chapter argues that lumber society on Burrard Inlet is best understood as the product of two forces, capitalism and the frontier,[2] which intersected in ways particular to this industry (logging and sawmilling), to this place (Burrard Inlet), and to this time (the early stage of industrial capitalism). Although settlement clustered around a single industry, the power of capital, expressed through policies of managerial paternalism, was sharply curtailed by the ethnically complex, relatively transient, geographically isolated, and generally unsettled nature of lumber society. The class tensions generated by industrialism were mediated by race, ethnicity, gender, and status. A complex pattern of identities resulted.

BURRARD INLET TODAY anchors a vast stretch of urban space along British Columbia's lower coast, but to Europeans in the nineteenth century – until the 1880s, at least – the Inlet was isolated. Travelling to Burrard Inlet from New Westminster, the closest urban centre, entailed a journey of nine miles overland through an 'almost impenetrable forest' or a voyage of thirty miles by water from the Fraser River to Burrard Inlet around Point Grey.[3] The Fraser was the main route from the capital at Victoria into the interior; Burrard Inlet, by contrast, was a dead end for European travellers. After Spanish and English explorers entered area waters in the early 1790s, few other outsiders came until the late 1850s, when the rush for gold on the upper Fraser heralded a permanent European presence.

Gold seekers camped briefly on English Bay, and elk that inhabited swampy land between Burrard Inlet and the Fraser River were slaughtered to feed hungry miners. In 1859 Captain George Henry Richards, commanding the HMS *Plumper*, surveyed Burrard Inlet, and in 1862 the coal he had discovered near Coal Harbour, just beyond the Inlet's entrance, attracted the first White settlers to the area. Europeans soon began to pre-empt land, and in early 1863 Oblate missionaries from New Westminster visited Salish communities on Burrard Inlet and English Bay. A more permanent Roman Catholic presence on the Inlet followed with the erection in 1866 of a mission chapel at Ustlawn (now St. Paul's Mission) on the north shore. Methodist missionaries arrived in 1864.[4]

The Burrard Inlet to which Europeans came in the 1860s was not empty. Salish-speaking Natives had harvested abundant fish and game for many hundreds, and perhaps thousands, of years. The group that eventually settled in the Inlet was the Squamish, one of the clusters of Gulf of Georgia Salish people whose original home centred on the Squamish River at the head of Howe Sound. Squamish territory extended from above the Sound southward along its shores into English Bay and Burrard Inlet. Another Salish group, the Musqueam, lived further south, near the mouth of the Fraser River.

Extensive middens at Whoi-Whoi, just inside the First Narrows entrance to Burrard Inlet near what is now Lumberman's Arch in Stanley Park, indicate that a significant number of Native people, probably Squamish, had used this site for at least 500 years. An even larger midden at Marpole, on the south slope of Point Grey in what is now Vancouver, indicates the presence of Musqueam extending back 2,000 years. Both the Musqueam and Squamish claimed the territories around English Bay, False Creek, and Burrard Inlet to be part of the social and economic space in which they fished, hunted, and lived. Both were correct, though only the Squamish could be found there during the period of European settlement.[5] Ethnographic and historical evidence suggests that the Squamish people traditionally migrated to Burrard Inlet and False Creek for food gathering in early summer and abandoned the area during the salmon runs of August and during the winter. As Cole Harris recently observed, in coming to Burrard Inlet the Squamish were not so much entering the territory of another people, the Musqueam, as 'moving within webs of social and economic relations that connected different individuals and people to each other and to each other's places.'[6]

Seasonal migration gave way to permanent settlement when the Inlet's two sawmills began employing the Squamish as labourers in the mid-1860s.[7] By 1881, more than 500 Squamish lived at or near Burrard Inlet, with 300 Musqueam further south. The area contained several settlements, occupied mainly by Squamish speakers: the rancherie, a collection of Native people immediately east of Hastings Mill on the south shore; Snauq on False Creek; Whoi-Whoi in Stanley Park; Homulcheson at the mouth of Capilano Creek across the First Narrows from Whoi-Whoi; the Mission Reserve at Ustlawn farther east along the north shore, one and a half miles before Moodyville; and the Seymour Creek village, still farther up the channel (see Map 1.1).[8]

The desire of Europeans to profit from Burrard Inlet's immense firs

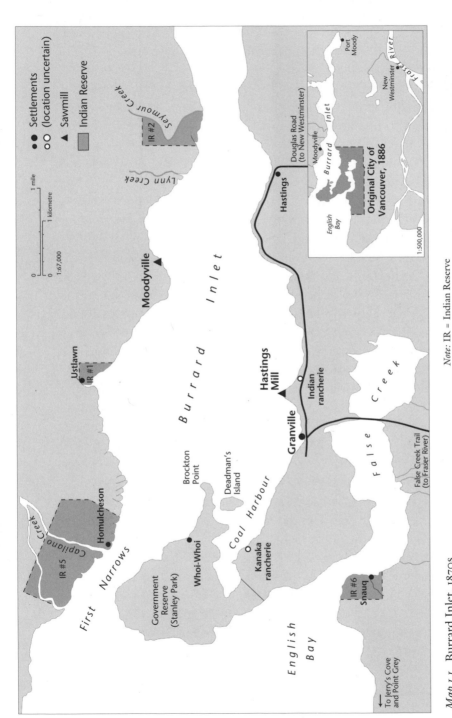

Settlements
- ● Settlements
- ○○ (location uncertain)
- ▲ Sawmill
- ▨ Indian Reserve

1 mile
1 kilometre
0
1:67,000

Seymour Creek

IR #2

Lynn Creek

Moodyville ▲

Burrard   Inlet

Ustlawn
IR #1 ○

Hastings ●

Douglas Road
(to New Westminster)

Hastings
Mill ▲
Granville ●
○ Indian rancherie

False   Creek

Brockton
Point

Deadman's
Island

Coal Harbour

Whoi-Whoi ●

Kanaka ○
rancherie

Homulcheson ●
IR #5

Capilano Creek

First   Narrows

Government
Reserve
(Stanley Park)

IR #6
Snauq ▨

English
Bay

False Creek Trail
(to Fraser River)

→ To Jerry's Cove
and Point Grey

Original City of Vancouver, 1886

Port Moody ●

Fraser River

New
Westminster ●

Moodyville ●

Burrard Inlet

English
Bay

1:500,000

Map 1.1 Burrard Inlet, 1870s

Note: IR = Indian Reserve

Source: Compiled from CVA, Major J.S. Matthews Collection photographs, Map
P.21 N.32 (base map), Map P.3 N.11, Map P.10 N.8, Map P.11 N.7, and Map P.23 N.3.
Spelling of Native names drawn from evidence in CVA, Matthews Collection, as
revealed in Map P.10 N.8.

and cedars upset the balance that had evolved over many years between Native people and the bountiful environment. Sawmilling in this 'lumberman's paradise' began in 1863, when two New Westminster businessmen erected a small water-powered mill on the Inlet's north shore. It became permanent at the end of 1864 when a party of entrepreneurs from New Westminster enriched by the Fraser River gold rush, assumed control. The key member of this group was an American from Maine named Sewell ('Sue') Moody. Buoyed by the injection of new capital from two Fraser Canyon stagecoach operators (William Dietz and Hugh Nelson) and from his agent in San Francisco (Andrew Welch), Moody quickly emerged as the largest lumber manufacturer in British Columbia.[9]

Moody met almost immediate competition from English capital. Captain Edward Stamp, a former English sea captain, had sailed to the northwest coast in 1857 to collect spars in Puget Sound. Four years later, he established a large sawmill at the head of the Alberni Canal on Vancouver Island. The failure of this venture did not deter him. In 1865 he formed a company in England, backed by capital of $100,000, to produce lumber in British Columbia. Stamp also secured from the colonial government of British Columbia the right to purchase or lease 16,000 acres of timber on the lower coast, and selected a mill site on a point of land along Burrard Inlet's south shore. Delayed by the failure of crucial machinery parts to arrive from England, Stamp did not begin cutting lumber for export until June 1867. After managing the firm for less than two years he retired, and shortly thereafter his company went into liquidation in England. The mill closed for a period in 1870 but opened again in August after being purchased by Dickson, DeWolf and Company of San Francisco. Known at first as Stamp's Mill, it now became the Hastings Sawmill Company, or Hastings Mill.[10]

As the reorganization of Stamp's mill attests, the forces that brought industrial capitalism to Burrard Inlet were distinctly coastal, with financial ties to San Francisco and London. Sawmilling originated along the southern coast in the 1820s. Early mills were usually small and geared to local markets, a pattern evident from California north to Oregon, Vancouver Island, and the Fraser River. But market forces around the Pacific soon generated more capital-intensive enterprises, of which the steam-powered sawmills constructed on Puget Sound during the 1850s by two lumbermen from Maine, Andrew Jackson Pope and Captain William C. Talbot, are an excellent example. After mid-century, west coast production of lumber grew rapidly to exploit a series of new market opportunities created by gold rushes in California and in the Australian colonies of New South Wales and Victoria, by sharply increased sugar production in Hawaii, by dramatic economic growth in Chile, and by increases in demand from Peru, Mexico, Tahiti, and China. At the centre of the expanding industry was San Francisco, an important market itself but also the location of regional entrepreneurship, capital, and trade.

Burrard Inlet's two sawmills were products of these influences. They were closely tied to San Francisco, large compared to the earliest BC mills, and oriented to export markets around the Pacific. Indeed, for twenty years after 1865, Burrard Inlet was the only important lumber exporting centre in the province. Over sixty vessels loaded there in the peak year of 1882. Sewell Moody in particular looked south for buyers, machinery, and supplies. He lost his life just beyond Cape Flattery when, during the night of 4 November 1875, the small ship on which he was sailing collided with another. Moody, who travelled constantly, had been on his way to San Francisco to market Burrard Inlet lumber.[11]

Moody's Mill – by the 1870s referred to as Moodyville – and Hastings Mill, both steam-powered and producing lumber for markets around the Pacific, were large by BC standards but smaller than some mills on Puget Sound. Moodyville's capacity of 100,000 board feet per day in the early 1880s was greater than that of its rival, and together the two Burrard Inlet enterprises employed from 150 to 200 workers, not counting longshoremen and loggers.[12]

Since sawmills were not sophisticated or complex industrial places they could rely on the workers available to them, often a mobile and ethnically heterogeneous collection of 'rough labourers.' Several sawmill occupations required special skill, among them engineering, saw filing, and blacksmithing, but many mill jobs could be done by unskilled workers. Sawmill workforces were also notoriously transient. An unmarried worker was likely to remain employed in a mill for no more than a few weeks, 'after which he would withdraw his wages and move on.'[13] R.H. Alexander, who became the manager of Hastings Sawmill in 1882, claimed that his millhands 'were largely composed of runaway sailors and Indians.'[14] The number of Native men who worked in the mills cannot be discovered accurately from the 1881 census, the earliest taken in British Columbia, but contemporary comments indicate that both Squamish and Musqueam people worked as millhands and longshoremen. Some Native workers came from even farther afield, one sawmill labourer a distance of 400 miles from his home on the north coast.[15] The Indian Reserve Commissioners reported in 1877 that sawmill labour and other forms of economic activity put between $80,000 and $100,000 annually into the hands of Burrard Inlet Natives; in return, the mill owners and shippers who visited the mills 'benefited in a corresponding degree ... by having a local source of labour constantly available.'[16] Both the Mission Reserve near Moodyville and the Indian rancherie east of Hastings Mill were products of the labour market created by the sawmill industry on Burrard Inlet.

In contrast to most sawmill and longshoring jobs, the 'responsible posts' generally belonged to White men of British cultural heritage.[17] Burrard Inlet loggers, who worked either for the mills or for independent logging contractors, were on average more highly skilled than mill workers and more likely to be of British origin. The highest paid camp workers were fallers and teamsters, the latter rewarded for coaxing oxen, acting in unison, to drag huge logs across greased skids from the forest to tidewater. Ordinary millhands toiled for twelve hours a day, 'minus one half hour for a hurried lunch,' in return for approximately $20 to $30 per month plus board. Fallers and teamsters could earn double that amount, or more.[18] Other forest industry workers probably made something in between, depending on the skill and status of the job.

Lumbering was the industry through which Europeans placed their imprint on the landscape of Burrard Inlet but in the 1870s it provided only limited and slow growth. Employment was either in logging and sawmilling or in servicing the forest industry. For a decade the settlement that clustered around Moody's Mill on the north shore remained the larger of the two population centres, 'a straggling little place' with workers' shanties strung along the waterfront and a few better homes on the hill behind.[19] Moodyville's population of 200 was linked almost entirely through work at the sawmill, which employed about 100 (see Table 1.1). As an urban space owned by private capital, Moodyville was from its inception a company-controlled community with virtually no independent merchant class. While its physical appearance was unprepossessing and its economic base limited, contemporaries viewed Moodyville as a socially progressive community with a school, a library, and a fraternal society, and

Taken in 1889, this photograph illustrates the ethnically diverse nature of Moodyville's workforce. Most of these longshoremen are Native and probably lived at the Mission Reserve more than a mile to the west. The supervisors to the left are White, and the man and the boy with the laundry are, typically, Chinese. (Bailey Bros. photo, City of Vancouver Archives MI.P.2 N.26)

Loggers working at Burrard
Inlet in the 1880s were, typically, White men of British
cultural heritage who had
come west from places such as
Maine, New Brunswick, and
Britain. They earned more and
enjoyed higher status than
mill workers and longshoremen. (Bailey Bros. photo, Vancouver Public Library 19767)

with a management-imposed policy that strictly forbade the presence of liquor. In the words of a young English sailor, James McCulley, who had jumped ship at Moodyville in 1875, 'there is a library and papers with reading room which is a great boon and places Moodyville far ahead of the neighbouring mills and villages which nearly all boast of a rum mill or two ... Nothing of the kind is allowed on Moody's land.'[20]

Although Moody was, in fact, forced to accept a hotel on north shore land in the mid-1870s, McCulley's 'rum mills' were to be found principally at two spots on the south shore: Granville, west of Hastings Mill just outside the boundary of company land, and Hastings, four miles to the east (see Map 1.1). Granville's life as a European settlement began with the construction of a saloon. An enterprising engineer and steamboat pilot named Jack Deighton, a Yorkshireman lured by gold first to California and then to the Fraser, saw an opportunity in meeting the recreational needs of thirsty mill workers and loggers. The site he chose in 1867 for the Globe Saloon, known popularly as 'Gastown' because of 'Gassy Jack' Deighton's willingness to express himself on any subject, was surveyed as a townsite three years later and given the legal name of Granville.[21] To the sailors and loggers of Burrard Inlet, however, Granville remained 'Gastown,' a place consisting mainly of saloons. Of its ten buildings in 1875, several of a 'rather primitive kind,' four were devoted to selling liquor.[22]

While initially smaller than Moodyville, Granville eventually outgrew its rival. The reason is simple enough: Granville's function as a service centre where loggers gravitated for recreation, equipment, and food gave it a

Table 1.1

Population of lumber society on Burrard Inlet excluding Native villages, 1881

	Total		Adults	
	M	F	M	F
Granville (and Hastings Mill)	170	73	126	40
Moodyville	135	61	108	30
Hastings	11	1	11	0
Logging camps	133	9	128	5
Visiting ships	92	5	90	5
Total	541	149	463	80

Note: The term 'adults' is defined as people of working age, i.e., 15-64.
Source: Data for Tables 1.1 to 1.3 drawn from Canada, Nominal Census 1881, microfilm C-13284, British Columbia, Division 187 (New Westminster), Subsection B (S.D. North), pp. 86-114

Granville, ca. 1884, crowded between forest and shore. This panoramic photograph illustrates Vancouver's birth as a village of shops and hotels that provided services to the fledgling forest industry of British Columbia's south coast. (City of Vancouver Archives DIST.P.30 N.19)

potentially broader economic base. That Granville's economy did expand is illustrated by an often-reproduced photograph taken in 1884. Later annotated by Vancouver archivist J.S. Matthews, it shows a pioneer settlement, 'crowded between forest and shore,' consisting of three hotels, two saloons, a dry goods business, a restaurant, a general store, a Chinese laundry, a Chinese wash house and general merchandise emporium, George Black's very substantial butcher shop, and a profusion of stumps, forest debris, and luxuriant skunk cabbage.[23]

Another constellation of people lived on company-owned land at Hastings Mill, an entirely separate place one-quarter mile east of Granville but closely linked to it. Here, amid the 'incessant rattle of machinery and cloud of escaping steam,' stood the cottages of married men, a bunkhouse for single men, the mill manager's residence, and the Hastings Mill store, the single most important merchant house on the south shore.[24] The Granville school also held classes here in a one-room building donated by the company.

East of Hastings Mill, Hastings had emerged as a distinctive place on Burrard Inlet in 1865 when a hotel was erected at the north end of the recently completed Douglas Road, built to connect the Inlet with New Westminster, the 'Royal City.' Initially called Brighton because it functioned as a summer resort and bathing spot for 'all the swells and their children' from the Royal City, Hastings (the name assigned to Brighton by the colonial government in 1869) remained into the 1880s little more than a stopping place that was galvanized into a few moments of activity each day when the New Westminster stage met the Burrard Inlet ferry. It boasted two hotels, the second constructed by Granville businessman and sports enthusiast George Black, but had no industries and virtually no families. Its population was eleven men and one child. This village, in other words, had developed little from a resort and ferry stop.[25]

The more complex nature of society at Granville compared to that at Moodyville is illustrated in the 1881 Canadian census: almost twice as many men of working age in Granville – which includes here both Granville proper and Hastings Mill – were small proprietors or white-collar workers. Skilled workers made up 22 per cent of the male workforce on the south shore compared to only 14 per cent across the water. A fragmentary middle class consisting of one doctor, one minister, four merchants, two butchers, one shoemaker, and five lodging house keepers lived at Granville;

Moodyville had only one hotel and one general store. The image of rum mills, then, while accurately portraying Granville's difference from Moodyville, should also be viewed as symbolizing something broader, the divergent functions of two communities operating within a common, lumber-extractive economy.

The social structure of these villages reflected the newness of European society on Burrard Inlet. Characteristic of resource-extractive settlements at an early stage of development are a marked imbalance between the sexes and a very young population. In the lumber villages of Burrard Inlet the number of men exceeded women[26] of all ages by a ratio of 2.3 to 1.0, and of working age, by 3.5 to 1.0. Yet such statistics still underrepresent the masculine character of society. They ignore the number of non-Native men who used the services of the villages but did not reside in them, men from the logging camps around the Inlet and crews from ships waiting to load lumber. The 1881 census lists five logging camps around Burrard Inlet with a total population of 142, all but fourteen of whom were adult men of working age. Ships docked regularly at Moodyville and Hastings Mill to load lumber – five such sailing vessels were at the Inlet when the census was taken – and brought almost entirely male crews for layovers lasting from one to several weeks. Wives and children accompanied the captains of these ships. When the crews of lumber vessels and logging camps are included in the calculation of Burrard Inlet's non-Native population, the imbalance between adult men and women increases to a ratio in excess of six to one. In the demographically more mature population of Native villages on the Inlet, the relationship between the sexes differed dramatically; adult women slightly outnumbered men.

The fact that males were disproportionately of working age (78 per cent) and single (54 per cent) adds to the impression that these lumber villages were on the margin of settlement society. By contrast, only slightly more than half of the much smaller female population was of working age; of these adults, a mere 6 per cent were single, the rest linked to men by marriage or common-law relationship. Burrard Inlet's lumber villages, then, contained a great many unattached men of working age but almost no single women. The impression of a rather rootless society with relatively few families and limited social permanence was reinforced by the movement of loggers and sailors in and out of Moodyville, Granville, Hastings Mill, and Hastings.[27]

Yet while single men of working age constituted the dominant social group in lumber society, women, children, and families were also present. Their increasing numbers by the 1880s served to lessen the raw edge of masculine dominance. Particularly in the early years, when few European women ventured to settle in such a distant society, White men formed relationships with Native women. Reminiscences by Burrard Inlet pioneers tell of many European men who lived with, or married, women of Native descent. For instance, sawmill owner Sewell Moody cohabited with a Native woman on Burrard Inlet while his wife of European descent lived in Victoria; the first wife of Granville hotel owner Joseph Mannion, a cultured man of literary ability and 'fond of good music,' was Aboriginal; so too were the first and second wives of saloonkeeper Jack Deighton, the second only twelve years old at marriage.[28] We cannot know for certain whether Emma Gonzales, who according to the 1881 census lived at Moodyville with Chilean-born millhand Pedro Gonzales and their two children, or Annie Larvieu, listed as sharing a household with the Quebec-born stoveman Onesam Larvieu and three Larvieu children, were of Native descent, but circumstantial evidence suggests strongly that they were. Combined with reminiscences, 1881 census data when interpreted in a speculative but reasoned manner[29] indicate that approximately 40 per cent of the women and children of Moodyville and Granville were either of Native or Mixed-Blood ancestry (see Table 1.2). Lumber society, it appears, was not as rootless as its gender imbalance would lead us to believe. Nonetheless, information on family formation, like data on age and gender, does reinforce the image of a society born in isolation and forged by the special circumstances of a particular place.

Women contributed to the region's economy as well, though the masculine nature of work in the forest industry limited female opportunities for wage labour. The 1881 census reveals that in the area's three lumber communities, only two women were employed for wages; both women were of Native descent and both worked as domestics.[30] Unfortunately, the census recorded women's employment very inadequately, particularly in their role as casual labourers. Thus, when in 1873 respectable European families – those who thought of themselves as being of good character – gave a party for the daughter of John Patterson, a stevedore, and Emily Susan Patterson, a midwife and lay nurse, they had Native women clean the Hastings Mill schoolhouse in preparation for the event; such short-

Table 1.2

Sex and race of people living in lumber villages[a] on Burrard Inlet, 1881 (by percentage)

	Working age (all)	Working age[b]		Children (all)	Children		Total population
		M	F		M	F	
Native descent[c]	12	4	36	41	42	40	20
Europeans and others[d]	89	96	64	59	58	60	80
Total %	101	100	100	100	100	100	100
Number of cases	315	245	70	136	71	65	451

Notes:

a Granville (with Hastings Mill), Moodyville, and Hastings

b Children: ages 0-14; working-age adults: ages 15-64

c Since the 1881 Nominal Census gives birthplace and ethnic origin but not racial descent, status must be inferred from the available evidence. I defined as being of Native descent those adults who had been born in British Columbia and were of British Columbia origin, and the larger number (mainly women) who had been born in British Columbia but for whom a place of origin was not given. These women might have been Native or Mixed-Blood, but the difference cannot be determined accurately, hence the use of the more general description Native descent. Children with one parent of Native origin and one of European were categorized as being also of Native descent. Where possible, names of people determined as being of Native descent were also checked against textual evidence, drawn mainly from the Matthews Collection at the City of Vancouver Archives. These data come from the European part of the 1881 Nominal Census (New Westminster, South District B) and not the separate Native part (New Westminster, Coast of Mainland D7), where the population of Burrard Inlet's Native villages was recorded.

d Includes: (1) those for whom a place of birth and place of origin were given in the 1881 census as Canada, United States, Europe, or a British possession; (2) Chinese; and (3) Blacks, of whom an unknown but small number (such as the Sullivan family) lived on Burrard Inlet.

Source: See Table 1.1

term employment at low-status jobs by women of Native descent probably occurred often on the Inlet. By contrast, European women worked mainly in the home and outside the market economy. Exceptions included women employed as prostitutes and as respectable but low-paid schoolteachers.[31]

Ethnic and racial diversity was another product of Burrard Inlet's unique history and geography. When surveyor George M. Dawson came to Moodyville at the end of 1875 he reported 'a very mixed assemblage of people. While Europeans or at least Whites fill the responsible posts, Indians (Squa'mich), Chinamen, Negroes and Mulattoes and half breeds and Mongrels of every pedigree abound.'[32] The point to be noted is how different Burrard Inlet appeared to Dawson from the more homogeneous societies of French and English Canada with which he was familiar.

The 1881 census confirms Dawson's impression of ethnic complexity (see Table 1.3). While a third of the non-Native population was British

Emily Susan Patterson served as
midwife and lay nurse to both
Native and European residents
of Burrard Inlet. She arrived
from Oregon in 1873 with her
husband, John Peabody Patterson, a stevedore. They lived first
at Hastings Sawmill and then
Moodyville. They belonged to
the management-centred White
community that constituted
Burrard Inlet's upper strata. In
1936 *Chatelaine* magazine recognized Mrs. Patterson's work as a
nurse in a poem entitled 'The
Heroine of Moodyville.' (City of
Vancouver Archives PORT.P.131
N.546)

born, the British formed a much less prominent cultural group on the Inlet than in some other parts of British Columbia, most notably Victoria. Eastern Canadians constituted one-sixth of the village populations and were especially prominent among skilled sawmill workers and area loggers. About one in ten Inlet residents hailed from the United States, their numbers also concentrated among forest industry tradespeople. Burrard Inlet loggers, a highly skilled group, were almost entirely of British origin (more than four-fifths) and came disproportionately from Ontario, Quebec, New Brunswick, and Maine. The British Columbia-born segment of Inlet society (one in six residents of the three lumber villages) was principally of Native descent. As noted earlier, women and children predominated in this

Table 1.3

Birthplace of working-age people[a] living in lumber villages, logging camps, and visiting ships on Burrard Inlet, 1881 (by percentage)

	Burrard Inlet lumber villages							Other	
	All lumber villages			Granville		Moodyville		Hastings[b]	Visiting ships	Logging camps
	All	M	F	M	F	M	F	M[c]	M[d]	M[d]
Canada										
(except BC)	17	19	10	19	13	13	7	73	4	56
British Columbia	16	8	40	10	25	7	60	0	1	3
Great Britain	34	35	30	33	38	40	20	0	30	24
United States	10	10	11	6	10	13	13	18	12	10
Europe	9	11	0	13	0	11	0	9	26	2
China	7	7	7	11	13	2	0	0	2	4
Sandwich Islands	3	4	0	6	0	3	0	0	0	0
West Indies	1	2	0	2	0	2	0	0	8	0
Central and										
South America	3	3	1	0	3	8	0	0	4	0
Other	1	1	0	0	0	2	0	0	12	0
Total %	101	100	99	100	102	101	100	100	99	99
Number of cases	310	240	70	125	40	104	30	11	90	128

Notes:
a Includes people of Native descent in lumber villages but excludes people enumerated in the Native section of the 1881 census for Burrard Inlet.
b Hastings, but not Hastings Mill; the population of the latter is included with Granville.
c Census takers found no women in Hastings.
d One woman (an American) was living on a ship; five (two from eastern Canada, two from British Columbia, and one from the United States) resided in logging camps.
Source: See Table 1.1

group, with few men of Native background living in Granville or Moodyville. On the other hand, a substantial if undetermined number of Native men, mainly Squamish from villages around Burrard Inlet, worked in the mills and thus contributed to the area's industrial life, though they remained socially and culturally separate from it.

An impression of ethnic diversity was heightened by the one in four non-Native men from places outside the sphere of British, Eastern Canadian, or American influence. Their numbers reflected the extent to which the male workforce moved in and out of the Inlet by sea from the four corners of the world. These workers included Germans, Swedes, Chileans, Filipinos, West Indians, Mexicans, Peruvians, Russians, and Chinese – what Hastings Sawmill executive R.H. Alexander referred to as a very 'motley lot.'[33] The crews of visiting ships, an important source of sawmill labour, were a noticeably varied group, with American, English, Scottish, Filipino, West Indian, and German sailors represented in the 1881 census. One-tenth of Granville's residents were Chinese, who also worked as cooks in logging camps around the Inlet. Unlike Moodyville, Granville provided job opportunities for the Chinese in petty trade and the service sector. Of particular note is the balance between Chinese men and women at Granville, a pattern that would change dramatically with the influx of Chinese railway navvies in the 1880s.

Workers from the Sandwich (Hawaiian) Islands formed one other distinguishable social group. Known as Kanakas, they had laboured for the Hudson's Bay Company and other employers up and down the north-west coast since the 1820s and constituted a small but important part of Burrard Inlet's social landscape. The census indicates that 3 per cent of the population of lumber villages were Kanakas, though the intermixing of Kanakas and Native people, a product of the relatively long tenure of Sandwich Islanders on the coast, undoubtedly extended Kanaka connections to a larger number. A group of Kanakas lived at Coal Harbour on the south shore, and a row of houses built on pilings along the shoreline east of Moodyville was known as Kanaka Row. The partner of Maxie Michaud, the Hastings hotel owner notorious for selling liquor illegally to Natives, was a woman named Frisadie, whose heritage was part Native and part Kanaka. Frisadie was one of the many people on Burrard Inlet whom the ethnocentric George Dawson would have labelled 'half breed' and 'mongrel.'[34]

THE SOCIETY FORMED by these various groups exhibited a relatively fluid but essentially hierarchical social structure. At the top were mill managers and logging camp owners, the principal employers in an economy narrowly based on the extraction, processing, and export of timber. The localized nature of Burrard Inlet's labour market meant that work relations between capital and labour were carried on face to face. This personal contact reinforced the discretionary power of managers and tied workers to individual bosses. Especially close to the managers were the managerial staff of the sawmills (accountants, bookkeepers, storekeepers, and tallymen), the highly skilled technical staff at the mills (engineers, machinists), stevedores who managed the loading of ships, entrepreneurs engaged in respectable business activities (such as better-class hotels and the butcher shop), and doctors who lived intermittently at Granville.

While including fragments of the upper class (mill managers), the middle class (managerial staff and small businessmen), and the lower class (machinists), this high-status group was also White, of British origin, and reasonably well educated. Its members were stable residents of the Inlet. In addition, by the 1880s they were almost always married to women of European rather than Native descent. In short, they formed a definable clique linked across class lines by a shared sense of their own respectability. The structuring of society on Burrard Inlet appears to have been a multifaceted process involving elements of social status, gender, ethnicity, race, and economic power.

Led by managers' wives, this group sought to solidify its prestige and influence at Burrard Inlet by adopting a lifestyle that would set it apart from the threatening mass below. Respectable families lived in detached houses, the two largest of which belonged to mill managers. Of these, the one constructed by Hugh Nelson on Knob Hill, located behind and above the mill in Moodyville, became the centre of high-status social activity, especially after 1882 when the Springers moved in.

Mrs. Springer, formerly Mrs. Richards, who was Granville's second schoolteacher and had married Ben Springer in one of the earliest 'Society' events of the 1870s, led the way in importing social rituals such as tennis parties, teas, and 'at homes' that aimed to enhance cohesion and identity among this small, exclusive group. As one observer of Burrard Inlet social life reminisced, Mrs. Springer 'gave quite delightful garden parties, house parties, and afternoon teas; played tennis, and on one occasion gave a very elaborate entertainment at her elegant home on the cliff of Moodyville, above the mill, and had an orchestra.' Mrs. R.H. Alexander led Society in a similar fashion on the south shore. Social activities with the officers of visiting sailing vessels and their wives offered this group additional chances for shared outings, whether at balls organized by ships' captains 'for the ladies and gentlemen of the Inlet and New Westminster' or on picnic excursions to nearby Granite Falls.

Until 1881, however, the elite lacked one instrument essential for defining status: their own church. Reluctant to attend the Methodist church in Gastown, the congregation of which was formed mainly by Native mill workers, they participated in Anglican services at the Masonic Hall in Moodyville and at the schoolhouse near Hastings Mill. This continued until St. James Anglican Church, sponsored by mill manager Captain James Raymur, opened in the spring of 1881 on Hastings Sawmill Company land. Former Methodists like Mrs. Springer now crossed the Inlet regularly to attend.[35]

This group saw itself as 'respectable,' and those around them as 'rough.' To be 'respectable' was to be of good character: pious, sober, honest, industrious, and self-sufficient. It was to show tangible evidence of material progress,[36] and, in this fragile society with its newly formed and polyglot population, to be White and of British or American background. The respectable included middling elements of society such as small businessmen – though not saloonkeepers, usually held in low esteem – and portions of the labour force, especially those workingmen whose education, background, and conduct led them to conform to the standards of Victorian morality. Loggers, mainly of British background and skilled, could be respectable; as one observer noted, 'They drank, but were not drunkards. They were a superior class of men.' Similarly, the former English sailor James McCulley, who praised Sewell Moody for the rational recreation that his library made possible at Moodyville, was respectable. By contrast, millhands, who were ethnically mixed and generally unskilled, were perceived as 'a roughish lot.'[37] Even rougher were the 'unruly seamen' who caused 'trouble and annoyance to the respectable portion' of Moodyville's population.[38]

The ethnocentric and racist overtones that the ethos of respectability assumed at Burrard Inlet found particular expression in negative perceptions of Native and Mixed-Blood people. Families created by men and women from European and Native cultural traditions, respectively, were quite common on Burrard Inlet, though for managers and the respectable element this was more a phenomenon of the 1860s and 1870s than of the 1880s. Europeans never fully accepted such liaisons as normal, particularly after more White women arrived. For example, women of Native descent were often referred to as 'squaws' and their European partners as 'squaw men,' pejorative terms that implied a departure from European cultural norms. Thus, R.H. Alexander viewed the community created by his European workers and their 'squaws' as 'curious.' The term 'Siwash,' commonly used by Europeans, was equally disliked by Natives. Jim Frank, a Squamish born at Burrard Inlet and employed by Hastings Sawmill, reflected later in life on how much he had hated being referred to by the derogatory term 'Siwash': 'I'm Indian, me Indian, not Siwash,' he asserted.[39]

In addition, women of Native descent, including the Native wife of Jack Deighton, were denied the right to inherit property from their dead, White mates. August Jack Khahtsalano, a Squamish, was born on the Inlet in 1877. Reminiscing about his youth, he said that when the White husband of an Native woman died, 'they kick the womans out ... because she's "just a squaw."'[40]

Respectable Whites held Mixed Blood people in particularly low regard. Comments in Department of Indian Affairs records emphasized the excessive drinking and generally debauched state of Mixed-Blood people.[41] Equally revealing is the patronizing tone of a Moodyville schoolteacher who described her students – of whom one-half to two-thirds were Mixed-Blood – as 'very careless and the majority backward although to be half breeds some of them are very nice.'[42] Such images suggest the stigma that Native blood carried among Whites. Europeans cast Mixed-Blood and Native people to the margins of what they considered respectable society, by which they meant White society of British origin. In so doing they defined people of Native descent living in lumber villages as a separate and lower-status community. Racial categorizations joined economic and social status as important sources of stratification at Burrard Inlet.

LED BY sawmill company managers, the 'respectable' group worked assiduously to hold together the mélange of people and cultures at Burrard Inlet and to encourage within the community law-abiding, sober, and orderly behaviour. Both in turn aimed to increase the efficiency of workers and to extract as much value as possible from their work. This leadership from above is best categorized as a form of paternalism: a method of organizing society into an organic whole by linking the social mass to their superiors, usually through face-to-face relations in intensely localized and isolated places. Historians have found that paternalism operated as a social system most frequently in rural and preindustrial societies, but manufacturers are also known to have introduced paternalistic policies during the transition to industrial capitalism. Such was the case at Burrard Inlet.[43]

Mill managers attempted to direct the moral and social behaviour of Burrard Inlet residents by three types of initiatives: organizational, legal, and recreational. Managers and their staffs strongly supported organizations that would promote rational social behaviour. For instance, the Mechanics' Institute of Burrard Inlet provided a library of books and periodicals, and Mount Hermon Lodge, a fraternal society, offered social assistance to needy members and their families. The Mechanics' Institute was run throughout its history by leading figures on the north shore, many of them in managerial positions at the mill. Lodge members included a range of working people such as carpenters, blacksmiths, and some millhands, as well as others in management and business. The names of almost all members of the Institute and the Lodge were of British origin, with Josiah C. Hughes, a clerk at Moody's Mill elected to the first provincial legislature after Confederation, heading both. The Hastings Literary Institute emerged on the south shore some time after the Mechanics' Institute on the north. Significantly, its president and secretary in 1882-3 were the manager and a clerk of Hastings Sawmill.[44] Mill managers took the lead as well in establishing public schools at Moodyville and Granville in the early 1870s and continued to direct school matters into the 1880s.[45]

In addition, the judiciary served as a useful instrument of power for lumber industry officials. In the 1870s the province's legal system retained from the colonial period strong roots within local communities, and in areas outside Victoria and New Westminster the justices of the peace, who as the lowest-ranking officers of the court were not professionally trained in law, were often members of the local elite.[46] Among the justices of the peace appointed at Burrard Inlet in the 1870s were Hastings Sawmill officials Captain Raymur and R.H. Alexander, Moodyville bookkeeper Ben Springer, and logging camp operator Jeremiah Rogers.[47] They sought to maintain law and order at a place where, according to one observer, a 'pretty hard crowd used to find their way ... from other parts [of the coast] to escape arrest.'[48] But it was moral behaviour, and particularly the sale of liquor to Native people, that most concerned local magistrates. Sewell Moody's attempt to limit access to liquor on the north shore has been noted. Captain Raymur had a tougher task, since his company did not own the land at Gastown or Hastings. After being appointed manager he expressed shock at what he called 'this aggregation of filth' at Gastown, proclaiming, 'I'll not permit a running sore to fasten itself on an industry entrusted to my care.'[49] To this end he fought hard as manager to prevent the licensing of additional outlets that would sell liquor past midnight or allow cards to be played on Sundays, and as magistrate he tried to stop the illegal sale of liquor.

Paternalism found its most imaginative expression, however, during the Inlet's celebration of Dominion Day. The settlement that formed in the 1860s around the north shore mill initially had an American orientation, and the American national holiday emerged as the Inlet's first mid-summer festival. The festivities were led by Sewell Moody, an American. But in 1873 R.H. Alexander, a Scottish-born but Canadian-educated bookkeeper at Hastings Mill, inaugurated a separate celebration to mark British Columbia's recent entry into the Canadian Confederation. For a short period celebrations on July 1 and July 4 competed but it was Dominion Day that grew and survived. Sponsored by the Hastings Sawmill Company, Dominion Day was, to quote one observer, 'always ... a specialty at Hastings Mill,' the sports and prizes 'ahead of anything else in British Columbia.' Crowds of up to 750 people gathered on the sawdust spit in front of the mill. Flags atop the mill and wharf greeted as many as 400 excursionists from Nanaimo and Victoria. Activities included running, jumping, sailing and canoe races, rifle shooting, climbing greasy poles and catching greased pigs, a band that played through the entire day, and a 'splendid dinner ... provided for everyone, free of charge by Captain Raymur,' the mill manager.[50] As evening approached, departing excursionists extended loud expressions of thanks to an appreciative Raymur. Other socially prominent residents supported these mill-directed initiatives.

The gendered nature of this support is worth noting, for while the 'respectable' tended to live in families, and thus to include women, the general workforce – the object of paternalism – was disproportionately masculine. Thus in 1879 the manager's quest for social harmony led a group of families to form the Coal Harbour Bachelors' Quadrille Club 'for the purpose of raising the moral standard of the community, and bringing the young of both sexes together ... to promote sociability, harmony and good fellowship.'[51]

The leadership of Mrs. Alexander was particularly noticeable. On Dominion Day she could be found singing 'with much taste' before a multitude of spectators drawn from all levels of Burrard Inlet society. More instructive of Mrs. Alexander's sense of herself as a moral and social leader is the story of how she intervened to stop racial 'rioting' east of Hastings Mill. One day early in 1886, after many navvies from discontinued construction sites along the Canadian Pacific Railway line had come down to Gastown, a crowd of 'tramping and shouting' men passed behind the mill on their way to the Chinese shacks to the east. Sensing their hostile tone, the manager's wife 'was fearless and went out with her apron on – she wore a big white apron, and ... reprimanded them severely.' The narrator, a local resident, leaves the impression that this charter member of the Inlet's upper class successfully restored order through her personal intervention.[52]

WHETHER PATERNALISM proved so effective, however, is open to more critical assessment. For while these various initiatives tell us much about the assumptions and identity of the Inlet's leaders, they indicate little about the community's response. Additional evidence, though fragmentary, suggests that economic power did not translate so easily into social and cultural control.

Four historical incidents, all revealed through fragments of stories left by residents of the time, help us to explore the complex nature of social relations on Burrard Inlet. The first tells of mill owner Sewell Moody's attempt to discipline Native employees who had acquired whisky from a visiting ship's captain. When a stern-looking Moody entered the Mission Reserve to berate the partying millhands for failing to show up for work, the Natives 'stripped him absolutely naked, put him at the head of the procession and marched him from "The Mission" to the [nearby] sawmill, singing songs, making all the noise they could ... three Roman Catholic priests following the procession carrying Moody's clothes.' Two days later the Natives marched back to beg the humiliated sawmill owner his forgiveness. This time the priests led the procession.[53]

The second story tells of how a 'young lady,' unmarried and probably from a genteel settler family in Victoria, came to observe an important Native ritual at Burrard Inlet. While visiting the Alexanders in 1877, she was invited to accompany them to an 'Indian war dance ... held deep in the woods on the waterfront near Hastings.' While the dance was 'not open to the public,' she gained access as one of a number of Europeans who had received special invitations; among them was her host, R.H. Alexander, who had been 'made a chief awhile ago for some service they esteemed.'[54]

The third comes from the Reverend Charles Montgomery Tate, a Methodist missionary who attended the Dominion Day celebrations at Hastings Mill on 1 July 1876. Of note are his comments on what came after the official, and mill-directed, program had been completed. In the evening 'people danced and drank whiskey until sober persons became scarce,' the Rev. Tate confided to his diary. 'The sight I beheld that night I think I will ever remember – white people and Indians drunk on every hand. What is the country coming to.'[55]

The final example is less a story than a short but instructive comment from an elderly R.H. Alexander while reminiscing about how different Burrard Inlet life had been before the advent of the railway, rapid urbanization, and a fully developed capitalist economy. On one occasion, he said, Hastings Mill had been forced to 'shut down for a couple of days because so many [millhands] were engaged in a particularly interesting game that was going on.'[56]

Together these stories suggest a complex pattern of social relations between elites and ordinary people on Burrard Inlet. At one level they reveal company power. In seeking the forgiveness of Moody for their indiscretion, Native mill workers seemed to buckle under to the moral authority of the church and the economic authority of the Moodyville Sawmill Company. The inclusion of Alexander in an important Native ritual could also be interpreted as an example of deference to European economic power and evidence of the loss of cultural autonomy.

Another reading is also possible. In both cases Natives may have been making concessions to preserve something more important, the continued viability of their traditional culture. The war dance represented only one example of Native cultural persistence on Burrard Inlet. Despite being declared illegal by the Dominion government in 1884, potlatching – the giving away of material goods as part of a ritual to announce and validate rights and status – continued there at least until 1889 and perhaps beyond.

The reason why Native men worked in the mills is suggested in another story, this one told by the Rev. George Grant while on an expedition to British Columbia from Central Canada in 1872. 'An old fellow, big George,' the ethnocentric Grant tells us, worked 'industriously at the [Moodyville] mill for years till he saved $2,000. Instead of putting this in a Savings Bank, he had spent it all on stores for a grand "Potlatch," summoning Siwashes from far and near to come, eat, drink, dance, be merry, and receive gifts. Nearly a thousand assembled.' Once the potlatch had finished, the penniless man 'returned to the mill to carry slabs at $20 a month.'[57] Simply put, for Natives, wage labour appears to have been incorporated into a constantly evolving but still vibrant traditional culture.

The persistence of separate social realities on the Inlet is also revealed in the stories of drinking and gambling. Lumber company attempts to control excess drinking and the sale of liquor to Native people were at best only partly successful, as the repeated liquor charges laid against hotel operator Maxmillian Michaud indicate.[58] More significantly, drinking was a crucial part of the recreational lives of men, whether Native or European, who worked on the industrial frontier, and the practice remained impervious to the reform-oriented goals of the managers. The gendered nature of drinking and gambling was a natural product of the social environment in which most male workers lived. While men with families resided in small houses, the majority of mill workers and loggers lived without female companionship, sharing all-male bunkhouses, mess halls, and twelve-hour work days. For single men Burrard Inlet life was generally quiet, indeed monotonous, though punctuated by periods of intense socializing. In the words of one Granville pioneer, the village was very quiet except on pay days when the loggers came in; then it was lively until they sobered up and went back to work. The Sunnyside Hotel in Granville, built 'on stilts over the beach,' was a favourite spot for single men when they were not working. Here they gathered around 'the one long table' to share meals, later spending the night dancing and drinking. Liquor was an essential component of this masculine recreational culture, and as the name of Moodyville's 'Maiden Lane' suggests, so too was prostitution.[59] One can argue, then, that the drinking that the Rev. Tate observed on Dominion Day was a natural part of the masculine world of lumber society and coexisted with, but was not superseded by, the rational culture of the 'respectable.'

The four stories evoke one other observation about the relationship of social groups at Burrard Inlet: like their influence over social and cultural practices, the ability of company managers to discipline workers was limited. The labour market in this coastal enclave retarded the formation of trade unions. The market's localized nature meant that work relations were carried on in a highly personalized manner between managers and workers, reinforcing the power of capital.[60] This personalized form of industrial relations may explain why no strikes are known to have occurred at Burrard Inlet until navvies who had recently arrived from inland railway camps led workers at Hastings Sawmill to walk out in the spring of 1886.[61] On the other hand, mill workers tended to move frequently, a pattern reinforced by the high wages offered along the labour-short northwest coast. Thus, transiency could serve as a ready form of protest against management controls, and the labour market offered plenty of job opportunities for transient workers. Despite his humiliation, then, Sewell Moody needed Native labour and could not simply fire all workers from the Mission Reserve who had defied his edict against taking liquor. Similarly, Alexander had no choice but to close Hastings Mill when his employees collectively decided to gamble rather than work.

THE MOST OBVIOUS FACT about Burrard Inlet society was the prominence of sawmills in settlement life. Resource-based communities emerged to extract wealth from British Columbia's rich forests. Burrard Inlet was not an agricultural society organized around a large number of small producers who lived in nuclear families and owned land. Rather, production was highly concentrated and, supporting the thesis that British Columbia has always been a 'company province,' settlement emerged out of the labour demands of industrial capitalism. Indeed, social organization can be described as a symbiotic relationship between a company-dominated clique of respectable families and a social mass drawn to the area by work in the mills, on the waterfront, and in the forests. At the centre of power and influence were mill owners or managers and their wives. Lumber society on Burrard Inlet, one could argue, was structured primarily by class.

But the foregoing has revealed a level of social complexity that qualifies such a thesis. The mill managers and their economic allies were part of the dominant British cultural group in British Columbia and thus were also defined by ethnicity. The upper group lived mainly in families, and the combination of British ethnicity and family organization significantly contributed to the group's sense of itself as respectable. Below the elite, lumber society lacked coherence. Complex identities united groups on some levels – the skilled and mainly anglophone loggers with the mill elite, or single loggers with the male sawmill workers – but divided them on others. Thus, single men such as skilled loggers from New Brunswick and unskilled millhands from Mexico shared a common masculine subculture but faced obvious differences of occupational status and ethnicity. Race divided workers fundamentally, as the segregated locations of the Chinese rookery at Moodyville and the Indian rancherie at Hastings Mill indicate. In other words, the industrial society that grew up around the Hastings and Moodyville sawmills was hierarchically structured along several axes, of which class was only one.

CHAPTER TWO

City Builders

D ominion Day on Burrard Inlet was an even bigger festival in the late 1880s than it had been in the 1870s, but the nature of the community being celebrated had changed dramatically.[1] Granville, formerly a village of several hundred residents, had transformed into Vancouver, a city exceeding 9,000. Now a two-day affair, Dominion Day activities included a long list of sporting events on land and water, visits by dignitaries and thousands of ordinary folk from New Westminster and Vancouver Island, a much-loved illumination of Vancouver at night, and a grand civic ball. But it was the parade through downtown streets – impossible in the harbour-oriented setting of Granville – that best illustrated change. A variety of voluntary associations participated, from corporations and small businesses to fraternal societies and trade unions.

The police and a grand marshal, R.H. Alexander, headed the 1889 parade, followed by an impressive military band and a 130-member garrison battery. Fire brigades from Seattle, Victoria, and Vancouver came next, the last of these proudly displaying its new hook and ladder truck and hose reel. Behind the Westminster Fife-and-Drum Band and carriages bearing political officials and leading citizens came the parade's highlight, a sixteen-foot-long 'Triumphal Car' that celebrated the now overwhelmingly British character of society along Burrard Inlet's south shore. Drawn by four horses and topped by a broad canopy and large Union Jack, the car featured ten women – the eleventh did not show up – dressed in white. They were to represent Canada's seven provinces and four territories. On a throne at the centre of these allegorical figures sat another woman representing Britannia, with a shield, a helmet, and a trident at her side. The symbolism was clear: the ethnic and racial diversity of lumber society had given way to a city that was both more populous and more British.

Having placed Vancouver and its institutions in their imperial setting, the 1 July parade then proceeded to reveal the city's inner workings. Ethnic ties were represented by the Sons of England and St. George's Society; community life by the Knights of Pythias, the Ancient Order of Foresters, and two baseball clubs; business by real estate, ice company, and confectioners' floats; industry by a float illustrating an operating foundry; and organized labour by marching typographers, longshoremen, cabinetmakers, carpenters, and plasterers, as well as by two cabinetmakers' floats. Lumber mills did not participate in the 1889 parade, but a year later the Hastings Sawmill Company entered a huge log pulled by four oxen. The oxen, in turn, were driven by one of the Inlet's longest-serving bull punchers. Business and labour were interspersed throughout the second half of the parades, neither having priority of place. Thousands of spectators, 'all respectably dressed and evidently impressed with their [own] importance in the community,' applauded the various groups of marchers.[2]

The nineteenth-century parade has been described as 'an organized body, usually of men, [who] marched into the public streets to spell out a common social identity.'[3] Such was the case with the Dominion Day parades of 1889 and 1890. No longer an expression of lumber company paternalism, Dominion Day had evolved into a grand celebration of urbanism and progress. Sponsored by the City Council, Dominion Day from 1887 to the early 1890s expressed both the boosterism of town-promoting entrepreneurs and the pride of ordinary citizens in their achievements as city builders. In this sense the parades in particular and the celebrations more generally reflected a unity of purpose that crossed class lines and encouraged widespread acceptance of civic leadership by leading businessmen. The parades also marked the distance that settled society on

Burrard Inlet had come since the 1870s. The sophistication of urban services, the diverse range of voluntary associations, and the new wealth so boldly displayed announced the birth of a Victorian city on the outer margins of the British empire.[4]

Yet beneath the consensus about economic and cultural values were hints of complexity and division. The Canadian Pacific Railway's absence from the parades reflected the inherent tension within capitalism between large, externally controlled corporations and smaller, locally centred businesses. The shared desire of these two groups to boost Vancouver – and to enhance the value of land – mediated tensions in the 1880s. It would not do so, however, once the real estate boom had passed. In addition, as Vancouver became more ethnically homogeneous, and the identity of the dominant group clearer, discrimination against ethnic and racial minorities became more pronounced. This behaviour expressed ethnocentrism. It also reflected the association of respectability with rootedness and families, the latter of which, overwhelmingly of British heritage, set the norms for respectable behaviour in the new city. Dominion Day had become, then, the instrument by which Vancouver's respectable residents – its stable, family-based, and culturally British population – celebrated their vision of an ideal society.

THE RUSH OF EVENTS that transformed life on the south shore of Burrard Inlet started with a land deal. In May 1884, Canadian Pacific Railway (CPR) officials began negotiating with the British Columbia government for a bonus of provincial land in return for making Coal Harbour the terminus, and when an agreement was struck the rail company came away with more than ten square miles of property. The 6,458 acres it received included 'an immense tract ... of largely untouched forest' south of False Creek, a smaller block of land behind and to the west of the old townsite of Granville, and 175 acres donated in small parcels to the east and west of Granville by private owners hoping to benefit from railway-stimulated growth (see Map 2.1). In return the railway company agreed to erect works, docks, and a station between Coal Harbour and English Bay and to complete the line from Port Moody by the summer of 1886. While railways in both American and Canadian cities received public and private grants of land to encourage construction, the CPR received much more land in Vancouver than did its counterparts south of the border.[5]

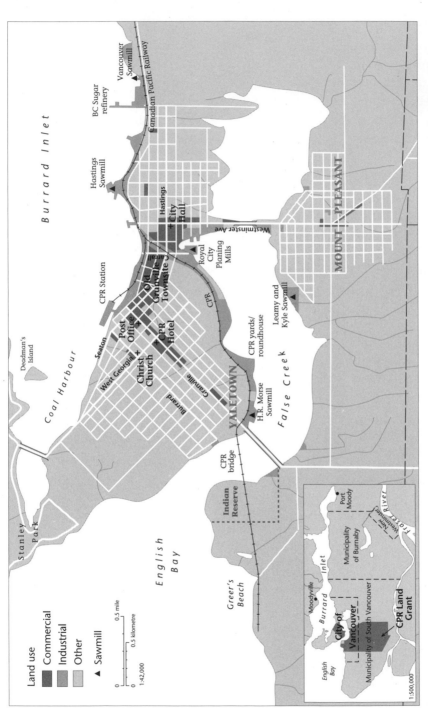

Map 2.1 Vancouver, 1890s

Source: Compiled from Bruce Macdonald, *Vancouver: A Visual History* (Vancouver: Talonbooks 1992), 22-7; CVA, Map no. 334; and *Williams' Illustrated Official British Columbia Directory, 1892* (Victoria: R.T. Williams 1892)

Land use

- Commercial
- Industrial
- Other
- ▲ Sawmill

Burrard Inlet

Vancouver Sawmill

BC Sugar refinery

Canadian Pacific Railway

Hastings Sawmill

Hastings

City Hall

Westminster Ave

Royal City Planing Mills

Leamy and Kyle Sawmill

MOUNT PLEASANT

CPR Station

Old Granville Townsite

Post Office

CPR Hotel

Christ Church

West Georgia

Seton

Deadman's Island

Coal Harbour

Stanley Park

Burrard

Granville

YALETOWN

H.R. Morse Sawmill

CPR yards/ roundhouse

False Creek

CPR

CPR bridge

Indian Reserve

English Bay

Greer's Beach

1:42,000

0   0.5 mile
0   0.5 kilometre

Burrard Inlet

Moodyville

Port Moody

Westminster River

Fraser River

Municipality of Burnaby

City of Vancouver

Municipality of South Vancouver

CPR Land Grant

English Bay

1:500,000

The Canadian Pacific Railway's plans generated a flurry of real estate speculation near Coal Harbour. In new western towns, where expectations of high financial returns from city building provided the 'indirect and intangible' element that stimulated rapid urbanization, much of the growth-generating activity centred on the sale and servicing of land. Some of the earliest speculators and migrants hoping to share the western terminus's 'inevitable prosperity' came from Victoria. Prominent entrepreneur Edgar Crow Baker typified the land grabbers who rushed to English Bay, Coal Harbour, and False Creek. Encouraged by A.W. Ross, a federal MP who had won and lost a fortune in the Winnipeg boom of 1881-2 and was closely connected to the CPR, Baker began purchasing land in the summer of 1884. Two years later he netted spectacular profits, in one instance selling for $2,000 English Bay lots that had originally cost $66. Other leading Victoria government officials, businessmen, and politicians, among them Premier William Smithe and John Robson, a long-time newspaperman and legislator, soon joined Baker. Canadian businessmen travelling across the west from one CPR-generated land boom to another also arrived.[6]

The CPR land deal shifted the focus of economic activity at Granville from servicing the lumber industry to servicing urban growth. To encourage investment in services and to proclaim the community's prominence, a movement to incorporate Granville as a city began in mid-January 1886 with a large assembly of villagers in Gastown. Members of the old community were conspicuous but so too were real estate and railway agents. The assembled group elected a committee of ten, six of whom were long-time Granville residents, to draw up a bill of incorporation. Three of the others, led by Land Commissioner Lauchlan A. Hamilton, had ties with the railway. The key figure was mill manager R.H. Alexander, who had actively promoted the idea of incorporation and who as chairman of the ten-man committee 'spent considerable time in seeing the act passed through the house at Victoria.' Alexander took with him to the provincial capital a petition signed by 125 people from Granville encouraging incorporation; the petitioners were all men and 'nearly all bore sturdy English names.' The business-oriented and mill-dominated upper stratum that for some time had dominated south shore society controlled the movement for incorporation. Behind the leadership of Granville's old guard, however, stood representatives of economic change.[7]

More than any other agency during the boom that lasted into the early

1890s, it was the CPR that shaped the transformation of Granville into Vancouver, or, as the place became known in popular discourse, the Terminal City. Like the hundreds of small investors drawn to Burrard Inlet in the mid-1880s, the rail corporation strove assiduously to return a quick profit from the land it held both inside and outside the city limits. This priority was not unique to Vancouver – urban land sales across the west provided an important source of income for the new and financially insecure rail corporation. But the CPR enjoyed an unusual opportunity to maximize income from land in Vancouver. On the prairies it marketed land in forty-seven towns along the main line in partnership with private investors through the Canada North West Company, while in some 800 villages and towns on branch lines the railway managed property through its Land Department. The CPR received only one-half the net proceeds from real estate sold by the North West Land Company, but in Vancouver, where the railway administered its land directly, profits accrued entirely to the corporation. Vancouver furnished the CPR's 'most spectacular' and most profitable venture in townsite promotion, generating returns that from 1886 to 1888 reached $868,059. By 1889, town lot proceeds in Vancouver exceeded returns 'in all other company towns combined.'[8]

Rail executives encouraged the improvement rather than speculative reselling of land. Consequently, the company's initial auction was a somewhat chastening experience for Harry Abbott, the CPR's chief executive officer in Vancouver. Finding that speculators had 'seized upon all the best ... sites without any intention of putting up buildings,' Abbott increased the prices and adopted a policy of offering generous discounts of 20 to 30 per cent 'on condition of building.'[9] Such improvements enhanced the short-term value of unsold CPR property and served the company's long-term interests of creating a transportation and commercial centre at its western terminus.

The company spared no expense to pull development towards its land west of the Old Granville Townsite. Upon Vancouver's incorporation, the CPR quickly assumed governmental functions in the westside area, spending the enormous sum of $235,000 from April to December 1886 clearing, grading, and constructing streets. Aided by interlocking corporate directorships, the rail company persuaded the Bank of Montreal to accept a new bank site on Granville Street, the central thoroughfare through company property.[10] CPR officials in Montreal and Vancouver, as well as company friends in Britain, were encouraged to invest along Granville, and by 1889 eastern executives Sir Donald Smith and Sir William Van Horne had completed Vancouver's two largest privately owned office buildings. At the height of land on Granville Street between Coal Harbour and False Creek the CPR erected a $200,000 hotel, for many years the city's most outstanding structure.[11] Next door the company placed an expensive opera house, at $100,000 costing double Vancouver's finest brick and masonry commercial block of the period. The opera house was, to quote its manager, 'far ahead of the actual requirements of the town' and like the hotel served primarily to advertise the CPR townsite.[12] Both also expressed William Van Horne's unlimited faith in Vancouver's future.

Commerce, manufacturing, and utility services concentrated to the east, as did the majority of residents. But here too city-building growth expressed an underlying unity founded upon the sale, servicing, and development of land. Real estate boosters served as leading advocates of business development that would broaden the community's service base and attract immigrants and capital. To do this they headed the city's most important civic organizations, the Board of Trade and the City Council. They also constituted early Vancouver's most active entrepreneurial group. An examination of the business affiliations of sixty-eight leading entrepreneurs between 1890 and 1893, and of the number of important companies they promoted, shows clearly that up to the depression of the 1890s real estate promoters led all others, including merchants and railway executives, in furthering business development.[13]

The achievements of two eastside real estate men, David Oppenheimer and Charles Rand, illustrate the nature of entrepreneurship during Vancouver's first expansion boom. The son of a Bavarian vintner, David Oppenheimer had left Germany in the 1840s. After stops in Louisiana, California, and the British Columbia communities of Yale and Victoria, he finally settled in Vancouver. Though engaged with his brother Isaac in early Vancouver's largest wholesale grocery firm, David focused on the family's considerable real estate investment. He served as president of the Vancouver Improvement Company, a syndicate formed in 1886 by prominent Victoria real estate speculators to control the largest block of land in Vancouver outside the CPR holdings. Oppenheimer divided his attention between public duties as mayor (from 1888 to 1891) and private promotion of land held by the eastside Vancouver Improvement Company. By the

CPR offices, Granville Street, 1892. The Canadian Pacific Railway greatly influenced Vancouver's layout and economy. The company put its stamp most firmly on Granville Street, located to the west of the old community of Granville on land granted by the provincial government to the CPR as a bonus for establishing its terminus at Coal Harbour. (City of Vancouver Archives CAN.P.67 N.46)

1890s this property had become Vancouver's industrial heart, serving as the location of a sugar refinery, a lime company, and a foundry. David's ancillary business interests enhanced his primary real estate and commercial concerns: he headed the New Westminster-based syndicate that built an interurban tramline between New Westminster and Vancouver and was a director of the Vancouver City Foundry and Machine Works Company. Isaac's role as president of the Vancouver Electric Street Railway and Light Company and director of small fruit canning and coastal shipping firms also bolstered the Oppenheimer family's influence in the utility and commercial sectors of the economy.[14]

Charles Rand was the Terminal City's most industrious entrepreneur. Born into a Nova Scotia shipbuilder's family, he settled in Vancouver in September 1887 to take charge of the local branch of the family real estate business, founded three years earlier in New Westminster. Rand Brothers soon carried out numerous large and extensive real estate transactions in the city and became agents for David Oppenheimer's Vancouver Improvement Company.[15] Charles Rand initiated more new businesses in early Vancouver than any other booster. He promoted gas and street railway utilities as well as Vancouver's first important shipping company, organized candy manufacturing and wholesale confectionery businesses, and served as chairman of the British Columbia Ironworks Company. His interests also extended to railways. He first incorporated and then became president of the ill-fated Burrard Inlet and Fraser Valley Railway Company, formed in 1892 to break the CPR's monopoly in the lower mainland. Real estate, shipping, utilities, railways, producers' and consumers' goods manufacturing – Rand's role as an entrepreneur ranged across a broad spectrum of business activity.[16]

In addition to promoting new enterprises, David Oppenheimer and Charles Rand also organized financial capital for investment in Vancouver. Frontier societies characteristically experienced a shortage of development capital, and business people who could attract money played a crucial role in boosting community growth. The more capital invested, either in land or businesses, the greater the multiplier effect throughout the local economy. David Oppenheimer channelled capital into Vancouver from Victoria and New Westminster through syndicates interested in city real estate and the interurban railway. More important was Charles Rand, who in partnership with his brother Edward established an office in London and travelled widely in search of British financing. They succeeded in encouraging English capitalists to invest extensively in Vancouver property. As a consequence of their contacts, three major businesses came to the Pacific coast between 1886 and 1892: the Ross-McLaren Lumber Company from the Ottawa Valley and two British financial companies, one specializing in loans and real estate.[17]

The link between finance and land also emphasizes the extent to which the urban real estate market supported economic growth in early Vancouver. Particularly important were non-banking financial institutions that directed local and external money into mortgages. J.W. Horne, said to have brought to Vancouver $1.5 million generated by successful investments during an earlier real estate boom in Brandon, Manitoba, created one such company, Vancouver Loan, Trust, Savings, and Guarantee. Capitalized through a subscription of stock worth $200,000, it sold real estate and lent mortgage capital. Similarly, by 1896 the British Columbia Land and Investment Agency, controlled in Britain, had become the largest financial house of its kind in the province. Speculative fervour affected even bankers. Essentially a promoter rather than conservative banker, the Scottish-born manager of the Bank of British Columbia, J.C. Keith, went beyond the already generous guidelines set down by the bank's British head office and made loans secured only by real estate at highly inflated prices. For his defiance of company policy the bank dismissed Keith in 1892.[18]

An examination of Vancouver's occupational structure in 1890 indicates that most other economic activity, in addition to real estate promotion and finance, occurred in response to land promotion and development (Table 2.1). Construction employed 15 per cent of the labour force, reflecting the extent of Vancouver's city-building boom between 1886 and 1890, when the total assessed value of buildings jumped from $1.6 to $12.0 million. Hotels and boarding houses employed a significant 8.5 per cent of the workforce and housed tourists, transient workers, and especially the large and as yet unsettled population of migrants who had come west in search of employment and fortune. More than 900 residents worked in commerce, constituting one in every five members of the local workforce. Their products ranged from dry goods and food to specialized items such as jewellery, glassware, and building supplies. Commercial establishments were small, employing fewer than ten workers. Only the prosperous Oppenheimer Brothers was bigger. The comparatively few workers and limited wage bill in the wholesale, as opposed to retail, sector of the grocery trade also indicate that Vancouver's merchants catered to city rather than to regional needs.[19]

Massive log booms and screaming saw blades would have suggested to contemporary observers that lumber was more than a local economic activity. Indeed, in 1891 mills in and around Vancouver cut 64 per cent of the timber logged in British Columbia, and Burrard Inlet's two largest plants, the Moodyville and Hastings sawmills, employed more than half the area's

Table 2.1

Occupational structure of Vancouver, 1890

Economic sector	Annual wages ($)	No. of employees	No. of employees as % of total
Manufacturing	874,000	1,637	32.6
Wood products	462,000	885	17.7
Salmon canneries	12,000	200	4.0
Foundries and machine shops	95,000	105	2.1
Other manufacturing	305,000	447	8.9
Construction	480,000	750	15.0
Transportation and public utilities	628,000	960	19.1
CPR	400,000	600	12.0
Steamship companies	75,000	150	3.0
Utilities	108,000	110	2.2
Other transportation	45,000	100	2.0
Service	1,102,000	1,669	33.3
Professions	77,000	97[a]	1.9
Hotels and boarding houses	257,000	125	2.5
Grocery trade			
Retail	143,000	195	0
Wholesale	20,000	25	19.2
Other commerce	492,000	742	0
Other services	49,000	116	2.3
Miscellaneous	64,000	69	1.4
Total	3,084,000	5,016	100.0

a   Includes eighteen 'medical men' listed in the Vancouver Board of Trade's publication of the survey (Vancouver Board of Trade, *Annual Report, 1891,* 40-1). No figures for medical men were given in the *Vancouver Daily World* newspaper report used for this table. The 1891 Nominal Census for Vancouver listed twenty-nine doctors, twenty-eight lawyers, nine dentists, seventeen architects, twenty-four clergymen, and fifty-three schoolteachers.

Source: Mayor David Oppenheimer's statistical survey of the Vancouver economy, presented to the Vancouver City Council on 5 January 1891 and reprinted in the *Vancouver Daily World,* souvenir edition, 11 April 1891, pp. 3 and 4

substantial sawmill workforce (Table 2.2).[20] Reflecting the impact of urbanization on the industry, however, the seven new mills constructed in Vancouver during the railway-generated boom catered to local rather than to traditional markets. The new mills were comparatively small, each employing less than one-third the number of loggers and millhands engaged by Hastings Sawmill. Most Vancouver mills also manufactured secondary wood products, such as sashes, doors, and frames, for domestic consumption. Thus, even though the lumber industry employed a substantial 17.7 per cent of Vancouver's workforce in 1890 (Table 2.1), lumber exports do not explain the city's economic expansion. The new mills were a product rather than a cause of Vancouver's population explosion.[21]

The CPR alone among Vancouver businesses created economic expansion independent of the land market. Being a transcontinental terminus, Vancouver assumed the role of breakpoint between different land and water transportation systems. Burrard Inlet's connections with the Far East, established previously by the lumber trade, expanded in 1887 when the *Abyssinia*, laden with mail, silk, tea, and general cargo, inaugurated the CPR's trans-Pacific steamship service to Vancouver. The first of a new line of ships, the *Empress of India*, arrived four years later. The transfer of goods between land and sea generated considerable economic activity, ranging from laundry cleaning and supply provisioning to operational maintenance and freight handling. In 1888, between regular maintenance and building

Table 2.2

Lumber industry in the Vancouver area, 1891

Sawmills and lumber manufacturing companies	Invested capital ($)	Annual wages ($)	Number of employees
Hastings Sawmill	500,000	150,000	300
Moodyville Sawmill	250,000	80,000	185
Royal City Planing Mills	185,000	72,000	90
Commercial Mills (Leamy & Kyle)	100,000	36,000	70
Morse & Boggs (H.R. Morse)	150,000	40,000	70
Vancouver Sawmill (Webster and Edmonds)	50,000	24,000	50
Cassady & Company	50,000	20,000	40
Vancouver Shingle Mill (Slater & Co.)	20,000	22,000	40
Vancouver Manufacturing & Trading Co.	35,000	18,000	40
Total	1,340,000	462,000	885

Source: See Table 2.1

projects, the CPR employed 800 workers, and this in a community of 8,000 to 9,000 people. Mayor Oppenheimer's 1890 survey identified the corporation as Vancouver's largest single employer. Only the lumber and construction industries spent more on wages (Table 2.1). Ultimately, however, the promotion and development of urban land, rather than other economic functions, explain business leadership in early Vancouver.[22]

THE TASK of servicing land fell within the jurisdiction of the municipal government. It controlled the pace and direction of development by providing funds for street improvements, offering fire and police protection for property, and determining the nature of water, light, and transportation utilities. Consequently, for a short period merchants, railway officials, and land promoters looked to civic government for the service infrastructure and financial support necessary for urban expansion. City Council became a focus of business power and enticed more business leaders to run for elective office than at any other time before 1913. Forty per cent of city councillors from 1887 to 1889 were drawn from among Vancouver's business leaders.[23] Real estate entrepreneurs and managers found civic government to be particularly helpful in advancing their commercial interests (Table 2.3). The two groups most active in early Vancouver politics were the CPR and the Oppenheimers, Vancouver's largest and second largest property holders respectively. These two factions, the former centred on the west side, the latter on the east, directed civic political life until the early 1890s.

Business leaders and property holders reinforced their economic control of the new city by limiting access to political power. Vancouver's 1886 charter had required that mayoral and aldermanic candidates – men only until 1917 – own Vancouver property assessed at $1,000 or lease property valued at $2,000, for aldermen all of it in the nominee's ward.[24] But in 1887 the provincial legislature mysteriously raised the qualifications for mayor and alderman without Vancouver City Council's approval. Business leaders R.H. Alexander, David Oppenheimer, and Lauchlan Hamilton, the first two of whom had close business and social ties with members of the provincial government, dismissed suggestions that they had secretly instructed the legislature to restrict the franchise in their favour, pointing instead to Nanaimo industrialist Robert Dunsmuir as the culprit.[25] Certainly, the violent expulsion of Chinese workers from Coal Harbour a month before –

Table 2.3

Direct participation in civic politics by Vancouver's ten major real estate owners, 1889

	Assessed value of Vancouver holdings ($)	Direct participation on Council
Residence or regional office in Vancouver		
Canadian Pacific Railway	1,700,000	L.A. Hamilton (Ald. 1886-7) Wm. Salsbury (Ald. 1889, 1893-4) J.M. Browning (Ald. 1890) H.E. Connon (Ald. 1892)
Vancouver Improvement Company	225,000	David Oppenheimer (Ald. 1887 and Mayor 1889-91)
Oppenheimer Bros.	150,000	Isaac Oppenheimer (Ald. 1887-9) David Oppenheimer (as above)
J.W. Horne	125,000	Ald. 1889-90
Dr. James Whetham	100,000	Ald. 1889
A.G. Ferguson	100,000	None
Bewicke & Wulffsohn	60,000	None
Residence or regional office unknown		
Isaac Robinson	125,000	None
H.A. Dewindt	60,000	None
Town & Robinson	60,000	None

Source: Assessed value of real estate drawn from Norbert MacDonald, 'The Canadian Pacific Railway and Vancouver's Development to 1900,' *BC Studies* 35 (Autumn 1977):18

discussed later in the chapter – had upset Dunsmuir and other Island members, who feared that such action threatened law and order.[26]

Whatever its motives, the legislature removed the leasehold provision for candidates in Vancouver altogether and doubled the ownership requirements to $2,000. It thus severely reduced the number of male residents capable of filling elective positions. The legislation also removed an 1886 provision that gave the vote to a significant group of male renters paying $5 per month or $50 per year for lodgings. The new provision maintained the requirement that voters own property assessed at $300 but sharply increased the financial requirements stipulated for leaseholders and renters. These severe restrictions remained unaltered until 1891, thus providing legal support for early political leadership by elite entrepreneurs.

Councillors achieved their goal of promoting development by borrowing heavily to construct streets and bridges that would open land for development, by giving a bonus to transportation and manufacturing companies, and by employing the city's credit to ensure the provision of necessary utility services. Leading capitalists dominated early decision making in these crucial areas. Between 1887 and 1889 four top businessmen, the most prominent of whom was David Oppenheimer, manoeuvred three general loan by-laws through Council; the city's entire credit could then be employed to finance more services at a faster rate than under the previously employed local debenture system of civic financing.[27] A series of by-laws were introduced to provide civic bonuses for enterprises ranging from smelting works and a foundry to the CPR workshops and roundhouse. All major bonusing proposals before 1891 came from business leaders on Council.[28] In addition, David Oppenheimer and J.W. Horne, the latter a leading real estate and utilities investor, initiated the young city's most important public utilities decision, the municipalization of the Vancouver Water Works Company.[29]

Elected CPR officials publicly acknowledged that their role in government was to represent 'the vast interests' of Vancouver's largest property owner.[30] Company representatives on Council demanded more civic funds for westside roads, defended the CPR's claim to own much of the city's Burrard Inlet waterfront, and boosted private companies in which CPR executives were interested.[31] The latter provides an excellent example of how railway managers used their political power for corporate and personal benefit. In February 1890 J.M. Browning, Vancouver City Council's finance chairman, directed the Council to bonus BC Sugar's anticipated new refinery in Vancouver. This he did while serving as CPR land commissioner and representative for the Montreal-based CPR executives who were financing the refinery enterprise. The development-minded councillors did not consider Browning's dual role as both a grantor and a recipient of the city's largesse a conflict of interest. A month after Council's decision to bonus the new company, Browning was named BC Sugar's first president.[32]

Underlying consensus within the business-dominated Council about the need to promote urban growth did not always ensure cooperation among boosters. Indeed, some of the most heated conflicts in early Vancouver occurred among the city's main business groups, who were divided by the sectional nature of the land market. So intense was passion over development issues that Charles Rand, the city's most vocal booster, was moved to urge citizens 'to pull for Vancouver irrespective of section.' Citizens in other cities were united, he proclaimed, but in Vancouver 'were all divided.'[33]

David Oppenheimer represented the contradictions of boosterism. At one level he embodied the hopes and aspirations of all town boosters, encouraging large-scale borrowing, supporting bonuses to industries, urging the municipalization of utilities, and enthusiastically advertising Vancouver. As mayor and Board of Trade president he could justifiably claim to have done his 'utmost to further the general interest of the City.'[34] Yet his record also reveals a consistent pattern of sectional partisanship. Differences with westside representatives over where to locate a rail bridge across False Creek or how to distribute public works appropriations soured political relations and turned City Council into a forum for open, and at times bitter, conflict.[35]

Sectional feeling about where to locate a federal post office illustrates how intense division between the two leading factions of city developers could be. In the spring of 1886 A.W. Ross convinced the federal government to locate a temporary post office on CPR land west of Gastown. To quote the MP, whose close ties to the rail company had earned him the title 'C.P.R. member of Parliament': 'I made the arrangement to move the P.O. up on the Company's property ... and had to use all my influence at Ottawa to keep it there against the wishes of the citizens.'[36] A storm of controversy accompanied the post office decision, promoting petitions from both eastside critics and westside supporters. Opponents presented a solid case, arguing that the Hastings Street post office site was relatively inaccessible to most residents. Indeed, as one of the founders of Vancouver's trade union movement in the 1880s later observed, 'at all elections' Vancouver workingmen, having grown 'very weary of walking' from their east- and southeastside homes to Vancouver's public offices in the western suburbs, 'stood by the east end ticket' headed by David Oppenheimer.[37]

But the logic of numbers in Vancouver could not counter corporate lobbying in Ottawa. As discussions turned to a permanent site, the CPR gained a tactical advantage by offering seven choice lots at Granville and Pender. It did so for a nominal fee, forgoing large real estate profits. Once more both sides organized massive petitions and public meetings, generating in the city an intensely fractious political climate. Considering a permanent post office on Granville to be 'of very great importance to the

David Oppenheimer, mayor of
Vancouver, 1888-91. (City of
Vancouver Archives PORT.P.662
N.500)

Harry Abbott, general superintendent of the CPR's Pacific
division, 1886-97. (Vancouver
Public Library 988)

C.P.R.,' Van Horne spared no effort to win a favourable hearing.[38] To silence local opponents he instructed Vancouver CPR superintendent Harry Abbott to intervene directly, and uncharacteristically, in local politics. At one point Abbott organized westside forces to capture a potentially hostile public meeting, having it pass instead the company's 'own resolutions.'[39] Ultimately it was Van Horne's personal intervention with federal officials, rather than west coast pressure, that swayed Ottawa's judgment in the CPR's favour.[40] In March 1890 the postmaster-general announced that a large and expensive structure would be built on Granville Street, in the heart of the company's townsite (see Map 2.1). The Canadian Pacific was indeed, as its detractors maintained, 'a power in the land.'[41]

The contrary tendencies of a business community united in support of rapid urban growth but sharply divided by conflicting interests and personalities are understandable when viewed as separate parts of a single process. Urban booms initially create conditions susceptible to economic and political control by major landholding interests. Thus, during the 1880s Vancouver's emerging upper class dominated both public and private spheres of authority.[42] Major issues of the day relating to the city's physical expansion greatly concerned business leaders and drew them into an active political role. In a political environment where other social groups had only minimal influence, municipal decisions were determined through public controversy between competing business leaders. In the 1880s conflict between landed interests enormously influenced Vancouver's spatial development, shaping its economic and social geography to the present day.

While disagreeing on particular issues, however, business leaders were of one mind about fundamental values and policies. Thus the mayor's success in promoting Vancouver through exhibitions and advertisements, his strong commitment to attracting industries, and his achievements in floating municipal debentures on foreign money markets benefited all boosters, especially the CPR. Top railway officials endorsed Oppenheimer's candidacy for re-election in December 1888 and again a year later. Harry Abbott led rail company support, sitting prominently by the mayor's side at a sumptuous banquet held to celebrate Oppenheimer's victory over a determined opponent. One of the mayor's harshest westside critics on the sharply divided Council that year, W.F. Salsbury, the CPR treasurer, joined the celebration.[43]

Culmination of the post office dispute offers perhaps the clearest understanding of the bounds within which conflict among business leaders occurred. The first public indication that the post office question was nearing resolution came prior to the December 1889 election, when Mayor Oppenheimer switched positions to favour a Granville Street location. He may have succumbed to CPR influence, or he may have changed his mind to gain westside support for the upcoming election fight. Certainly, in abandoning the eastside position he accepted a fait accompli. After the federal government announced its choice in March, the Board of Trade and several prominent businessmen followed the mayor's lead by accepting the inevitable in the name of unity. Board president R.H. Alexander reluctantly agreed to the Granville Street site for 'patriotic' reasons, stating that he hoped 'City interests might not be jeopardized.'[44]

SOCIAL DIVISION along class lines was more worrisome to civic leaders than was division among business groups. The first instance of overt conflict between those who owned or controlled the means of production and those who sold their labour occurred at a point of symbolic significance in Vancouver's history: the first civic election. After the bill to incorporate Vancouver as a city received royal assent on 6 April 1886, plans to elect a municipal council were begun. An obvious candidate for mayor was R.H. Alexander, the most powerful representative of capital on Burrard Inlet in the early 1880s and a man well connected to the provincial elite in Victoria. Major property owners in Vancouver and Victoria, including the CPR, supported Alexander. A number of prominent Victoria investors came by boat on the morning of 3 May to cast ballots on his behalf. He was challenged by Malcolm MacLean, a Scots-born and Ontario-raised real estate agent who represented the interests of small businessmen, including both Granville pioneers and the newly arrived and mainly Canadian real estate element.[45]

Crucial to the election's outcome was a strike by millhands against Hastings Sawmill in early April, the first known labour conflict of this kind in the history of Burrard Inlet mills. Fighting for a ten-hour workday, the workers challenged the traditional twelve-hour day that had long prevailed up and down the coast. The strikers were neither the mill's Native or Chinese workers nor its older European hands but former navvies recently hired by Alexander after being laid off by railway contractors along the recently completed CPR line. They brought with them new ideas about what constituted a fair day's wage, notions that would profoundly unsettle old ways on Burrard Inlet. The Knights of Labor, a trade union organization that flourished during the 1880s among industrial workers in eastern North America, had entered British Columbia in 1883 and created a number of assemblies, including two along the CPR line at Kamloops and Yale.[46] Knights of Labor organizers and members were among the White railway navvies who migrated to the coast. Their presence signalled the inception of a new pattern of labour relations based much less on a personal bond between worker and manager and much more on the collective interests of labour and capital. Alexander's intransigence, his arrogant claim that to maintain the old twelve-hour day he need only hire more Natives and Chinese, and his alleged statement that Canadian workers were nothing but 'North America Chinamen' infuriated the strikers and made them implacable political enemies of the boss-who-would-be-mayor. Some men voted more than once, which may account for MacLean's narrow victory over Alexander, 242 to 225.

Whether aided by corrupt electoral practices or not, the tide of change was with the workers. Having lost the first dispute, labourers struck again in June 1887 for a ten-hour day and closed four sawmills. This time they won.[47]

Three strikes in 1889 hinted at the issues that capital and labour would contest over the next quarter century. A six-day walkout in July pitted 228 unionized carpenters against contractors and sash and door factory owners over the workers' demand that the normal workday be reduced from ten to nine hours. Carpenters struck for and got nine hours on construction projects but factory owners retained the ten-hour day, conceding only that carpenters employed in sash and door plants might leave work three hours early on Saturdays. Unionized printers won a short strike at the *Vancouver Daily World* newspaper over control of the work process. A fifty-six-day walkout by longshoremen in the fall over wages and union recognition proved less successful.[48]

Disputes about wages and working conditions are a staple of industrial economies and have been a recurring feature of labour relations in Vancouver. At their core was the issue of how to determine the value of labour once it had ceased to be an autonomous factor of production and had become a commodity for sale. The walkouts by longshoremen and carpenters reflected this ongoing concern. But the 1889 work stoppages revealed as well the much deeper struggle for control of the labour process.

The issue of control was most evident in the typographers' strike: a compositor was fired for contesting the right of management at the *World* to make alterations to the style board, prompting seventeen typographers to walk out. This conflict over the seemingly trivial matter of 'who would make the correction from lower case "i" to capital "I" in the word "independence"' was a power struggle over control of the work process. The same issue found different expression in the longshoremen's strike, where workers demanded that the stevedoring company recognize their union and hire labour through a union-controlled hiring hall rather than on an individual basis. To fight this demand the company recruited 'scab' labour from ports on Puget Sound to replace the striking longshoremen. It also asked Mayor Oppenheimer to provide police protection for the non-union substitutes. Not surprisingly, Oppenheimer, a high-profile member of the city's emerging upper class, supported management.[49]

Nonetheless, the tendency of industrial societies to divide along the fault line of class remained weak in early Vancouver. One reason was the city's social structure. Put simply, while very different in size and function from the lumber village it replaced, Vancouver retained important elements of its frontier past. Its youthful and predominantly male population continued to characterize Vancouver as a city being formed, not a city firmly established. As was the case in Granville, over half the people of Vancouver at census time in 1891 were working-age men (Table 2.4). Adult women remained a distinct minority in the new city, despite increasing proportionately by 5 per cent during the 1880s. They formed a particularly small part of the working-age population that lived without a spouse and resided outside of a family structure; the city had 527 unattached women compared with 4,619 men of similar status, a ratio of nine to one. The waterfront remained a predominantly masculine social world as the former Gastown area evolved into a district of hotels and boarding houses. More than four-fifths of the population sheltered there were male, most of them unattached men of working age. The waterfront section of town had the lowest percentage of family men – husbands with wives, as defined in Table 2.5 – of any part of the city. Yet men living outside of a family structure were so pervasive in early Vancouver that they could not be accommodated by one district alone. Consequently, they exceeded the number of family men in other parts of the city as well. Vancouver's population also remained young, the average age in 1891 (25.4 years) being virtually identical

Table 2.4

Population structure of Granville (1881) and Vancouver (1891)

	Granville 1881	Vancouver 1891
Children as % of total population	31.7	25.8
Working-age population as % of total	68.3	73.5
Working-age men as % of total	51.9	51.6
Working-age women as % of total	16.5	21.6
Mean age (total population)	25.8	25.4
Mean age (working-age men)	35.8	32.0
Mean age (working-age women)	30.9	31.1
Number of cases	243	13,647

Note: Children: ages 0-14; working-age adults: ages 15-64
Sources: Canada, Nominal Census 1881, Division 187 (New Westminster), Subsection B (S.D. North), pp. 86-114; and Canada, Nominal Census 1891, District 2 (New Westminster), Subdistrict C1 (Vancouver City)

Table 2.5

Ethnicity and family[a] in Vancouver, 1891 (by percentage)

Birthplace	Granville total 1881 population	Vancouver total 1891 population	Vancouver family population		Vancouver non-family population	
			Men (husbands)	Women (wives)	Men (adult)	Women (adult)
Canada (BC)	36.6	8.7	1.1	3.2	1.0	5.5
Canada (except BC)	15.6	42.5	43.7	45.5	35.6	39.7
Great Britain	23.0	29.1	41.5	36.4	31.9	36.2
United States	5.8	7.9	7.1	9.5	5.5	11.4
Europe (except the UK)	6.6	4.4	5.4	4.7	6.3	6.1
China	7.8	6.1	0.3	0.2	17.3	0.4
Other	4.5	1.2	0.9	0.5	2.4	0.8
Total %	99.9	99.9	100.0	100.0	100.0	100.1
Number of cases	243	13,647[b]	1,707	1,707	4,619	527

Notes:

a 'Family' has been defined as men or women living with a spouse in Vancouver when the census was taken in the spring of 1891. 'Family' spouses were identified by linking last names of adult men and women who lived in the same household and who had household relationships that made it possible for them to have been spouses; for instance, the status of 'wife' for women and 'head of household' for men was a common combination. 'Non-family' has been defined as men or women without a spouse in Vancouver at census time. For instance, many married men had come to the city without their wives, the large number of married Chinese men (271) without wives (only ten married Chinese women were listed as living in Vancouver) being the most obvious example. These men have been included in the 'non-family' category. Of necessity, this method of defining 'family' has left out some adults linked to family members in other ways, such as adult siblings or single parents and their offspring.

b The city's population totalled 13,673, but the birthplace of twenty-six was unknown to the census takers.
Sources: See Table 2.4

with that ten years earlier (25.8 years). The relatively rootless character of this instant city reinforced the power and authority of the business community, its most structured part.

The organizational advantage that Vancouver's social structure offered to business leaders is evident in the early histories of the Vancouver Board of Trade and the Vancouver Trades and Labor Council (VTLC). Established in September 1887 to create a favourable environment for business activities, the Board of Trade expressed the functional and symbolic authority of business. The conclusion of a recent study on Canadian boards of trade – that before 1920 such boards were key institutions in the city-building process, consistently influencing municipal councils to 'help local business' – is pertinent to Vancouver. Headed by business leaders, the Board of Trade quickly entered debate on civic issues, opposing the CPR in one instance and actively promoting a campaign to boost investment in another.[50]

By contrast, the VTLC, whose goal was to advance 'in every way ... the material welfare of workers,' was much slower to organize and a much weaker organization once formed. In December 1888 unionized typographers formed a committee to inquire into the feasibility of uniting local unions into a city labour council, but another year passed before printers, carpenters, plasterers, painters, and members of the Knights of Labor achieved their goal. Limited mainly to skilled craftsmen, the Council did not include the large number of unskilled labourers who crowded the city's boarding houses and hotels. In addition, the newly created and insecure VTLC, unlike the Board of Trade, played little part in Vancouver's legislative process, limiting its advice mainly to pleas that the city government and private employers not hire Chinese labour.[51]

The history of these two organizations underscores the point that in a society where most people had recently come from somewhere else, and where economic and social connections were being created anew, the boom-town atmosphere favoured an elite of businessmen who commanded the organizational skill and access to capital required for successful boosterism. Businessmen quickly formed a complex network of personal connections through their many joint ventures and the Board of Trade.[52] Most leading managers and entrepreneurs had arrived in the city by 1887 and remained there for the next half-dozen years. By contrast, working people were a larger and more transient group whose complexity and mobility made developing social and political ties beyond a limited part of the working

A pioneer bachelors' hall, Vancouver, 1890. In the late 1880s
Vancouver attracted thousands
of young people who hoped
to find jobs and establish new
lives in the far west. Men
without families predominated.
(Bailey Bros. photo, Vancouver Public Library 13196)

class very difficult. The extent to which the rootlessness of boomtown Vancouver retarded the development of social networks among working people is evident in the attempts of printers and longshoremen to establish trade organizations. In May 1887 seventeen printers met to form Vancouver's first union local, after which they sought affiliation with the International Typographical Union. But the new charter did not arrive, and when the following January nine printers again started the process of creating a union, only two of the original seventeen remained in the city. In a similar manner, longshoremen 'were very migratory ... and new ones kept coming and going,' making the process of institutional formation very difficult.[53]

A second explanation for the weak challenge of working people to business leadership in early Vancouver, and for the limited extent of open conflict between classes in the new city, is to be found in the ideological orientation of western immigrants. Carl Abbott, an American historian, has argued that nineteenth-century cities were viewed 'primarily as a series of economic possibilities, [where] every new warehouse and every new citizen was simultaneously a confirmation of achievement and a promise for the future.'[54] Belief that society was marching inexorably towards improvement and advantageous change – in other words, that society was 'progressive' – was pervasive, as was faith that economic expansion would reward hard-working and resourceful individuals, and through them society as a whole. This faith was especially widespread in western boom towns such as Vancouver. The desire of migrants, bent on personal gain, to exploit the economic opportunities offered by rapid urban growth crossed class lines and created an ethos that linked people behind the common goal of advancing their city. Thus, just as the *Vancouver News*, a business-oriented newspaper, could proclaim that 'progress is our watchword,' so could George Bartley, a typographer and leader of Vancouver's fledgling labour movement, proudly describe his community as 'a progressive and up to date city.' Both statements reflect a belief that the city-building process benefited all.[55] In 1889 the *Daily News-Advertiser* similarly spoke of common values when remarking on 'the healthful competition and keen desire ... among all the classes [in Vancouver], even the poorest, to better their condition.'[56]

WHILE THE ECONOMY served more to unify than to divide Vancouver residents in the late 1880s, ethnicity and race structured identities in more ambiguous ways. The railway brought in its wake thousands of people, mainly of working age, who dreamed of jobs and wealth. Many had crossed the continent. Most were either British-born or hailed from British stock (88 per cent). Eastern Canadians formed the largest single group (42.5 per cent), with lesser numbers born in Great Britain (29.1 per cent), China (6.1 per cent), and the United States (7.9 per cent). Indeed, Canadian-born citizens, excluding those born in British Columbia, were almost three times as prominent in Vancouver as they had been in Granville a decade earlier (Table 2.5). By contrast, British Columbians formed a much smaller proportion of the population in 1891 (8.7 per cent) than they had in 1881 (36.6 per cent). The difference reflects demographic change within the settlement community on Burrard Inlet: 40 per cent of women and children in the lumber communities of Moodyville and Granville had been born in British Columbia, many of Native descent. By contrast, few Vancouver women were local, and few women or female children in the city were of Native birth or origin. The partial integration of European and indigenous people that had occurred during the initial phase of European settlement on Burrard Inlet had given way – first among managers and skilled workers in lumber society and by 1891 across all strata of the urban population – to a pattern of social and cultural separation. In contrast to its predecessor, Vancouver was, in ethnic terms, a relatively homogeneous community.

An increased level of racial intolerance by Whites against non-Whites accompanied this demographic shift. The best known conflict occurred early in 1887 near Coal Harbour, where a gang of Chinese workers were clearing 350 acres of West End land. In January a group of White residents met at City Hall to establish two committees, one to raise funds that would induce the Chinese to leave town and another to encourage employers to replace Chinese with European labourers. Among the committee members were respectable city leaders such as Mayor Malcolm MacLean, magistrate J.J. Blake, hardware merchant Thomas Dunn, and capitalist A.G. Ferguson. A crowd of 600 'citizens' cheered the first twenty Chinese to depart, testifying to the popularity and success of the initiatives. Support for anti-Chinese policies continued to flourish among Whites, though the movement now passed out of the hands of respectable civic and business leaders. Four additional meetings, all well attended, were held in January, and 'citizens ... continued to paint white crosses on establishments that were said to deal with Chinese.' The defiant rejection of community standards by John McDougall, a contractor, led to a large public meeting on the evening of 24 February, after which mobs of angry men – mainly transients – pulled down, burned, or ransacked the shanties of Chinese labourers at Coal Harbour and at Carrall Street, in what is now Chinatown. As Kay Anderson notes in *Vancouver's Chinatown*, 'the riot marked the first act of physical violence against the Chinese in Canada.' The provincial government then passed 'An Act for the Preservation of Peace within ... Vancouver,' depriving the city of its police and judicial powers, and dispatched forty special constables from Victoria to control Vancouver's 'mobs.'[57]

The city's Native residents also came under attack from the now overwhelmingly White majority. White attention focused on the Indian rancherie – described as 'a long low building built in a sort of trestle and divided into cabins' – located to the east of Hastings Sawmill.[58] Before the railway came, the rancherie had been a centre for Native mill workers. It became thereafter part of a 'regular town of shacks' constructed by the growing number of Native people living in the area. Through the early months of 1887 Vancouver newspapers carried numerous stories on the 'revelry, rioting and shooting' at the rancherie, and local clergy spoke out against Native women coming into the city from up the coast to engage in prostitution. On 12 July the city's chief of police visited the rancherie and, to end the ongoing 'nuisance,' expelled its occupants.[59]

These incidents demonstrated racial impulses that were very much part of the culture of western Europeans. Sentiments similar to those expressed in Vancouver were to be heard in many lands where late-nineteenth-century Europeans, burdened with a sense of cultural and racial superiority, sought to impose their values and institutions on non-European peoples. Yet it is reasonable to argue that this process of racial aggression also took on a meaning particular to British Columbia. Anderson suggests that this meaning is to be found in the way that Vancouver's newly formed British majority used racial categories to consolidate its identity as the city's dominant group. Outbursts against Chinese and Aboriginal people coincided with the emergence of a more ethnically homogeneous society on Burrard Inlet's south shore. Racial identification allowed the British-, Canadian-, and American-born residents of all three classes to concentrate into a 'counter-idea' everything that was thought to conflict with their notion of an ideal community.[60] Attacks on minorities were the cultural equivalent of squabbles among businessmen in municipal government: both were part of the process by which power and position were distributed within the emerging city.

Ethnicity and race would remain important sources of status in Vancouver to the First World War, though perhaps less so than in the turbulent 1880s. However, as the city aged and social relations became more stable, the role of family, and the difference between family and single status, would also increasingly separate citizens from non-citizens. Though the mobs who attacked Chinese dwellings in February 1887 expressed anti-Chinese sentiments widely shared among the city's White majority, the transient men who participated were not respectable. Indeed, it was precisely the need to control this element that led the Protestant churches, the Women's Christian Temperance Union, and the Independent Order of Good Templars to campaign determinedly against the hotels and saloons that proliferated as the population grew.[61] George Pollay, a carpenter at the Royal City Planing Mills on False Creek and an active member of the city's single tax movement, undoubtedly reflected the views of many respectable workingmen when he spoke out publicly against saloons in the city.[62] The Indian rancherie was threatening to the British majority not just because of its racial character but also because the drinking and fighting that went on there 'greatly alarmed the people living in that vicinity,' and challenged their notions of respectability.[63] The boundary separating those who could claim to be a 'citizen' of Vancouver from those who could not was being set down through this discourse on liquor just as it was through the rhetoric of racial exclusion.

The Dominion Day parades of 1889 and 1890 should be viewed, then, as an expression of the aspirations and sense of place of those residents who saw themselves as respectable and were accepted as such by their peers. They were people like William Pleming, an English-born carpenter, churchgoing family man, and activist in Vancouver's fledgling labour movement, who would later recall the thrill of being a 'pioneer' in Vancouver, of driving back the forest, of establishing the province's mills and factories, and of creating a city.[64] Such residents enjoyed the status and power of being part of the city's cultural majority, and by joining voluntary associations such as fraternal societies, trade unions, churches, and reform organizations they planted roots in the community.

One such organization, an American-based fraternal society called the

Knights of Pythias, aimed to promote among its members friendship, brotherhood, 'and citizenship.' By marching on Dominion Day the Knights asserted metaphorically their claim to be accepted as respectable and permanent 'citizens' of Vancouver.[65] Businessmen and workers, both immensely proud of the city's growth, paraded together because they shared this sense of respectability. Beyond the consensus, however, lay different visions of how Vancouver society should be organized and what role capitalists and common people should play in it. These differences would set the agenda for civic life in Vancouver for much of the 1890s.

CHAPTER THREE

Monopolists and Plain People

The municipal election of December 1889 marked the beginning of an important change in Vancouver's civic life. William Templeton, a retail grocer and member of the middle class, challenged David Oppenheimer, an upper-class businessman and politician, for the position of mayor. Several aldermanic candidates and many enthusiastic supporters backed Templeton. At a time when development issues dominated the political agenda and power was shared by two business factions, Templeton and his band of vocal dissenters introduced a new language to Vancouver politics: the language of social and political conflict. Recognizing that Oppenheimer's support was 'highly respectable,' they portrayed themselves as friends of the worker. Templeton was running to serve 'the working and middle classes,' they exhorted. 'He represented the bone and muscle of the City,' not its business aristocracy. Oppenheimer's backers deprecated 'the cry of "class" which had been raised,' but they also sensed that Vancouver's political terrain was shifting, with business control of civic power being challenged from below. The confrontation drew virtually every business leader into open support for the mayor, who won the election and retained control of City Council.[1]

The election marked a new stage in the structuring of society. The squabbles among prominent businessmen that had characterized civic politics in the 1880s was giving way to a political discourse that pitted the leading entrepreneurs and corporate managers against the respectable middle stratum of Vancouver society. Both interests and ideology separated the two groups. Whereas leading businessmen represented large investments of capital – often originating outside the region – and the fostering of regional growth by a close alliance of business with the provincial or federal governments, the middling group emphasized small-scale enterprise, the small producer, and community ties. Significantly, while Templeton's remarks suggested that social hierarchy was to be defined by economically based classes, the reality was more complex. The emerging middle stratum included people of both the middle and working classes.

THE ECONOMIC and social structures that nourished political dissent in Vancouver are best understood as part of a trend in North American capitalism of the period: the rise of 'big business,' where small, locally based, and individual or family-owned enterprises were giving way to large, incorporated, and bureaucratic organizations. American business historian Alfred Chandler suggests that as businesses became large their structure passed through four stages. The first he terms 'personal enterprise.' Here, even when traditional partnerships 'began to incorporate, their capital stock stayed in the hands of a few individuals or families.' These locally based businesses remained single-unit enterprises that 'rarely hired more than two or three managers.' Next came 'entrepreneurial or family capitalism,' when the enterprise required more managers than a family or associates could provide but those who had built the enterprises continued to hold the majority of stock, to maintain a close personal relationship with their managers, and to have a major say in the management decisions. In the final two stages of growth, businesses that had been highly personal and often limited to a home community or region became increasingly impersonal and bureaucratic, extending their geographic range of operations, capital requirements, and managerial needs far beyond the reach of individual families or networks of friends. In return for raising the large pools of capital required to finance expansion, banks and other financial institutions placed representatives on the firms' boards of directors and thereby acquired a say in top management decisions. This third stage, known as 'financial capitalism,' gave way to the fourth, 'managerial capital-ism,' when ownership became widely scattered and clearly divorced from management. This final stage existed when salaried managers both deter-mined long-term policies and managed short-term operating functions.[2]

Most business activity in early Vancouver was controlled by locally cen-tred entrepreneurs who headed firms at the initial two stages of Chandler's typology. Real estate, utility, commercial, manufacturing, and service sec-tors of the economy were entirely or predominantly owned and managed by Vancouver businessmen, and to a lesser extent by entrepreneurs from the nearby communities of Victoria and New Westminster. The biggest of the Vancouver-centred businesses, such as BC Sugar, had reached the entre-preneurial or family capitalism stage of development. Formed by Benjamin T. Rogers and financed initially by Montreal and New York capitalists, BC Sugar had as its first president the CPR land commissioner, J.M. Browning, who represented the outside investors. But Rogers soon gained financial control of the profitable firm, which by the turn of the century had evolved into a classic example of family capitalism.[3] Lumbering was similar. After the Beecher and Hendry families of New Westminster and Vancouver bought Hastings Sawmill in 1889, all lumber companies in Vancouver except the London-controlled Moodyville sawmill were owned and man-aged by regional capitalists, and remained at the earlier stages of organiza-tional development. During the late 1880s, David Oppenheimer was clearly the most powerful of these local businessmen.

In the following decade a severe economic downturn weakened Vancouver entrepreneurs. Some adjustment following the rapid growth of the 1880s was to be expected. As the Winnipeg boom of 1882-3 had illus-trated, real estate bubbles were destined to burst. Signs that Vancouver's growth-leading property industry was in trouble came as early as March 1890, when J.M. Browning noted how quiet business was in the Terminal City. Victoria, in contrast, was enjoying 'quite a boom.'[4] Vancouver's frag-ile economic base made the city especially vulnerable to the widespread depression that started in industrial countries in 1893. Land sales and con-struction in Vancouver virtually ceased. The Canadian Pacific Railway, unable to sell townsite lots as individual units, closed its Vancouver land office, fired Browning, and to lessen taxes tried to sell off a significant por-tion of its city land in a single chunk.[5] The city's street railway companies and Oppenheimer Brothers collapsed, while Vancouver's largest lumber company, the local gas utility, and a small but soon-to-be-successful enterprise, the Union Steamship Company, barely escaped bankruptcy. One group of Vancouver businessmen contemplated abandoning the city as a lost cause.[6] Many citizens did, lured away by better prospects in Cariboo and Kootenay mining. Among them was Charles Rand, maestro to Vancouver's symphony of growth in the eighties, who moved first to Sandon, British Columbia, and then to Spokane, Washington.[7]

Business people did not suffer alone. Comments by observers at mid-decade tell of extensive hardship for wage earners, especially those engaged in construction. In the spring of 1891 and again in 1892 construction workers protested publicly the lack of jobs, claiming that in the former year up to 40 per cent of carpenters and 20 per cent of bricklayers had been without work.[8] By March 1896 at least half the city's carpenters were unemployed, and of those working none received the standard wage. Almost all construction work was being carried out by subcontracting – by which men pooled their wages – and on a piecework basis. This strategy significantly diminished hourly rates of pay. Over the previous twelve months not more than a score of bricklayers and plasterers had found employment. In lumber mills and sash and door factories working conditions had become desperate. Employees laboured ten to twelve hours per day 'at extremely low wages.' We have had a 'very hard time of it' for the past two years, an employer stated in 1896. 'A very large number of our best workingmen, including the skilled as well as the unskilled, have gone into the upper country.'[9] Indeed, the number of wage earners who left the city during the depression must have been large, though the extent and character of outmigration is statistically undocumented. For many who stayed, economic prospects were grim. As Lady Aberdeen, wife of Canada's governor-general, noted after a visit to the city in November 1894, 'The place seems improved and the streets are being laid with asphalt – but the times are v[ery] hard, and there are great numbers of people out of work.'[10]

The history of Vancouver utility companies, an important field of investment for city-building entrepreneurs, underlines the tenuous state of local business during the 1890s. The city's gas, light, water, telephone, and street railway companies had all been founded by Victoria, Vancouver, and New Westminster capitalists. Yet by 1898 only the gas company remained in the hands of regional investors. The City of Vancouver assumed control of the waterworks in 1891 and the two bankrupt street railway and electric light companies were taken over, first by a mixed consortium of local and British capitalists and then, in 1896, by the British Columbia Electric Railway Company (BC Electric). The latter was a London-based corporation headed by mining promoter R.M. Horne-Payne. The BC owners of Vancouver's utility companies had been unable to cover the losses they incurred during the economic slide of the early 1890s. In October 1897 Johannes Buntzen, a BC Electric manager, wryly observed, 'Vancouver is not a wealthy town – at any rate not yet.'[11]

As the fate of the utility companies suggests, the depression accentuated the real nature of corporate power by weakening the competing influence of local entrepreneurs. By virtue of their small-scale and recent creation, Vancouver-centred businesses had been relatively insecure, even during the boom. Local entrepreneurs had attracted investment money through personal networks of friends and acquaintances, which necessarily limited the volume of capital they could accumulate. In addition, the city's short history had lessened the possibility of accumulating capital through retained earnings. Undercapitalized local businesses were vulnerable in a severe economic downturn, especially since so much early growth had been tied to the sale and development of land. The Oppenheimers and Rands saw their wealth and influence disintegrate in the 1890s like sandcastles beneath a rising sea. By contrast, while the CPR suffered a serious erosion of profits, it had the financial strength to ride out disastrous returns in particular parts of its operation, such as Vancouver real estate.

John Hendry, head of the New Westminster-based British Columbia Mills, Timber, and Trading Company (BCMTT), which owned three sawmills in the area, would certainly have testified to the relative power of external capital in the 1890s. As a contemporary observer put it, BCMTT 'got into financial trouble. Sweeny [manager of the Bank of Montreal] ... was one of the directors. They [BCMTT] wanted to get rid of Alexander [manager of Hastings Sawmill], but Mr. Sweeny said "No ... So long as you have an overdraft Alexander must remain on board." He had confidence in Mr. Alexander. If it had not been for Sweeny the mill would have collapsed.'[12] In other words, to save his business a BC industrialist had been forced to accept a key managerial decision made by an eastern banker.

In the public mind, however, real power rested with the CPR. Historical circumstance offered much to justify such a perception. The money invested and people employed by the CPR had constituted the city's most important initial source of economic growth. The corporation's legal status, its ability to shape Vancouver's spatial organization, and its social leadership extended this influence into the 1890s.

Two conflicts between the city government and the CPR illustrate how legal and statutory protection set the rail company beyond the influence of community control. First, when in 1891 Vancouver City Council asked the railway company to provide 'proper and modern gates' to protect the public against the 'great danger to both life and property' caused by exposed train crossings in the city's core, the CPR replied with an unqualified 'no.'[13] Referring to provisions of the Dominion Railway Act of 1888 that placed the adjudication of disputes between the national railway and municipal governments in the hands of a committee of the federal cabinet, Harry Abbott stated that in previous decisions the Railway Committee had adopted the principle that local governments were responsible for at least as much of the cost of street barriers as rail companies. Furthermore, he went on, why should the CPR incur such cost to protect citizens in Vancouver when the company had received so little from the city, and the community so much from the railway? Did property in Vancouver not owe its 'value almost entirely, if not solely, to the existence and operation of the C.P.R.?'[14] In 1904 City Council was still pressing a recalcitrant Canadian Pacific Railway Company to protect the public at level crossings.[15]

Judicial interpretation of the 1881 act under which the CPR had been incorporated also favoured the company. This legislation granted the CPR the right to hold waterfront land 'to such extent as shall be required by the Company for its Railway and other works.' When the city government argued that the act did not give the company unrestricted access to the foreshore along the railway right of way, the CPR disagreed. To provide public access to the harbour, the municipality acted unilaterally by constructing a road up to and over the CPR's rail line embankment at the bottom of Gore Street. The company then took the city to court. The case eventually reached the Judicial Committee of the Privy Council (JCPC) in London, Canada's highest court, where in 1894 counsel for Vancouver argued that a victory for the railway would not only block access to the waterfront on this specific street but would in effect give the CPR virtual 'control of the whole harbour along which the City of Vancouver is built.' The JCPC upheld the company's case.[16] By 1899 the city and the CPR were again at odds over the public's right to control and use the ends of streets along the harbourfront on Burrard Inlet.[17]

The CPR's power also seemed more obtrusive in the 1890s than earlier because it was now less closely linked to the private interests of local business. In the first years after 1886 Vancouverites shared the goal of advancing personal prosperity by promoting urban growth. This city-building ethos led to the accommodation of factions within the business community that fought over specific policies but shared a common desire to boost Vancouver. The dramatic collapse of the real estate market uncoupled this link between local and external capital, a change illustrated by the rail corporation's view that direct representation on City Council, from which its last representative departed at the end of 1894, was no longer necessary. The CPR now functioned in Vancouver more exclusively as a large transportation company whose freight rate and waterfront land-use policies often ran counter to the collective interests of local business. The separation of community from corporate interests was expressed clearly by CPR president Thomas Shaughnessy at a public meeting in Vancouver in 1898: 'The company wished to meet the views of the City,' he stated, 'so long as its own interests were not jeopardized thereby.'[18]

Not surprisingly, it was the families of Canadian Pacific managers and rail company friends who combined economic power with social prestige to lead the process of social stratification in early Vancouver. To some extent the CPR's social influence was indirect. Expectations that Vancouver would be more than just a speculative 'instant city' because of the rail company's prominent role in promoting it undoubtedly made the coast city appealing to young men with talent and connections, such as Henry Bell-Irving and B.T. Rogers, who were looking for a place to make their mark in business. Railway construction also drew company-employed doctors, engineers, and contractors westward to the line's terminus, where they formed some of Vancouver's most prominent business and Society families.[19]

But the CPR also acted in a deliberate manner to employ social status as an instrument of economic advantage. Corporate executives encouraged business leaders and wealthy citizens to settle on company property, thereby enhancing corporate prestige and profits. Townsite promotion focused on Granville Street, at the centre of a 480-acre block of company real estate located between Burrard Inlet and False Creek. The CPR erected its hotel and opera house at the height of land on Granville. In addition, company managers sought to attract to Granville Street capitalists with ties to the upper levels of the social status structure in Britain and Canada, and by December 1888 they could boast that two knights of the realm, two English lords, and two professors had erected commercial structures there. Indeed, one disgruntled investor complained that, lacking 'a very long Pedigree' and being 'Canadian without a title,' she had been thwarted by the company in her bid to invest 'on aristocratic Granville Street.'[20] To the west of Granville along the bluffs overlooking Burrard Inlet, the company fostered Seaton Street (now West Hastings), Vancouver's first high-status neighbourhood, where CPR executives and other business and social leaders built expensive homes. Company managers and friends also pulled business and professional families westward by leading the formation of Vancouver's second Anglican congregation, Christ Church, and the construction of a fine sandstone cathedral on prime railway company land two blocks west of the Hotel Vancouver.[21]

The company's social pretensions naturally led it to support the movement by top businessmen to define themselves as a social status elite. In the 1880s businessmen formed a number of recreational clubs and organized the city's premier sporting body, the Brockton Point Athletic Association. In 1889 several businessmen started planning 'a first class social club' that would emulate the high-status business and social clubs of other major North American cities. Finally established in 1893, the Vancouver Club's promoters and executive represented a who's who of elite businessmen.[22] In addition, a fully integrated social elite required institutions for the socialization of children. Consequently, in 1890-1 Dr. James Whetham, 'an enterprising land developer from Ontario,' set up Whetham College 'especially for the secondary education of gentlemen's sons.'[23] The school was backed by leading businessmen David Oppenheimer and J.C. Keith, along with the CPR's chief engineer for the Pacific division, Henry Cambie. Charles Whetham, brother of James and former teacher at Upper Canada College, came west to run it.

Giving personal expression to the CPR's social aspirations were company manager Harry Abbott and his wife Margaret, who headed virtually every one of the young city's high-status social and cultural organizations. Both had privileged backgrounds. Harry Abbott, who as manager of the transcontinental railway's Pacific division held 'the most responsible [position] of its kind on the entire line,' had gained an engineering degree from McGill University. His father had graduated from Glasgow University and his brother, J.J.C. Abbott, was in 1891-2 the prime minister of Canada. The father of Margaret Abbott, the Honourable Justice Sicotte, had served with John A. Macdonald as co-leader of a government in the Canadas before Confederation.[24]

Once in Vancouver the Abbotts quickly assumed the mantle of social leadership. Harry helped found the Vancouver Club, presiding over it during the organizational stage to 1893 and becoming vice-president and president thereafter. He also served as the first president of both the Boating Club and the Lawn Tennis Club, the latter second in prestige only to the Vancouver Club. In 1894 the Abbotts were named honorary vice-presidents of the newly formed Art, Historical and Scientific Association (AHSA), which historian Ian Hunt describes as 'in many respects the city's premier cultural organization before the First World War.' At their Seaton Street home the Abbotts entertained all travellers of note to Vancouver, including Governor-General and Lady Aberdeen, Archduke Francis Ferdinand of Austria, explorer Sir Henry Stanley, and Sir Robert Baden-Powell, founder of the Boy Scout movement.[25] As one visitor to the city observed, in Vancouver the railway seemed to control everything.[26]

THE ECONOMIC CLIMATE of the early to mid-1890s, then, led to the decline of locally based enterprises dependent on a vibrant real estate market and rapid population growth while enhancing the business, economic, and social influence of Vancouver's one large corporation, the CPR. This dichotomy significantly affected the city's political climate. Local business leaders lost their capacity to retain control of civic decision making, and the CPR, which no longer needed to be directly involved in city government, exercised its powers in other ways.[27]

The resulting political vacuum at the municipal level reinforced the inclination of society's middling stratum to use elective office to advance its interests and express its vision of community. The political thrust of the respectable middle of society spread from the civic to the provincial and then the federal level, revealing broad support for a movement that challenged the power of upper-class business leaders. The movement's active members were, to some extent, 'populists,' for they saw themselves as representatives of 'the people' in opposition to a powerful, business-centred, minority.[28] The term used here is 'reformers,' a more inclusive description that refers to their shared desire to remake society in such a way as to preserve the values and practices that they believed were being destroyed by economic change.

The unifying core of the reformers' thought is what scholars refer to as 'the producers' ethos': the belief that labour was the source of all wealth and that employers and workers were united as creators of wealth. The farmer, the craftsman, and the small businessman shared a common identity as producers. They believed profoundly in the ideal of economic independence and, among wage earners, often hoped themselves to become employers. Their enemies were large companies, *rentier* capitalists, financiers, and speculators, all of whom profited from the work of others. In opposition to the 'producing classes' stood the 'capitalists' and 'monopolists,' who upset the harmony of interests that united producers – the producers' ethos 'recognized no permanent or irreconcilable differences between an employer and his employees' – and divided capital from labour along class lines. The term 'monopolist' referred increasingly to the new captains of industry, often now financiers, who presided over large and heavily capitalized manufacturing enterprises.[29] By the 1890s reform-minded critics of modern capitalism from locations as diverse as Australia, California, and Ontario believed that 'the growth of monopolies, economic and political, was the central evil of ... advancing capitalist society.' As a consequence, ordinary people tended to rank capitalists at the top of what Australian historian Peter Love has called 'a hierarchy of moral turpitude.'[30]

Central to the producers' ethos was a clear concept of what constituted a good, or moral, society. A product of influences from the American republican and British radical traditions of the late eighteenth and early nineteenth centuries, this ethos included the notion of a 'fair' return for one's labour, with 'fair' defined by traditional practices rather than by the competitive forces of the labour market. Of particular importance was faith in what Craig Heron has called the 'full promise of liberal democracy,' a philosophy of political equality for all men (though not women) regardless of property or status. The parliamentary system should make political power accessible to all through a broad franchise and should guarantee political liberties. The same egalitarian impulse conditioned sharp criticism of social privilege, leading reformers to demand free and ready access to education, recreational space, and jobs.[31] Society's fundamental social boundaries were defined in moral – and racial – terms. By contrast, the term 'class' carried an essentially negative connotation. In contemporary language the 'plain people,' or 'masses,' were juxtaposed against the self-serving elite, or 'classes.' American historian John Gilkeson has appropriately labelled those who shared this ethos a 'moral community of producers.'[32]

The newspaper clippings gathered through the 1890s for the Vancouver Trades and Labor Council (VTLC) by Harry Cowan, a printer and member of the Council executive, indicate the astonishing range of influences from across North America and parts of the British empire that served to sharpen the moral sensibilities of Vancouver's community of producers. Ethical criticism of capitalism by Christian reformers featured prominently, as did the utopian ideas of Edward Bellamy, Henry George, and Eugene Debs. Of these, George's proposal for reforming capitalism by replacing all taxes on labour by a single tax on land, which he thought would siphon off profits gained unfairly by speculation, was particularly popular. Stories about temperance, cooperatives, free silver, and direct legislation are also to be found, reflecting varying levels of support for these ideas among Vancouver reformers. Indeed, it appears as if in Vancouver, as in Toronto, reform thought in the 1890s was characteristically a 'diverse and contradictory mélange of earnestness, fad, and fantasy.'[33]

Reform leaders were, in occupational terms, primarily middle rather than upper or working class. In addition to William Templeton, they included William Brown, real estate businessman; Charles L. Queen, liveryman; G.I. Wilson, salmon canner; Dr. J.T. Carroll, medical doctor and single-tax reformer; Charles W. Murray, accountant; John McDowell, draying business proprietor; the Reverend George Maxwell, Presbyterian minister; the Reverend George Pedley, Congregationalist minister; and Francis Carter-Cotton, former member of the British diplomatic corps and owner/editor of the *News-Advertiser*. These men came together as a political group in the December 1889 civic election and gained momentum in the spring of 1890 when Carter-Cotton ran for a seat in the provincial legislature. Backed by a broad movement of working- and middle-class supporters and claiming great 'sympathy with workingmen,' he swept into the legislature at the head of the polls.

Carter-Cotton's organization was then put to effective use in December 1890, when the opposition forces routed Oppenheimer's candidates at the aldermanic level, failing only to dislodge the mayor. The battle of reformers versus the 'classes' was fought again a year later when Dr. Carroll challenged David Oppenheimer's successor, a small businessman named Fred Cope. Business leaders rallied behind Cope, the reformers behind Carroll. In January 1892 Cope won the mayoralty by a slim margin but failed to regain control of the Council. Reformers continued to fight remnants of the 'same old gang' for the rest of the decade.[34]

Middle-class leadership of the opposition forces should not be interpreted as synonymous with middle-class dominance, however, for the politics of the 1890s included an important role for workingmen. Reluctant to participate directly in elections, Vancouver's fragile trade union movement endorsed only a handful of candidates, all but one at the civic level, between 1891 and 1895. Nevertheless, by passing resolutions and declaring platforms they helped focus public debate on reform issues.[35] On one occasion VTLC's platform was deemed important enough to be debated by the City Council. In the municipal election of 1892 both mayoralty candidates – the business representative and the middle-class reformer – accepted the labour platform. Typically, the Trades and Labor Council under president George Bartley refused to take a stand about the mayoralty candidates but it did endorse a labour candidate for alderman. Its influence peaked at mid-decade when the VTLC and a new labour reform organization, the Nationalist Party, drafted a joint platform for the 1896 dominion election. From this came the reformers' greatest triumph, the election to Parliament of the Reverend George Maxwell.

Maxwell's political career illustrates the prevailing influence of producerist values on Vancouver's public life in the 1890s. Described in his obituary as a 'patriotic Scot and passionate admirer of Robert Burns,' Maxwell was the son of a Scottish miner and had begun working in a mine himself at the age of eleven. His self-image as a 'son of labor' and a staunch friend of those who toil, which he articulated often while living in Vancouver, reflected his early experience.[36] He emerged from a period of formal education in literature, philosophy, the classics, and theology to become an ordained minister of the established Church of Scotland, and in December 1890 after preaching in Ireland, Scotland, and Quebec took charge of Vancouver's eastside First Presbyterian Church. In 1892 Maxwell revealed both the anti-elitist and moral tendencies of his reformism by arguing for separate labour representation on City Council and attacking the spread of prostitution into the neighbourhood of 'respectable residences.'[37] That same year, while claiming to be an 'old country conservative' and a British free trader, he rejected the Canadian Conservative Party; its high tariff served only the 'enrichment of the capitalist,' he argued, and its close links to business made it a party of moral decay and the protection of privilege.[38]

In April 1893 Maxwell became an important figure in local politics by organizing a public rally to air mainland grievances against the provincial government of Theodore Davie, and in 1894 he guided formation of the Nationalist Party. Although it was described by one commentator as British Columbia's first real labour party and drew its membership primarily from among wage earners, the Nationalist Party had no direct ties to the trade union movement and owed its character very much to the leadership of Maxwell. The Nationalists then joined other opponents of the provincial government to endorse three candidates for the general election of 1894: Francis Carter-Cotton; Robert Macpherson, a carpenter; and Adolphus Williams, a lawyer. All were elected. At the end of 1895 the Nationalists and the VTLC created a joint platform that offered a classic statement of reform thinking. It argued for greater political democracy, day rather than contract labour for municipal workers, a direct tax on land but not on improvements to land (single tax), municipal government ownership and operation of all city utilities, the creation of free public recreational space in Stanley Park, free school books and supplies, and opposition to charitable giving to the poor. The following year a coalition of Nationalists, federal Liberals, and supporters of D'Alton McCarthy – an MP from Ontario who led the anti-Catholic 'Equal Rights' movement – nominated Maxwell to run against a Conservative in the federal riding of Burrard, a difficult constituency extending over 1,500 miles from Vancouver in the south to Atlin in the north. Elected by a slim majority in a three-way contest, Maxwell soon emerged as an Independent with close ties to the Liberal Party.[39] He would be re-elected as a Liberal in 1900.

Reformers also opposed the Victoria-centred provincial government, with which Vancouver's business leaders were politically connected. Voters had elected Carter-Cotton to one of two Vancouver seats in the provincial contest of June 1890. In 1894, joined by Maxwell and the Nationalists, reformers took all the Vancouver seats, now three in number. Their pro-government opponents were direct descendants of the alliance of development-oriented businessmen organized to support Oppenheimer's clique in the late 1880s and to elect his successor as mayor in January 1892.

A leading figure of this group was J.W. Horne, real estate and street railway company promoter who had reputedly brought more than $1 million with him from earlier town-building investments in Manitoba. Elected to the provincial legislature as an Independent in 1890, Horne became, to quote his principal opponent, 'one of the most slavish supporters of the Government.' In 1894 Horne demonstrated this connection by campaigning openly under the Citizen's Ticket banner for the incumbent provincial administration.[40] Other government supporters from among the city's upper class included David Oppenheimer; Robert Tatlow, connected socially to CPR management; Dr. J.M. Lefevre, employed by the CPR; and Charles Doering, a brewer.

The series of governments that managed the province's affairs from 1883 to 1898 were dominated by business interests centred in Victoria. As Margaret Ormsby has noted, 'business men and large property-holders sat in the House ... and every prominent business man was known to the legislators.' Their political beliefs emphasized the exploitation of regional resources through the provision of public concessions to private interests. A huge concession went to Vancouver Island colliery owner Robert Dunsmuir, himself a member of the Legislative Assembly, in return for which he constructed a railway from Esquimalt, near Victoria, to Nanaimo. Dunsmuir netted a princely empire of 1.9 million acres of land, a legacy that contributed significantly to his emergence in the late 1880s as British Columbia's wealthiest man and principal monopolist.[41]

One reason why Dunsmuir had come to symbolize immoral – as opposed to small scale and hence acceptable – capitalism is revealed in the 1884 submission by the Nanaimo lodge of the Knights of Labor to the Royal Commission on Chinese Immigration. The monopolization of resources by wealthy employers, it argued, left 'no hope of a number of small, independent companies being formed to work our mines.' By granting a vast railway reserve to Robert Dunsmuir, the government had prevented any competition in the Vancouver Island coal mining industry and had determined that miners would 'forever remain in the subordinate position of employees.'[42] Monopolies and privilege blocked upward mobility, an important value shared by working- and middle-class members of the producers' community. The other major beneficiary of government largesse, usually given as bonuses of land, were railway companies, of which the CPR was the leading example.

The concentration of wealth in the hands of a limited number of so-called 'monopolists' inevitably focused the anger of Vancouver's reformers on the Victoria-centred government that had granted the resources and on the railway and land companies that had received them. Thus the platform that led Carter-Cotton to victory in 1890 included a rousing condemnation of 'avaricious corporations' and a call to end the bonusing of speculative land companies. The moral vision of small producers found similar expression in a letter of the same period by five Vancouver workingmen to the president of the Vancouver Trades and Labor Council; it too demanded that political power be kept from the hands of 'moneyed rings and monopolistic combinations.'[43]

At the civic level the ideology of producerism translated most forcefully into a political movement rather than a cultural or social one, and no issue served to politicize Vancouver citizens more directly than the relationship between utility companies and the municipal government. It brought into focus the desire of ordinary people to maintain their economic independence and local autonomy and to have a city government that represented the interests of the whole community. Both were threatened by the growing power and increasing authority of large corporations.[44]

Franchises for water, gas, and street railways had been much sought in the 1880s. Investors received favourable treatment from a city government more interested in rapid economic growth than in the defence of civic authority. But by 1891, as Carter-Cotton was to write in the *News-Advertiser*, the general direction of opinion was towards greater regulation, and perhaps even public ownership, of 'enterprises that concern the whole community.' Reformers now talked of 'the people's rights' to good services and to the control of city streets. 'Public opinion was ... changing with regard to the privileges being granted to corporations,' Alderman Brown stated in June 1891; no longer were the sweet deals that business leaders had negotiated in the 1880s to be tolerated. Unlike the CPR – a huge corporation controlled from outside the region – Vancouver's first utility companies had all been financed by local or regional capitalists, and franchises had been granted by the municipal government. Even local capitalists were 'not popular among the general population.' Consequently, utility enterprises and their Vancouver investors represented both practical and enticing targets for the city's reform-minded moral community of producers.[45]

From 1892 to 1896 the street railway company and city government fought constantly. After the Vancouver Street Railway and Light Company had passed into the hands of its bondholders, both the shareholders and bondholders – overlapping but different groups – looked to the civic government to protect their investments. City taxpayers would have none of it. In May 1893 they opposed a financial guarantee to bondholders. The following year they rejected an offer to purchase the company, fearing that the price was too high for their debt-burdened city. Concern about taxes had prevailed despite public enthusiasm for government ownership of utilities.[46]

Every new line of track also proved contentious. While the company's charter had given it control of some routes for thirty years, new routes or duplicate tracks were to be granted by the city street by street. Debate over lines proposed for Powell, Granville, and Robson streets consumed endless hours of Council time at mid-decade, drawing out clearly different philosophies about the rights of corporations both public (city government) and private (incorporated businesses). Often heard was the refrain that utility company managers were trying 'to run the City.' As usual, Carter-Cotton put the issue most clearly: 'Is the City to own and control its streets or are they to be under the control of private individuals or corporations? Are they to be utilized for the general advantage and convenience of the community or are they to be under the control of private parties?'[47] Ultimately, advantage lay with the private investors whose interests were protected by the franchise provisions of the original charter and by a provincial government friendly to business. Over the next five years the local manager of BC Electric, the highly bureaucratic British corporation that assumed control of Vancouver's street railway system in 1896, completely outmanoeuvred city government representatives to protect the company's interests.[48]

It was street lighting, however, that most thoroughly divided Vancouver's upper class from its producers' community. Unlike the original street railway franchise, the street lighting contract signed at the end of 1889 was to terminate in five years. Consequently, by the spring of 1894 street lighting appeared to offer a very real possibility for municipal ownership and thus for a direct challenge to monopoly capitalism. The fact that New Westminster had successfully created a municipal lighting company made the idea even more enticing for reformers. After having been urged for some time by City Council's Fire, Water, and Light Committee, a by-law to raise $100,000 for a municipal street lighting company was approved by ratepayers in October 1894. The resulting controversy was intense. Shareholders in the bankrupt Vancouver Street Railway and Light Company – the same company that Council was negotiating with over street railway licences – mounted a concerted and ultimately successful campaign to force the City Council to negotiate a new contract with them and thus preserve the value of their investment in the existing lighting system. Having failed to defeat the by-law, frustrated business leaders turned in January 1895 to the provincial government, where they succeeded in having added to the city charter new provisions that made a municipal company virtually impossible. Thwarted at this turn, the Council then chose an alternative strategy, that of leasing the franchise to a private American firm. The latter proved to be a 'bogus' enterprise, leaving Council no choice but to negotiate an agreement with the British investors who had taken over the Vancouver Street Railway and Light Company. The provincial government's role in protecting the interests of utility company investors had proven crucial in stifling the will of Vancouver's reform-minded electors.[49]

The producers' community did, however, win one small skirmish with the elite over utilities. Vancouver's water system, which began to carry north shore water into the city in March 1889, was purchased by the city government two years later. Strongly supported by all factions in the business community, Vancouver's first example of municipal ownership had been motivated by the pragmatic goal of boosterism and had not been contentious.

But as the city's political climate changed, water joined light and street railways in the arena of ideological conflict. The issue centred on who should manage the water system: elected aldermen from the middling stratum of Vancouver society or upper-class businessmen. In 1893 several of the latter proposed that an elected commission administer the water service. While initially accepted by the City Council, some of whose members did not seem at first to understand its implications, the plan provoked a sharp confrontation in early 1894 between business leaders and reformers. According to the by-law written by Alderman W.F. Salsbury, the CPR's representative on Council, three individuals elected in city-wide contests would constitute a board of water commissioners. They were to have 'supreme' control over the system's physical works and revenue. The commission idea would allow the 'best men' – 'men of ability,' as Salsbury described them – to serve in a limited capacity as civic administrators with-out having to dirty their hands with the grime of day-to-day municipal politics. In January 1894 three of Vancouver's most prominent social and business leaders, all members of the upper class, were elected as water com-missioners: former CPR railway contractor and wealthy property owner A.G. Ferguson; lumberman R.H. Alexander; and CPR chief engineer H.J. Cambie. But also elected was a City Council animated by the ethos of pro-ducerism. They were much less accommodating than their predecessors to a raid by 'monopolists' on municipal government authority and by month's end had drained the commission of its power to control water revenues. All three commissioners resigned in protest and Council repealed the com-mission by-law.[50] Later that same year the two leading protagonists in this political fight – Salsbury, a Vancouver Street Railway and Light Company shareholder and strident defender of the property rights of its investors; and Joseph L. Franklin, an English-born master craftsman, contractor, trade unionist, and 'father' of the by-law – would battle again to create a municipally owned lighting system.[51]

PARADES HELD at the end of summer to celebrate Labour Day also demonstrated the values and outlook of ordinary people, though in cul-tural rather than political terms. Processions served the same function as reformist rhetoric, giving expression to the ethos of producerism that linked blue- and white-collar workers, lower-status professionals, and small businessmen in opposition to Vancouver's capitalist class. Parades simply communicated their message in a different manner: through symbolic rather than verbal signifiers.[52]

Workers in the Maritimes had been proclaiming the dignity of labour through public processions and picnics since the 1840s, but unofficial recognition of Labour Day did not begin until the 1880s. In the United States, Labor Day celebrations began in New York in 1882 and were being celebrated throughout the country by 1886.[53] British Columbia's first Labour Day started before noon on Saturday, 6 September 1890, with a parade of working people through the streets of Vancouver. Sporting con-tests and speeches followed at the Brockton Point grounds in Stanley Park. The form that Vancouver's celebrations took thereafter varied. Parades were held in eight of twelve years from 1890 to 1901, with speeches given at the beginning of the decade but not at the end. In September 1894 the

Dominion Government officially designated the first Saturday in September as a time for recognizing working people across the country. Vancouver's trade union movement continued to organize processions in the early 1900s, but despite greatly increased numbers of workers in the city these parades fell short of their predecessors in physical scale and ideological significance. A *Vancouver Daily World* editorial of 1908 observed that 'recreation pure and simple has taken a larger and larger place in the occupations of the [Labour Day] holiday, until but the slightest trace remains' of the old features of the celebration. By the 1920s 'the parading business' had almost gone out of fashion.[54] In short, the role of the Labour Day parade in expressing a particular philosophy of social relations was very much a phenomenon of the 1890s.

To some extent Labour Day was a successor to the big Dominion Day celebrations of 1889 and 1890. The most outstanding feature of each was a large procession through city streets. The principles governing the organization of both sets of parades were similar: bands and officials led the procession, followed by an organized sequence of marchers with banners or floats to mark the identity of each group. Both included a mix of participants from the working and middle classes, and the latter contributed floats that advertised Vancouver businesses, especially small service operations such as laundries, hotels, and grocery stores. Both types of parade also celebrated ties to the local community.

But important differences also marked the two celebrations. Dominion Day parades featured a greater diversity of associations and greater participation by prominent citizens, whereas Labour Day processions gave a central place to working people. In addition, although the Dominion Day festivities of 1889 and 1890 had been intended to encourage civic boosterism and to solidify participants' claim to citizenship, the holiday evolved into a more narrowly commercial enterprise of military pageants and sports sponsored and promoted by middle-class hotelkeepers and journalists. By contrast Labour Day, especially the parade, was less an instrument of civic consensus than a means for ordinary but respectable people to assert their civic identity.[55]

Most obviously, Labour Day parades expressed the class identity of Vancouver's working people. Labour Day was a direct outgrowth of the emergence of a city-wide labour council in 1889. In addition, the parades clearly expressed what Bryan Palmer has called 'the dignity and essential

Labour Day, 1892, the Bakers'
Union. (City of Vancouver
Archives PORT.P.1653 N.944)

In 1890 Vancouver's fledgling
trade union movement established one day in late summer
to celebrate the 'dignity and
essential place of productive
labour.' The celebrations,
which featured a parade, also
expressed the pride of
respectable working people in
their place as citizens of
Vancouver. Labour Day
parades flourished until the
turn of the century.

The Longshoremen's Union
and its float, the SS *Umatilla,*
in the Labour Day parade of
1898. (City of Vancouver
Archives STR.P.371 N.329)

place of productive labour.' For instance, in 1898 local stevedores constructed a forty-foot replica of the SS *Umatilla,* a ship that connected
Vancouver and San Francisco. The miniature vessel belched steam along
the entire route of the Labour Day procession, with upwards of 140
marching longshoremen eyeing their creation proudly from behind. The
parade of 1899, described as the largest in the province to that date, featured six floats on which craftsmen presented working demonstrations of
their skill. These displays expressed such artisanal values as self-help and
mutuality, the latter of which also animated a number of schemes by
Vancouver-area workers in the 1890s for commercial or industrial cooperatives. In this sense, Palmer was correct to see in Labour Day parades a
claim to respectability that was particular to the wage-earning class and
that could potentially motivate its members to take collective action to preserve rights inherently opposed to the interests of capital.[56]

The most overt expression of class identity on Labour Day occurred in
1893, when more than 500 striking fishermen from Steveston, accompanied
by their fife-and-drum band, triumphantly joined Vancouver's Labour Day
procession. The parade in this instance turned into an explicit statement
that workers' lives and interests were different from, and potentially
opposed to, those of their employers.[57]

But Labour Day parades also represented something else: the fractur-
ing of Vancouver society along social status rather than class lines. Wage
earners defined themselves as 'plain people' and thus identified with other
'plain people' of the middle class. Labour Day parades offered a visual representation of ordinary people's faith in the value of small-scale and locally
based capitalism and their rejection of the 'unfair' piling up of wealth and
power by heavily capitalized corporations. Seen from this perspective, the
well-scrubbed longshoremen who marched through the streets of
Vancouver during the city's first Labour Day parade, 'their badges
trimmed with gilt lace and their handsome silk banners beautifully
inscribed with suitable design,' were asserting two identities concurrently:
a class identity and a claim to social recognition as small producers and citizens of Vancouver. Labour Day parades represented Vancouver's middling
stratum on display, where workers joined with small producers of the middle class to challenge upper-class conceptions of economic and social relations. Local businesses such as the British Columbia Ironworks Company,
sponsor in 1899 of a float that showed skilled artisans at work mending

boilers, joined readily with labour in these industrial processions; the city's largest corporation and most obvious monopolist, the CPR, did not.[58]

PARADOXICALLY, debate that divided the upper class from the producers' community over the nature of Vancouver society and its institutions also united them as citizens who claimed the right to engage in public discourse. Not sharing this right, and thus marked off as a separate and lower stratum of 'outsiders,' were the transients and 'foreigners' who lacked the skill, the permanence, or the British ethnic heritage to be considered citizens. The marginalization of these groups, which had begun during the first stage of industrialization on Burrard Inlet in the 1870s and had gained momentum during the city-building years of the 1880s, continued to influence the structuring of Vancouver society in the 1890s. When presenting its vision of social relations on Labour Day, Vancouver's middling stratum thus not only challenged upper-class values but also distanced itself from residents who formed a separate social grouping below it.

For working people, life in Vancouver from the early to mid-1890s was not easy. Survival was particularly hard for those people who could not look after themselves. Such was the case with a man named Ross, aged sixty, who lived 'in absolute poverty ... in an old open shack without [a] stove.' He was 'very weak and without food or neccesary [sic] clothing.' Single women with dependent children were particularly hard pressed. The seventy-one-year-old Mrs. Pollard and her young granddaughter were forced to ask for charity when Mrs. Pollard's unemployed son returned to the old country – from which they had all recently emigrated to find work. A middle-aged woman named Howard, abandoned by her husband and unable to pay the rent, sought help from the city when she feared being turned out into the street. A Japanese man, found neglected, starved, and dying in a logging camp near the city, could have testified eloquently to the burden of being Asian, as well as unemployed, in winter.[59]

Poverty's bite penetrated deeply not only because of the economic conditions of the time but also because of widely held views about its origins. Based on the notions that people were responsible for their own well-being and that material deprivation was usually a social manifestation of moral bankruptcy, respectable members of all three classes responded similarly to the plight of the poor. Support for the truly deserving poor, especially women and children, was acceptable but aid to able-bodied men unaccompanied by work would, it was feared, erode the work ethic and lead to a more permanent state of pauperization. The VTLC was as firm in its opposition to indiscriminate philanthropy as was the business community and strongly disapproved of what it called 'doles of charity.' To systematize and limit the distribution of relief to the unemployed and poor, City Council established a separate Relief Committee in February 1894 and the Protestant churches formed a Relief Association in December 1895. The 'classes' and the producers' community in Vancouver shared the Relief Association's goals of minimizing the evils of private charity and begging, and of discriminating between 'worthy and unworthy mendicants.'[60]

Perhaps the most potent symbol of social marginalization in the 1890s was the shack, a flimsy, usually one-room, and often jerry-built dwelling that was to be found located illegally along the shorelines of Burrard Inlet or False Creek. The term 'shack' could refer to a cabin on land, a boathouse, or a cottage perched atop pilings over the foreshore, the area between the high and low watermarks. Marginal housing was very much a part of Vancouver's early history, and of the BC coast more generally, where people lived either by choice or necessity literally on the edge of respectable society. Shacks were an especially prominent feature of Vancouver's social landscape in the 1890s, with one source in 1894 identifying 364 shacks on the various foreshores of the city.[61]

The sequence of events that led to the removal of shack dwellers remains obscure, but circumstantial evidence suggests that large property holders featured prominently. The Vancouver Board of Trade called for the removal of shacks in the spring of 1891, and the CPR cleared forty squatters from company land seven months later. A Supreme Court ruling that permitted the clearance of Vancouver's foreshore lands was to have been implemented in September 1893 but for humanitarian reasons was delayed until the following summer. A series of evictions followed, the 'emissaries of destruction' in one instance removing over 100 shacks in a single day.[62]

At one level the issue of shacks divided economic and social leaders from the producers' community, as did so many issues in the 1890s. The different sensibilities of the two groups were revealed when, armed with a petition of more than 600 names, many of them belonging to working people, Francis Carter-Cotton succeeded in having implementation of the court order delayed from September 1893. As Carter-Cotton argued, the occupants of shacks included 'many honest and hardworking men' who would have had no way to provide shelter for the winter if evicted so late in the season. Similarly, Joseph Franklin, reflecting the worker's natural distrust of state authority, spoke strongly against a massing of police 'to overawe the people' as the shacks were being torn down.[63]

At the same time, reformers who owned or rented enough property to vote were ambivalent about squatters, an ambivalence that quickly turned to opposition when squatters and the unemployed were identified as members of an ethnic minority. Thus, when the issue of relief assistance for unemployed Italian labourers was raised in the City Council, Joseph Franklin argued that 'citizens' should be given preference. He defined 'citizen' in a narrow political sense as anyone who could vote, but his actions betrayed a different understanding of the term. The two Italians he identified as unsuitable for relief assistance were citizens by his own definition, both meeting the property and residency requirements for inclusion in the Vancouver Voters' List. What they were not, however, was people of British heritage. Two other men, F. Murrell, an Italian labourer, and King Bill, 'a coloured gentleman,' were even less likely to meet Franklin's unstated assumptions about citizenship because they were poor and transient as well as ethnically or racially different from the city's dominant group. Both shack dwellers unsuccessfully resisted the destruction of their waterside homes in 1894.[64]

Members of respectable society sympathized even less with the city's most fully marginalized residents, the Chinese men whose dilapidated cottages reinforced deeply held and very negative racial stereotypes about Asians. The by-law of May 1893 that made illegal the erection of laundries or wash houses anywhere except in the vicinity of Dupont Street reinforced a process already underway, the segregation of Chinese residents into a distinct area of Vancouver that, as City Health Committee minutes reveal, became officially designated in the mid-1890s as 'Chinatown.' Kay Anderson sees this naming as part of the process by which the European majority categorized the Chinese as 'other,' a process that also found expression in the campaign to remove Chinese shacks from the city's shoreline. Even more than the cabins of European squatters, the shacks into which Chinese men had crowded were seen to be unclean and unsanitary and thus a threat to public health. In response to negative descriptions of Chinese housing 'and to an examination of the south side of Dupont Street by city health officials in 1896, four rows of wooden shacks and cottages ... were destroyed in the latter part of the decade.'[65]

As these accounts of the administration of relief and the removal of shacks illustrate, the philosophical and political separation of Vancouver's upper stratum from its producers' community must be placed within the context of the enduring presence of a third stratum of people, who for reasons of transiency, poverty, or ethnic heritage were not fully acknowledged citizens. Ethnic and racial minorities, especially Asians, were the most obvious outsiders in a city where power was rooted culturally in the hands of the British majority. Business leaders and reformers, the latter including members of both the middle and working classes, were uniformly of British cultural heritage. A study of twenty leading members of the Vancouver Trades and Labor Council in the 1890s shows that all were of British origin. Of these, two-thirds were British by birth – most of them English – and the remainder Canadian and American. In addition, almost half were Anglican and all but two were skilled craftsmen.[66] In other words, trade union leaders, who expressed the values of producerism with such clarity, were among the most privileged and respectable members of the working class. As such they stood apart from working men and women whose lack of occupational skill or plain bad luck had prevented them from putting down roots in the community.

One final point about the structuring of social boundaries in the 1890s should be noted. Throughout the decade, the dialogue of the respectable was primarily a dialogue of men. Women did not enjoy the full benefits of citizenship any more than poor, transient, or non-White men. In other words, sex was an important source of social marginalization. But the position of women in the social structure was more complicated than that of the shack dwellers because women shared the status, though not the power, of their husbands and fathers. A fundamental characteristic of patriarchal society, this construction of female status through family associations meant that women both could and could not participate in Vancouver's public life. Denied access to politics, the women of respectable upper-, middle-, and working-class families, especially the upper, could still influence the ordering of society in other ways, such as through participation in voluntary associations. Mrs. R.H. Alexander, for example, enjoyed high status and considerable influence first in Granville and then in Vancouver through her place in a prominent business family. But as the social distress of Mrs. Pollard and Mrs. Howard illustrates, their sex also left women vulnerable to economic and social marginalization.

TO SUMMARIZE, Vancouver became a more complex city in the 1890s than it had been during the boom years of the 1880s. Strikes, Labour Day parades, and the water commission plan revealed underlying tensions between the upper and working classes. A second pattern of relationships featured three broad strata – upper, middling, and lower – that overlapped with but were separate from the class system. The status and class structures intersected most fully at the top, where social leaders in the new and relatively unformed city of Vancouver were almost entirely prominent businessmen and their families. The two structures overlapped less fully as one moved down the status hierarchy. Skilled tradesmen, for example, defined themselves through workingmen's institutions and practices, yet shared with members of the middle class an identity as 'plain people.' Public life in the early to mid-1890s revolved around conflict between ordinary people and elites and owed more to status than to class relationships. That was to change, however, as Vancouver emerged 'from the fading beams of the nineteenth century' a city increasingly conscious of, and divided by, class.[67]

CHAPTER FOUR

Capital and Labour

Conventional wisdom holds that in the early years of the twentieth century, British Columbia workers expressed a relatively high level of class feeling. Travellers of the period identified relations between capital and labour as British Columbia's distinguishing feature. Once west of the Rockies an easterner 'finds himself confronted with a new set of moral and social problems,' the Rev. S.D. Chown, a leading social critic from Ontario, commented during a west coast visit in 1904. The 'most insistent question of the common people is not, what have you to say about temperance or prohibition, but, what is your message in respect to capital and labour; what is your scheme for bettering the material conditions of the people, and producing peace and good will between the employer of labor and his employees.'[1] British writer J.A. Hobson concurred: 'Nowhere else in Canada is the labour question so prominent, nowhere else is class sentiment of employer and employed so much embittered.'[2]

The industrialization of British Columbia through the extraction and processing of resources had accelerated in the 1890s. The growing tensions between workers and managers that resulted from the intensification of industrial production, especially in the fishing, coal mining, and hard rock mining industries, struck observers like Chown and Hobson as British Columbia's defining characteristic. As the province's largest city, and from the late 1890s the centre from which the region's economy was managed, Vancouver naturally reflected and was influenced by this regional trend. Changes within the structure of capitalism at the national and international levels also affected the social relations of production on Canada's west coast. Consequently, Vancouver did become more clearly divided along class lines in the 1897-1903 period. The higher incidence of industrial conflict and the increasing prominence of the language of class in politics clearly distinguished the city of the twentieth century from that of the nineteenth.

IN THE FALL of 1897, Vancouver's leading salmon-canning agent, Henry O. Bell-Irving, wrote to his cousin and financial broker in London, John Bell-Irving, that 'Vancouver's going steadily ahead, and a great increase in population may be expected shortly on account of the gold excitement.' 'Property is going up [in price] like smoke,' he asserted a month later; 'all points to a lively time here in the spring.'[3] The letters are significant for two reasons. First, their upbeat tone suggests that Vancouver had turned the corner from depression to renewed economic expansion. More importantly, they indicate that prosperity was returning to Vancouver through links to the natural resource economy of the far west, in sharp contrast to the inward-looking and speculative nature of growth a decade earlier.

Certain sectors of the provincial economy expanded enormously in the 1890s and in so doing helped pull Vancouver out of the depths of economic depression. The output of salmon from canneries on the Fraser River and to a lesser extent on more northerly waters such as Rivers Inlet jumped by more than 160 per cent over the course of the decade, as did the output of Vancouver Island coal from mines at Nanaimo, Wellington, and Cumberland. In addition, the importation of hydraulic mining technology from California generated new investment in Cariboo gold mining. One of the few success stories in Vancouver at mid-decade was the British Columbia Iron Works Company, which prospered in response to growth in local steam shipping and cannery enterprises and the beginning of a 'new era of scientific mining in the up-country.'[4]

Klondike mining also stimulated Vancouver's economy. Every one of the passengers arriving at San Francisco and Seattle from the Klondike in

July 1897 'seemed to have struck it rich,' setting in motion what has been called 'North America's last "old-fashioned" gold rush.'[5] While Seattle's established links with Alaska and Vancouver's lack of shipping connections to the north gave the Puget Sound city a huge commercial advantage during the early period of the Klondike rush, Vancouver did receive a commercial lift from the opening of this new mining frontier, as Bell-Irving's reference to 'gold excitement' suggests.

Less immediate were influences on Vancouver from the resource-extractive economy of southeastern British Columbia, where hard rock mining and smelting in the Rossland-Trail area flourished at mid-decade, and coal mining in the Crowsnest Pass began at the end. With expansion of the prairie wheat economy and the Klondike rush, the Kootenay boom drew commercial, financial, and transportation enterprises west and heightened new awareness among eastern Canadians of business prospects in British Columbia. Interest in mining generated a migration of business people and branch companies to Vancouver, which offered the better growth potential of British Columbia's two major cities. The Imperial Bank had anticipated the flow of Canadian businesses to Vancouver by establishing a branch in 1895; three other Canadian banks, including the Canadian Bank of Commerce, followed in 1898. During the next five years a covey of eastern fire and life insurance companies and several wholesale and manufacturing firms also organized west coast branches in the Terminal City.[6]

Growing links between city and hinterland resulted in the restructuring of Vancouver's wholesale trade. Commercial success did not come immediately. With few exceptions, of which Oppenheimer Brothers was the most outstanding, Vancouver's early merchant houses had employed a limited number of workers and served local customers. Vancouver's $4 per ton cost advantage over Victoria for freight to interior parts of the province failed initially to overcome the island city's advantage of established connections, and at mid-decade Victoria remained, in the view of contemporaries, 'the chief centre of wholesale supply for the province.' As economic growth on the mainland outstripped that on Vancouver Island, however, Vancouver's geographic advantages over Victoria undermined traditional commercial practices. Thus by 1897 a number of Vancouver firms were competing successfully for a share of the province's business.

New shipping ties also brought coastal British Columbia more firmly within Vancouver's orbit. The Union Steamship Company led the way, extending service in the 1890s from coastal logging camps to Skeena River canneries and to the Yukon via Skagway. A variety of other vessels – from ships operated by the coast's largest firm, the Canadian Pacific Navigation Company, to a growing fleet of small steamers, barges, and scows – supplemented these connections. The Union Steamship Company and the CPR opened service from Vancouver to the Klondike in 1897 and 1898 respectively. By offering lower transfer costs for this expanding mainland and coastal trade and providing better commercial connections to the region, Vancouver finally broke the capital city's commercial hegemony. In 1899 Vancouver surpassed Victoria as British Columbia's principal port of entry and over the next decade opened a substantial lead. Vancouver's new 'merchant princes,' who included W.H. Malkin, Robert Kelly, E.J. McFeely, Charles Woodward, and Henry Stone, emerged as a powerful group within the city's upper class.[7]

Lumber was the sector of the economy that most directly tied Vancouver's recovery to the region's expansion. Sawmilling in Vancouver had grown in the 1880s as local construction boomed and had suffered correspondingly in the 1890s with the boom's collapse. But provincial logging and wood product manufacturing rebounded spectacularly after mid-decade, replacing salmon canning and coal mining as the 'king of the industries' on the coast. Lumber production grew in part to meet the construction needs of an expanding urban population. In Vancouver the population doubled from 1891 to 1901 and more than tripled again in the next decade. Large-scale immigration during the Laurier years also substantially increased the provincial population (Table 4.1).

Equally significant, however, was the influence of continental integration in reorienting lumber exports from markets around the Pacific Rim and in Britain to markets in the province's interior and on the prairies. In

Table 4.1

Population growth in British Columbia, Victoria, and Vancouver, 1871-1921

	1871	1881	1891	1901	1911	1921
British Columbia	36,247	49,459	98,173	178,657	392,480	524,582
Victoria	3,270	5,925	16,841	20,919	31,660	38,727
Vancouver	0	0	13,709	27,010	100,401	117,217

Source: Sixth Census of Canada, 1921, vol. 1, tables 1 and 12, pp. 3 and 234

particular, the more than one million immigrants who settled on the prairies from 1896 to 1913 created an almost insatiable demand for cheap building supplies. By the prewar period two-thirds of the province's lumber output found buyers east of the Rockies. The demand was supplied from mills both in southeastern British Columbia, where large-scale production was new, and on the coast, where the industry had traditionally centred. Thus, for instance, in response to the opening of the prairie market, Vancouver entrepreneurs James and Robert McNair and E.H. Heaps established shingle and sawmill companies that grew into million-dollar corporations.[8]

Expansion of both local and export markets for coastal lumber had a tremendous impact on the city. It reaffirmed the status of Burrard Inlet, now joined by False Creek, as the geographic centre of British Columbia's largest industry. In the years 1900 to 1907 local mills logged approximately 39 per cent of all timber cut in the province; of ten companies that led the payment of timber royalties to the provincial government at the end of the decade, seven were from Vancouver. The Vancouver-New Westminster area could claim nineteen saw and shingle mills in 1900, fifty-four in 1906. Indeed, wood manufacturing formed Vancouver's only really large industry: of a total industrial labour force of 9,777 workers in Vancouver and the immediate area in 1911, the logging and wood product industry employed over 6,000. Five Vancouver lumber companies became giants by BC standards, boasting assets that before the prewar downturn ranged as high as $8 million. Indeed, half of the city's eight largest provincially incorporated companies belonged to the forest sector.[9]

Changes in the structure of capitalism at the national and international levels accompanied and aided Vancouver's economic revival. Virtually every Vancouver lumber company and most of the city's wholesale firms were headed by entrepreneurs who had created their own businesses and lived in the city. In this sense, economic integration of city and region significantly reinforced the business segment that had been seriously weakened by the land boom of the 1890s: entrepreneurial capitalists who owned and directed locally based companies. But large corporations of transcontinental stature were also extending westward, led by the CPR in the 1880s and Canadian banks a decade later. Perhaps the most important incursion of 'big business' into Vancouver in the late 1890s occurred in 1896 when British capitalists consolidated the electric light and street railway services of British Columbia's three major coastal cities into one large, bureaucratic corporation, the British Columbia Electric Railway Company.

Salmon canning offers an especially important example of the relationship between external capital, corporate restructuring, and Vancouver's rise to metropolitan status. Control of salmon canning began to shift from Vancouver Island to the mainland in the early 1890s, when the number of Fraser River canneries owned or managed in Vancouver jumped from two to fifteen. Leading the change in 1891 was Scottish-born Henry Bell-Irving, who, through family connections in Britain, successfully amalgamated nine canneries, seven of them on the Fraser River, into a limited liability company, Anglo-British Columbia Packing. The significance of this reorganization is suggested by canning historian Keith Ralston. New entrants into the industry were not set up or financed in the old way, through merchant houses in Victoria. Now, typically, a limited liability company was formed, and most new entrants had their headquarters in Vancouver. Also locating in the Terminal City were cannery agents such as William Farrell, George I. Wilson, and Bell-Irving, who acted on behalf of external investors in managing BC canneries.

The influx of Canadian investment capital, primarily from banks, that started at mid-decade encouraged excessive expansion of fish-canning capacity in the 1899-1901 period. The expansion provoked a fundamental restructuring of the industry in 1902 when two Canadian banks and a Toronto stock promoter amalgamated thirty-four canneries – twenty-four on the Fraser River and ten in northern waters – into one large limited liability company, the $4 million British Columbia Packers Association. As a 'big business' at the third, or 'finance capital' stage of organizational development, BC Packers chose to manage its geographically dispersed canneries from Vancouver, increasingly connected to business in eastern Canada, rather than from Victoria, traditionally tied to San Francisco and London.[10]

The stimulus provided by the economic integration of city and hinterland spread down through the Vancouver economy, generating new business activity in services to the resource sector, such as metal shops and stores specializing in loggers' equipment, and to the city's increasing population, such as tailor shops, street railway lines, and new homes. Construction and real estate again emerged as buoyant sectors of the economy, though they remained less dominant than in the 1880s.

Hastings Sawmill, Vancouver, 1912. From the 1860s to the 1920s, settlement on Burrard Inlet was closely tied to the history of the sawmill. Acquired in 1889 by New Westminster lumberman John Hendry, Hastings Sawmill remained up to the First World War Vancouver's largest industrial enterprise. Hendry moved from New Westminster to Vancouver in 1903. One historian has written that the career of John Hendry, 'the foremost industrial entrepreneur in the Canadian West by the turn of the century,' symbolized Vancouver's development. (Leonard Frank photo, Jewish Historical Society of British Columbia LF 32826)

The number of both small employers and big businesses grew, creating a hierarchy of firms that can be grouped into three categories. Externally controlled corporations constituted the first group, led by the CPR, Canadian banks, street railway and telephone companies, BC Packers, and one or two other businesses such as the equipment firm, Canadian General Electric. These corporations were organized at the third or fourth stages of Chandler's business typology: highly bureaucratic, heavily capitalized, controlled from outside the region, and run locally by career managers. Although very powerful, they remained few compared to smaller firms headed by individual entrepreneurs.

Second were locally controlled 'big businesses,' led by wholesale and resource industry companies, especially lumber. Around the turn of the century this group also included a few companies of increasing size and importance in other sectors, including metal manufacturing (Vancouver Engineering Works and Ross and Howard), confectionery (BC Sugar and Ramsay Brothers), and liquor (Vancouver Breweries). They included as well businesses financed outside the region but controlled locally, such as the canning agency H.O. Bell-Irving and Company and wholesalers Evans, Coleman and Evans. While big by local standards, these enterprises were still run by the individuals or families that had established them. Consequently, they represented entrepreneurial rather than finance or corporate capitalism.[11] The owners and principal managers of firms in both of these first two business categories were key members of the city's upper class.

Economic growth also encouraged expansion of the middle class, spawning many small businesses that were not heavily capitalized and employed few workers. This third group prevailed especially in areas such as retailing and manufacturing, servicing the needs of local city dwellers. Typical were saloons, hotels, grocery stores, real estate agencies, tailor shops, and bakeries.

As VANCOUVER'S business community grew in size and complexity, so too did its need for wage labour. In fact, proclaimed Edmund Walker, president of the Canadian Bank of Commerce, 'The labour question lies at the bottom of everything connected with material progress in British Columbia.'[12]

Businessmen shared two basic assumptions about how a labour force was to be organized and controlled. First, employers urged that an ample supply of cheap labour be available to ensure economic expansion. Of particular concern to managers were labour shortages during periods of rapid growth; these favoured workers, allowing them a choice of jobs and the ability to drive up wages. Thus in 1901 and 1906 industrialists lamented the dearth of cheap labour for British Columbia's resource industries, claiming that a tight labour market slowed the influx of capital and made local products uncompetitive. Even more threatening for some high-status observers was the shortage of inexpensive domestic workers, which menaced 'the stability of the home' and retarded the 'physical and social development of white residents.' A reserve labour supply would keep the wheels of industry turning smoothly and maintain upper-class social standards.[13]

Essential to preserving a competitive labour market was an open immigration policy. From the time of CPR construction in the 1880s, Asians had provided the most readily available pool of semi- and unskilled workers, and controversy about their role in British Columbia's development continued to resonate through provincial history into the 1890s. Vancouver alderman James Fox, a contractor, articulated the assumptions behind capitalists' demand for Asian labour as follows: 'We have an extensive province without a population. Shall it remain in its primeval state ... with its forests of wealth rotting, with its vast treasures of riches lying hid, with its pastoral lands arid wastes, with its waters stinking with fish undevoured ... Shall we linger along ambitionless ... and pass away without employing that power that Heaven has placed in our hand'?[14] Certainly not, asserted Fox, but the province lacked sufficient labour to carry out this development. He suggested as the solution an influx of up to two million Chinese workers who would open British Columbia's treasure house and generate untold wealth. CPR president William Van Horne similarly supported an open immigration policy and sharply criticized anti-Asian legislation that prevented it. Looked at from a 'practical and selfish point of view,' he argued, restricting competition from Chinese labour retarded development of resources 'to the material disadvantage of the very working-men it is intended to help ... It is sad to see our laws prostituted to a race prejudice.'[15]

Second, owners demanded complete control over the work process. For them the economic role of capital superseded that of labour. Consequently, the owners of capital should be left alone to determine whom they would employ, the level of remuneration, and working conditions. Whether proprietors of small tailoring shops or managers of

American-controlled fishing companies, capitalists iterated that they refused to be dictated to by workers.[16] In the words of a Vancouver sheet metal shop owner, 'we have a right to run our own businesses along lines to suit ourselves.'[17]

Workers viewed these issues differently. Recognizing that capitalism had reduced labour to a commodity to be bought and sold, they strongly rejected the owners' demand for an open and unregulated labour market and forcefully opposed the immigration of unskilled workers. A bit later J.W. Wilkinson, secretary of the Vancouver Trades and Labor Council, would explain why market vulnerability led workers to oppose immigration: 'We are working men and the only way we have of getting our livelihood is by selling ourselves from day to day, wherever we find someone to hire it ... The price we can get will determine to a large extent the standard of living we shall enjoy.' Whether constituted of Asians arriving on their own resources or of 'the industrial garbage of the Old Country' sent by benevolent societies, an influx of unskilled labour threatened to undermine the job security and living standards of settled White workers. This attitude may seem selfish, Wilkinson conceded, 'but in the struggle for existence matters are very often reduced to the ethics of the jungle.'[18]

The employers' notion that with the ownership of capital went the unquestioned right to control the labour process also ran hard against the workers' unshakable belief that it was they who supported the capitalists, and not capitalists the workers. Drawing on the deeply rooted traditions of their crafts, skilled tradesmen in particular expressed the desire to 'be on equal terms with their employers.'[19] To attain this relationship would require that wage earners be protected from undue competition for their jobs, be paid 'fair' and 'proper' wages determined by traditional practices, and retain substantial control over the work process.[20] Crucial to achieving these goals was gaining owners' acceptance of trade unions, through which workers could voice their concerns and protect their interests. Trade unions directly challenged employers' power, however, and were usually recognized only when workers could enforce their will by successfully withdrawing their labour.

Yet trade unions were growing lustily at the turn of the century. The 1890s depression had almost destroyed Vancouver's fledgling labour movement but starting in 1897 renewed prosperity stimulated a trade union renaissance, giving new life to suspended locals and generating even among less skilled workers the enthusiasm and market strength to organize. No authoritative statistics on the number of city locals formed or percentage of the workforce unionized are available for this period, but province wide the labour movement expanded from 100 locals in 1900 to 216 in 1903. Evidence presented in James Conley's comprehensive examination of working-class formation in the lower mainland suggests that unionization was also a powerful force in Vancouver. Indeed, Conley writes, the years 1900 to 1903 represented one of two periods of 'intense working-class mobilization and collective action' in Vancouver; the other came at the end of the First World War.[21]

The changing balance of supply and demand for labour offers the most obvious explanation for the timing of this surge of labour militancy. A shortage of workers was unquestionably the union movement's best friend, and by the early 1900s improved economic conditions had severely tightened Vancouver's labour market. Naturally, then, wage earners were delighted that, in the words of one observer, 'nearly every man who wants to work can get it ... So far as demand for men and wages go things were never better in Vancouver.'[22] An advantageous labour market and high expectations triggered workers' demands for better wages, hours, and working conditions. It also whetted their desire to unionize.

To understand the character and extent of this mobilization requires a short discussion of the structure of Vancouver's wage labour force, for what stands out for the prewar period as a whole is the barrier to class formation imposed by conflicting identities within the wage-earning population. One source of division was occupational status. Skilled workers enjoyed higher status, more job security, and greater income than unskilled. A study of the annual earnings of family heads in a select number of occupations in 1911 confirms this (Table 4.2). It reveals sharp differentiation by income. Highly trained members of the railway running trades, led by locomotive engineers, formed the working-class elite in Vancouver as elsewhere in Canada, earning almost double per year what unskilled labourers did. Skilled trainmen and electricians earned more than salesmen, despite the latter's higher status as white-collar workers. Experiencing less competition from novices learning their trade on the job, bricklayers and plumbers accumulated higher yearly incomes than did carpenters. At the bottom of the income hierarchy were labourers. Lacking specialized skills they had to accept lower hourly wages and lower annual incomes than skilled craftsmen. The table documents an income structure roughly similar to that a decade earlier, when the *Labour Gazette* reported skilled carpenters and machinists in Vancouver earning respectively $3.00 and $2.75 per day, semi-skilled scaffoldhands and hod carriers $2.50, unskilled builders' labourers $2.00, and common labourers in saw and shingle mills (often Japanese) $1.00 to $1.50.[23]

Job regularity also influenced total earnings. Certainly, tradesmen could expect greater job security and thus higher annual incomes than unskilled workers but the relationship was not always straightforward. In 1911, for example, carpenters commanded an hourly wage of 50 cents compared to 35 cents for street railway conductors and motormen. Yet the annual incomes, as documented in Table 4.2, were almost identical. The phenomenon is explained by the more secure and less seasonal employment offered by the British Columbia Electric Railway Company.[24]

In fact, seasonal fluctuations had a major influence on annual wages, creating patterns of differentiation that overlapped with but did not entirely match those defined by skill. Winter unemployment plagued Canadian workers from Montreal's docks and Cornwall's cotton mills to British Columbia's logging camps. The building trades were especially vulnerable to unemployment, even in Vancouver, where rain hampered large street, sewer, and water line projects. During four months in 1903 wet con-

Table 4.2

Average annual earnings of heads of Vancouver families in specified occupations, 1911

	Earnings ($)
Trainmen	1,213.59
Electricians	1,022.64
Salesmen	1,022.44
Bricklayers, masons, and stone cutters	973.82
Plumbers and gas fitters	963.67
Chauffeurs	955.38
Bakers	927.11
Carpenters	914.75
Street railway employees	895.47
Domestic and personal	868.36
Painters and decorators	857.24
Labourers	629.30

Source: Sixth Census of Canada, 1921, vol. 3, p. xx

ditions restricted Vancouver construction workers and machinists to twelve days' employment in thirty. Both skilled tradesmen and unskilled labourers endured layoffs, storing up 'like the squirrels' in the summer for the seasonal unemployment that would inevitably follow.[25]

In addition to earning power, status also differentiated skilled from unskilled workers. Specialized skills protected craftsmen from the competition of unskilled labourers as well as the opposition of employers. Skilled tradesmen carefully guarded control over the pace of work and especially the training of apprentices and hiring of helpers, which had traditionally been the prerogative of carpenters, machinists, moulders, printers, and other tradesmen rather than of employers. Much of the impetus behind trade union organization among skilled workers in nineteenth-century industrial societies had resulted from a defensive struggle to preserve this power, which defined them as a distinctive stratum at the top of the working class. The struggle continued in Canadian cities, including Vancouver, in the early 1900s. In addition, skilled workers strongly believed in advancement according to merit and thus insisted on wage differentials that, in the words of Craig Heron, 'recognized their exalted status over helpers and labourers ... In this sense they were quite willing to accept some limited degree of hierarchical stratification.' This consciousness of economic privilege often blunted their enthusiasm for organizing the unskilled.[26] In particular it reinforced the desire of White, skilled workingmen to protect their privileged position in the labour market from the competition of wage-earning Asians and women.

The deeply entrenched ethnocentrism then pervading White society forced Asians to the margins of Vancouver's economy. Here they sold their labour at one-half to two-thirds the value of White labour or engaged in petty commerce. The Asian portion of Vancouver's lumber industry workforce, especially Japanese men – who were considered to work harder than the Chinese or Whites – increased from the 1890s to the First World War. More generally, over half of all Asians worked as labourers in resource industries. Some, such as the Chinese cannery workers who butchered salmon prior to canning, had acquired considerable skill. Most, however, laboured at routine and unsophisticated tasks. The Chinese became especially prominent in small business, providing service as grocers, launderers, pedlars, shopkeepers, and restaurateurs either to the White community or exclusively to a Chinese clientele. While ethnocentrism and the single, sojourner status of most Asians segregated them from White workers, regardless of skill, segregation ultimately rested on the hardpan of racial prejudice. This prejudice greatly impeded the ability of White workers to see Asians in class terms or to actively include them in Vancouver's blossoming trade union movement.[27]

Women, too, made up a distinct part of Vancouver's workforce, exhibiting employment characteristics common in other cities and particular to the west coast. As Table 4.3 illustrates, in 1911 women constituted only 12.7 per cent of Vancouver's overall paid labour force and an even smaller proportion of its factoryhands. Reflecting the resource-extractive economy of the surrounding region, Vancouver provided a disproportionate number of jobs for men. By contrast, women were much more likely to work as factoryhands in Toronto, a larger city with a higher ratio of jobs for women in the clothing, textile, tobacco, and food-processing industries. British Columbia's comparative disadvantage as a location for end product manufacturing – the result of remote location, small population, and discriminatory Canadian tariff and freight rate policies – particularly affected Vancouver, preventing it from becoming an important manufacturing centre for consumer goods, like Toronto.[28]

Employment for Vancouver women was also conditioned by the widely held view that women belonged in the home, where they were to support the principal breadwinner and nurture the children. If economic necessity required that women work for wages outside the family, suitable job choices extended from this domestic role into health care and education, personal service, clerical labour, and certain kinds of manufacturing. Based on the assumption that 'men and women were suited to different

Table 4.3

Wage-earning women in Vancouver, Toronto, and Winnipeg, 1911

	Women as % of total city workforce	Women as % of manufacturing portion of workforce	Women as % of urban population
Toronto	25.3	25.5	50.6
Winnipeg	18.3	17.2	45.3
Vancouver	12.7	9.6	39.9

Sources: Women as percentage of total workforce: *Fifth Census of Canada, 1911,* vol. 2, table 6; includes females ten years old and over. Women as percentage of urban population: *Fifth Census of Canada, 1911,* vol. 1, table 1; takes into account females of all ages, including children.

types of employment,' wage-earning women were segregated into a very few occupations, characterized by 'low wages, irregular work and dull, dead end tasks.' James Conley has noted that most women employed for wages in Vancouver were young, and turnover was high. Women also enjoyed few opportunities for promotion to skilled or managerial positions. These several factors – a life cycle that took women when still young out of the workforce to marry and have children; values that limited the ability of women to gain occupational skills and thus acquire power in the workplace; and a general disinclination on the part of male unionists to organize lower-status women workers – created a solid barrier against the unionization of women.[29]

Two additional occupational groups enjoyed distinctive identities in Vancouver. One of them, white-collar office workers and retail clerks, made up about 20 per cent of Vancouver's labour force in 1911. They shared with skilled manual workers a similar relationship to the productive system – both worked for wages – but differed profoundly by identifying their interests with management rather than with other members of the working class. In November 1900 George Bartley, editor of the *Independent,* a labour paper that served as official voice of the VTLC, and a staunch supporter of the union cause, reflected this fact in a scathing critique of the 'wage-working "gentleman" [who] look[s] down upon the horny-handed son of the toil.' Being able to dress as well as his employer and to 'appear in society with neat hands and a fair complexion,' the bookkeeper or salesclerk might be able to enjoy outward distinction of dress but was 'a wage slave as well as the manual laborer, if only he could realize it.' Bartley's outburst indicates that white collar workers, of whom 40 per cent by 1911 were women, believed that they enjoyed much higher status than blue-collar wage earners. They did not see themselves as participants in a 'class struggle' and exhibited little interest in joining trade unions.[30]

The other group, which was predominantly male, was made up of seasonal workers. These migrated between the city and jobs on the transcontinental railway, and coastal fishing and logging camps. By 1900 new railroad and shipping ties had solidified Vancouver's earlier function as a labour distribution and service hub. As Eleanor Bartlett notes, the 'province's resource industries were active primarily in spring, summer, and early fall. When winter closed these operations, the workers flocked to Vancouver to find other work or to spend their unemployment.'

Vancouver's mild climate and terminal location further enhanced the city's image during winter as a 'mecca of the unemployed.' Spring and summer brought their own employment rhythm, with many men leaving for resource industry jobs while others arrived to construct roads, street railway lines, and sewers. Whether skilled loggers or unskilled labourers, seasonal wage earners joined Vancouver's workforce for only a portion of each year. Seasonally determined transiency meant irregular employment, fluctuating income, and marginal integration into the city's working class. It also retarded the development of shared identities and institutions by settled urban workers and unsettled seasonal migrants.[31]

The disproportionate level of economic and cultural resources commanded by skilled workers helps to explain their lack of empathy for less advantaged members of the working class. Skilled workers could more easily than the unskilled disrupt production without being replaced. Craft traditions also encouraged the cohesion of skilled workers into unions. Not surprisingly, one study has found that, prior to the First World War, the Vancouver workers most likely to be unionized were metal tradesmen, cigar makers, printers, electrical workers, building tradesmen, and street railway employees. All but the last would be classified as skilled. Another has concluded that from 1889 to 1913, printers, machinists, and carpenters contributed 75 per cent of all VTLC presidents, with craftworkers in the building trades the Council's most active regular members. All of the VTLC executive were men of British heritage and thus members of the city's ethnic majority. To quote James Conley's summary, 'Skilled, white, male workers, generally of British ethnic origins, were ... the most strongly mobilized members of the Vancouver working class.'[32]

For this privileged group, unions provided varying degrees of protection against disability, illness, unemployment, and old age. They also reinforced class awareness by organizing a variety of social activities, giving form to identities rooted in artisanal tradition and workplace experience. While Sunday parlour recitals, picnics, and balls provided family entertainment, many gatherings reflected the male-centred character of craft culture. A machinists' 'stag picnic' pitted journeymen against apprentices on the baseball diamond, and a freight handlers' smoker featured speeches, songs, and recitals. When Vancouver's two carpenters' unions held jointly organized smokers, the men would 'don their "boiled" Sunday shirts' and assemble for an evening of food, beer, fun, and cigars, the latter 'often

A telephone operator, ca. 1915. The coming of the telephone provided women with a new opportunity for employment. However, work in this industry, as in others, was structured by gender. Women were relegated to routine tasks that required little skill and provided little chance for advancement. The attempt by female operators to form a union succeeded briefly in 1903 but was crushed in 1907. (City of Vancouver Archives CVA 17-57)

rolled especially for the occasion and always bearing the blue union label.'
The machinist union's masquerade ball of November 1901, held to raise
money for striking brothers in Seattle, articulated unambiguously the fraternal values of mutuality, cooperation, and equality that animated much
of the associational life of skilled artisans.[33]

What makes trade union formation between 1898 and 1903 so remark-
able is the degree to which it extended beyond this advantaged group, creating a potent thrust for class unity. Even though women, Asians, office
workers, millhands, and retail clerks still rarely joined unions, the incidence of union formation among workers outside the British, skilled, male
group testifies to the widespread desire of semi- and unskilled working

Table 4.4

Yearly level of strikes in Vancouver, 1901-14

	Number of strikes	Number of strikers[a]	Striker days[b]	Largest strikes (and striker days involved)[c]
1901	3	165	1,773	3 strikes (unknown)
1902	11	524	3,782	telephone linemen/operators (420)
1903	10	1,311	51,719	UBRE sympathy strike (38,075)
1904	3	99	2,324	halibut fishermen (1,300)
1905	5	189	2,873	painters (1,425)
1906	4	159	5,709	telephone operators/electrical linemen (4,082)
1907	5	1,440	30,585	carpenters (27,000)
1908	0	0	0	–
1909	6	428	5,896	longshoremen (2,700)
1910	7	627	12,077	machinists/engineers (7,170)
1911	6	6,046	257,112	building trades sympathy strike (241,216)
1912	9	1,168	78,818	halibut fishermen (74,200)
1913	5	416	5,864	granite cutters (2,500)
1914	2	80	691	sheet metal workers(100)
Total	76	12,652	459,223	

Notes:

a These yearly figures are based on hard data for 52 strikes and a statistical average of 55 workers for each of the
remaining 24, for which no information was available. In calculating the average I deleted the 10 largest strikes
(each involving more than 199 workers) and averaged the number of strikers in the remainder.

b I employed the same technique for 26 strikes for which information about striker days was unavailable, calculating an average of 591 striker days for 40 other strikes, each of which involved no more than 2,499 striker
days of work.

c Only hard data, not the calculated averages, are listed.

Sources: Canada, Department of Labour, Strikes and Lockouts Files, original and revised RG 27, National
Archives of Canada; Canada, Department of Labour, *Labour Gazette* 1-15 (1901-15); and local newspapers
and labour papers

people to assert their power in the workplace and thereby limit the power of capital. At least seventeen unions were created at the turn of the century by these outsiders, among them shingle weavers, mill workers, factory woodworkers, confectionery labourers, laundry workers, freight handlers, builders' labourers, general labourers, civic employees, and retail clerks. Of eleven leading members of the VTLC from 1898 to 1903, four represented this recent wave of unionization among semi- and unskilled workers.[34]

The extent of labour militancy is revealed in Table 4.4, which documents a total of seventy-six strikes for the period 1901-14. The cycle of conflict peaked in 1902 and 1903, not to be exceeded again until the end of the war. What has been called British Columbia's 'first great sympathy strike' occurred in 1903 when over 600 members of several unions walked out to support the strike of freight handlers and clerks, members of the United Brotherhood of Railway Employees (UBRE), employed by the CPR. None of these unions represented the skilled elite that had generally led the fight for workers' rights in early Vancouver. In addition, for the years 1901-3 issues involving a clear challenge by strikers to management's power – trade union recognition and command of the labour process – were much more often the subject of contention than the straightforward economic question of wages, again suggesting a heightened level of militancy. The point is underlined by a comparison of strikes for the three-year periods ending in 1903 and 1912, which reveals that issues of control were two and a half times more frequent than the issue of wages in the earlier period but merely of equal significance in the later years.[35]

In defence of capitalist hegemony, employers launched what historian Andrew Yarmie has called an 'outright war against unions.'[36] The mobilization of business to meet labour's challenge was influenced by the structure of capitalism in Vancouver. Upper-class entrepreneurs heading regionally centred companies and managers heading externally controlled 'big businesses' responded to different manifestations of stress within the capitalist system. Business factions meshed in 1903 and 1904 to form a powerful, and class-specific, answer to labour militancy.

As travellers to the region have observed, British Columbia experienced both political and social upheaval around 1900. Political instability reflected the evolution from a highly localized region of discrete communities into an increasingly integrated society of provincial scope; social unrest resulted from an intensification of capital investment and the separation of capital and labour. Major strikes over wages or trade union recognition occurred in the hard rock mines of the Slocan and Rossland in 1899 and 1901, in the Fraser River fishery in 1900 and 1901, and on the coal fields of Vancouver in 1903, deeply embittering relations between employers and employed. The shock of industrial strife was magnified by collapse of the highly personalized and localized system of government that had prevailed at the provincial level in British Columbia since Confederation.

Business leaders felt particularly threatened by the political and economic instability that accompanied the increased pace of industrialization in British Columbia. The two concerns intersected most dramatically in 1899, when leaders of the Western Federation of Miners in the Kootenays convinced the newly elected MLA from Nelson, Fred Hume, to introduce into the divided and politically unstable assembly an amendment to the Metalliferous Mines Inspection Act to limit work in hard rock mines to eight hours per day, down from ten. The act passed without dissent but businessmen were outraged. A Vancouver entrepreneur referred to it as the 'foolish 8 hour law' and a Rossland mine manager proclaimed that labour now 'can and is dictating terms [to the Legislature] without qualification.'[37]

The bill ignited a seven-month strike over wages at silver-lead mines in the Slocan Valley (where owners lowered wages to be commensurate with the reduced hours) and indirectly encouraged profit-starved British owners of the overcapitalized Le Roi and War Eagle-Centre Star mines at Rossland to impose a contract wage system on its miners. They refused to accept it, and another long and bitter work stoppage resulted. Rossland lawyer and mining promoter T. Mayne Daly reflected the business community's view of the overall labour question in the province when exclaiming in 1903, 'Unhappy British Columbia! What a turmoil things have been in since 1897.'[38]

Labour conflict in another resource industry, the Fraser River fishery, gave this general sense of turmoil concrete meaning for Vancouver businessmen. Canners and fishermen drifted apart during the 1890s, each side developing a collective identity in opposition to the other. At the centre of contention was control of fishing licences. The canners wanted to continue receiving licences from the dominion government and hiring fishermen to use them, the principal form of licence distribution until the 1890s. Fishermen argued that they, rather than canneries, should be licensed, after which they would sell salmon to canners at a negotiated price. By 1900 independent, or 'free,' fishermen controlled nine of every ten licences. By heightening 'in both canners and fishermen an awareness of their respective interests,' writes Keith Ralston, this struggle over fishery regulations polarized the two 'into opposing groups.' The first organizations of canners and fishermen emerged prior to a fishing strike in 1893 but did not survive. Five years later escalating conflict over licences and prices led the canners to reorganize by forming the British Columbia Salmon Packers' Association. In self-defence White fishermen then unionized and Japanese fishermen, who by now held 40 per cent of the Fraser River licences, formed a benevolent association that provided some of the functions of a trade union. Strikes followed, closing the fishery for parts of the next four summers. Conflict during the 1900 strike was particularly intense.[39]

This process of class formation on the Fraser increased the sensitivity of Vancouver business people to unions. As noted earlier, in the 1890s new salmon-canning investment tended to be routed through Vancouver, and it was representatives of this external capital, rather than the older generation of canners working though Victoria merchants, who fought most aggressively in the 1890s to maintain high profits. Especially prominent were the Bell-Irving brothers, Henry and Duncan, the former of whom had risen to become an industry leader because of his understanding of finance capital. Henry organized substitute workers to defeat striking fishermen in 1893 and with Duncan united canners to lobby Ottawa and then break the solidarity of striking fishermen at the end of the century.[40] It was also Henry, 'an advocate of the hard line in past disputes,' who, along with fellow Vancouver businessman William Farrell, orchestrated the dispatch in late July 1900 of the Sixth Regiment – the Duke of Connaught's Own Rifles to intimidate striking fishermen in Steveston. Headed by Lieutenant-Colonel C.A. Worsnop, a socially prominent Vancouverite, and C. Gardiner Johnson, a cannery shareholder and leading Terminal City businessman, this militia company was closely tied to the upper stratum of Vancouver society. Vancouver's Board of Trade also considered the salmon-fishing and -canning industries its areas of concern and, already upset over the success of Kootenay miners in legislating a shorter work day, enthusiastically backed the canners in the 1900 strike.[41]

The extent to which class tensions on the Fraser reverberated back into the city is suggested by the behaviour of Joseph Russell, a lawyer and

Vancouver police magistrate viewed by city workers as extremely biased against members of labour organizations. Russell's conduct during the 1900 strike confirms that workers had reason to question his impartiality. When six White fishermen appeared in a Vancouver court on charges arising out of the conflict, Russell, present in the public gallery as an observer, became so involved in the proceedings that he interrupted defence counsel and forced the presiding magistrate to clear the courtroom. The next day a man uttering something about cannery monopolists accosted Joseph Russell on Powell Street and, pistol drawn, threatened to blow his head off. A useful clue to Russell's behaviour is to be found in a recently published account of the family law firm; Joseph, it seems, was not only an officer of the state but an active capitalist who served from 1899 to 1910 as 'local manager and legal counsel for the Canadian Canning Company, Ltd., a London-based company which owned three operations on the Fraser River.'[42]

Local capitalists, though acutely aware of the changing character of industrial relations in British Columbia, were initially divided into various groups and lacked the means to coordinate their response to labour. Small companies that employed skilled labour found it particularly difficult to resist the unionization trend. Lumber companies kept unions out of their mills through a combination of factors, including the unskilled nature of most mill work and management's deliberate policy of dividing the workforce by race.[43] Large, externally controlled corporations had the wealth and power to control their workers in more sophisticated ways. BC Electric, for example, implemented a program of paternalistic policies, including union recognition and profit sharing, that successfully created in the early 1900s a sense among its workers and managers that all were part of 'a united family.'[44] BC Electric's approach to labour relations was the exception, however. Far more representative was the militant stance of the CPR, which adamantly refused to negotiate with trade unions unless forced to do so. By 1900 it had come to accept the right of its most skilled workers to belong to unions but continued to reject any such rights for the unskilled. As a national corporation, the CPR had power that local companies did not, especially the ability to organize strikebreakers – a key weapon in their battle against unions – in a national or international labour market. By contrast, regionally centred employers tended to limit their search for replacement workers to the lower mainland and Puget Sound.[45]

Not surprisingly, then, it was Vancouver's biggest 'big business,' the Canadian Pacific Railway, that broke the upward spiral of trade union growth and militancy. In the early 1900s the company fought a series of strikes with its skilled shop workers over wages, union recognition, and the increased employment of apprentices and unskilled helpers for jobs originally held by skilled tradesmen. In a tight labour market these machinists, boilermakers, and other 'allround mechanics' did well until 1903, but a counter-offensive by the corporation successfully lessened the workers' control over production thereafter.[46]

Less skilled freight handlers and clerks also prospered in the early 1900s and in 1902 formed a local of the UBRE, an affiliate of the American Labor Union (ALU). Business found the ALU threatening because it organized workers by industry rather than by skill, and thus spread unionization to workers usually ignored by the mainstream labour movement in North America. It certainly frightened the CPR, which set out to stop the new organization at Vancouver, where it had first taken hold. Vowing to 'spend a million dollars to kill the UBRE,' the company provoked a strike on 27 February 1903 by forcing union members to walk out in defence of an unfairly dismissed clerk. Not even the sympathetic strikes of longshoremen, messengers, teamsters, and steamshipmen could limit the force of corporate influence. Faced with aggressive CPR tactics, including espionage, the importation of strikebreakers, and the murder of labour leader Frank Rogers, the Vancouver-centred strike collapsed, destroying the UBRE and three other unions with it.[47]

The UBRE strike left workers with strong memories of 'the old 1903 spirit of B.C. unionism' but it left capital with something much more substantial: enhanced power. In addition to stemming the tide of unionization among semi- and unskilled workers, the UBRE strike pulled together Vancouver's fragmented business groups into a single organization, the Employers' Association of Vancouver. Founded during the UBRE strike in May 1903, the Association emulated similar organizations recently formed in the United States and Toronto. General anxiety borne of several years of political instability and trade union growth in British Columbia made businessmen receptive to the idea of fighting labour through group action. So, too, did fears that the concurrent strikes in Vancouver and at the Dunsmuir coal mines on Vancouver Island represented a socialist conspiracy to damage western Canada's economy. At the root of this fear was the

Longshoremen at work, early 1900s. Heavy work, long hours, and uncertain employment characterized work on Vancouver's docks. The limits of human strength and endurance determined the speed at which a ship was loaded; machines and tools merely supplemented the strong backs and iron muscles of the 'man along the shore.' Longshoremen were some of Vancouver's most militant workers, striking at least ten times between 1889 and 1913. But the unskilled and casual nature of their employment made unionization difficult. (P. Timms photo, Vancouver Public Library 2886)

fact that the unions leading both strikes, the UBRE in Vancouver and the Western Federation of Miners on the island, were American-based industrial unions under socialist leadership. Class feeling among the business community was further heightened, then, by the perception that the strikes represented a fundamental challenge to the province's economic and political order.[48]

The Employers' Association proposed to return to the owners and representatives of capital the 'right to manage.' To achieve this goal they aimed to terminate 'closed shop' agreements and thus open unionized firms to both unorganized and organized workers. R.H. Sperling, general manager of the British Columbia Electric Railway Company, put the owners' case succinctly: in each case where the unions had secured a closed shop they had driven up wages and 'imposed numerous working conditions which ... [were] very unpalatable to the employers.' To end this condition the Employers' Association vowed to import and subsidize strikebreakers, lobby governments in opposition to union demands, and pursue legal action against 'the leaders of mobs' and people who threatened business property. The Association initially listed 103 members, all of whom employed five or more 'hands.'[49] Victory for Vancouver's open shop movement came quickly when in early 1904 the Vancouver Engineering Works, backed by the Association, forced striking boilermakers and machinists to accept the opening of its plant to non-union tradespeople. Other metal shops in Vancouver soon implemented open shop rules as well.[50]

Increasing ties between lawyers and businessmen assisted upper-class resistance to the demands of labour. Lawyers shared the commitment of entrepreneurs and corporate managers to free enterprise and the pursuit of private wealth. As Jonathan Swainger writes in a thoughtful study of early twentieth-century lawyers in the Alberta town of Red Deer, 'The lawyer, like most of the adventurers and settlers who came to the west, subscribed to the image of an individualistic entrepreneur prospering in a new land.' Economic interests also linked business and professional people in more practical ways. Lawyers melded into the capitalist class with particular ease because their interests and expertise led them either to serve as agents and facilitators of business or to become entrepreneurs themselves. In addition, changes in the legal status of companies and the subsequent emergence of large, heavily capitalized, and bureaucratic corporations created demand for the expertise of legal specialists.[51] In British Columbia, the mining and salmon-canning industries passed through a significant period of capital consolidation from 1889 to 1902, and externally controlled corporations dominated the fields of banking, transportation, and utilities. All brought lawyers into the mainstream of business promotion or management.[52]

POLITICS IN VANCOUVER illustrate the heightened tensions between what the dominion labour commissioner, E.P. Bremner, called British Columbia's 'two great classes.'[53] In 1900 the Vancouver Trades and Labor Council became actively involved in politics, nominating two candidates for the provincial election and establishing a separate workers' party, the Vancouver Labor Party (VLP). Shortly thereafter it united with federal Liberals to co-sponsor the re-election of MP George Maxwell. The Council backed three more candidates indirectly through the VLP in the 1903 provincial contest. Labour candidates were joined in the political arena by a new set of participants, the socialists, who ran a single candidate in the 1900 general election and three more in the next. Although only Maxwell succeeded in getting elected to public office, labour and socialist candidates in Vancouver garnered 15 per cent of the provincial popular vote in 1900 and 25 per cent in 1903. Many upper-class Vancouverites would have agreed with New Westminster MP Aulay Morrison that there appeared to be 'a [political] ... movement on the part of Labor people to "Laborize" ... British Columbia.'[54]

Labour activism represented both a continuation of and a departure from the reform impulse of the 1890s. Continuity was exemplified by the philosophical orientation of two institutions created by workers in 1900, the *Independent* and the Vancouver Labor Party. Established in March 1900 by George Bartley and co-sponsored by the VTLC, the *Independent* for more than two years presented a strong independent voice for Vancouver labour. The Labor Party was formed by the VTLC to overcome the perception that VTLC-sponsored candidates represented only the interests of skilled labour and thus to attract the support of unorganized workers. The VLP described its goals in the language of labour reform, which reflected the assumptions of the producers' ideology. Thus Bartley spoke of the *Independent*'s desire to reach out to 'plain people, whose sympathies are co-ordinate in the work of trades unions and social reformers.' Similarly Francis Williams, a tailor, leading political activist for the VTLC, and one of the Council's labour candidates in each of the 1900 and 1903 provincial elections, urged the creation of a separate labour party 'with a liberal platform.' The names he suggested for the Vancouver Labor Party – 'Reform league' and 'People's league' – evoked the sense of mission that had animated the broadly based movement against elites and monopolies a decade earlier. The platform of the VLP did as well, with its emphasis on direct democracy, government ownership of all public resources, a tax on land values, abolition of Asian immigration, the eight-hour day, and day labour for all government works. Its policies were liberal, reformist, and evolutionary.[55]

What differentiated provincial politics in 1900 from 1890 was the desire of many labour men to speak for themselves, apart from connections to middle-class reformers. As early as the mid-1890s the middle- and working-class strands of Vancouver's reform impulse had begun to separate when Francis Carter-Cotton argued against candidates for City Council running as representatives of a single class and when William Brown made known his distaste for trade unions.[56] As the labour movement gained strength and workers new confidence, wage earners began to assert an identity independent of their erstwhile middle class allies. This change is evident in the language used by politically active leaders of Vancouver's trade union movement in the year 1900. The intensely anti-socialist J.H. Watson, an American Federation of Labor union organizer, encouraged workers to recognize that they had 'certain distinctly class interests.' Francis Williams urged that the VLP be 'out and out for class legislation.' At a rally for George Maxwell, Harry Cowan asserted his independence from Liberal Party support for Maxwell by emphasizing that he spoke as 'a labor man.' In a provincial by-election at the end of the year Robert Macpherson, elected an MLA as a reformer in 1894 and oppositionist in 1898, also strongly asserted his working-class identity by promising to serve as 'a straight Labor man.'[57]

The degree to which Vancouver politics tended to realign along the axis of class for a short but turbulent period around 1900 is also suggested by the working-class orientation of city Liberals. National party affiliations had not yet been introduced at the provincial level and were weak at the federal, as exemplified by Maxwell's identity as an Independent Liberal. By 1900, however, a move was afoot to stabilize provincial politics by introducing national parties, and this was achieved in 1903. In this period of political flux, support for Liberals in Vancouver came substantially, but not exclusively, from lower-status occupational groups, while Conservatives were the party of business and the professions.[58] The anti-elitist tone of Liberalism was reinforced by the emergence of Joseph Martin – a partisan Liberal and lawyer formerly noted for his stand against French-language education and public funding of confessional schools in Manitoba – as MLA for Vancouver in 1898 and premier of the province for several months in 1900. Martin's three Vancouver running mates were Liberals known for their sympathy for labour. In addition, a meeting 'called by unorganized labour' and attended by 200 to 300 citizens during the election showed strong feeling that 'Premier Martin's platform [is] the best for the workingman.'[59] Unfortunately for the ticket, Martin's irascible character limited his support. Nonetheless, Martin's group took 39 per cent of the Vancouver popular vote and won two of four seats. Exceeding 50 per cent, the combined Liberal, Labor, and Socialist popular vote represented a broad wave of support in Vancouver for candidates sympathetic to working-class concerns. George Maxwell's easy re-election later in the year similarly tapped the wellspring of labour reform sentiment in the city.

The inclination of federal Liberals in Vancouver to support the interests of labour and federal Conservatives those of capital is illustrated in the bitter antagonism between George Maxwell and Henry Bell-Irving over fisheries issues. Maxwell, an Independent Liberal MP with strong connections to working people and recipient in 1896 of political support from Fraser River fishermen who lived off-season in Vancouver, stated flatly, '*I am* [the] Minister of Fisheries within our constituency' and as such 'am not going to give any man a ... licence who is not a supporter of the [Laurier] government and of myself.' Bell-Irving, an ardent Tory, not surprisingly considered both Maxwell and Martin to be 'out and out blackguards.' Maxwell spoke out strongly in support of striking fishermen, and the canners responded with a concerted but unsuccessful effort to thwart his bid for re-election to the House of Commons.[60] Throughout the 1890s and early 1900s, in fact, BC canners overwhelmingly supported the Conservative Party and fishermen the Liberals.[61] In so doing the two groups reinforced the tendency of politics in turn of the century Vancouver to be structured along class lines.

Socialists at first reinforced this tendency, contributing to class polarization especially through their leadership in the labour movement. Two Vancouver socialists, Frank Rogers, a one-time seaman and then longshoreman, and Will MacClain, a machinist, were the two most powerful spokesmen for striking fishermen during the course of the 1900 strike, and Rogers actively supported the UBRE during the strike of 1903. In 1901 British Columbia socialists established their own journal, the *Western Clarion*, in Vancouver. Reflecting the growing strength of socialist support among miners in the Kootenays and on Vancouver Island, city socialists also gained increasing influence within the VTLC. Two related events particularly symptomatic of the growing radicalism of British Columbia's labour movement under socialist influence were the VTLC's vote early in 1903 to endorse industrial rather than craft unions and its decision in April to walk out of the Trades and Labour Congress of Canada when the latter refused to follow its lead by endorsing industrial unionism. As historian Thomas Loosemore reminded us many years ago, industrial unionism implied 'a broad class outlook rather than narrow group interests,' and thus was implicitly radical.[62]

More importantly, the advent of socialist politics in British Columbia spurred the upper class, led by resource industry entrepreneurs, to react and defend British Columbia capitalism. The introduction of national party affiliations in provincial elections and a militant counter-offensive by capital against trade unions were two results. In addition, the Liberal Party in Vancouver moved to the political centre and by 1908 was 'controlled not by labor but by commercial interests.'[63] The weakening of the Liberal left and marginalization of labour represented the political equivalent of capital's economic campaign against unions. In effect, then, as labour's economic and political strength grew in the 1898 to 1903 period, and as the conditions that led labour to challenge business also spawned a socialist critique of capitalism, powerful elements within the upper class organized to defend their economic interests. They did so by political as well as economic means.

CHAPTER FIVE

Incorrigible Optimists

Vancouver changed greatly between the late 1890s and 1913. Most obviously different was the concentration in Vancouver of transportation, wholesaling, and resource management companies that operated throughout the region. The city's growing population also required a greater variety of retail, manufacturing, and professional services. The market for services encouraged expansion and diversification of the city's upper and middle classes.

But continuity accompanied change. The economic functions of resource promotion and extraction still linked the budding metropolis to its roots in the forest industry, and speculation, now a regional phenomenon, again became a major source of growth. Indeed, so powerful was the fever of speculation in Vancouver from 1909 to 1913 that people of all classes were drawn in by its hypnotic promise of instant wealth. The shared experience of playing the capitalist game of investing in land or other resources weakened, temporarily at least, the thrust towards class separation that had gained momentum at the turn of the century.

THE INFLATED PROSPERITY that accompanied Vancouver's formation had evaporated by the early 1890s, and many residents departed as quickly as they had come. Nevertheless, by 1897 the city was growing again and continued to do so until a minor downturn in 1907 and a major collapse in 1913. Persistence rewarded pioneers who had stuck with the city through the troubled 1890s, for the tide of provincial growth clearly favoured the Terminal City. Large-scale immigration into Canada from the late years of the century to 1913 did for British Columbia what the CPR's arrival in the 1880s had failed to do, stimulate a widespread expansion of the provincial economy. Population statistics reflect the region's dynamism (see Chapter 4, Table 4.1). Increasing by 80,000 people in the 1890s, British Columbia's population swelled a further 214,000 in the following decade. While the West Kootenays stagnated, the Crowsnest Pass, East Kootenay, and Boundary districts flourished. The Okanagan continued its transformation from ranching to fruit farming, and the north coast gained economic importance as the salmon-canning industry decentralized from the Fraser River to northern waters. Railway construction, ranging from Great Northern branch line extensions in the province's southeastern region in the late 1890s to new transcontinentals from 1908 to 1915, boosted provincial growth. Construction generated jobs for workers, markets for urban distributors and manufacturers, and speculative profits for land and resource investors. Immigration and investment flowed especially along the Grand Trunk Pacific route from Edmonton through Prince George to Prince Rupert and along the Canadian Northern Pacific line from Edmonton through Kamloops to Vancouver. Farther east, more than one million prairie settlers created an almost insatiable demand for British Columbia shingles and wood. Lumber shipments inland by rail from coastal and southeastern parts of the province jumped dramatically to consume approximately two-thirds of British Columbia's lumber output at the height of the prewar boom. With its mainland location, natural harbour, and CPR connection, Vancouver was ideally situated to manage and service this expanding provincial economy.[1]

Having surpassed Victoria as British Columbia's largest city in the late 1890s, Vancouver quickly blossomed into a metropolitan centre more than three times as populous as its rival. The Canadian census of 1911 records 100,000 people living in the city of Vancouver, with an additional 30,000 or so in the surrounding suburbs of North Vancouver, South Vancouver,

Table 5.1

Structure of Vancouver's economy compared to seven other Canadian cities, 1911

	Total workforce	Percentage population increase over previous decade	Percentage of total workforce by occupational category[b]				
			Construction	Commerce (trade and merchandising[c])	Professions	Transportation	Manufacturing
Calgary	21,320	893.7	20.8	15.2	6.8	12.6	15.1
Vancouver[a]	50,628	271.7	17.6	17.0	7.8	9.8	18.6
Winnipeg	62,265	221.3	17.2	21.1	7.5	13.7	17.6
Toronto	169,520	81.9	11.7	20.4	7.0	7.1	34.9
Montreal	183,257	75.7	13.3	18.6	6.0	10.4	33.1
Hamilton	37,428	55.7	10.8	13.4	4.4	6.5	50.7
Victoria	15,479	51.3	16.6	13.9	7.5	17.2	20.7
London	19,615	21.9	7.6	17.8	6.1	9.2	42.3

Notes:

a Population statistics for Vancouver refer to Vancouver proper and not to North Vancouver, South Vancouver, Burnaby, or Point Grey.

b Data include both employers and employees.

c Data for banks, insurance companies, and loan, trust, and real estate companies are not included.

Source: Fifth Census of Canada, 1911, vol. 1, table 13 and vol. 6, table 6

Burnaby, and Point Grey. Growth continued for another two years, during which Vancouver's numbers increased by a further 20 per cent. One suspects that the outlying suburbs grew at least as quickly. At the high point of the prewar period, then, Greater Vancouver could boast a population of more than 150,000, making it Canada's fourth largest city and a close rival of Winnipeg for third place.[2]

Table 5.1 places Vancouver's economy in comparative perspective. It suggests two patterns of economic activity among the cities examined. In one, Vancouver belongs to a category of metropolitan centres that directed commerce for part or all of the country. Vancouver was in the middle of this group, with trade employing a larger portion of the workforces in Winnipeg, Toronto, Montreal, and London, and transportation a greater percentage in Calgary, Winnipeg, Montreal, and Victoria.[3] An obvious explanation for Vancouver's middle position within the commercial and transportation hierarchies is to be found in the limited extent to which it functioned as a central place. Whereas Winnipeg served as a commercial centre for much of western Canada, and Montreal and Toronto for the nation as a whole, Vancouver's hinterland was more sharply circumscribed. Freight rates restricted Vancouver's commercial ties for the most part to British Columbia, which remained relatively small despite rapid growth before the war.[4] Vancouver was an important provincial centre but not a transprovincial or national one.

Yet despite these limitations, other evidence underlines the importance of trade and transportation to Vancouver. In the transportation sector, Vancouver not only remained the terminus of the Canadian Pacific Railway but was about to become that of the Canadian Northern Railway and to be connected to the United States by the Great Northern. An extensive network of shipping ties linked the city to the province's north coast. In trade, more than 8,600 workers out of a total workforce of 50,628 were engaged in some kind of commercial activity by 1911, whether as employers or as employees. Merchants constituted the largest single group of business leaders, with seventeen of ninety-one top businessmen occupied in the wholesale trade and three in retail. Vancouver's second generation of merchant princes, several of them well established by 1900, continued to expand their operations across the province as new participants, including eastern companies, established large provincial operations in the coastal city. Of these various enterprises, Frederick Buscombe and Company became western Canada's largest china and glass distributors, McLennan and McFeely emerged as the biggest glass wholesale hardware business west of Winnipeg, the eastern-based Canadian Fairbanks Morse Company claimed to have the 'Largest Machinery and Mill Supply House' in British Columbia, and Evans, Coleman and Evans, importers of British industrial supplies, boasted of being British Columbia's 'principal commercial firm.'[5]

The manufacturing and construction categories of Table 5.1 suggest a different pattern of growth among the eight cities surveyed, one more regional than national in character. In contrast to trade, the levels of work that manufacturing provided for the gainfully employed of western cities was dramatically different from eastern cities. This part of Vancouver's economy shared much with that of Winnipeg but less with the more heavily industrialized economies of Montreal, Toronto, and Hamilton. In 1911 proportionately more than twice as many Vancouver workers as their Toronto counterparts toiled in wood manufacturing and lumber plants, a reflection of the obvious importance of forest-related production in the coast city. By contrast, a Toronto worker was three times as likely to labour in clothing and related industries and twice as likely to find employment in metal manufacturing firms.[6] As the table reveals, industrial jobs in Toronto and Montreal exceeded manufacturing work in Vancouver by a ratio of almost two to one.

British Columbia enjoyed a comparative advantage in national and international markets for its primary resources, to which only limited value had been added. The huge Hastings Sawmill on Burrard Inlet and the several saw, shingle, and sash and door mills that lined False Creek testified to the pervasive influence of forest wealth on Vancouver's economy. As a thinly populated region far removed from major markets and lacking a freight rate structure that favoured the eastward flow of high-value goods, however, British Columbia did not experience the scale or locational economies required to manufacture highly processed items competitive beyond provincial boundaries. Small by national standards, the city's consumer goods plants, engineering works, and clothing shops served mainly local or regional needs. BC Sugar, by far Vancouver's largest consumer goods manufacturing company, was the single important exception, refining sugar from the South Pacific for markets across the province and beyond the Rockies.

The construction industry also engaged a higher proportion of the workforce in western than in eastern centres, though the differences were less dramatic than for manufacturing. Construction employment was greatest in Calgary, Vancouver, and Winnipeg, the three fastest growing cities listed in Table 5.1, and not surprisingly these places were located in western Canada. Rapid population growth stimulated widespread construction in Vancouver and caused the value of building permits from 1908 to 1912 to increase by 223 per cent. 'Thousands of carpenters, bricklayers, stonemasons, electricians, plasterers, painters, plumbers, [and] other craftsmen,' along with their helpers and labourers, built 'houses, offices, shops, warehouses, and factories' across the city. The census of 1911 for Vancouver lists 5,600 construction workers, of whom carpenters made up almost half. Another 1,800 men worked as general labourers, probably on such labour-intensive projects as water line excavation and street repair. Prewar construction changed the face of downtown Vancouver through the erection of several landmark buildings, including the provincial courthouse (now the city art gallery), the fourteen-storey steel-framed Dominion Trust Building, Dominic Burns's Vancouver Block (topped by its well-known clock), the World Building on Pender Street (now the Sun Tower), and another CPR station. The previous one – Vancouver's second – had opened little more than a decade earlier.[7]

As Vancouver's economy expanded it also grew more complex. The increasing prominence of lawyers, clergymen, doctors, teachers, architects, and other professionals in the city provides the most striking example. Whereas professionals constituted slightly less than 4 per cent of Vancouver's workforce in 1891, the proportion had doubled by 1911 (3.7 per cent versus 7.8 per cent).[8] One obvious explanation for the shift is the area's greater population. Another is metropolitanism. Vancouver had emerged as a 'mother city,' providing specialized services for the region.[9] As suggested in the previous chapter, Vancouver's function as a business management centre increased employment for lawyers. The move to Vancouver from New Westminster by Justice Aulay Macaulay Morrison and his family in 1904 after more than a decade of lobbying by the Vancouver Law Association for a resident Supreme Court judge marked the Terminal City's coming of age as a legal centre. Prominent New Westminster lawyer Robie L. Reid followed in 1905, leaving behind twelve years of legal experience in the Royal City. As the decade progressed, observers noted a 'large exodus' of lawyers from places such as Nelson and Rossland to Vancouver, where the province's legal business was 'being centralized.'[10] The Roman

Catholic church followed, moving its archdiocese from New Westminster to Vancouver in 1909 due to the latter's 'growing size and importance and greater facility of approach.' Doctors and architects organized professional associations in the city in 1899 and 1908 respectively. In the field of education, Vancouver emerged as a provincial leader with the opening there of British Columbia's first Normal School in 1901 and McGill University College in 1906. Soon after, the McBride government chose crown land at Point Grey on Vancouver's western edge as the site of a provincial university. Protestant churches established colleges in Vancouver in 1908 (Presbyterian), 1911 (Anglican), 1912 (Methodist), and 1913 (Anglican again).[11] The relatively equal proportion of professionals in seven of the eight cities listed in Table 5.1 indicates that Vancouver had become a substantial, and in some ways typical, urban place offering a wide range of professional services.

If expansion of the professions increased the complexity of Vancouver's upper class, the status group to which most members of the professions sought to belong, an examination of the financial wealth of selected categories of businesses suggests a similar broadening of the city's middle class. *Bradstreet's Book of Commercial Ratings* for 1911 offers a comprehensive though incomplete picture of the many grocers, artisans, drygoods merchants, and confectioners who were part of the economy's rapidly growing retail and service sector (Table 5.2). At the heart of Vancouver's middle class – where they joined contractors and real estate agents – were merchants and master craftsmen, whose shops seldom commanded financial resources larger than a few thousand dollars. The most numerous worked in the retail trade, where almost all businesses were small. Rapid population growth had encouraged commercial specialization, spawning single-product wholesale firms that together sold a variety of products, from fresh produce and electrical supplies to cigars and liquors. Yet fewer than one in eight wholesale houses in 1911 commanded financial resources of $100,000 or more, and these large companies, headed by upper-class entrepreneurs well established in the city by 1902, sold hardware, industrial supplies, or groceries throughout the province. Recently formed, highly specialized, and relatively small, Vancouver's many other wholesale firms lacked the hinterland connections required for extensive corporate growth.

So too did Vancouver's manufacturing enterprises, a point suggested earlier by Table 5.1 and supported again in Table 5.2 by evidence from the

Bradstreet credit rating books. In 1911 the typical manufacturer of industrial equipment or supplies was worth less than $20,000, or approximately half the value of local sawmill and salmon-canning firms. Only in the lumber industry did a significant number of companies command resources of more than $100,000. Additional evidence from the Canadian census shows that the region's twenty-three log product plants averaged 235 workers, while among secondary industries boiler and engine manufacturing firms employed eighty apiece and other industries considerably fewer.[12] Almost all capital goods for BC industries came from outside the region, with local machine shops limited mainly to supplying supplementary items and modifying imported machinery. Plants manufacturing consumer goods were of equally modest size. As early as the 1890s the bulk and perishability of

Table 5.2

Hierarchy of commercial, industrial, and construction businesses in 1911 (by wealth of median firm[a])

	Number of firms in category	Wealth of median firm ($)	Percentage of firms with wealth over $100,000
Lumber: manufacturing and commerce	53	35,000-50,000	26.4
Salmon canning	17	35,000-50,000	5.9
Commerce: wholesale	153	10,000-20,000	13.1
Manufacturing: non-consumer	41	10,000-20,000	7.3
Construction	31	10,000-20,000	6.5
Manufacturing: consumer	90	5,000-10,000	12.2
Commerce: service[b]	231	2,000-3,000	2.2
Commerce: retail (non-grocery)	449	2,000-3,000	.7
Commerce: grocery	311	500-1,000	0
Artisan[c]	200	500-1,000	0
Commerce: confectionery	151	0-500	0

Notes:

a Bradstreet's, the source of these estimates of wealth, rated most Vancouver businesses in certain economic categories, excluding utility companies, real estate firms, banks, non-banking financial companies, and Vancouver-based enterprises speculating in hinterland resources. In short, the book excludes most large, externally controlled corporations such as the CPR and the BC Electric Co. and leaves out almost entirely the speculative component of Vancouver's business community. Furthermore, many companies are listed without wealth and credit data, including some local firms and most externally controlled ones. The table draws on estimates of wealth for 1,727 firms, or 73.7 per cent of the total number listed by Bradstreet's for Vancouver.

b Includes businesses ranging from restaurants and undertakers to plumbing and heating firms and hotels.

c Includes artisans listed as sheet metal worker, upholsterer, butcher, baker, blacksmith, tinsmith, painter, printer, jewellery maker, plumber, tailor, engraver, lithographer, boat builder, gunsmith, carriage maker, and pattern maker.

Source: Bradstreet's Book of Commercial Ratings: Dominion of Canada (New York: Bradstreet Company 1911), 174:52-73

many consumer products and the simple technology required to make them had induced local production of candy, canned fruit, bakery products, beer, and tailored clothing. Such import substitution industries thrived in the prewar period. Yet both industrial equipment manufacturing companies and consumer goods firms were generally small.[13] In other words, when measured in economic terms most manufacturing enterprises, like virtually all retail and many wholesale firms, were relatively small in scale and local or regional in geographic reach.

VANCOUVER'S ECONOMIC HISTORY is only partly told by statistics, however, for numbers merely hint at the speculative ethos that animated the city's expansion. As the provincial labour movement's official journal observed, Vancouver was particularly dependent on both 'building and real estate speculation for its main industries.' A number of influences came together to create a boom that extended geographically beyond the city to encompass large sections of the province. At its core was the belief that riches could be had quickly through the buying and selling of land and other natural resources. In the words of one observer, the Rev. R.J. Wilson, this expectation had produced 'in British Columbia, as in no other part of Canada ... a culture based on flamboyant paganism, the worship of the almighty dollar.'[14]

Vancouver's prewar boom owed its timing and strength to a much broader range of influences than had sustained its predecessor of the 1880s. Expansion of Canada's rail network after 1906 represented a major component of the national investment surge induced by rapid development of the prairie wheat economy.[15] More importantly, it generated a speculative climate that enveloped the province. As the *British Columbia Financial Times* noted in May 1914, Vancouver's exceptional growth rate during the previous few years had not been founded 'upon the excellent future prospects for increased development of existing territory.' Rather, it rose from 'expectations ... that enormous new areas of varied agricultural, mineral and timber resources in British Columbia were about to be opened by the building of ... two new Canadian transcontinentals.'[16] Speculation was most intense along the routes of the national railways, especially the Grand Trunk, and the coastal termini of the two lines.

Government policies intensified resource speculation. In an attempt to increase timber revenues, the government in 1905 abolished existing timber leases and established in their place a new special-licence system that made licences transferable, renewable, and hence marketable as speculative commodities. Large quantities of timber passed into the hands of heavily capitalized syndicates.[17] In addition, Premier Richard McBride reinforced the boom mentality by making railway development the central platform of his 1909 and 1912 election campaigns. He offered generous bond guarantees to the Canadian Northern and Pacific Great Eastern railways, the latter an exclusively provincial line intended to link Vancouver with the northern interior. A special condition written into British Columbia's agreement with the Grand Trunk Pacific had given the province a half interest in many townsites along the line. This put the provincial government squarely on the side of those who would profit from northern land speculation. In Vancouver, crown land sales at Point Grey, Kitsilano, and Hastings Townsite gave new impetus to the metropolitan real estate market. In the view of Montreal's *Journal of Commerce*, by giving away to speculators 'the lands of the Province, as well as fishing, timber, and mineral rights,' the McBride government had mortgaged British Columbia's future.[18]

Easy money joined boundless optimism as another essential element of Vancouver's prewar boom. City entrepreneurs established a number of loan and trust companies that channelled BC savings into regional investments, especially city mortgages. As often happens in new regions, however, demand for investment money far exceeded local supply, forcing the largest of these financial companies to raise capital in England. British capital imports into Canada rose dramatically after mid-decade, increasing sixfold from 1907 to 1913. Equally important was British willingness to venture into the private sector. While still preferring conservative investments in social overhead projects, British moneylenders showed an uncharacteristic willingness to lend non-ownership portfolio capital to private industrial enterprises in eastern Canada and to mortgage and resource companies in the west.[19] The availability of inexpensive British financial capital allowed BC businesses as diverse as the Dominion Trust Company and E.H. Heaps and Company, lumber manufacturers, to expand rapidly. Americans also greatly facilitated expansion of the BC lumber industry by investing directly, as owners, in mills.[20]

Vancouver managed much of the province's speculative investment. By the eve of the First World War, Vancouver headquartered just over half of British Columbia's provincial and two-thirds of its extraprovincial and foreign

companies. Local businessmen opened a stock exchange in 1907 to promote mining properties, giving the city a role previously monopolized by
Spokane, London, and eastern centres. In 1911, Vancouver contained proportionately twice as many brokers and brokerage clerks as any other
Canadian city, a measure of the importance to Vancouver of speculation in
natural resources. Many of these brokers also joined the 'floating army of
land sharks' who 'swarm[ed] hungrily' about the city, selling real estate.[21]

In his short career as a British Columbia entrepreneur, George H.
Salmon demonstrated the speculative orientation of much business growth
in Vancouver during the boom. A chemist by trade, Salmon came to the
city in 1908 and immediately purchased fifty acres of land in North
Vancouver for $100,000, of which the initial payment was 1 per cent. He
subdivided the property and within ninety days netted a profit of $90,000.
Salmon then bought 4,000 acres of land on Lulu Island at the mouth of
the Fraser River. With returns from this property, he formed the
Dominion Stock and Bond Corporation, a real estate, mining, and stock
promotion company of which he was the majority stockholder. Price
Ellison, the provincial minister of finance, was named president, thus giving the company credibility. Like many other Vancouver entrepreneurs,
Salmon then extended his business operations beyond the lower mainland
to include speculation in hinterland resources. After purchasing 2,700 acres
of land for $79,000 at Fort Fraser, he developed the town by establishing a
sawmill, building a hotel and general store, and grading streets. With
returns from this investment, which exceeded $1 million, he purchased
more land in the Nechako Valley and in the Cariboo. At the height of the
boom Salmon, a demonstrably successful businessman, moved into a new
home on Davie Street opposite B.T. Rogers's 'Gabriola.' But success seems
to have been short lived. By 1917 he had left Vancouver, and by 1920 street
directories registered no trace of his business empire.[22]

For others as well, life in Vancouver's fast lane was a thrilling but brief
ride to economic disaster. As novelist Bertrand Sinclair was to observe in
The Inverted Pyramid – a scathing critique of the social and ethical character
of speculative capitalism in British Columbia – land and resource promoters tended to forget 'that whatever goes up must come down.'[23] They were
soon reminded. The crash of 1913-15 destroyed inflated land values, personal reputations, and wealth in a matter of months.

J.C. Keith had always been a speculative investor, having been fired in

1892 from his job as Vancouver manager of the Bank of British Columbia for improperly lending money secured only by real estate. But his business practices seemed to pay off. At his death in 1914 he left wealth estimated initially at $580,700, the only real estate entrepreneur to place among the business community's twenty top wealth leavers (see Table 5.3). When the estate's real worth was finally determined some thirteen years later, however, debts of almost $1 million remained. Keith's business empire, inflated by exaggerated land values and heavy mortgaging, paid creditors no more than two cents on the dollar.[24]

Francis Carter-Cotton's economic decline into insolvency was less precipitous but no less significant. As newspaper editor and publisher of the *Daily News-Advertiser*, Carter-Cotton had been Vancouver's leading intellectual and a prominent reformer of the 1890s. Still active in provincial politics a decade later, he had increasingly turned his attention to business, specializing in land promotion and non-banking finance. The bulk of his property 'was heavily mortgaged,' and in 1919 he too left an insolvent estate drained by declining land values to a level almost $160,000 below the break-even point.[25]

But the failure that best symbolizes the loose investment practices of many Vancouver businessmen was the collapse in 1914 of Dominion Trust. Trust companies, unlike banks, could lend money secured by real estate.[26] In the prewar decade they therefore took on the increasingly important role of channelling local capital into land, company stocks, and timber limits, and especially into mortgage loans on property. They acquired funds by selling shares and debentures in their own companies, by managing estates, and by more sophisticated forms of capital accumulation such as the sale of guaranteed investment securities. Big companies like Dominion Trust also began to act like banks by taking deposits. Boosters of the time praised trust companies for being both more flexible than banks, thus investing money in the local land market where demand was high, and very safe. As one Vancouver commentator put it, these scientifically run businesses, managed by 'experts' using 'modern business and financial methods,' are 'permanent,' and never die.[27]

More insightful is the critical perspective of Bertrand Sinclair who, looking back from the 1920s, saw prewar trust companies as nothing more than glorified pawnbrokers, money grabbers, and 'damned parasites.'[28] For Sinclair, Dominion Trust symbolized these unsavoury qualities. Its history

A real estate office, North Vancouver, 1912. During the prewar boom, real estate speculation became a passion for almost everyone in Vancouver, or so it seemed. The buying and selling of land spread into outlying areas around the city. The North Vancouver business illustrated here is typical: a small enterprise, locally owned, that sold suburban land. (City of Vancouver Archives BU.P.681 N.570)

supports his contention. Founded as a small local firm in 1903, Dominion Trust within a decade had become a national company with branches in British Columbia, the Prairie provinces, and Prince Edward Island. It claimed assets worth $5 million and boasted as its corporate symbol the tallest office tower in Vancouver.[29] But the company engaged in highly speculative lending practices, investing large amounts of the funds it held for clients into real estate and other speculations, and lending money secured only by real property.[30] The largest single borrower, who received more than $1 million, was upper-class businessman Alvo von Alvensleben, the son of a Prussian aristocrat, one of prewar Vancouver's leading boosters, and a man CPR president Thomas Shaughnessy described uncharitably as 'a hare-brained speculator, and nothing more.'[31] When the boom collapsed, so did the value of real property that Dominion Trust had accepted as security for loans. Land and resource investments created by funds held in trust for clients also lost much of their value. Adding to the problem were the financial practices of vice-president and general manager William Arnold, who admitted privately that he had 'committed acts' for which he could 'go to the penitentiary.'[32] On the morning of 12 October 1914, six weeks after the first revelations of trouble at Dominion Trust, the thirty-two-year-old Arnold lay dead in a Shaughnessy Heights garage, having shot himself in the heart. Death came, in the coroner's words, from the 'accidental' discharge of a pump shotgun![33] Eleven days later Dominion Trust closed its doors, leaving liabilities that exceeded assets by more than $2 million. Arnold, the consummate speculator once hailed as 'an energetic young man of great financial ability,' was now condemned as 'dishonest,' 'criminal,' a 'scoundrel.'[34]

The larger significance of these losses can be traced through a survey of the probate records of Vancouver's business leaders and subleaders. Comprising declarations of real and personal property at death, probates offer a glimpse of the scale and composition of society's wealth.[35] The probate records of sixty-three business leaders and another eighty second-level businessmen form the substance of Tables 5.3 and 5.4.[36] They indicate that the most likely way to get rich in Vancouver was to be an industrialist or wholesaler and that real estate, non-banking finance, and retail commerce offered less assured routes to wealth. The point is emphasized by the virtual destitution of second-level businessmen in these categories after the crash. The lack of enduring wealth generated by real estate and non-banking finance, sectors that employed one-quarter of all prominent Vancouver businessmen, seriously limited the city's capacity to accumulate capital.

In addition, almost all local entrepreneurs appear to have invested in land, mining stocks, timber limits, or companies promoting them, and this further broadened the impact of the prewar crash. Even the productive sectors of the resource-based economy were affected. While John Hendry's estate was large by local standards, for example – at three-quarters of a million dollars it stands sixth in the top fifty fortunes documented in Table 5.3 – it was probably much smaller at his death in 1916 than it would have been several years earlier. For a generation Hendry had owned the province's largest lumber company. He had also emerged as a business figure of national prominence, serving as president of both the Canadian Forestry Association and the Canadian Manufacturers' Association. But just as the prewar construction boom had given 'a great impetus' to British Columbia's lumber industry, so too did its collapse diminish the industry 'very materially.' Hendry's estate also listed substantial stock investments in land, mining, and power companies, nineteen of which were almost value-less when he died.[37] By contrast, sugar manufacturer B.T. Rogers, an uncharacteristic Vancouver capitalist, mainly avoided speculative investments and died a millionaire.[38]

Table 5.3

Largest estates left by pre-1914 Vancouver business leaders and subleaders[a] who died before 1940[b]

		Principal occupation to 1913	Net assets ($)	Death
1	Walter C. Nichol	Newspaper publishing	2,780,519	1928
2	Benjamin T. Rogers	Secondary manufacture (sugar)	1,238,168	1918
3	William Braid	Wholesale commerce (food) Secondary manufacture (liquor)	830,919	1924
4	Robert Kelly	Wholesale commerce (food)	800,202	1922
5	E.J. McFeely	Wholesale commerce (hardware)	767,506	1928
6	John Hendry	Primary manufacture (lumber)	725,784	1916
7	Chas. M. Beecher	Primary manufacture (lumber)	693,943	1906
8	Richard Marpole	CPR manager	588,545	1920
9	J.C. Keith	Bank manager, real estate	580,700	1914
10	Wm. H. Barker	Primary manufacture (salmon canning)	551,909	1929
11	Charles Doering	Secondary manufacture (beer)	486,400	1927
12	William L. Tait	Primary manufacture (shingles)	432,388	1919
13	J. Duff Stuart	Wholesale commerce (stationery)	403,696	1936
14	Dr. J.M. Lefevre	Utilities (telephone)	360,618	1906

		Principal occupation to 1913	Net assets ($)	Death
15	Fred Buscombe	Wholesale commerce (housewares)	356,798	1938
16	H.O. Bell-Irving	Primary manufacture (salmon canning)	339,346	1931
17	William Farrell	Utilities (telephone)		
		Wholesale commerce (industrial supplies)	306,881	1922
18	Wm. G. Mackenzie	Wholesale commerce (hardware)	255,694	1922
19	Dominic Burns	Secondary manufacture (meat packing)	240,728	1933
20	Jas. S. Emerson	Primary manufacture (lumber)	211,973	1921
21	Harry Abbott	CPR manager	211,166	1915
22	Jas. W. Horne	Real estate, non-banking finance	209,585	1922
23	Wm. H. Armstrong	Construction	201,428	1922
24	Geo. I. Wilson	Primary manufacture (salmon canning)	199,605	1924
25	John F. Ross	Secondary manufacture (iron)	194,232	1912
26	John Hanbury	Primary manufacture (lumber)	187,501	1928
27	F.C. Rounsefell	Real estate	186,780	1938
28	J.W. Hackett	Primary manufacture (lumber)	180,766	1918
29	Alfred Wallace	Secondary manufacture (shipbuilding)	169,731	1929
30	William N. O'Neil	Wholesale commerce (builders' supplies)	165,447	1934
31	Chas. A. Godson	Wholesale commerce (metal)	163,409	1926
32	Homer N. Galer	Non-banking finance	156,834	1930
33	Rt. P. McLennan	Wholesale commerce (hardware)	154,266	1927
34	William Salsbury	CPR manager	142,007	1938
35	Robert J. Ker	Wholesale commerce (grain, flour)		
		Secondary manufacture (flour, cereals)	136,563	1919
36	Robert J. Leckie	Wholesale commerce (industrial supplies)		
		Secondary manufacture (boots and shoes)	129,047	1932
37	Robert G. Tatlow	Real estate	123,472	1910
38	David Robertson	Primary manufacture (lumber)	119,671	1933
39	J.D. McCormack	Primary manufacture (lumber)	115,480	1935
40	David E. Brown	Real estate	111,822	1926
41	Charles D. Rand	Real estate	108,946	1914
42	Dr. D. Bell-Irving	Primary manufacture (salmon canning)	105,403	1929
43	Harry L. Jenkins	Primary manufacture (lumber)	97,115	1921
44	S.O. Richards	Real estate	96,705	1910
45	R.H. Alexander	Primary manufacture (lumber), manager	94,605	1915
46	Campbell Sweeny	Bank manager	91,522	1928
47	Wm. W. Montelius	Retail commerce (pianos)	86,838	1927
48	Dr. D.H. Wilson	Non-banking finance	85,796	1926
49	H.T. Ceperley	Real estate	83,698	1929
50	William Murray	Bank manager	81,988	1914

Notes:

a The methods used to define and research Vancouver's business leaders and subleaders are discussed in the Introduction.

Table 5.3, continued

b The probate records of several other potentially wealthy Vancouver businessmen who were prominent before 1914 but who died after 1939, the cut-off date for this study, have not been incorporated into Table 5.3 (or 5.4). Among them are wholesale merchants William H. Malkin, R.V. Winch, and Henry A. Stone, and lumbermen E.H. Heaps, A.D. McRae, and James A. McNair. The probate record of retail merchant Charles Woodward (d. 1937) could not be located. McRae left an estate in 1946 worth $447,889 (net).

Source: With one exception, probate records read for Tables 5.3 and 5.4 were drawn from British Columbia Attorney General, Estate Records, BCARS, BC Supreme Court, Vancouver Probates (GR 1415), Victoria Probates (GR 1304), or New Westminster Probates (GR 1422). Frederick Buscombe's probated will was read at the Court Registry in New Westminster.

Table 5.4

Wealth of Vancouver business leaders and subleaders[a] (by probate records at death)

Principal area of business before First World War	Business leaders 1890-3 and 1910-13		Business subleaders 1890-3 and 1910-13	
	Average net assets ($)	Number	Average net assets ($)	Number
Secondary industries	443,647	7	181,988	5
Primary industries: fish and lumber[b]	341,602	8	137,492	9
Wholesale commerce	309,705	11	133,266	12
Utilities and transportation[b]	153,519	9	181,552	2
Banking	140,477	7	41,966	2
Real estate and non-banking finance[b]	116,042	15	4,129	25
Retail commerce	15,066	1	-10,239	12
Professions	0	0	75,312	7
Other business types	774,094	2	24,961	2
Average size of estates	257,182		61,978	
Total number of cases		60		76

Notes:

a The methods used to define and research Vancouver's business leaders and subleaders are discussed in the Introduction.

b If broken down into more specific occupational categories the totals would read as follows. For real estate and non-banking finance: *leaders,* real estate 13, promotion: all others 0, non-banking finance 5; *subleaders,* real estate 14, promotion: all others 3, non-banking finance 9. For primary industries: *leaders,* lumber 6, fish 2; *subleaders,* lumber 6, fish 3. For utilities and transportation: *leaders,* utilities 2, transportation 7; *subleaders,* utilities 2, transportation 0. Totals in the real estate and non-banking finance category have been adjusted to avoid calculating twice the net estate of businessmen occupied in both real estate and non-banking finance (for leaders, two cases) or of prominent businessmen in this category for both the earlier and later periods (for leaders, one case). For a fuller discussion of how business categories such as 'non-banking finance' and 'promotion: all others' are defined, see Robert A.J. McDonald, 'Business Leaders in Early Vancouver, 1886-1914' (PhD dissertation, University of British Columbia 1977), appendix B, pp. 471-2.

Source: See Table 5.3

The buying, selling, and financing of land and resources had a profound impact on Vancouver. By leaving business wealth vulnerable and insecure, it sustained a level of fluidity that we generally associate with relatively new, or frontier, societies. Such uncertainty did not preclude the development of a social hierarchy in the city but did limit the degree to which wealthy families became entrenched. Perhaps this is why, when writing about the Canadian establishment of the 1970s, Peter Newman could find among British Columbia's corporate leaders few families whose prominence in the province stretched back further than three generations.[39]

Working people also embraced the speculative ethos of the time, though the extent to which they did so is less easily measured than it is for upper-class businessmen. Literary evidence is suggestive. In 1912 a writer in the *British Columbia Federationist* bemoaned the poor electoral support for Socialist candidates in the recent provincial election. The reason, the author suggested, was that 'capitalist "prosperity"' had been 'boomed in the ears of the [wage] slaves until many of them thought they were included in it, and ascribed their hard struggle for existence to just a run of bad luck.' As a result, 'the fever of speculation ... seized the workers as well as the rest,' many of them investing 'their scant savings in a house and a lot.' In testimony presented to the provincial Commission on Labour, Charles Cassidy, a member of the Stonecutters' Union, spoke of knowing 'quite a few working men' who had wanted to buy lots but were unable to raise the capital necessary to do so. Cassidy himself had purchased a thirty-three-foot lot for $750. Novelist Bertrand Sinclair portrayed Vancouver as a society in which shoe clerks, 'dreaming of the quick turnover and the long profit,' would 'go without lunch to make payments on plots of land in distant suburbs.'

South Vancouver seems to have been full of such dreamers. A suburb that grew rapidly in the prewar years, it was, in the words of print shop owner and local resident Alfred H. Lewis, 'the home of the industrial classes.' In this community of respectable working- and middle-class people, many of them recent arrivals from Britain, 'everybody went wild ... over the inflation of [real estate] values. A few people preached caution but their voices were weak. From the artisan who owned a 33 foot lot, to the large speculator who owned 50 and 100 acres, the slogan was progress.' In April 1918 the Board of Taxation, appointed by the recently elected Liberal government to explore a drop in provincial tax receipts of more than 50 per cent since 1912-13, produced its first report, which traced the financial shortfall to the boom years when 'the wage-earner, the man in the street, and even farmers ... lost all sense of proportion in respect to land values.' A 'wild riot of borrowing and spending' followed. When the inevitable collapse occurred, South Vancouver could not fund its debt and went into receivership. The South Vancouver reeve who had first responded to the clamour for sidewalks, roads, and water lines, and who had sharply increased the municipality's debt as a consequence, was W.A. Pound, a card-carrying member of the typographical union.[40]

A study of applications for the purchase of crown land in British Columbia during a one-week period at the height of the boom puts flesh on the skeleton of contemporary observations. The data were published by the Ministerial Union of the Lower Mainland under the title *The Crisis in B.C.: An Appeal for Investigation*. Summarized in Table 5.5, they reveal the active participation of British Columbia's working class in the provincial land market. The acreage applied for by nurses, stenographers and clerks, industrial workers, mechanics, and labourers was almost 45 per cent of the total; when adjusted to delete an unknown number of applications by male clerks and contractors who would have considered themselves to be middle class, the working-class proportion of the total is reduced somewhat but remains at approximately 40 per cent. A surprisingly high proportion of the applicants were women, some of whom, such as nurses, were also members of the working class. A large share of the applicants, more than 45 per cent, lived in Vancouver and the surrounding area; the remainder came from other British Columbian, Canadian, and foreign locations.[41]

While Table 5.5 leaves much unexplored – the total number of applicants in each occupational group, the average size of grants applied for, the ultimate disposition of the applications – it nonetheless makes clear one essential point: ordinary people were caught up in the speculative hysteria of the period. One such person was John Fay, a Vancouver butcher who on 27 June 1912 applied for 640 acres of land near Tsa-cha Lake on Vancouver Island. Fay's application was organized by agent James Scott, whose clients for land in the Tsa-cha Lake area included eight other working people, among them three hardware clerks, a miner, a single woman, a steward, a foreman, and a sailor. When the boom collapsed, the 'multitude of clerks and artisans' who had 'lost their ... all' would have included many like John Fay.[42]

Table 5.5

Occupations of land purchase applicants in British Columbia for the week ending 3 October 1912 (by quantity of land applied for)[a]

	Land applied for (acres)	Percentage of land applied for
Merchants and manufacturers	54,260	11.7
Professional men	49,991	10.8
Real estate agents and brokers	34,955	7.5
Farmers and ranchers[b]	24,079	5.2
Women	99,260	21.3
Married	48,402	10.4
Unmarried	36,490	7.8
Widows	10,569	2.3
Nurses	3,799	0.8
Clerks and stenographers[c]	40,056	8.6
Industrial workers	93,450	20.2
Contractors	5,520	1.1
Cooks	4,720	1.0
Loggers	5,549	1.2
Miners	7,120	1.5
Prospectors	5,590	1.3
Shoemakers	5,600	1.2
Various	59,351	12.8
Mechanics	34,360	7.4
Carpenters	11,010	2.4
Machinists	3,480	0.7
Mechanics	2,560	0.6
Printers	10,440	2.2
Various	6,870	1.5
Labourers[b]	34,274	7.4
Total	464,685	100.1

Notes:

a While the author of this table is not identified in Ministerial Union of the Lower Mainland of B.C., *The Crisis in B.C.: An Appeal for Investigation* (Vancouver: Saturday Sunset Press 1916), it was probably Moses B. Cotsworth, who was described at the outset of the pamphlet as having organized its facts (p. 2). I have retained the occupational categories as presented by Cotsworth, while slightly rearranging their order. The table summarizes occupational references from 1,052 land purchase applications listed in the *British Columbia Gazette* for a one-week period in the fall of 1912.

b The original included the phrase 'mostly in cities.'

c The original included the phrase 'partly women.'

Source: Ministerial Union of the Lower Mainland of B.C., *The Crisis in B.C.: An Appeal for Investigation* (Vancouver: Saturday Sunset Press 1916), 32

IN PREWAR BRITISH COLUMBIA this economic dynamism reinforced the liberal myth that hard work and individual effort would lead to material success and moral fulfilment. The belief that material success was a moral right, given hard work, has been identified as one of the defining characteristics of the newly emergent middle class in nineteenth-century industrial societies, and limited evidence suggests that, among leading business people at least, such was also the case in Vancouver. The ethos was most clearly articulated in 1907 by Henry Bell-Irving in a letter to his sons at Loretto, a private school in Scotland. 'A man is the maker of his own fortune,' Bell-Irving wrote; 'he is either self made or never made. By industry, application, and good use of his leisure time, he may become almost anything he pleases.' Self-denial, application, and 'incessant work' were essential ingredients of success.

The biographical sketch published in 1914 of John Dougall, an alderman and hotelkeeper in early Vancouver and then successful foundry owner in Victoria, reiterated the belief that 'self-reliance and unfaltering industry' were the foundation of 'honorable principles' and economic success. The mythical quality of this self-image is evident in emphasis on a rags-to-riches progression through life. W.H. Malkin was described at his death as an 'immigrant farm boy who became a millionaire merchant,' even though his father had been a prominent earthenware and tile manufacturer in England. Particularly insightful is the biographical sketch of Alvo von Alvensleben, published in *British Columbia Magazine* in 1911. Since von Alvensleben came from Prussian nobility, to have emphasized his 'poor immigrant background' would have stretched credibility. Yet the writer cleverly made virtue of necessity by arguing that von Alvensleben's aristocratic background was 'as notable as the fact that Andrew Carnegie was once a messenger boy, or that Edison was a newspaper boy.' The myth of the self-made businessman had to be reasserted, even if von Alvensleben was an obvious exception.[43]

The reality, of course, differed from the myth. As numerous studies of urban elites have shown, business and social leaders generally came from advantaged backgrounds.[44] Vancouver was no exception. Particularly significant is the high status of Vancouver's first group of business leaders. A social profile of twenty-one such individuals for the period 1890-3 shows that the fathers of most had worked mainly as businessmen or professionals. Almost half had received some university-level education, and none had been limited to elementary school. When apprenticeship in a profession is also considered, the proportion of those educated beyond high school surpassed half, exceptionally high for late-nineteenth-century Canada. Moreover, a quarter of these top businessmen had attended high-status private schools such as Toronto's Upper Canada College. Over 60 per cent claimed membership in the Anglican church, generally the denomination of socially prominent Anglo-Canadians. Just one individual belonged to the collective category of lower-status Roman Catholic, Methodist, and

Table 5.6

**Education of Vancouver business leaders, 1890-3 and 1910-13
(by percentage of known cases)**

	Business leaders 1890-3	Business leaders 1910-13
Elementary	0	27.5
Secondary (total)	45.5	48.2
Secondary (high status)	27.3	12.0
Postsecondary	54.6	24.8
Number of cases, data known	11	58
Number of cases, data unknown	10	33

Note: The methods used to define and research Vancouver's business leaders are discussed in the Introduction.

Table 5.7

**Occupations of fathers of Vancouver business leaders, 1890-3 and 1910-13
(by percentage of known cases)**

Father's occupation	Business leaders 1890-3	Business leaders 1910-13
Business: large or noted	44.4	22.7
Business: small	0	2.3
Business: size unknown	22.2	11.4
Professions	22.2	25.0
Military/public official	0	6.8
Clerical	0	0
Farmer	11.1	29.5
Skilled/semi-skilled	0	2.3
Other	0	0
Number of cases, data known	9	44
Number of cases, data unknown	12	47

Note: The methods used to define and research Vancouver's business leaders are discussed in the Introduction.

Table 5.8

Religious affiliations of Vancouver business leaders[a], 1890-3 and 1910-13, compared to city as a whole (by percentage of known cases)

	Vancouver 1891	Business leaders 1890-3	Business leaders 1910-13	Vancouver 1911
Anglican	28.0	61.1	39.7	26.2
Presbyterian	24.6	16.7	25.6	26.3
United[b]	0	5.6	10.3	0
Methodist	16.3	0	9.0	14.1
Roman Catholic	11.5	0	6.4	10.2
Baptist	5.1	5.6	3.8	6.1
Other Protestant	6.5	0	5.2	—
Jewish	0.7	11.1	0	1.0
Jossist, Buddist, Confucian, Chinese[c]	6.6	0	0	—
Number of cases, data known	13,490	18	78	100,401
Number of cases, data unknown	183	3	13	—

Notes.
a The methods used to define and research Vancouver's business leaders are discussed in the Introduction.
b 'United' refers to the United Church of Canada, formed in 1925, and is the religious affiliation mentioned in obituaries for men who died after that date. Earlier, such businessmen would probably have belonged to the Presbyterian or Methodist Churches, the two principal denominations that joined to form the United Church.
c The 1891 Nominal Census assigned these religious designations to people of Chinese heritage. The *Fifth Census of Canada 1911* did not list eastern religious affiliations. These probably approximated the proportion of Vancouver's population that was of Asian origin (6.1 per cent in 1911).
Sources: Vancouver 1891: Nominal Census 1891; Vancouver 1911: *Fifth Census of Canada 1911*, vol. 2, table 6

Baptist denominations. By contrast, for the city as a whole in 1891 Anglicans constituted just over a quarter of the population and Roman Catholics, Methodists, and Baptists almost a third (see Tables 5.6 to 5.8).

Henry Bell-Irving was one of these socially advantaged entrepreneurs. An Anglican, he had come from a prominent landed and business family in the Scottish lowlands, had received training as a professional engineer, and had raised investment capital through relatives 'in the old country [who] were fixed financially and had wealthy friends.' Hard work and character had allowed Bell-Irving to make the most of his exceptional inheritance but he was not 'self-made.'[45]

Nonetheless, business leaders from the 1910-13 period did come from a distinctly lower status than their predecessors from 1890-3. Whereas all of the earlier group had been educated beyond the elementary level and 55 per cent beyond high school, almost three of ten members before the war had received only an elementary education and only a quarter had undertaken postsecondary studies. Family backgrounds changed too. Of the 1890s' group about whom father's occupation is known, six had come from business families (67 per cent) but only one from a farm background (11 per cent). By contrast, the percentage of prewar business leaders who came from business families declined to half that of the earlier period while the proportion of men from farms almost tripled. The same shift among business elites from higher- to lower-status social backgrounds is reflected in religious affiliations. More than six of every ten members of the 1890s leadership group belonged to the prestigious Anglican church, compared to only four of ten just before the war. By contrast, the percentage of business leaders to be found as members of Roman Catholic, Methodist, and Baptist churches rose three times, from 5.6 to 19.5 per cent.

This trend differs from our understanding of elite formation, which usually emphasizes the more privileged nature of recruitment through time. William Acheson, for example, found that 'the high degree of social mobility' that marked Canada's industrial leaders in 1885 had narrowed by 1910.[46] Historians of other western cities have concluded that social prominence flowed from business success in the west, and that hierarchical structuring in cities like Calgary or Denver increased through time as a result of the new wealth generated there.[47] By contrast, Vancouver was hierarchical from its inception. Why the difference?

In part the contrasting pattern is explained by the inordinate influence of the CPR on Vancouver's early history. Building on the foundation of a small business community centred by mill manager R.H. Alexander and his wife, the Canadian Pacific Railway had deliberately fostered a graded society at its Burrard Inlet terminus. Thereafter, the combined influences of rapid population growth and substantial speculative investment had opened business opportunities to men – for business leaders were almost entirely men[48] – from lower-status backgrounds. The social and economic advantages enjoyed by prominent businessmen were thus less striking during the prewar boom than they had been a generation earlier. The difference reinforced the popular faith in the idea of progress and boosted the incorrigible optimism of Vancouverites during the boom.

The extent to which working people also believed that Vancouver would provide material improvement and social mobility for all is hard to ascertain. The preceding discussion of speculative investments suggests, however, that for a short period at least they saw in the existing economic system hope for economic betterment. The increasing numbers of workers attracted to the west coast by its high wages during the prewar boom also reveals that confidence. Moreover, there were to be seen around the city many examples of workers who had experienced substantial upward social mobility, mainly from the upper working class into lower middle class.[49] Several former tradesmen previously active in the local labour movement had established their own shops. By the war, typographer Harry Cowan owned a printing business; cigar maker John Crow had established the Old Crow Cigar Factory; John Towler had moved from bricklaying to poultry ranching; and Joseph Dixon had advanced from carpenter to contractor and then to manufacturer of office and store fixtures. An unskilled laundry worker, C.N. Lees, was able to finance a tea and refreshment parlour at English Bay. Even Ralph Smith, former miner, president of the Trades and Labour Congress of Canada (1898-1902), and Nanaimo representative in the provincial legislature (1898-1900) and federal parliament (1900-8), had by 1913 become a second-level business leader in the Terminal City. He headed a financial and insurance business and was known to be 'widely interested in mining properties.'[50] Contemporaries could easily have interpreted such experiences, whether typical or not, as demonstrable evidence of a society open to economic improvement.

Particularly revealing is the occupational history of Frank Woodside. Born into a family of Prince Edward Island farmers, Woodside left home at age sixteen to work for two years in the lead and silver mines of Colorado before migrating in 1896 to the Kootenays. He resumed mining and joined the Western Federation of Miners, serving as secretary from 1900 to 1902. Woodside participated actively in trade union affairs. He successfully lobbied the provincial government to pass the eight-hour bill of 1899, directed union strategy in the Rossland strike of 1901, and represented Kootenay miners at the Kamloops convention that formed a provincial labour party in 1902. Shortly thereafter he left Rossland for Vancouver, where he took up selling insurance and real estate. He invested in land, including mining properties in the Kootenays and suburban lots in Hastings Townsite, to the east of Vancouver. He fought successfully to have Vancouver annex the area and in 1912 became its first representative on City Council. He was also instrumental in founding the British Columbia Chamber of Mines, which he served as president for much of the

1920s. Once a leading spokesman for labour, Woodside ended his career as a prominent capitalist.[51]

Such evidence illustrates that Vancouver was still a new city and that class boundaries were flexible, particularly during periods of rapid growth. Vancouver to 1913 remained a society in the making rather than a society made. As with business people, however, so with working people, opportunity for social mobility was more myth than reality. A study of the career paths of Vancouver Trades and Labor Council leaders for the decades before and after 1900 is instructive. Of twenty VTLC leaders for the period 1890-9, ten eventually owned businesses (50 per cent). Cowan, Crow, Towler, and Dixon, cited above, are examples. Of the twenty-two for the next decade, the number drops to seven, four if we omit those who had left the Council by 1901 and whose labour movement ties extended back into the 1890s rather than forward into the 1900s (18 per cent).[52] In other words, the career paths of labour leaders were marked by less opportunity for social mobility than those of top business leaders. Such evidence is consistent with earlier discussion of the growing class awareness of working people at the turn of the century but inconsistent with suggestions that by the early 1910s people across social strata embraced the ethos of speculative capitalism, from which high expectations of economic improvement flowed. The contradiction is rooted in the divergent realities of myth and lived experience. Both affected how Vancouver people acted and thought.

BRITISH COLUMBIA'S prewar boom lasted about five years. At its peak, commentators already noted a 'surplus of skilled men in the district.'[53] The arrival of transient workers and immigrant families increased the demand for jobs far beyond supply, and unemployment became a companion of progress. High prices on the coast also accompanied high wages, sapping people's incomes. By late 1913 large numbers of idle men could be found walking the streets of Vancouver looking for work. As the collapse gained momentum through 1914 its impact resonated from one corner of the province to the other.[54]

The trouble started in Europe, where the Balkan wars gave rise to panic on European money markets, diminished security prices, and restriction of further lending abroad. British confidence in Canadian investments declined, and as credit tightened real estate offices across Canada began closing in the fall of 1912. Yet the collapse in Vancouver did not come immediately. The value of building permits issued in 1913 dropped to almost half that of the previous year but still exceeded the total for 1909. British funds continued to find investment possibilities in western Canada. The great influx of immigrants in 1913 – the largest number in a single year in Canadian history – also generated short-term economic growth.[55]

When the business cycle ended, British Columbia experienced a more profound dislocation than its prairie neighbours. Historians of western Canada tend to define 'west' as 'prairie west' and to ignore British Columbia, but the prewar period offers an excellent example of how historical patterns sometimes found distinctive expression in 'the west beyond the west.'[56] In the Prairie provinces the economic downturn was mainly an urban phenomenon that affected real estate and construction. Continued investment and growth in the agricultural hinterland partly offset reduced building activities in cities. By contrast, British Columbia's prewar boom had been province wide, and because speculation had fuelled growth in both the country and the city, the decline in tax revenues that accompanied collapsing land and timber limit values was broadly based and precipitous.[57] The leading resource industry of each region responded differently to the recession as well. Whereas the prairie wheat economy continued to grow through 1913 and 1914, and was given a tremendous boost by the war, British Columbia's forest product industry declined as investment and construction in cities lessened. The outbreak of war further reduced construction and real estate investment in western centres but provided little alternative income for lumber producers from war contracts.

Winnipeg's recession has been described as 'a reduction in the rate of expansion, rather than an absolute decline'; Vancouver's economy actually got smaller.[58] The value of building permits issued in Vancouver declined from $19.4 million in 1912 to $1.6 million in 1915. The city's construction boom slowed to a virtual halt. Rents for commercial property dropped by 50 per cent, and the vacancy rate for office space reached 80 per cent. Many property owners could meet neither their tax nor their mortgage obligations. Trust companies were especially vulnerable: fifteen of the nineteen financial institutions with which Vancouver business leaders and subleaders of the 1910-13 period were associated and which had been organized during the boom did not survive the war. By October 1914 the number out of work in and around Vancouver had reached 15,000, a total swollen by the influx of unemployed from other parts of the province.[59]

Many of the people drawn to British Columbia by visions of prosperity and material success only a year or two earlier were forced to leave. Building tradesmen, mechanics, stenographers, and factory operatives led the exodus, departing for locations as far away as Australia and New Zealand and as close as the prairies. The war also siphoned off some of the surplus population. Construction workers and real estate agents alike joined the armed forces for economic reasons. When prosperity finally returned to Vancouver in the summer and fall of 1916, the city of 122,000 had become a community of 96,000, 20 per cent less than at its peak.[60]

The significance of this outmigration is to be found within the larger context of Vancouver's economic growth since the 1890s. At one level Vancouver functioned as a metropolitan city, managing resource industries, directing transportation and commerce, and providing a growing range of business and professional services for the region. At another it continued to be a city on the frontier, a new society far different from Burrard Inlet's nineteenth-century lumber communities yet still subject to the vicissitudes of a regional economy narrowly based on resource extraction and promotion. While structured in complex ways, Vancouver society remained fluid.

CHAPTER SIX

The Wealthy Business and Professional Class

I n the years leading up to the First World War, prosperity and the speculative nature of Vancouver's economy blunted the social impact of economic differentiation and kept class boundaries relatively open and flexible. Just as the growing scale of economic activity divided workers from bosses – with both groups seeking to control the process of wealth production and the product of their labour – so the expansion of wealth increased the possibility of enhancing one's social position within the community. Growth and prosperity greatly facilitated the desire of people to set themselves above one another by means of lifestyle, education, or social connections. The result was a structuring of Vancouver society according to the criteria of mutual regard and prestige – 'status' – as well as relationship to the means of production – 'class.' Status was powerfully influenced by class: occupation affected income and the freedom one had to make choices about lifestyle and social relationships. But as the following three chapters will demonstrate, the nature of those choices also reflected non-economic influences, of which education and family status were the most obvious.

The report of a Vancouver social survey carried out by the Methodist and Presbyterian churches in 1912 provides a framework for understanding how status relationships structured Vancouver society. It found 'three distinct social grades' in the city: 'the wealthy business and professional class, the artisan or moderately well-to-do class, and the immigrant section.'[1] What the report calls 'classes' were really status groups, grounded not in relations of production but in patterns of consumption.[2] In the upper stratum were the families of prominent businessmen and professionals who, benefiting from greater than average wealth and searching for social recognition, constructed a way of life that sharply differentiated them from the lower middle and lower strata. Leisure, housing, neighbourhood, philanthropy, and culture all became instruments of social definition. The resulting status system consisted of a highly fluid pattern of relationships best conceptualized as a finely graded hierarchy of prestige descending from a small group of early business families. At this topmost level high social status and high class position most often overlapped. Thereafter, class determined social status less predictably, with status more the function of education and family history and class defined by economic role. Differences should not be exaggerated, because business and professional families, regardless of status, shared an unquestioning faith in the capitalist system and a common ethnicity. At the same time, status was immensely important in structuring the social networks through which Vancouver people carried on their daily lives.

LED BY sawmill managers' wives, respectable, White, and family-based residents of Burrard Inlet had begun to separate themselves socially from the lumber settlement's ethnically mixed and working-class majority in the 1870s. The coming of the CPR ignited a firestorm of population growth that shifted the business community's economic centre from lumber mills to the railway but did not lessen the impulse among economically advantaged residents to mould themselves into a distinctive social clique. In the late 1880s the families of leading businessmen began to take on the characteristics of an integrated social group, aided by the privileged educational and family backgrounds of railway managers and several independent entrepreneurs. Centring this overlapping group were pioneer business families with CPR connections, including the Abbotts, Cambies, Rogerses, and Sweenys. The Alexanders and Beechers represented lumber. In the

1890s high-status private schooling and intra-elite marriages – a daughter of the Alexanders and a son of the Abbotts, for instance – started to knit the core families into an identifiable and self-conscious whole.[3]

The diary of Mrs. B.T. Rogers, who exemplified the early connection between business leadership and social prominence, reveals a world enclosed by walls of privilege that restricted social intercourse to a particular circle of original families. Business wealth aided the development of a genteel lifestyle among this clique. Rogers exemplified the link. At the end of the 1890s, his sugar refinery now 'exceedingly prosperous,' he hired a coachman to drive Mrs. Rogers around town for shopping and calling and commissioned Samuel MacClure, British Columbia's premier residential architect, to design a spacious new family home.[4]

This set of business families evolved into a larger status group around 1900. Economic depression had slowed the transformation but the prosperity generated by mining booms in the Kootenays and Klondike at the end of the 1890s encouraged greater numbers of upper-class families to display their claims to gentility. Of particular importance was the emergence of lawyers from the shadows of business leaders to claim social recognition. Edward P. Davis and John Senkler, both graduates of Upper Canada College and the University of Toronto, had arrived in 1892 and 1893 respectively, but only at the century's turn could they boast secure practices and the wealth required to sustain a socially active lifestyle.[5] Reinforcing the original core of socially prominent business families were more recent migrants from advantaged backgrounds who entered the city continuously from the late 1890s to the end of the prewar boom. As British traveller A.G. Bradley observed in 1903, the 'better classes' were 'very strongly represented' among the predominantly eastern Canadian and old country immigrants to Vancouver.[6]

The most important of these new arrivals were Sir Charles Hibbert Tupper and Lady Tupper. A Harvard-trained lawyer and former federal cabinet minister, Sir Charles had come west in 1898 while still a member of parliament for the Nova Scotia riding of Pictou, which he represented for another six years. His father, Sir Charles Tupper, was a father of Confederation, minister in the governments of Sir John A. Macdonald, Canadian high commissioner in London, and briefly in 1896 prime minister of Canada. He was also leader of the Opposition in the House of Commons from 1896 to 1901. Lady Tupper's father, James McDonald, also a former

Conservative MP, served as chief justice of the Supreme Court of Nova Scotia from 1881 to 1904.[7] The Tuppers' political background gave them enormous prestige in Vancouver, as the Abbott family's association with national affairs and the CPR had earlier. The Tuppers quickly assumed a prominent role in defining Vancouver's status elite and set the pace for a new residential clustering of prominent families by constructing a house on the edge of Stanley Park. At some point the Tuppers headed or participated in virtually every prestigious social and charitable organization in the city.[8]

The social system that this mix of established business people, rising professional and commercial families, and socially advantaged migrants created in turn of the century Vancouver shamelessly emulated 'Society' in London, New York, and other metropolitan centres to the east.[9] The instruments for systematically defining high social status had emerged in the mid- to late nineteenth century in the United States and Great Britain amid the swirl of rapid social change that accompanied industrialization. Entry into the newly defined status elites was voluntary and associational. Prominent families who successfully drew around themselves the boundaries of social distinction sought a lifestyle based on shared values and intimate access to one another.[10]

In a very deliberate manner they set about creating in Vancouver a 'high society.' The Vancouver Club and the Vancouver Lawn Tennis Club, organized during the city's first surge of growth, continued to lead fashionable behaviour through the 1890s and beyond.[11] New private schools opened, among them Crofton House, begun as Miss Gordon's School for Girls in 1898. With many daughters of prominent local families in attendance, it gave special attention to manners, deportment, and other elements of social etiquette.[12] Four boys' schools also operated for brief periods around 1900, three of them on the city's west side.[13] Increasingly popular were rounds of afternoon visits by socially active women. Regulated by a complex system of leaving and receiving cards derived from England and the United States, 'at homes' transformed informal social intercourse into a formal ritual for defining status.[14] In addition to 'calling,' tennis tournaments, croquet matches, and garden parties necessitated large, well-staffed residences reasonably proximate to one another. To accommodate these demands, a new high-status neighbourhood of homes boasting features such as mahogany staircases, solid oak billiard tables, conservatories, and extensive gardens and lawns emerged after 1898 in a discrete area of the city bordering on Stanley Park and English Bay. People called it the West End.[15]

Society became visible to all through the development of social pages in city newspapers. In February 1900 the *Vancouver Daily Province* first devoted a regular column 'entirely to the goings on in the social world'; the *Vancouver Daily World* soon followed.[16] By recording the endless at homes, 'ping-pong teas,' tennis tournaments, and trips to the opera of the socially prominent, columnists like the *Province*'s Julia Henshaw, herself renowned as a Society hostess, patron of the arts, and writer, helped create a social elite by naming its participants. The naming became explicit in 1901 when the *World* listed, as 'a kind of social register,' 201 hostesses and their receiving days.[17] Newspaper social pages also reveal the layers of prestige developing within Society as prominent families formed cliques of relatively higher or lower status. While the precise structure of these cliques has yet to be determined,[18] Lady Tupper's presence at a social event clearly marked it with cachet. Newspapers also encouraged local emulation of metropolitan practices by introducing big city language to Society page discourse. Writers talked of the West End as 'Vancouver's Nob Hill' and 'residential quarter,' the place 'where dwell the "upper ten," the wearers of purple and linen.'[19] Those who attended a ball organized in October 1901 by the prestigious executive of the Women's Exchange became what a local newspaper labelled 'Vancouver's "400,"' a reference to Mrs. Astor's effort in the 1880s to create an enclosed status group in New York.[20]

IN THE DOZEN YEARS that followed the ball, the number of business and professional families in Vancouver grew rapidly, and the impulse for social differentiation continued apace. The scramble for status found public expression in an increasingly conspicuous consumption of goods and services designed to convey the impression of material well-being. Sustained economic growth contributed not only to 'the piling up of money' but, as writer Stephen Leacock observed for Montreal at this time, to 'the growth of luxury' as well. In a bigger and wealthier Vancouver, evidence of personal success came to mean fast cars, fashionable recreation, and expensive homes.[21] The motor car was a toy for the rich during the early years of the century. Business leader W.H. Armstrong is reported to have acquired the city's first car in 1899, and both B.T. Rogers and Alvo von Alvensleben gained notoriety by roaring about in their 'snorting motor[s]' at speeds that exceeded forty miles per hour. But as the number of automobiles registered in British Columbia jumped during the boom years, the motor car lost its status-defining appeal. Other forms of recreation proved to be more exclusive. Yachts served as a much surer barometer of wealth than did motor cars. The Royal Vancouver Yacht Club was formed in 1903, and the purchase of expensive vessels became more frequent as the decade progressed. In January 1912 Thomas Langlois of the BC Permanent Loan Company followed many others when he '[broke] into the yachting game on an ambitious scale' by ordering a sixty-foot, twin-screw, crude oil-fuelled boat.[22] The Pacific Coast Lawn Tennis Championships held on Denman Street courts remained popular, though the number of Society men and women for whom riding was considered a necessary accomplishment increased sharply, challenging the status of tennis.[23]

Travel also provided ready and conclusive evidence that business and professional families had succeeded in the marketplace. Resort vacations and motor trips in California became popular in the early years of the century, and the 'epidemic of wanderlust' that broke out among the well-to-do in 1910 carried some social status leaders to more distant lands as well.[24] One of the most adventurous was Amelia Davis, wife of noted lawyer E.P. Davis and 'socially prominent' in her own right as chatelaine of a fashionable waterfront home in Point Grey, on the city's west side. With two sons, she trekked across India in the early months of 1912. Such extended travel set the Davises apart from others who could afford to go no further than Pasadena. So too did Henry Bell-Irving's purchase of Pasley Island in Howe Sound, near Vancouver, for his family's private recreation, and B.T. Rogers's trip around the southern perimeter of the United States in a private rail car, accompanied by family and servants.[25]

No form of conspicuous consumption could match that of a new home, however. Just when the West End – where big houses and expensive gardens were mainly to be found – had solidified its reputation as a neighbourhood of prominent business and professional families, the area began to decline. Apartment blocks appeared among the majestic mansions, challenging the association of single-family houses with normal family life. The CPR's plans to develop 250 acres of company land on the rise south of False Creek, announced in 1907, and the opening of a bridge across the creek at Granville Street two years later gave Vancouver's wealthy status

Vancouver Society at play, 1914. 'Until very recently,' the *Vancouver Province* wrote in April 1913, 'riding was not considered a necessary accomplishment.' But the institution of a horse show and the establishment of a riding academy, both with the 'fashionable support' of Vancouver's 'money spending and pleasure loving class,' quickly turned riding into an instrument to display wealth and claim social recognition. Women of 'prominent social standing,' such as those photographed here, figured conspicuously in the scramble for status in prewar Vancouver. (Leonard Frank photo, Jewish Historical Society of British Columbia LF 84)

seekers a timely alternative.

Designed by Montreal landscape architect Frederick Todd to unsettle 'all previous ideas of where a fine house should be built,' Shaughnessy Heights represented a deliberate attempt by the CPR to manipulate standards of fashion for profit. To create a unique 'aesthetic environment' that would accord prestige to Shaughnessy, the corporation spent more than $1 million laying out tree-lined streets and broad boulevards that curved along the natural contours of the terrain. Building lots could be no smaller than one-fifth of an acre, and the minimum price for a house was set at $6,000. To the south the company constructed a ninety-acre golf course and country club.[26] In Shaughnessy Heights, business and professional families would find 'greater amenities and fewer threats of encroachment by business and the lower social orders' than in the rapidly changing West End.[27]

Socially prominent Vancouverites flocked to the area. By 1914 approximately one in five of the city's leading business and professional families had moved to new homes in Shaughnessy Heights or, in a few cases, to homes in more rural areas west and south in Point Grey.[28] Often designed by architects, Shaughnessy houses were heavily influenced by styles from different periods of English history. Featuring combinations of broad eaves, gabled roofs, bay windows, and fieldstone, shingle, or half-timbered exteriors, many hinted at country manors and a way of life that predated the hustle and bustle of the industrial age. 'Hycroft,' a neoclassical mansion completed in 1912 for lumber baron A.D. McRae, stood out as a conspicuous exception to the predominance of English stylistic references. Boasting a grand porte-cochère, Italian garden, twelve fireplaces, and interior plasterwork by sculptor Charles Marenga, McRae's $250,000 home expressed in exuberant fashion the prewar business community's boundless optimism.[29]

A garden party held in Kerrisdale, southwest of Shaughnessy Heights, illustrates the important role that family dwellings played in creating a high-status way of life. The many 'cars ... driven over suburban roads' to Alvo von Alvensleben's 'country home' began to deposit their occupants in the middle of the afternoon, the *Province*'s social page writer observed, and as afternoon turned to evening additional guests arrived, 'each soon to be carried away by the spirit of cordiality and revelry which pervaded the scene.' Lawn tennis, the novel contest of clay pigeon shooting, and walks about the spacious lawns and gardens entertained the guests until seven, at which time dinner was served. At dusk the gardens 'were illuminated with Japanese lanterns swung in graceful lines among the trees and shrubbery,' and dancing followed, accompanied by the music of two orchestras. A 'very charming ... "Parisian cafe"' in the garden with 'tête-à-tête tables' and ample refreshments invited talk and merriment to a very 'late hour.' A long list of Vancouver's notables, all named in the newspaper story, attended.[30]

Families also expressed their social aspirations through private schooling. Schools that required fees provided public confirmation of a family's economic security and linked both children and parents with other families of genteel status. The degree to which private schools served either to facilitate social mobility or to preserve inherited status depended on the kinds of education that parents could afford and, in the case of the best schools of eastern North America and Britain, could gain access to through family name and connections. One observer claimed that a 'large and increasing number of families in the Coast Cities' were sending their children, 'at great expense, to be educated in the East or in the South,' draining Vancouver's wealthy of $200,000 a year in fees. A number of local institutions were created to meet this demand, but like Whetham College of the early 1890s and almost all of the handful of schools created at the turn of the century, their stability was tenuous and their existence usually short.[31]

The memoirs of Hugh Keenleyside, who went on to achieve distinction as a Canadian diplomat after growing up in Vancouver, illustrate how one family employed education to raise its social status. Hugh came west from Ontario as an infant in 1899 after the North American Life Assurance Company promoted his father, Ellis William Keenleyside, to the position of manager for British Columbia, a position he held for almost forty years. Margaret Keenleyside, née Irvine, also from southern Ontario, was the daughter of a skilled toolmaker who found work as a shop foreman for the CPR after coming to the coast. Both sides of the family were intensely religious, the paternal side Methodist, the maternal side Baptist. In 1908, after living for several years in a respectable but not prestigious part of the West End, they built a new home in the western part of Kitsilano, south of English Bay, an area to which streetcar service was about to begin. Reflecting the family's growing affluence and desire to express its success with visible symbols of prosperity, the Keenleyside home and surrounding grounds included a grass court for tennis, a small rose garden, a stable for two ponies, electric lights and a telephone, a sunroom-conservatory, an 'enormous granite fireplace,' five bedrooms, a parlour, and 'a handsome hall of red mahogany.' Hugh's mother participated actively in the ritual of social calling and with the aid of 'a succession of Japanese servants' received at home once a month.[32]

The Keenleysides occupied a solid foothold in the upper ranks of the middle class and clearly aspired to raise their social status. A private education for their children offered one way to achieve this goal. Unable to afford a school away from the city, they had to settle for local institutions. After starting at a public school Hugh entered New College, a private institution located in the West End and run by two young Englishmen educated at New College, Oxford. He then entered Langara, a boys' school, formed in 1911 along with Braemar, a school for girls, in the vicinity of Shaughnessy Heights. Both were part of Western Residential Schools, a company described by Jean Barman as Vancouver's 'first major private educational enterprise of the new century.' With seven of twelve directors drawn from among prominent Vancouver businessmen, the company reflected the aspirations of new money rather than the interests of old families. Langara attracted the sons of middle-rank families such as the Keenleysides but not the offspring of wealthier and more established families such as the Bell-Irvings and Sweenys. They sent their sons to England.[33]

As THE KEENLEYSIDE FAMILY's history illustrates, money was necessary for a high-status lifestyle, its importance reflected in the social survey designation of upper-stratum families as 'wealthy.' But a closer examination of wealth holding at the upper levels of Vancouver's social system reveals that top businessmen commanded far greater riches than did their social status counterparts (see Table 6.1). The wealthiest families were those who combined business and social success. Much poorer, by contrast, were the many Society families headed by men who owned or managed smaller businesses or worked in one of the professions and who in class terms would be defined as upper middle rather than upper class. As revealed in Table 6.1, professional men who had achieved social success but were not leaders in business left estates that averaged $31,334. This amount equalled only one-eighth the size of estates left by prewar business leaders ($264,384) and one-twelfth that left by top businessmen who were also members of Society ($366,254). In other words, many families at the top of

Vancouver's social status hierarchy were neither prominent in business nor particularly wealthy. What, then, explains the existence of a social status elite separate from, though overlapping with, the upper class?

An explanation is to be found in the contrasting social backgrounds of Vancouver's business and social leaders.[34] The men who headed Society families were well educated. Two out of three had received some postsecondary training, an extremely high ratio for the period. Equally important, one in four had attended a high-status private school such as Toronto's Upper Canada College. The group's occupational status helps explain the extensive education that its members had received. More than one-third of the men who headed Society families worked in the professions, and half were themselves the sons of professionals. By 1914 Vancouver was no longer 'purely a business town.'[35] Its social leaders had broadened from an elite of business families into a 'wealthy business and professional class.'

By contrast, leading businessmen generally came from less advantaged backgrounds than the occupationally mixed social leaders, and the differences offer additional insight into the complex gradations of prestige that marked the city's entire upper stratum. Education again stands out.

Table 6.1

Comparison of wealth held at death by business and social leaders (by probate records)

	Average net assets ($)	Number of cases
Overlapping social leaders (1910-14) and business leaders (1910-13)	366,254	25
Business leaders (1890-3)	292,462	13
Business leaders (1910-13)	264,384	47
Business leaders without social leaders (1910-13)	190,136	19
Social leaders (1910-14)	151,283	84
Social leaders without business leaders (1910-14)	60,194	59
Social leaders, primary occupation as professional (1910-14)	31,334	22

Note: Probate records were read for business leaders of the 1890-3 and 1910-13 periods and social leaders of the 1910-14 period who died before the end of 1939. Subleaders are excluded from the study. Because of the cut-off date, the table excludes the records of several wealthy business leaders who died after 1939 (wholesale merchants Wm. H. Malkin, R.V. Winch, and Henry A. Stone and lumbermen E.H. Heaps, A.D. McRae, and James A. McNair). The table examines the wealth of men, but not women, at the head of business or society families. The methods used to define and research Vancouver's top businessmen are discussed in the Introduction. Social leaders are defined in the text of this chapter and in Robert A.J. McDonald, 'Vancouver's "Four Hundred": The Quest for Wealth and Power in Canada's Far West, 1886-1914,' *Journal of Canadian Studies* 25 (Autumn 1990):56 and 70 n. 10 (where they are called a 'social elite').
Source: See Table 5.3. The probate records of retail merchant Charles Woodward (d. 1937) could not be located.

On average, Society men were much better educated than top businessmen of the prewar period. A larger proportion of them had attended private secondary schools of high status (25.8 per cent compared to 12.0 per cent) or received some university or professional training (66.8 per cent versus 24.8 per cent), and a lower proportion had been limited to elementary schooling (3.7 per cent versus 27.5 per cent). Family background as measured by the occupational status of fathers reveals similar differences. The chance that a member of either group had come from a business family was roughly equal (42.4 per cent for men in Society families, 36.4 per cent for business leaders), and working-class parents were, with the exception of one top businessman, unknown. But while Society men emerged almost entirely from urban families, 30 per cent of leading businessmen grew up on farms. The number of fathers in each group who had attained positions in the professions, the military, or public life differed substantially (57.1 per cent of fathers of professional men compared to 31.8 per cent of fathers of business leaders). In addition, the religious affiliation of Vancouver's socially prominent was decidedly Anglican, the church of the upper class in Britain. By contrast, business families expressed a greater range of religious preferences, reflecting their more varied status. Differences are especially sharp when the overlapping group of business and social leaders – forty-two of ninety-one business leaders in prewar Vancouver were also members of Society – is removed from the discussion and one considers only the business leaders who had not achieved a place in Society and the social leaders who had not become top businessmen.[36]

From this perspective, Vancouver's social status leaders appear as a collection of families headed by men who had been educated well beyond the high school level and top businessmen appear as a group more consistently from relatively humble circumstances. Wealth measured success for the latter but not the former. This evidence suggests that the social status elite was not so much invented in Vancouver as reassembled there; in coming to the west coast, Vancouver's social leaders were seeking first to consolidate, and then to express, their existing social position.[37]

The complex relationship between class and status is illustrated in the histories of two second-level business leaders, John Campbell and William Arthur Ward. The business roles of both men placed them in the lower reaches of the upper class. Campbell headed a family-run storage company and, starting in 1907, served as shipping master for the Port of Vancouver, an appointment acquired through Liberal Party connections. William Arthur Ward chaired the board of directors of the British Columbia General Development Syndicate, a limited liability company that held Kootenay timber and land for English investors. Ward's speculative enterprise claimed prewar assets worth twice those of Campbell's business ($378,888 versus $187,487), and neither man invested extensively in other companies. Both died in the early 1930s leaving minuscule estates, Campbell of $10,000, Ward of debts that exceeded assets by more than $40,000.

Despite parallel roles as capitalists, the two men lived very different lives. One came from Ontario's labour aristocracy, the other from Victoria's business and social elite. John Campbell's father, a skilled artisan, had built carriages in Woodville, Ontario. After attending public schools to age fifteen, John followed his father by apprenticing as a blacksmith. He then left Ontario for the United States, where he worked for two railway companies and rose to the level of foreman of the blacksmithing department of the Wabash Railway before heading to the Klondike in 1898. He never got there, settling in Vancouver along the way. By contrast William Ward was, so to speak, to the manner born. The son of a leading banker and landowner in Victoria, Ward attended a prestigious boys' school in Port Hope, Ontario, before rounding out his education in England and France. In 1907 he moved to Vancouver. At the height of the prewar boom Campbell, who had wed years before, lived in a modest area near the centre of the city. Describing himself as a 'man of domestic tastes' who 'divides his time largely between his home and his office,' Campbell participated actively in two fraternal lodges, St. Andrew's Presbyterian Church, and the Liberal Party but claimed no other club associations. Ward, on the other hand, resided in the West End, attended the high-status St. Paul's Anglican Church, belonged to three golf clubs and two prestigious men's clubs, and with his wife was listed in the *Vancouver Social Register and Club Directory*. Ward had chosen to be part of Society. Campbell and his family remained in the social status group below.[38]

FAMILIES WHOSE education, connections, and histories provided sophisticated indices of status tended to reject claims for social recognition based on wealth alone. They sought to preserve family status acquired through ascription rather than achievement. For this purpose social leaders created rituals and institutions as much to protect existing status as to promote status mobility.

The restrictive tendencies of exclusive clubs provided excellent sources of protection from pretenders attempting to buy social recognition. Indeed, several studies have argued that in major North American cities during the industrial age, metropolitan clubs provided the best index of a family's social standing.[39] Led by the Vancouver Club, social clubs had been defining status in Vancouver since the 1880s, and expansion of the city's club hierarchy mainly reinforced an established pattern. A whole series of new business and social organizations emerged in the prewar decade, ranging from middling-status commercial associations like the Western Club and the Progress Club to higher-status social organizations such as the Connaught Skating Club and the Shaughnessy Heights Golf Club.

The status-defining function of clubs can be illustrated by studying how the city's two most important business clubs, the Vancouver Club and the Terminal City Club, sorted top businessmen – they accepted only men – of the prewar period into discrete groups. The Vancouver Club, formed in 1889 but firmly established only in 1893, remained the city's premier, and most exclusive, metropolitan club. By contrast, the Terminal City Club, which emerged in 1899, was much more open.[40] Both catered to the interests of business and professional men, and both combined social and business functions. Their clientele differed sharply, however. Seventy-one per cent of the prewar business leaders and subleaders who belonged to the Terminal City Club were not members of the Vancouver Club, and 73 per cent of those in the Vancouver Club did not belong to the Terminal City. Terminal City Club members were more active in speculative real estate and resource promotion enterprises, in financing speculative schemes through the many trust and loan companies that flourished in the prewar period, and in the retail trade. Vancouver Club members were more likely to work in the banking, urban utility, or transportation sectors of the economy, or in the professions. Most revealing is that over 50 per cent of the Vancouver Club members were primarily occupied in companies with assets greater than $1 million, almost twice the proportion of prominent businessmen in the Terminal City Club.[41] Entrepreneurs heading resource companies and wholesale firms belonged in roughly equal proportion to the two clubs.

Social background was a more compelling agent of differentiation. The Vancouver Club had always defined itself as a first-class social club that would emulate the high-status business and social clubs of other major North American cities, and its admission policies aimed to bring this about by excluding men who had not attained a high social standing. Prospective members of the Vancouver Club were to be thoroughly investigated before being admitted, had to be nominated by two club members, and would be denied admittance if opposed by one in six. The policy was effective. By 1914 half the leading businessmen who belonged to the Vancouver Club could boast of some university training, while fewer than one in five of their counterparts in the Terminal City Club could make a similar claim. The former were more likely to be members of the Anglican church, by a ratio of almost two to one (62 per cent to 34 per cent) and less likely to belong to the Methodist, Roman Catholic, or Baptist church. Terminal City Club members were half as likely to have been raised in professional families and more than twice as likely to have been raised on farms. Top businessmen in the two clubs clearly moved in quite distinct social circles.[42]

Clubs played such a crucial role in defining status during the prewar period that a closer examination of memberships allows us to speculate on the overall size and structure of the city's 'wealthy business and professional class.' An innovation of the period, the social register of clubs and associations, provides the means. At the end of the nineteenth century, elite directories began to appear in major cities to help sort out the status implications of club proliferation. Socially prominent families in New York, Boston, and Philadelphia led the way by publishing social registers designed to identify Society members and to control the flow of new entrants into the status elite.[43] Vancouver received two such directories before the war, the *Elite Directory of Vancouver* of 1908 and the *Vancouver Social Register and Club Directory* of 1914. The latter is more comprehensive. Describing its role as primarily that of publishing – and thus identifying – the names of families and persons active in Vancouver's social life, the *Social Register* was not unduly restrictive and, one can reasonably guess, includes the majority of families who wanted to be considered part of the city's upper stratum. Of its 2,491 entrants, 2,270 consisted of married couples. The list included only 221 single men or women. Thus named were 4,761 people, almost all of them married. When we consider that many of these families would have had children or close relatives living in the city, the total size of Vancouver's upper stratum approximates 8,000.[44]

This stratum was divided into levels of status, and cross-referring the register and various club lists allows us to tease out of the larger group a sense of the complex nature of Vancouver's status hierarchy. Because Vancouver's status leaders were an associational elite, created through a process of socialization in a select number of voluntary associations, their composition can be identified from lists of club members. For the 1910-14 period memberships of husbands or wives either in three of the city's eight most prestigious clubs or, alternatively, in the *Vancouver Social Register and Club Directory*, the restrictive Vancouver Club, and one other prestigious club can be interpreted as indication of high social status. The 302 families and individuals so identified constituted Vancouver's 'Society,' comparable to the 'Four Hundred' prominent families identified a generation earlier by Ward McAllister as New York's fashionable elite.[45] When husbands, wives, and children are considered, we can assume that Society families equalled perhaps 1,000 individuals, about one-eighth of the upper stratum as a whole.

WHETHER ESTABLISHING or solidifying their place in Vancouver's status hierarchy, families depended on the active participation of women. To be respectable required attachment to a family unit, a condition that severely diminished the social standing of both single men and single women. Industrialization had led to more sharply defined roles for each of the sexes, with convention dictating that the public sphere belonged to men and the private to women. The accelerated scale of economic activity during the Victorian era increased the importance of home as a haven from business. It was the task of women to keep at bay the amoral world of business by maintaining moral vigilance at home. Victorians viewed such vigilance as the foundation of a proper moral order,[46] and the language of separate spheres for men and women continued to be heard in twentieth-century Vancouver. Thus, just as Donald Stewart, a wealthy steam laundry operator of middling social status, could speak of 'finding his truest happiness at his own fireside,' so too could Hugh Keenleyside write of his mother's 'great help' in assisting his father 'to keep the business world out of his home life.' Margaret Keenleyside also 'maintained the little family customs at Christmas, on birthdays, and so on that meant so much' and contributed to the family's collective identity.[47]

By the early 1900s women had become much more active than in mid-Victorian times in public life outside of the home but continued to operate within the confines of a social system that prescribed separate roles for men and women.[48] At first Vancouver women confined their public activities to respectable church organizations and temperance societies. In the early 1890s, for instance, a local branch of the Women's Christian Temperance Union worked 'to enhance and protect the purity of the City' by expunging 'rude pictures' from cigar store windows and banning the sale of intoxicating liquor.[49] Then, in 1894, highly educated and economically advantaged women organized the Art, Historical and Scientific Association and, independently of men, founded the Vancouver Local Council of Women (LCW). The two would remain leading cultural and social reform organizations respectively for the next generation. Led by Lady Reid, wife of Sir John Reid, formerly of the Royal Navy, and Mrs. Anna Beecher, wife of Hastings Sawmill owner C.M. Beecher and one of the city's wealthiest women, the LCW fought initially to advance the cause of women as public figures – urging that they be allowed to run for elective office as school trustees, for example – while reaffirming traditional notions of women as 'homemakers.'[50]

The system of formal social intercourse known as 'at homes' reflected the most direct link between domestic and public roles. By creating intimate associations through a formalized ritual of visiting, socially prominent women were able to transform their function as homemakers into an instrument for locating families within the city's fluid status hierarchy. The social visibility of women in city newspapers, where long lists of names served to place families within spheres of influence, was especially important in marking the coming together of a status elite. While membership in the Vancouver Club reflected a significant measure of social acceptance for a business or professional man, he would remain on the social margins of the upper stratum unless connected by ties of family and home to men of comparable prestige.

In the years leading up to the First World War women continued to expand the range of activities that took them out of the home and into the public realm. Organizations such as the Connaught Skating Club and the Shaughnessy Heights Golf Club involved women with their husbands as families. Many other associations were gender specific. Auxiliaries to the Vancouver General Hospital, St. Paul's Hospital, the Seaman's Institute, and the Society for the Prevention of Cruelty to Animals attracted women from some of Vancouver's most prominent families during the prewar boom.[51] Like men, women also created status-defining women's clubs and associations. Formed in 1905, the Women's Musical Club catered to women 'from Vancouver's most prominent families.' Historian Ian Hunt writes that, because of their 'class origins and socialization,' Musical Club members assumed that 'only they possessed the sensibilities necessary to best appreciate and understand "good" music.'[52] Two other associations for socially prominent women, the Georgian Club and the Athenaeum Club, followed at the end of the decade. The former described itself as Vancouver's 'first ladies' social club'; the latter catered to adult women who were 'engaged professionally in art, literature, science or handicrafts' and were interested in 'the welfare, development and educational process of women.' Both signified a growing feminist consciousness among the educated and high-status women of Vancouver. Other organizations such as the Women's Canadian Club, formed in 1909, and the Local Council of Women drew members from a broader, though still mostly upper-middle- or upper-class, social base. These various organizations allowed women to advance their own status in Vancouver society and to enhance the prestige of their families.[53]

CULTURE PROVIDES another prism through which to observe the structuring of Vancouver society into a multilayered hierarchy of status. The upper stratum sought to foster art, music, science, and intellectual discourse as a means to counter the city's 'busy commercialism.' Cultural leaders, often top businessmen or their wives, typically enjoyed the benefit of good educations and prestigious family roots. Their efforts to cultivate the higher elements of British civilization and culture served to lessen in the public mind their own association with business and to distance them from ordinary people whose lives were more fully concerned with daily subsistence. In this sense, being an active supporter of art, music, or the opera defined status in much the same manner as a winter expedition to some far-away land or membership in a prestigious social club.[54]

French cultural theorist Pierre Bourdieu suggests a reason for the association of high status with high culture. 'Art and cultural consumption are predisposed, consciously and deliberately or not, to fulfil a social function of legitimating social differences,' he asserts. They do so because taste classifies, and artistic taste, and therefore the cultural competence to recognize artistic meaning, is acquired socially. Preferences in literature, painting, and music 'are clearly linked to educational level ... and secondarily to social

Daughters of the British
Empire, 1914. The photograph
illustrates the associational life
that was an important source
of high status among middle-
and upper-class families.
(Leonard Frank photo, Jewish
Historical Society of British
Columbia LF 45032)

origin.' Competence in the high arts, then, serves to demonstrate one's ability to rise above the mundane routine of daily life and display an appreciation of refined, disinterested, and economically unnecessary pleasures.[55]

In early Vancouver the ability to paint or to show an understanding of art provided an important benchmark of cultural competence. CPR land commissioner L.A. Hamilton decided to preserve on canvas the picturesque features of the Government Reserve at the entrance to Burrard Inlet, thus demonstrating his artistic and cultural sensibilities. In 1889 socially prominent pioneers formed an art association, the membership of which reached sixty-eight in 1890. Its goal was to cultivate a taste for art, particularly needed, one anonymous member noted, in a young and growing city 'where all are alive to the business interests.' In rejecting the association's request for civic space to begin an art gallery, Alderman Fox retorted that 'art was for the rich.' So, it seems, was membership in the art association. Leading CPR executives figured prominently, as did two socially active women, Annie Webster and Gertrude Mellon, both wives of former British naval officers.[56] The association died in 1892 and art became one component of a broader organization, the Art, Historical and Scientific Association (AHSA), formed two years later. Leading figures in the Studio Club, founded in 1904 to encourage artistic endeavour, were also well-educated members of the city's business and professional community. Emily Carr, hired by the Club to teach its members how to paint, described them derisively as 'a cluster of society women who intermittently packed themselves and their admirers into a small rented studio to drink tea and jabber art jargon.' Leadership then passed to the British Columbia Society of Fine Arts, whose patrons included Charles H. Tupper, Harry Abbott, J.C. Keith, A.L. Russell, and F.C. Wade. Its members were all part of the group of powerful families that belonged to both the upper class and to High Society. The Vancouver Operatic and Dramatic Society, the Vancouver Women's Musical Club, and the company formed in 1911 to raise money for a new opera house were similarly cultural associations of the socially prominent.[57]

The AHSA was less dominated by leading business families but more explicit in articulating elitist values. As Ian Hunt has shown, one of the Association's functions was to allow members to define themselves as culturally superior to the 'great masses of the people.' More British than the business community as a whole, AHSA members also more openly questioned the excessive materialism of the Pacific metropolis. Members hoped in particular 'to cultivate a taste for the beauties and refinements of life' among people otherwise concerned with 'the materialising struggle for existence.' To civilize society, and implicitly to control deviant behaviour by promoting the rational use of recreational time, they opened Vancouver's first museum in 1905.[58]

A practical example of how cultural attitudes shaped social action is demonstrated by the attempt of Vancouver's social status leaders to civilize the city's masses through beautification, and thus to impose its idea of social order upon people of the lower middle and working classes. The impulse for beautification accelerated in the prewar decade as high-status members of Vancouver's business and professional community moved to control the aesthetic and social blight that attended rapid urban growth. The movement they created was called City Beautiful. It had become popular elsewhere in the early twentieth century, including eastern North America and to a lesser extent Britain. It spread to Canada from Chicago's World Fair of 1893, peaking between 1910 and 1913. The urge to beautify also drew inspiration from the British Garden City movement of the same period. Conceptually ill defined, City Beautiful focused on the need to improve the aesthetic qualities of urban places. Improvement would result from the removal of visually disruptive elements such as billboards and smoke, the introduction of gardens and greenery, and the addition of architectural monuments. Grand buildings designed in the neoclassical style would enhance civic pride and add visual variety.[59]

Scholars have interpreted City Beautiful supporters variously as boosters concerned mainly with economic growth, unselfish and public-spirited philanthropists, and reformers intent on restoring to society social cohesion and the dominance of middle- and upper-class values.[60] The different strands of Vancouver's City Beautiful movement exhibited booster, cultural, and reform motives. The commercial thrust for beautification was advanced first by the Vancouver Tourist Association, formed in 1902 to represent the booster interests of mid-sized, locally based businesses in advertising, real estate, and tourism. Vancouver's most intellectual newspaper, the *News-Advertiser*, defined the movement in cultural terms. It promoted the idea of overcoming the city's utilitarian ugliness – and what one City Beautiful promoter called its 'packing-box style of architecture' – by planting trees and lawns in public spaces, including boulevards. In May

1905 this sentiment led West End ratepayers to form the Vancouver Garden City Association for the purpose of improving 'the general appearance of the city.' Led by prominent business personalities, the organization clearly reflected the values and interests of Vancouver's 'wealthy business and professional class.'[61]

The beautification movement continued to evolve over the next several years and reached a crescendo in the winter of 1911-12, at the peak of the prewar boom. One impetus came from a private company's proposal of August 1910 to run electric trolleys around the circumference of Stanley Park, Vancouver's recreational jewel. In response to 800 blue- and white-collar wage earners who petitioned City Council to put the tramway proposal to a vote, the proponents of city beautification were forced to mount a concerted effort to block the proposal and thus defend the natural character of the 960-acre park. In a January 1912 plebiscite Vancouver's lower middle- and working-class east and southeast wards marginally approved a proposal – somewhat different from the original – calling for a municipally owned tramway in Stanley Park; West End voters stood massively against the plan, thus ensuring its defeat.[62]

City Beautiful ideas, already popular in business and professional circles, received a boost in 1912 with the arrival from England of Thomas Mawson, one of Britain's most successful park designers. Commissioned by the Vancouver Board of Park Commissioners to present advice on the entrance to Stanley Park, where the 1888 bridge was collapsing and the Coal Harbour tidal flats were foul-smelling and unsightly, Mawson offered three plans: one to retain a tree-fringed waterline on the north side of a lagoon at the park entrance; another, far more utilitarian than the first, to create playgrounds for children and playing fields for adults by filling in the upper end of Coal Harbour; and a third, designed in the 'Grand Manner,' to feature three majestic neoclassical buildings surrounding a circular pond. At the centre was to be a statue atop a 'great shaft.'[63]

Reaction to the three plans illustrates the relationship between culture and status. Vancouver's upper stratum divided into two groups, a high-status clique of twenty-one business and social leaders who, while supporting the aesthetic goals of City Beautiful, rejected Mawson's beautification plans and mounted an uncompromising defence of the area's wilderness qualities; and a larger number influenced by the reformist assumptions of the City Beautiful movement and favourable to Mawson's first or third proposals.

The twenty-one defenders of an unimproved park were a privileged group whose numbers included four bankers, a dentist, an architect, two engineers, and two other university graduates. Two of Vancouver's first CPR officials, engineer H.J. Cambie and treasurer W.F. Salsbury; newspaperman Francis Carter-Cotton; the city's most active supporter of amateur sports, banker Campbell Sweeny; and Society leader Sir Charles Hibbert Tupper all belonged to this set. They were directed by F.C. Wade, a university-educated lawyer and writer 'well-read in legal lore, history, and the English classics.' Superior education and extensive travelling had familiarized the group with the Romantic tradition in art and literature and sharpened its emotional attachment to the peninsula's natural forest. They were members of Society and close to the top of Vancouver's upper stratum.[64]

The larger and more reform-minded group that dominated the Board of Park Commissioners consisted of mid-level businessmen and professionals. In 1910-13, for example, six Board members were middle class and one was an upper-class businessman, Jonathan Rogers. None belonged to Society. They believed that Stanley Park should be kept as natural as possible – opposing a tramline and commercial sports in the park, for instance – but required beautification at the entrance and the addition of tennis courts, putting and bowling greens, children's play apparatus, and other play facilities. They were much influenced by the ethos of progressivism, the broad intellectual movement that placed increasing value on economic, social, and political efficiency and the need for experts, such as Thomas Mawson, to bring it about. The underlying goal of this quest for efficiency was, to use the language of American historian Robert Wiebe, a 'search for order' in the face of mounting disorder caused by rapid social change.[65]

The Board not only supported Mawson's plans to improve Coal Harbour but also embraced the ideas of American playground movement reformers. In 1912 the Board established Vancouver's first fully equipped children's recreation area at McLean Park in Strathcona, to the east of Chinatown. McLean Park represented the culmination of a reformist strand of thinking that linked City Beautiful ideas of aesthetic improvement with the goal of bettering society by altering the moral behaviour of children.

The Local Council of Women (LCW) most fully articulated this goal. In 1897, for instance, LCW president Anna Beecher had spoken of the Council's desire to 'take care of the weaker classes' and to civilize the poor by encouraging 'greater taste for profitable reading.'[66] Similar assumptions animated the arguments of LCW leaders when, in January 1912, they initiated the founding of a City Beautiful Association.[67] Linking beauty with moral behaviour, LCW spokeswoman Mrs. J.O. Perry asserted that beautification would have a 'wholesome moral effect' on the city. The LCW were particularly troubled by the delinquent behaviour of juvenile boys who had capitulated to the lure of the streets; to keep them busy, and to help develop their 'artistic senses,' the Council proposed that youths be encouraged to garden. It also came to believe that supervised play would control city youth and successfully encouraged the Board of Park Commissioners to create supervised playgrounds. High-status supporters of City Beautiful, such as F.C. Wade, embraced the movement's goal of promoting Vancouver's 'higher development' through beautification but opposed the application of reform principles to Stanley Park, which they viewed as a cathedral of nature. Mrs. Perry and other LCW leaders, who in the prewar period belonged mainly to the outer circle of status in the upper stratum, more closely linked parks with reform.[68]

A wider cultural gulf separated the city's social status elite – including both park romantics or park reformers – from its common folk, a division evident in the language of debate generated by the tramline scheme and Mawson's plans for the entrance to Stanley Park. At one extreme were the purists who found abhorrent the thought of a tramline carrying 'thousands of people with lunch baskets and bottled beer into the park's recesses.' Their reaction to Mawson's idea of a sports stadium at the park entrance was even more hostile. Thousands of 'people, fans, rooters and all' would crowd into the stadium, they argued, 'chewing gum and howling with leather lungs.' Peacefulness, rest, and quiet, the people's 'greatest recreation' in Stanley Park, would be lost to the 'raucous shouting of a frenzied baseball multitude rending the quiet air.' The social distance between upper- and lower-status residents implied by such language echoed the desire of LCW reformers to civilize the masses by encouraging them to read and garden.

By contrast, the Vancouver Trades and Labor Council, which most forcefully articulated the views of ordinary people, presented a more utilitarian perspective. Vancouver lacked free athletic space, it asserted, and should adopt Mawson's proposal to fill and use in a practical manner the upper end of Coal Harbour. In addition, Park Board policy discriminated in favour of the rich by allowing buggies and motor cars to reach the far corners of Stanley Park while denying 'plain every-day people' a tramway that would carry them beyond the crowds that clustered near the park entrance. They scoffed at artfully contrived landscape forms and argued that Vancouver was already surrounded by 'water space'; what it needed was more 'playing space,' not a Coal Harbour lagoon or ornamental pool. Summarizing labour's attitude to parks, VTLC secretary J.H. McVety concluded that Stanley Park 'should not be treasured as a holy retreat, but should be a practical breathing spot, and should be considered at its used value.'[69]

In suggesting that the phrases 'holy retreat' and 'practical breathing spot' framed debate about Stanley Park, McVety hinted at broad cultural differences among Vancouver citizens. At one extreme were residents of wealth, education, and considerable worldly experience who saw themselves as sophisticated cosmopolitans of refined taste. For them Stanley Park was a thing of beauty, to be valued for its aesthetic and spiritual qualities. Trades and Labor Council members, on the other hand, were people of more limited wealth and education whose identities were rooted in the local community and whose values and tastes reflected the daily struggle for material well-being. In between the cosmopolitans and the locals were people whose outlook was a mixture of the cerebral and the practical. The movement for civic beautification, for instance, came initially from the upper levels of Vancouver's 'wealthy business and professional class' but, increasingly during the prewar decade, from people of more middling social status as well. City Beautiful reformers rejected the crass materialism of the VTLC but embraced a more practical, and less romantic, view of parks than the cultural leaders.

WAS STATUS just a social expression of class? The question is an obvious one, given that class and status identities both took on much sharper definition during the period around 1900. At the very top, status leaders were mostly members of the upper class who shared an identity as the principal owners of the means of production. Within this group, bonding among wealthy business and professional families provided a social context for economic unity. Key participants in the canners' confrontation with fishermen in 1900, for example – Worsnop, the Bell-Irvings, Farrell, Gardiner Johnson – were all prominent in the movement to create a Society in turn of the century Vancouver.

The connection between class and status during this period is illustrated especially in the business connections of socially prominent professional families. Joseph Russell functioned as a lawyer, a magistrate, a member of Society, a stout opponent of organized labour, and an agent for salmon canners. Sir Charles Hibbert Tupper, who with Lady Tupper led the way towards the creation of a high-status stratum of Society families in the early years of the century, also worked closely with business through his function as a lawyer. Having 'laboured hard for the canners' while federal minister of fisheries to 1894, Tupper joined the industry in 1899 when his Vancouver law firm became agents for Wurzburg and Company, salmon canners, with Tupper as Wurzburg's vice-president. The link between business and the legal profession is perhaps best reflected in the career of E.P. Davis, a socially prominent lawyer who, after turning down a chance in 1898 to become chief justice of the Supreme Court of British Columbia, remained closely tied to the CPR as its legal counsel.[70] In other words, through their economic and social behaviour Vancouver lawyers helped to integrate the upper portion of the upper class and to expand the capacity of businessmen to defend their class interests.

Beyond the inner clique of overlapping upper-class and High Society families, the relationship between class and status becomes complex, however. Upper-class economic position did not automatically translate into a high-status social life. When their economic interests were threatened, such as from a militant and increasingly socialist labour movement in the early 1900s, professionals and businessmen thought and acted in class rather than status terms. Indeed, the potential for class mobilization was always greater at the top of Vancouver's social structure than at the bottom because economic and social identities corresponded so closely. A shared British heritage and a common practice of living in family units reinforced this potential for class mobilization.

But for much of their lives such questions were not of pressing concern to members of the upper stratum, especially when exaggerated prosperity seemed to hold out the hope of material well-being for residents of all classes. In this environment other forms of identity gained importance. Vancouverites were people of multiple identities, and the relationship among those identities shifted in meaning and character according to the context of the time. Much of the meaning came through differences of lifestyle and associational patterns that reflected both class position and non-economic influences. It was precisely the significance accorded distinctions of status that James S. Woodsworth found so reprehensible in

CHAPTER SEVEN

The Artisan or Moderately Well-To-Do Class

Louis D. Taylor and Henry H. (Harry) Stevens rose quickly and almost simultaneously to positions of political leadership in prewar Vancouver. Defeated in January 1909 in his first bid to become mayor, Taylor triumphed a year later. He held office on six additional occasions until bowing out at the end of 1934. Stevens also entered electoral politics in the civic contest of 1910, winning a place on City Council for Ward 5 (Mount Pleasant), where he lived. Returned the following January, he then surprised political observers by taking the Conservative Party nomination and the seat for Vancouver City in the federal election of 1911. Stevens represented Vancouver in Parliament for nineteen years and the constituency of Kootenay East for another ten. He retired from electoral office in 1940.

The two men came from similar circumstances and in the prewar period followed remarkably parallel careers. His early life in Michigan marked by poverty, Taylor arrived in Vancouver in 1896 penniless but armed with a high school education. He helped bring the *Province* newspaper to Vancouver from Victoria in 1898 and served as its bookkeeper and circulation manager before moving on to buy the *Vancouver Daily World* in 1905. He did so with two partners and 'less than $600 to his name.' Under Taylor's direction the *World* became one of Vancouver's shrillest boosters, reflecting through its stories and real estate advertisements the city's promotional spirit. In 1912 Taylor erected for the *World* a tower that stood briefly as the tallest building in the empire. But like other speculative ventures of the period, both the tower and the newspaper fell victim to general economic collapse and passed into the hands of bondholders.[1]

Harry Stevens similarly emerged as a promoter and newspaperman. Born the son of a greengrocer in Bristol, England, he came first to Ontario and then in 1894 to the Okanagan, where he started his working life as a grocery clerk. Prospecting and mining in British Columbia's Boundary country were followed by a stint in the American army that took him to the Philippines and China during the Boxer Rebellion. After coming to Vancouver in 1901, Stevens again entered the grocery trade while learning accounting and bookkeeping at night. Like Taylor, he became caught up in speculation and promotion, establishing his own real estate and brokerage business and serving as director or president of four small companies. One of them, a trust company, collapsed along with many such businesses after the boom.

Taylor and Stevens were not wealthy and did not move socially in high-status circles. Promotional organizations like the Progress Club and Vancouver Exhibition Association appealed to Taylor, as did the Terminal City Club. He either did not want to join, or was rejected by, the more prestigious Vancouver Club. An active Mason and member of the Orange Lodge and Sons of England, Stevens also belonged to the Terminal City Club but not its more prestigious rival.[2]

Politically their relationship was more complex. Taylor was a strong Liberal who openly identified with the interests of workingmen. His connections to labour went back at least to the fall of 1900, when he served on the campaign committee of the Vancouver Labor Party. By 1909 he had emerged as 'the dominant power in the local [Vancouver] Liberal Party' and had created an organization called the 909 Club. The Club was to work 'through the labor unions' to advance Liberal Party fortunes in the provincial election and Taylor's mayoralty aspirations thereafter. Its impact is unknown but Taylor did receive working-class support when elected as mayor in 1910 and 1911, including endorsement by the Vancouver Trades and Labor Council in 1911.[3]

Election poster for L.D. Taylor, ca. 1910. L.D. Taylor's message of 'A Full Dinner Pail' and 'Fair Play' is an appeal to working-class voters. Material well-being was an ever-present concern of people who worked for hourly wages and lacked job security. The word 'fair' evokes a standard based on custom rather than the market and recalls the cultural heritage of skilled artisans. (P. Timms photo, Vancouver Public Library 7274)

Taylor's first two campaigns established him as a populist critic of Vancouver's business and social leaders. His opponent, the socially prominent businessman C.S. Douglas, stood for business issues, including economic promotion and the extension of city boundaries. Taylor emphasized concerns popular with working people, including the eight-hour day for civic workers, the exclusion of Asians from city jobs, and public rather than corporate control of street ends along Vancouver's waterfront. Taylor presented himself as a man of the people; Douglas presented himself as a successful businessman. Douglas's supporters portrayed Taylor as a 'demagogue' bent upon setting 'class against class,' while Taylor characterized Douglas as a 'society mayor' behind whom lurked 'powerful interests.' Taylor's response to the charge that he was a 'socialist' is particularly instructive. Yes, he responded: 'If a Socialist is a man who stands by what he thinks right and does not fear to express his opinions irrespective of monopolies, corporations, and other similar influences, who dares to speak on behalf of the masses of the people, then I am a Socialist.'[4] Douglas and his principal supporter, the business-oriented *Province,* concluded that Taylor owed his 1910 victory to 'the solid Socialist vote' from eastern and southern wards; the *Western Wage-Earner,* backed by trade unionists, agreed that 'Taylor's victory was due in no small measure to the support of ... members of organized labor.'[5]

In contrast, Stevens was an active Tory who built his career around the policies of moral reform and Asian exclusion. An English Methodist, he began in 1903 to participate in 'campaigns for closing down the Chinese gambling dens, the red light district and Vancouver's rough saloons.' To promote these causes he joined with other moral reformers to start the *Western Call* – a weekly newspaper for the Mount Pleasant district – and later the Good Government League.[6] One of the League's targets was Mayor Taylor, a Lutheran, whom it accused of being allied with the city's liquor interests. In addition to being an enthusiastic anglophone who believed in the superiority of all things British, Stevens argued throughout his political career that unless Asian immigration was stopped, China's 'teeming population' would threaten the British character of British Columbia. According to one source, Stevens's stand on immigration 'played a large part in his election to Parliament in 1911,' appealing to the ethnocentrism that permeated both working- and lower middle-class cultures. Taylor avoided crusades for moral regulation and supported Asian exclusion but did not emphasize it.[7]

Yet when we move beyond these policy differences to the values that the two men articulated we find many similarities flowing from a common reservoir of nineteenth-century reform thought. Both saw themselves as spokesmen for ordinary people and opponents of monopoly capitalism. Taylor defined his opposition to Douglas in the language of 'monopolies' and 'masses' that would have sounded very familiar to producerists of the mid-1890s. His refusal to dress formally, even when greeting Prime Minister Sir Wilfrid Laurier, and the red tie that was a constant part of his attire served to link him symbolically with the people and distance him from Vancouver's status leaders.[8]

Stevens too saw himself as an ordinary man representing ordinary folk. His family background, his Methodism, and his occupations as grocery clerk, bookkeeper, and real estate salesman rooted him solidly in the middling stratum of society. He built his political career in Mount Pleasant, a mixed neighbourhood of blue- and white-collar workers. Furthermore, his 1898-9 winter spent mining at Phoenix, British Columbia, had introduced him to trade unions – he served as secretary of the Phoenix local of the Western Federation of Miners – and to the economic plight of wage earners. One result was sensitivity to the long hours endured by Vancouver grocery clerks in the early 1900s, which he attempted to lessen by organizing the clerks into a trade union. Like Taylor, indeed like labourist members of City Council in the decade after 1900, Stevens supported day labour for civic workers.[9] The Phoenix experience also sharpened his antipathy to socialism, however, and reinforced his faith in private enterprise.

The seeming contradiction of sympathies for both trade unions and capitalism becomes more understandable in light of another aspect of his social philosophy: the capitalism he embraced was that of small businesses and local communities. He viewed the 'independent-citizen-businessman' as 'probably the finest expression of democratic life to be found anywhere.' Yet as he argued in 1910, 'the sacredness of private interests must be subservient to that of the public good.'[10] Thus, as a young politician he advocated public ownership of utilities and opposed corporate control of Vancouver's waterfront. More concretely, after being elected to Parliament he succeeded in having the Conservative government of Robert Borden build a state-funded grain elevator on Burrard Inlet – critics labelled it 'Stevens' Folly' – and open to public use the ends of five streets along the CPR-controlled waterfront. The populist character of his politics found expression again in the mid-1930s when he initiated a national inquiry into the pricing policies of Canada's large corporations.[11]

What, then, are we to make of these political stories? How do they help us to understand the values, attitudes, and social relationships of people in the middle of Vancouver's status hierarchy, people whom the social survey report of the Methodist and Presbyterian churches described as Vancouver's 'artisan or moderately well-to-do class'? While L.D. Taylor and H.H. Stevens differed sharply on moral questions and party politics, with Stevens expressing middle-class values through his politics and Taylor those of the working class, the two men shared an antipathy to monopoly capitalism, a commitment to localism, an ethnocentric view of Asians, an enthusiasm for real estate boosterism, and an identification with the common people. From this perspective Taylor and Stevens represented aspects of a culture and a way of life that were more populist, or of 'plain people,' than they were class based. The fact that economic interests could also divide these 'plain people' along class lines merely underlines a central point: the meaning that Vancouverites conferred on different parts of their lives varied according to the circumstances of time and place. To understand this complexity requires consideration of both class *and* status identities. This chapter examines the malleable nature of social boundaries among Vancouver's middling people, exploring first the divisive influence of labour issues, then the integrating force of status aspirations.

THE SEPARATION of Vancouver's producers' community along class lines had been hinted at as far back as January 1894, when Francis Carter-Cotton, a reformer whose ownership of the *News-Advertiser* placed him in the upper class, expressed disapproval of workingmen using class-specific language in civic elections. Class tensions became clearer at the end of the decade when William Brown, a prominent middle-class reformer, drifted away from his wage-earning friends within the producers' community over labour issues. Indeed, in November 1902 the Vancouver Trades and Labor Council directed its municipal affairs committee 'especially to oppose' the re-election to City Council of William Brown on the grounds that he stood 'against the aspirations of organised labor.' A rising wave of strikes that peaked in 1903 provided the context within which reform-minded producerists of the early to mid-1890s now divided by class.[12]

In the decade that followed, strikes continued to divide bosses from workers. As shown in Chapter 4 (Table 4.4), the number of labour conflicts recorded in Vancouver fluctuated considerably in response to shifts in the business cycle. A buoyant economy led to increases in the number and size of strikes in 1906-7 and 1910-12, whereas recession sharply undermined the capacity of workers to withdraw their labour in 1908 and for several years starting in 1913. Wage increases were hard won and easily threatened by the cyclical nature of economic growth. As one Vancouver carpenter observed in evidence presented to the BC Commission on Labour, 'in 1907 we had a strike and settled for $4.25 [per day] under an agreement which lasted until 1908. Conditions got bad and the contractors gave notice that wages would be reduced to $3.50, but things were in such shape with men out of work so long during the winter and trade affairs so bad in general that men had to accept this. They got $4.00 in 1909 and $4.25 in 1911.'[13] Thereafter, surplus labour and collapse of the real estate market once again reversed the fortunes of city carpenters.

Management's belief that ownership carried with it the right to manage without interference from labour found expression in a strike of June 1909 between the New England Fish Company and halibut fishermen. Alvah Hagar, New England's manager, asserted his right to continue employing one 'solitary non-union man,' Paddy Shean, even though the company's seventy-one other halibut fishermen – the majority of whom had been with the firm for up to fifteen years – belonged to the Pacific Halibut Fishermen's Union and were calling for a closed shop. Unionized workers asserted their rights by refusing to join a crew that included Shean. A strike ensued. Hagar replaced the strikers and successfully defended what he believed to be his prerogative.[14]

The city's largest labour conflict before the war, a general strike in 1911 of more than 4,000 building trades workers, centred on wages and control of the labour process.[15] Starting as a demand by carpenters for a fifty-cent per day wage increase, the dispute quickly escalated into what union leader J.W. Wilkinson characterized as a fight over the 'broad principle of closed shop versus open shop, capital arrayed against labor.'[16] The Master Builders' Association, representing large construction companies that were growing at the expense of small carpenter-contractors, took the occasion of the carpenters' request to declare itself in favour of the open shop. Over the following five weeks building labourers and electricians also struck against the open shop and for wage increases, and on 5 June the individual strikes broadened into a general withdrawal of labour by construction workers, including many non-unionists.

Both sides had prepared for a showdown. In 1909 the Building Trades Council, a general body of construction unions, had reorganized 'with ten of thirteen eligible unions as members.' It then reintroduced a working card system that James Conley describes as 'in effect and intention a union shop in the building trades, in which no tradesman would work on a construction site where any other building trades worker was not a union member in good standing.' On the other side, owners and managers revitalized the Vancouver Employers' Association, which had experienced declining membership since 1904. The 'escalation of the employers' tactics from reactive to active' was encouraged by an open-shop movement in the United States that included, in February 1911, a conference of Pacific coast employers at Portland, Oregon. Representatives from the Vancouver Employers' Association attended. A campaign to increase membership, with 'control of the workshop ... presented as the key issue,' followed. So too did aggressive resistance to the striking construction workers. Aided by a labour market glutted with building trades workers, the employers prevailed. Stronger unions were able to preserve closed-shop agreements with some contractors; the weaker trades were not. The carpenters agreed to an hourly wage of $4.25 per day, thus returning to the level they had achieved in 1907.[17]

Yet despite the best efforts of leading employers, Vancouver's trade union movement flourished during the prewar boom. In 1911 the Canadian Department of Labour reported that more than 7,000 Vancouver workers, about 22 per cent of the city's wage earners, belonged to a trade union. Some women, such as tailors, joined mixed unions while others formed gender-specific organizations for waitresses (1910), garment workers (1913), and home and domestic employees (1913). Lower-status workers found a new champion in 1907 when the Industrial Workers of the World (IWW), a union intent on fundamental change through direct confrontation with capital, began to organize unskilled labourers and immigrants who remained outside the labour movement's mainstream. Its lumber handlers and longshoremen's union, which embraced eighteen different nationalities, was 'the first IWW local to conduct a strike in western Canada.' In July 1910 unorganized Italian and English road construction labourers sported IWW buttons as they moved about city streets protesting a wage cut. Still, the vast majority of unionized workers were male, skilled, and of British heritage.[18]

The growing separation of capital from labour in turn of the century Vancouver found political as well as economic expression. For working people this expression took two forms, one at the civic level, another at the provincial. On City Council working-class attitudes and values were expressed forcefully by four aldermen who, elected for a total of sixteen years from 1903 to 1911, worked together as an identifiable pro-labour clique. Although drawing on the philosophical traditions of producerism they spoke in a language much more class specific than that of reformers a decade earlier. In this sense, producerism lived on in civic political discourse, though in a truncated form as the expression of artisanal traditions and values. Producerism had evolved into labourism.[19]

Sitting for wards distinguished by upper working- and lower middle-class voters, the four aldermen – John MacMillan, a builder; John Morton, a carpenter and contractor; Robert Macpherson, a carpenter; and Francis Williams, a tailor – provided an oppositional minority to Council's business-oriented majority.[20] They continued to draw upon the cultural traditions of skilled artisans by demanding 'just' employment practices and 'fair' compensation for workers. These values translated into strong political support for the idea that civic government should hire its labourers directly rather than through private contractors and that hours of work for civic employees should be reduced to eight hours per day.[21]

Labourists of the 1900s, like their predecessors in the 1890s, also continued to fight for the control of civic institutions by elected members.[22] Economic privilege remained as unacceptable as political inequality, and concentrations of economic power, such as private control of the ferry to North Vancouver, were strongly opposed. Such attitudes led R.H. Sperling, general manager of BC Electric, to portray MacMillan as a man who 'will give the company as much trouble as possible,' and Morton, sitting for the Mount Pleasant area where the 'labour vote' was strong, as a 'consistent enemy of the Company.'[23] Supported by many local businessmen, labour aldermen also led the fight against alienation to private lumber companies of street ends and water lots on False Creek, rights that companies acquired through connections with the granting government in Ottawa.[24] The same egalitarian impulse led labourists to fight the elitist assumptions of progressive reformers. Labourists opposed, unsuccessfully, the transfer of management of the Vancouver General Hospital from City Council to a board of appointed business and professional social leaders. They also articulated ideas about recreational space that challenged the growing popularity in prewar Vancouver of controlled playgrounds and uplifting landscapes. From the early 1890s to 1913, the Vancouver Trades and Labor Council consistently advocated, instead, the need for recreational space that was free and readily available to all.[25]

More dramatic, though less broadly based, was the emergence of a socialist movement that aimed to destroy capitalism rather than to reform it. Socialist candidates first challenged the right of labour reformers to speak for working people in the provincial election of 1900, and an articulate and aggressive cadre of socialist leaders dominated many working-class institutions in the following decade. They edited the *Western Clarion* from 1901, the *Western Wage-Earner* from 1909 to 1910, and the *British Columbia Federationist* thereafter. They presented the only distinctly 'leftist' candidates in regional and federal elections, and garnered from 10 to 13 per cent of the Vancouver vote in provincial elections between 1903 and 1912. Candidates labelling themselves the representatives of 'labour' took 15 per cent of the vote in 1903 but thereafter virtually abandoned the provincial field in Vancouver to the socialists. The labourist voice, and the values of producerism that echoed from it, remained to be heard in City Council. Because socialists wanted to overthrow the capitalist system, they looked to the senior levels of government where the productive system was managed. They saw civic issues as unimportant. Labour reformers, on the other hand, accepted capitalism if the power of big capital could be controlled.

The Vancouver Trades and Labor Council provided a particularly important forum for socialists. James McVety and Parm Pettipiece dominated the VTLC from 1905 to the war, while Jack Kavanagh and Victor Midgley played supporting roles. Socialists on the Council also promoted industrial unionism, thus challenging the conservative philosophy of 'business unionism' that dominated the national labour movements in Canada and the United States. Socialists led the VTLC out of the Trades and Labour Congress of Canada in 1903 and sponsored the Vancouver resolution that set off the second BC campaign for industrial unionism before the First World War.[26]

Socialist influence in public affairs reminded Vancouverites that their city had changed profoundly over the course of a decade. In 1910, middle-class citizens responded to growing economic and political tensions by establishing a branch of the Industrial Peace Association, a San Francisco-based organization that aimed to 'bring about a more harmonious relationship between masters and men.' The branch consisted principally of merchants and clergymen, the economic and moral leaders of Vancouver's increasingly self-conscious middle class. The Association's executive proposed a settlement for the 1911 general strike and found support from employers but not from workers. Pronouncements against unions and socialists by P.H. Scullin, 'father' of the industrial peace movement along the Pacific coast, suggest why labour rejected such mediation efforts: the Industrial Peace Association was more an agent of class interests than a neutral umpire in the game of labour relations.[27]

Trade unions were not part of the lives of small business people, shopkeepers, commercial travellers, school teachers, and most sales persons and office clerks. Rather, the growing size and assertiveness of the trade union movement served to heighten class differences between wage earners on the one hand and salaried workers and small proprietors on the other. This sense of difference ignited George Bartley's sarcastic comment, noted in Chapter 4, that in turn of the century Vancouver clerks identified with their business superiors rather than with their working-class equals. Joining an occupational organization has been described as 'a defining as well as an identifying act' in late nineteenth-century America,[28] and must have been so for the 'large number of clerks' who met on 1 June 1899 to form a clerks' association in Vancouver. Coming two months after another group had organized the city's first union of retail clerks, the timing provides a revealing glimpse of how social change forced white-collar workers to locate their place in an increasingly class conscious society. The contradictory response of clerks contrasted with the unambiguous identity of merchants. When faced with a growing labour movement and the emergence of socialist groups that questioned the fundamental tenets of private ownership, merchants and shopkeepers associated unreservedly with other employers. The Vancouver Merchants' Association, formed in July of 1900, included both externally controlled and locally based retail firms.[29]

The segmentation of Vancouver's producers' community into distinctive occupational groups can be observed with particular clarity in the realm of civic boosterism. Initially, locally based entrepreneurs saw themselves as part of a broadly based coalition. Thus, when in 1896 a group of businessmen met under the direction of real estate entrepreneur C.D. Rand to promote Vancouver's economic development, trade union representatives participated. Rather than be exclusive, the new association aimed to unite different elements of the city's middling stratum including local merchants, manufacturers, professional men, mechanics, labourers, and 'citizens', for the purpose of fostering trade, promoting settlement, gaining more favourable freight rates, and encouraging the establishment of industries. The groups identified came mainly from the working and middle rather than upper classes. They represented a wider social base than the Board of Trade, which promoted the interests of Vancouver's largest, and upper-class, business enterprises.[30]

After 1900 city boosters continued to establish organizations separate from the Board of Trade but these associations now typically excluded working people. Representatives from the real estate, non-banking financial, newspaper, hotel, and service sectors figured prominently. From 1902 to 1913 the Vancouver Tourist Association, organized to promote tourism and the commercial and industrial growth of the city, displaced the Board of Trade as Vancouver's leading booster organization. Other groups such as the Hundred Thousand Club and the Vancouver Ad Club emerged from the same social stratum for similar purposes. The founders and builders of the Vancouver Exhibition, inaugurated in August 1910 at Hastings Park on the city's east side, were mainly small real estate company entrepreneurs and newspapermen. Many other specialized business organizations also emerged, among them associations of lumber and shingle manufacturers. None articulated a sense of community that included the working class.[31]

VANCOUVER HAD EMERGED from the nineteenth century a more class-conscious city. Yet although the foregoing discussion indicates that economic change heightened class identities, a somewhat different sense of relationships emerges if we move away from the subject of work to explore other aspects of people's lives. This approach reveals a more complex pattern of identities among ordinary people, one in which social boundaries are structured simultaneously by class *and* status. Family status, neighbourhoods, fraternal societies, and ethnicity all linked the city's 'artisan or moderately well-to-do' residents in ways that crossed class lines.

From its inception, settlement on Burrard Inlet included large numbers of men living apart from families and without roots in the community. In the lumber villages of Moodyville and Granville, being part of a family – and being White – was an important requirement for access to the inner circles of power that centred around the mill managers. Arrival of the CPR and rapid urbanization not only brought large numbers of transient men to the Inlet but also expanded the number of families. The transformation of Burrard Inlet society that accompanied urbanization led middling-status families to distance themselves from the 'rough' world of loggers and sojourning labourers, almost all of whom were either unmarried or living apart from their families.

This process of defining family status as normal and men without families as outsiders is really the subtext of a debate in the late 1890s over the issue of whether the city should license for the waterfront area a music hall that sold liquor. Proposed in 1896, the music hall venture generated intense discussion for more than two years between social and business leaders on the one hand and the defenders of moral purity, drawn mainly from the middle class, on the other. At the centre of the debate was the issue of whether Vancouver would cater to the needs of the 'travelling miner and artisan,' and the loggers who had always been so much a part of settlement society on Burrard Inlet, or protect the values of family and clean living. Influential supporters of the music hall bristled at the 'gloomy fanaticism' of the moralists and argued that 'people who had been out in the woods all the year did not want to go to the Free Library and church all the time.' But music hall opponents carried the day, rejecting the idea in a plebiscite of March 1898. The proposal was repudiated most forcefully in the working- and middle-class east and southeast areas of the city, somewhat less so in the business, waterfront, and westside wards. Opponents triumphed again, after a brief debate, in July 1901.[32] In the following decade the social practices of transient men in Gastown remained an issue of periodic concern to moralists, particularly after such 'nuisances' as shooting galleries, slot machines, and moving picture houses appeared in the area.[33]

Led by Protestant church leaders – especially Presbyterians and Methodists – and moral reform organizations, this process of equating respectability with pietistic values and family organization could be seen as the vehicle through which the middle class asserted its class identity. Furthermore, working people played little part in the music hall debate, and what evidence we have of working-class opinion indicates support for the proposal. Rejection of the music hall appears to have been primarily a middle-class thrust.

Yet moral questions did not always divide society so clearly by class. George Bartley, editor of the labour newspaper the *Independent,* found disgraceful the inordinate attention given by local politicians in turn of the century Vancouver to moral rather than to labour issues. He conceded, however, that working people were 'divided on the liquor question just as they are on religion.' One labour activist of the period, Francis Williams, knew exactly where he stood on moral issues: as an enthusiastic Methodist known for singing and preaching to Native people from the False Creek shoreline of the Kitsilano Reserve, or Snauq, Williams was a strong supporter of moral restraint. Other labour leaders took a less moralistic stance against liquor, arguing in one instance that Gastown's 'skidway saloons and home-brew dynamite' retarded the ability of loggers to organize.[34]

The view that normal society centred on the family, and that to be outside of a family was to be on the other side of an important conceptual boundary, provided an obvious source of cohesion among respectable members of Vancouver's lower middle and upper working classes. Dr. W.J. McGuigan, a Roman Catholic physician who had arrived on Burrard Inlet before the railway but had never become part of the city's elite, articulated the middle-class perception of this boundary in a City Council debate over the early closing of saloons. Clearly separating the status of married men from single, he argued that on the basis of seventeen years' experience he 'did not think that there were many married men who visited the saloon after 6 P.M. ... Those that usually visited the bars at night were of the floating population, and with them it was not always a question of drinking ... They had no [other] place to go.' Similar assumptions about the normative status of the family animated the thoughts of J.W. Wilkinson in testimony presented to British Columbia's Commission on Labour in March 1913. Trained as a carpenter but now an executive member of the Vancouver Trades and Labor Council, Wilkinson portrayed 'the essential unit of the community' as a 'man who is living here and married and has interests here. He is the man on whose activity the well-being of the community is established.'[35]

These two observations start with the assumption that social organization is defined by the family status of men. This view is hardly surprising, given our understanding of the patriarchal, or male-controlled, nature of

Canadian society during the industrial era. In addition, men were expected to be family breadwinners and thus to have economic interests, such as jobs or property. Less commonplace is the association of 'community' with marriage, family, and rootedness. Wilkinson in particular appears to have been defining Vancouver's floating population of male sojourners and seasonal workers as antithetical to the community's well-being and thus threatening to the social order. He was drawing here a social boundary that is better understood in terms of status than of class, with his 'essential units' being families of both the working and middle classes.

The gendered nature of Wilkinson's portrayal of Vancouver society – it was the man's activities that determined the well-being of the community as a whole – leaves understood but unstated the fact that women, like men, threatened social norms if found outside the family. Here again, assumptions crossed class boundaries, for it was in the home that family men, whether of the upper, middle, or working classes, expected women to be. Some women laboured for wages before marriage to sustain themselves while single, and some worked afterwards due to the loss of male support. Others had no choice but to supplement a husband's meagre income. But the family ideal remained the same across the class divide: a husband earning sufficient income to provide a decent living for the whole family, thus fulfilling his manly duty of being the breadwinner; and a wife working at home to nurture and care for the children, and make the best use of her husband's wage.[36] In addition to accepting this division of roles between the public and private spheres, women were to conduct themselves with the humility and decorum expected of 'true womanhood.' Women who moved outside their expected place in public threatened the proper functioning of society and hence moral order. Thus, just as the Women's Christian Temperance Union expressed middle-class concern about the portrayal in cigar store windows of women partially dressed in men's attire – 'from the sight of which a right-minded person of either sex will instinctively recoil' – so did members of the Journeymen Barbers' Union make clear to the BC Commission on Labour that working around 'some of the dirty old bums' one found in barber shops was not appropriate for women. Apart from an obvious desire to protect their jobs in a trade already threatened by cheap 'coloured' labour, two barbers expressed a widely perceived concern that working in a masculine environment outside the home would have a 'bad moral effect' upon women. As one of them commented rhetorically to the male commissioners: 'I don't think you would choose a lady barber for a wife.'[37] Sometimes the threat posed by women who were 'out of their place' cut to the heart of patriarchal power, itself an important source of cohesion among respectable elements of Vancouver society. The response of Frank Woodside, the former Kootenay miner and union leader now serving as an eastside Vancouver broker and alderman, to suggestions that women be appointed as public officials within the civic adminstration is instructive. Many men already 'were at home rocking the cradle and washing the dishes, while the wives were employed outside at a salary,' he asserted; such activity should not be encouraged.[38]

Because prostitutes dramatically flouted sexual propriety, public response to prostitution reveals much about community standards of respectable behaviour. Prostitution had been part of settlement society on Burrard Inlet since industrial labour first entered the area, and the continued sexual imbalance of Vancouver's population – in 1911 three males for every two females among the population as a whole, with an even greater imbalance among adults – provided a continuing demand for the sexual services of women. The obvious link between the surplus of unattached men and prostitution was illustrated during the prewar boom, when Vancouver was flooded with working-age men looking for jobs. One irate observer recounted seeing 'a swarm of men going [to] the houses on Shore Street as if to a baseball match ... At one time there were as many as fifty men standing in the lane.' So brisk was business that additional women had to be sent for.[39]

As in many North American cities of the period, civic authorities in Vancouver responded to prostitution by tolerating it despite periodic outbursts of fervour by church-centred moralists, who urged that it be stamped out. But it was countenanced only when located in socially marginal areas of the city: first in Chinatown, then on Shore Street, two blocks further south, and finally for a year or so on Alexander Street, near the waterfront (Map 7.1). Dominated by Asians, non-British Europeans, and single men, these districts stood apart from the homes of White families of British origin.

When, in 1906, prostitutes began moving to Park Lane, near the homes of respectable working people, area residents, moral crusaders, and property owners' associations responded angrily to what they saw as an 'outrageous [threat] to public decency.'[40] American historian Neil Shumsky suggests why. Red light districts 'clearly demonstrated the difference between acceptable and unacceptable behavior and thereby set boundaries for respectability.'[41] They also served to control individuals who refused to keep sexual activity within the family and the home. Though Shumsky emphasizes the middle-class character of this ideology, his argument is consistent with evidence indicating that Vancouver's family-centred working class was equally concerned to differentiate itself from the city's rougher elements. In 1913, under pressure from moral reformers, Vancouver police stopped tolerating segregated districts and closed the brothels. They succeeded only in dispersing the prostitutes.

The neighbourhoods that respectable families wanted to keep free of prostitutes and their customers consisted of detached dwellings with surrounding grounds. While underestimating tenancy and exaggerating ownership, geographer Deryck Holdsworth has convincingly argued that relatively low land costs and cheap building materials made single-family dwellings the city's dominant housing form in the early years of the century. Jill Wade has shown that, in 1921, 'single houses made up 88.7 percent of Vancouver's 21,489 dwellings,' a proportion lower than it would have been had the southern municipalities of South Vancouver and Point Grey, 'where detached houses predominated,' been included in the study. Vancouver was indeed, as Holdsworth describes it, an 'emphatically suburban' city.[42]

Among those who were able to fulfil their deep-seated desire to live in a single-family cottage surrounded by gardens for fruit, vegetables, and poultry was the Jesse Enefer family. As recounted by Holdsworth, Enefer, a labourer, arrived in Vancouver in 1908 and lived first in rooms near the waterfront while working for the McDonald Marpole Coal Company. City directories indicate that in 1910, now working for a plumbing contractor digging pipelines, he and his family fulfilled their dream of owning a suburban house by moving a distance of 3.5 miles to East 48th Avenue in South Vancouver, a separate municipality to the southeast of the city. Three years later they moved again, this time eleven blocks further south to a house in the Grimmett area at the bottom of Main Street. Five other house-owning members of the Enefer family, all of them labourers, lived in the same neighbourhood. Vancouver was small enough that wage earners could reach work in the heart of the city from the suburbs by foot and

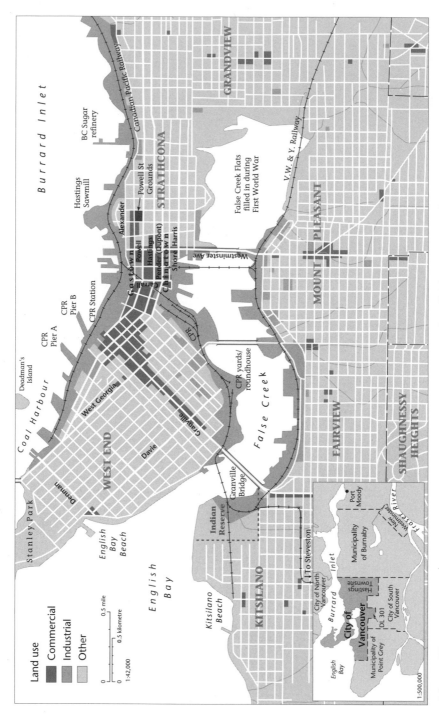

Land use

Commercial

Industrial

Other

1:42,000

0   0.5 kilometre

0   0.5 mile

Burrard   Inlet

BC Sugar
refinery

Canadian Pacific Railway

Hastings
Sawmill

Coal Harbour

Deadman's
Island

CPR
Pier A

CPR
Pier B

CPR Station

CPR

Stanley Park

WEST END

West Georgia

Denman

Davie

Granville

*English
Bay
Beach*

*English
Bay*

Kitsilano Beach

KITSILANO

Indian
Reserve

Granville
Bridge

To Steveston

False Creek

CPR yards/
roundhouse

Alexander

Powell

Hastings

Pender (DuPont)

Cordova

Carrall

Shore Harris

Gastown

Chinatown

Powell St
Grounds

STRATHCONA

False Creek Flats
filled in during
First World War

Westminster Ave.

V.W. & Y. Railway

GRANDVIEW

MOUNT PLEASANT

FAIRVIEW

SHAUGHNESSY
HEIGHTS

1:500,000

Burrard   Inlet

Port
Moody

Municipality of Burnaby

Hastings Townsite

New Westminster

City of North
Vancouver

City of
Vancouver

City of South
Vancouver

DL 301

Municipality of
Point Grey

*English
Bay*

Fraser River

Map 7.1 Vancouver, 1910s

Source: Compiled from CVA map collection, Maps 204 and 561, and from Bruce
Macdonald, *Vancouver: A Visual History* (Vancouver: Talonbooks 1992), 34–5.

streetcar in thirty minutes, an important factor in making single-family housing accessible to working people.[43]

In this low-density environment, respectable working- and middle-class families lived together in mixed neighbourhoods to the south and east of the downtown core. Contemporary and historical commentators portray Fairview Heights, Mount Pleasant, Grandview, and South Vancouver as neighbourhoods of middling status. Variations occurred among them, with the east tending to be more working class and the west more middle and upper class.[44] South Vancouver accommodated labourers and carpenters, dairy farmers, and builders but is most accurately described as home of the 'industrial classes.' The expanding westside neighbourhood of Kitsilano was more uniformly white collar.

Housing styles reflected these nuances, eastside dwellings tending to be of 'an unpretentious though useful type,' while Kitsilano featured the California bungalow. Noted for its 'broad verandahs, decorative brick porch supports, exposed rafters and shingled siding,' the California bunga-low appealed to wealthier families of middling status.[45] Yet despite differences, these neighbourhoods all featured some measure of mixing across class boundaries. As well, the suburban cabin, the California bunga-low, and the upper-class mansion all 'presented tangible signs of success in the general struggle for security and competence' in Vancouver; in doing so they helped to sustain what Graeme Wynn has called a 'loose partner-ship between the city's rich and powerful elite and its larger, less-favoured population.'[46]

The cottages and bungalows of South Vancouver, Grandview, and Mount Pleasant differed fundamentally, however, from the lodging houses, cheap hotels, shacks, and aging houses of Vancouver's original business and residential core. Here, geographic concentration accentuated the marginalization of transients, non-British 'foreigners,' the elderly, and the poor. In the words of the 1913 report of the Methodist and Presbyterian churches, the lodging houses of the 'immigrant section of the city,' filled with 'homeless men,' were "'not to be compared" with the homes of other working people.'[47]

Men who lived with their families in respectable neighbourhoods also mixed socially in fraternal lodges. Emerging in eighteenth-century Europe, fraternalism represented an attack on the hierarchical ordering of society. Through a complex series of rituals, lodges idealized the artisan as a social metaphor for brotherhood and social equality. The Masonic order put great stress on the meaning of ritual, and quasi-Masonic benevolent societies emphasized sociability and mutual benefit provisions such as insurance for ill health and death.[48] All functioned in secret to give members a sense of belonging, of being part of an 'extended family.' As American historian Mary Ann Clawson has argued, by idealizing the status of the craftsman they also articulated in a social setting the values of producerism, the leather apron worn by Masons, for instance, 'symbolizing the moral worth of economically productive activity, including manual labor.' Fraternalism 'idealized cross-class relationships,' denying class difference among the self-employed, clerks, artisans, and respectable workingmen and offering instead 'gender and race as the most logical and legitimate categories for the organization of collective identity.'[49]

Fraternalism thrived in Vancouver. *Henderson's Greater Vancouver, New Westminster and Fraser Valley Directory 1911* lists sixty-four male and four female lodges in the city, plus an additional twelve ethnic associations such as the Sons of England. Of the male lodges, eleven belonged to the Masonic Order; the remainder are best categorized as 'benevolent societies.' Among these were seventeen lodges of the Loyal Orange Lodge, eleven of the Independent Order of Odd Fellows, seven of the Foresters, and four of the Modern Woodmen of America. Determining their social makeup is more difficult. Biographical data on the social behaviour of Vancouver elites suggest that fraternalism was a much more important part of the associational lives of civic politicians, who were usually both *in* the middle class and *of* middling social status, than of Society leaders, who almost never entered local politics. Seventeen per cent of the male heads of Society families belonged to a fraternal lodge compared to 65 per cent of aldermen and mayors. More significantly, fraternal lodge affiliations represented only 5 per cent of the voluntary associations to which Society men and women belonged but more than 40 per cent for local politicians. By the early 1900s the club and the fraternal lodge had come to symbolize distinctive patterns of sociability among the top and middle strata of Vancouver society.[50]

The occupational status of three groups of lodge members in and around Vancouver supports the contention that fraternalism brought together in a social manner respectable men – and a few women – of both the middle and upper working classes. As indicated in Table 7.1, members of the Mount Hermon Masonic Lodge, the Orange Lodge, and the Knights of Pythias Lodge worked in roughly equal measure in white- and blue-collar occupations. The greatest difference was the three-to-two majority within the Knights of Pythias of clerks, managers, and small entrepreneurs over plumbers, carpenters, BC Electric employees, and other respectable workingmen. Such evidence is spotty and may not typify fraternalism in Vancouver as a whole. Some lodges may in fact have reinforced rather than softened class lines, as Bryan Palmer and Gregory Kealey have suggested for working-class fraternalism among skilled artisans in late nineteenth-century Toronto and Hamilton. One such example in Vancouver occurred at the top of the social spectrum, when in 1888 prominent businessmen formed the Cascade Lodge as an alternative to the more plebian Mount Hermon Lodge, active on Burrard Inlet for fifteen years.[51] Nonetheless, evidence presented in Table 7.1 bolsters recent work by American scholars who portray fraternal societies as linking men of middling status. John Gilkeson has observed that in nineteenth-century America 'gentlemen opted for more exclusive clubs' while 'the self-employed commonly

Table 7.1

Occupational status of fraternal lodge members in Vancouver and New Westminster (by percentage of known cases)

	White collar (%)	Blue collar (%)	Number known	Number unknown
Mount Hermon Masonic Lodge (Vancouver and Moodyville), new members, 1895-6	45.0	55.0	20	3
Orange Lodge (Vancouver), members at special meeting, August 1902	55.5	44.4	63	19
Knights of Pythias Lodge #6 (New Westminster), members, 1914	61.3	38.7	62	18

Note: The Mount Hermon Lodge belonged to the Masonic Order; the Orange Lodge and Knights of Pythias did not. Fraternal society records for Vancouver are fragmentary. The Mount Hermon Lodge records for the post-1886 period list members who joined during a one-year period only. The Orangemen studied here were identified from a published list of Vancouver Orange Lodge members who gathered for a special dinner given in honour of the Orange Lodge provincial secretary of Manitoba. The Knights of Pythias Lodge #6 was a branch from New Westminster, Vancouver's neighbour. Fourteen Knights of Pythias members from outside the Lower Mainland are excluded from the table; seventy-six from New Westminster and four from Vancouver are included.

Sources: Mount Hermon Lodge, Annual Return to the Grand Lodge of British Columbia, 28 April 1896, BCARS, Add. MSS 002, Freemasons Records, box 4, folder 3; *Vancouver Daily Province,* 13 August 1902, p. 2; and Knights of Pythias, Royal Lodge no. 6, *25th Anniversary of Royal Lodge, No. 6, Knights of Pythias, Roll Call, 8 June 1914,* CVA, Pamphlet 14-1.

socialized with wage earners in lodges of all orders.' The same appears to have been the case in early twentieth-century Vancouver.[52]

Religion and ethnicity also profoundly influenced the structuring of identities. A flood of English-speaking migrants to the south side of Burrard Inlet in the mid-1880s had firmly established British institutions and British values as Vancouver's cultural norm. More than 80 per cent of this predominantly anglophone population in 1911 was Protestant, with only 10 per cent Roman Catholic and approximately 6 per cent of Asian religious affiliations. Whereas in eastern North American cities religious affiliation often reinforced class and ethnic identities, especially where large numbers of workers were 'immigrant' and Catholic and the middle and upper classes were native born and Protestant,[53] in Vancouver no such Catholic-Protestant dichotomy separated the working from the middle class. Rather, more subtle differences within the anglophone majority reinforced status divisions between the more predominantly Anglican upper stratum and the more Methodist and Presbyterian middling stratum. Religion most fundamentally divided Vancouver residents at the bottom of the status hierarchy – within the working class – by separating the respectable and Protestant majority from Roman Catholic Italian labourers and non-Christian Asians.

For the most part born in Britain, Canada, the United States, or outlying parts of the empire to parents of British origin, Vancouver's respectable majority also shared the political, social, and economic privileges that came with being Anglo-Canadian. The rest of the population was constituted of outsiders. The rights of citizenship were, of course, distributed unequally between the sexes, women in a dependent role and men enjoying the full rights and benefits of enfranchisement. A substantial number of the British majority were also disenfranchised by their occupational mobility and lack of roots within the community. Loggers are an obvious example. In addition, ethnocentrism divided people along racial and ethnic lines that did not correspond exactly with the boundary of respectability. Again, single men of British birth or heritage would have felt a sense of cultural legitimacy in relationship to ethnic minorities such as the Italians or Chinese while still being denied, for social reasons, full entitlement to the status of respectable citizens. Nonetheless, with the exception of a limited number of northern Europeans, who were easily accepted by the dominant group, ethnicity separated the majority of Vancouverites, who were of British origin, from the minority, who were not. Respectable workers might disagree with businessmen about the relative power of labour and capital in the workplace but as British subjects they shared with them the feeling that they were entitled to participate fully in the construction of society and its institutions. Ethnic identity, then, must be seen as another bond that linked respectable people across class lines.[54]

The social survey report of 1913 used language that divided the upper- from middle-status groups in material terms, and defined the 'business and professional class' as 'wealthy' and artisans or people of similar status as 'moderately well-to-do.' Making these impressionistic categorizations more concrete is difficult, especially for the second group, whose members had lower individual profiles within the city than business and social leaders and whose wealth at death is thus more difficult to trace.

Nevertheless, the probate records of nine labour leaders whose occupational, residential, and associational characteristics correspond to the portrait of middling-status people presented above offer a general though highly tentative profile of the material foundation of respectability.[55] Eight took a leading role in the Vancouver Trades and Labor Council up to 1901 but only one thereafter. All were skilled or semi-skilled workers while active in the trade union movement, and all were White men of British heritage. They had families in Vancouver (eight of nine are known to have been married), lived in houses in respectable neighbourhoods (especially along the slopes to the south of False Creek), and participated actively in fraternal societies. Four of the nine later moved out of the working class to become businessmen, suggesting that, as a group, they straddled the boundary between Vancouver's lower middle class and upper working class.[56]

Not surprisingly, they left much less wealth at death than Vancouver's business or social leaders. With estates averaging just over $13,000, their net wealth at death was one-twentieth that of top businessmen (see Chapter 6, Table 6.1). Indeed, if we look at the median value of estates among the nine – thus discounting the estate of almost $60,000 accumulated by the carpenter turned office and store fixtures manufacturer Joseph Dixon – the figure drops to $7,158.40. Household goods and furniture are listed in only two of the probates; the amounts were modest, equalling $500 for the skilled cigar maker and then cigar manufacturer John Crow, and $150 for the bricklayer and poultry farmer William Towler. Almost as

This family's enthusiasm for the coronation of George V, 1911, illustrates the importance of British values and institutions to the identity of Vancouverites. The crowded site of the house suggests that the family were of middling social status, and probably members of the lower middle class. (P. Timms photo, Vancouver Public Library 7577)

valuable as furniture in Towler's estate was a collection of stuffed birds, which he willed to the city museum. Unlike members of the upper stratum, this group of nine kept their wealth mainly in real estate. They did not actively invest in company stocks or bonds but did own real property; six of the nine held more than one building lot. Real estate constituted an average of 87 per cent of the net value of their estates.

For William George, a shoemaker and trade union leader of the early 1890s who went on to serve for seventeen years as a city construction foreman, property was not only a speculative investment – he owned several lots – but the foundation of a valued home life. With a solid income from a respectable job, George was able in 1902 to buy a piece of property in Burnaby where he built 'a beautiful home' and pursued his passion for gardening. He did not invest in capitalist ventures, join prestigious clubs, enter his name in the *Social Register*, or engage in the conspicuous consumption of leisure. Like other members of the group, he lacked the means to do so. He probably also lacked the desire.[57]

THE FOREGOING DISCUSSION of identities among Vancouver's working and middle classes only begins to draw out the larger meaning of the early political careers of L.D. Taylor and H.H. Stevens, detailed at the outset of this chapter. Many aspects of the relationship between the two politicians and their electorate remain to be explored in greater detail, especially those concerning race and religion. But the general importance of these political stories to our understanding of how social boundaries emerged in early Vancouver is clear enough: the city's 'plain people' shared a lifestyle and outlook that melded them into a distinctive social stratum that coexisted with overlapping relationships based on class. Since the 1890s class identities had sharpened in Vancouver, a fact reflected in the prewar history of labour conflict and leftist politics and in the class symbolism and rhetoric employed by Taylor. Even so, a variety of influences served to integrate respectable citizens across class lines. Connections of family, neighbourhood, associational life, and ethnicity, as well as a shared antipathy to elites at one end of the social spectrum and to the floating and 'immigrant' population at the other, linked people of respectable but middling status in practical ways that softened, and at times made unimportant, the contradictions inherent in capitalism. Vancouver's middling stratum provided the foundation upon which Taylor and Stevens built their political careers, and the policies and outlook of the two men represented both the commonalities and the contradictions of the status group. In other words, identities within Vancouver's 'artisan or moderately well-to-do' stratum were complex, and the social boundary of class should not be accepted uncritically as a 'master category' for analyzing their lives.

CHAPTER EIGHT

The Immigrant Section

I n a recent study of racial discourse in British Columbia, Kay Anderson argues that identities are the product of both self-definition and classifications ascribed from without: 'Whereas the former are predicated on subjective or inclusive processes ... the latter are based on processes of exclusion.'[1] The role of exclusion is especially important to an understanding of the third, or lowest, stratum of Vancouver's status hierarchy. Constituted of residents who for reasons of racial identity or ethnicity were considered 'foreign,' who worked at the lowest-status jobs, who lived in a masculine environment of multiple-unit dwellings in the oldest parts of the inner city, or who were poor, this third stratum, which the social survey report of 1913 labelled 'the immigrant section,' formed a single entity only from the perspective of the majority. By according low status to ethnic minorities, seasonal labourers, and the poor, members of both the 'wealthy business and professional class' and the 'artisan or moderately well-to-do class' sought to secure their own identities as respectable citizens.

Race and ethnicity served as the most significant sources of status differentiation. Anderson argues persuasively that in the late nineteenth century, race functioned as 'an influential language with which to cement the collective sense of an in-group.'[2] In this capacity it served to establish the dominance of British cultural values and institutions and to marginalize people of colour such as the Chinese, Japanese, Sikhs, and Natives. But racial categorizations were also used to define southern Europeans – whose skin colour was white – as 'non-White.' In other words, racial concepts were socially constructed rather than biologically based, a characteristic that facilitated their function as an instrument of status. 'Race' is employed in this sense throughout the following chapter.

Members of the upper- and middling-status groups did not differentiate themselves from the city's lower stratum in racial terms alone. Family status also mattered a great deal. Single men lacked roots in the city and thus stood apart from the family-centred 'in group' that set behavioural norms. Poverty reinforced race, ethnicity, and family status as sources of marginalization, with many of Vancouver's poor also being 'foreign' men who lived in the city without family. The following chapter explores the process by which the majority of Vancouverites came to stigmatize ethnic and racial minorities, single men, and the poor as 'immigrants,' and thus as everything that they themselves were not.

WHEN THE CANADIAN CENSUS was taken in the spring of 1911, more than 85 per cent of all Vancouver residents claimed birth in Canada, Britain, European parts of the British empire, or the United States, with half of this group being Canadian. Residents born in Great Britain constituted the largest number of non-Canadians (30.6 per cent of the city's total population) and Americans the second largest (10.4 per cent). People who did not speak English or more generally claim British heritage were, in the language of the majority, 'immigrants' or 'foreigners.' Forming at census time only 12.4 per cent of city residents – though their numbers would have been higher in the wet months of winter when loggers, fishermen, millhands, and construction labourers converged on the city – 'foreigners' made up a surprisingly small proportion of Vancouver's population. In other words, prewar Vancouver appears to have been a relatively homogeneous city.[3]

In the construction of boundaries between Vancouver's 'in group' and 'outsiders,' however, ethnic minorities had an influence far beyond their numbers. The racial classification of being 'White' or 'non-White' exerted particular force in defining status. Racist attitudes by Whites of European background in British Columbia towards people of colour, especially Asians, have received considerable scholarly attention from historians and sociologists.[4] Of these studies, Anderson's argument that the socially constructed category of race provided a language through which Europeans of British heritage solidified their power over the 'new' settler society of British Columbia is persuasive. Drawing on the work of Edward Said and emphasizing the enduring nature of European discourse on 'Orientalism', Anderson suggests that Europeans had long expressed in various forms the sense that their culture was different from that of Eastern peoples. Expansion out of Europe increased economic contact between East and West and exaggerated the perception of difference between themselves (the civilized Christians) and others (the barbaric infidels). A new wave of expansion in the eighteenth century, the rise of a more aggressive form of European imperialism, and the growing application of scientific reasoning to social analysis in the nineteenth led to greater emphasis on 'race' as an expression of human differences. Migrating to the BC coast in the age of Charles Darwin and the 'White Man's Burden', English-speaking settlers brought with them the belief that their culture and their institutions were superior to all others. So pervasive was the 'race idea' among White migrants to British Columbia, says Anderson, that in testimony given to the Royal Commission on Chinese Immigration of 1884-5 almost every one of forty-eight witnesses 'traded freely in the language of racial types, racial instincts, and racial antipathy.'[5]

What Anderson adds to this familiar story is how settlers of British heritage used the ideology of race to secure their place as the dominant group in British Columbia. Brought to the coast as part of their cultural baggage, racial ideas became an instrument through which settlers secured their collective identity. Representing the interests of European settlers, provincial politicians used the racial idiom 'to concentrate into a "counter-idea" everything that was thought to be in conflict with the building of an ideal community.'[6] The ideals, of course, were British and included private holding of land, British law, the English language, and an enduring faith in the idea of progress. All levels of government passed discriminatory legislation that confirmed the difference between those who had the political and social rights of citizens and those who did not. For the Chinese this legislation included bills that restricted their right to vote in provincial elections and consequently to join the professions of pharmacy or law, to

Table 8.1

Select examples of birthplace of Vancouver's 'foreign' population, 1891-1911

| | Number | | | | | Percentage of total Vancouver population | | | |
	Chinese	Japanese	Italians	Scandinavians[a]	Total	Chinese	Japanese	Italians	Scandinavians[a]
1891	838	0	122	165	13,673	6.1	0	0.9	1.2
1901	1,800	1,010	101	379	27,010	6.7	3.7	0.4	1.4
1911	3,364	1,841	1,922	1,888	100,401	3.4	1.8	1.9	1.9

a Includes Swedes, Norwegians, Danes, and Finns.

Sources: Canada, Nominal Census 1891, District 2 (New Westminster), Subdistrict C1 (Vancouver City) and Norbert MacDonald, 'Population Growth and Change in Seattle and Vancouver, 1880-1960; *Pacific Historical Review* 39 (1970):310

acquire crown land, to work underground in coal mines, to be hired on public works projects, to hold a liquor licence, or to obtain a hand-logger's licence. In this region of recent settlement, racial identity provided a powerful instrument for the definition of status.[7]

In Vancouver the process of racial categorization focused especially on Asians, who were the largest and most visible non-British group. The Chinese established their presence early, continuing to settle in Vancouver after the riot of February 1887 and reaching 6.7 per cent of the city's population by 1901 (Table 8.1). A surge of Japanese immigration into British Columbia at the turn of the century created a solid Japanese presence as well, bringing Asians to more than 10 per cent of Vancouver's total population. Another large influx of Japanese workers in 1907 – more than 5,000 to the province in the first six months of the year – and, for the first time, immigrants from India, created tensions that led to an anti-Asian riot on 7-8 September in Chinatown and the Japanese quarter.[8] But migrants of European heritage, whether from eastern Canada, Britain, or the United States, also flocked to Vancouver. As a consequence, the city's Asian population dropped as a percentage of the whole, equalling about 6 per cent in 1911. Nonetheless, Asians remained Vancouver's most identifiable outsiders.

No group was more obviously 'foreign' to the majority than East Indian immigrants, almost all of whom were Sikh men of working age. Small in numbers, they nonetheless stimulated a large reaction from the city's cultural majority. Peter Ward has argued that popular conceptions of India depicted it as 'a land of teeming millions, of filth and squalor, of exotic, peculiar customs' whose people were 'a lesser breed of men.' The poverty, occupational roles, distinctive customs – including the wearing of highly visible turbans – and family status of Sikh immigrants strengthened racial stereotypes. Although 40 per cent of the first 5,000 East Indians to arrive in British Columbia between 1904 and 1908 were married, women and families stayed behind. The men came from the Punjab area of northern India intending to sell their labour for wages. They did this by gravitating to the arduous and rough work of handling lumber. The 684 Sikhs remaining in Vancouver at census time in 1911 were poor and lived in some of the city's oldest, most dilapidated buildings. The combination of racial perceptions, cultural distinctiveness, and degraded social conditions led health officials such as Robert Marrion to see 'Hindoos' as 'worse than the lowest class of Chinamen.' The desire of one faction in India to promote the violent overthrow of British rule reinforced Eurocentric attitudes about Sikhs. Racial tension culminated in one of the most dramatic confrontations in Vancouver's history, the *Komagata Maru* incident of 1914 in which '376 Indians (mostly Sikhs) on the steamer *Komagata Maru* were refused entry and sent back to the orient' after two months' detention in Vancouver harbour.[9]

The stereotypes through which the White majority viewed Asians have been examined by various authors, including Peter Ward and Patricia Roy. Four stand out. One stereotype is the perception at the time that hordes of Asian immigrants might inundate British Columbia and destroy its collective character as a land of White, European-based settlers. The second is an emphasis on the vastly different cultures and institutions of Asians, which, it was believed, insulated them from the influence of White society and made them unassimilable. The third is a focus on the willingness of Asians to work for less than what White workers considered a 'fair' wage, thus lowering the European community's standard of living. The fourth stereotype is the assertion that Asians, especially the Chinese and Sikhs, were 'unclean, diseased, and a threat to public health.' Overlooked were the facts that discriminatory legislation limited Asian immigration, that many Asians did not intend to stay in North America permanently and thus had no reason to want to assimilate, that European prejudice contributed to the segregation of Asians in discrete areas of the city, that Asians generally did not compete with Whites for employment but took the unskilled and rough jobs which, in a tight labour market, White workers avoided, and that the perception of unclean habits was contradicted by the reality of upper-income European families willingly accepting Chinese men into their homes as houseboys and cooks. The stereotypes, in other words, were irrational constructions, drawn from long-held images of the 'Oriental' but given new meaning by province-building European settlers in prewar British Columbia.[10]

The meaning of racial classifications is perhaps best examined in the context of the terms 'immigrant' and 'foreigner,' which conveyed a more general meaning than 'race.' Whereas 'race' usually implied distinctions of colour, 'immigrant' and 'foreigner' categorized both Asians and certain European groups as non-British, and consequently as outsiders. Thus, for instance, when moral reformers spoke of Vancouver's 'many foreigners

The *Komagata Maru* incident of 1914 illustrates dramatically the role that ethnocentrism played in separating Vancouver's cultural majority, who were mainly of British stock, from its minorities. The Sikhs in this photograph, who are dressed to go ashore, typify the people categorized by the majority as 'foreign' and 'immigrant.' (Leonard Frank photo, Vancouver Public Library 6231)

from [continental] Europe and the Orient,' they had in mind 'Greeks going around the streets on Sundays selling ice cream' and 'colonies of Italians, Greeks and other foreigners congregated in ... common-lodging houses,' as well as Chinese men trooping to gambling clubs in Chinatown. Families recently arrived from the British Isles, by contrast, were insiders, and were readily accepted as citizens.[11]

The term 'foreigner' became associated especially with Italians after Italian labourers – the vast majority of whom were men – flooded into the city during the prewar boom. For a short period in the summers of 1910 to 1913 Vancouver's Italian population, which had jumped from 100 to 1,900 in the decade after 1901 (Table 8.1), surged again to exceed 4,000, and perhaps 5,000. Italians had become very visible, and very threatening, to the city's British character. Italian stereotypes bore a close resemblance to those used to describe Chinese and other Asian workers. As seasonal workers who lived in crowded and unhealthy conditions Italians were said to threaten the public health of the city as a whole. In a classic application of ethnic stereotypes, a Dutch-born longshoreman told the BC Commission on Labour that 'Italians live on macaroni and the Russians on salt herring and bread ... That is impossible for us.' In other words, by underconsuming they could work for low wages and thus provide 'unfair competition' to respectable workers, just as Chinese sojourners were said to do.[12]

From this perspective, designations like 'foreigner' and 'Asian' conveyed meaning that transcended physical differences. 'Race' is a 'socially imagined rather than biological' reality that serves 'to designate collectivities' in a positive or negative manner. As theorist Robert Miles argues, when a dominant group ascribes biological characteristics to some other group it is necessarily defining itself by the same criterion, the opposites bound together with 'each giving meaning to the other in a totality of signification.' In this sense being White or non-White was not so much about colour as about status, with 'whiteness' the designation for insiders.[13] Thus, when an aldermanic candidate spoke in December 1911 of 'too many white men' remaining idle while 'Italians' worked, one of the city's few middle-class Italians correctly discerned that Italians were being classified 'as colored men.' Alderman Crowe used similar language in City Council a few months later.[14] The status-defining function of the term 'foreign' is suggested as well in a report of 1911 by Vancouver's Health and Plumbing Inspector, Robert Marrion, who associated 'foreign' not only

Labourers, George Street, South Vancouver, ca. 1914. In the early years of the century much construction work still depended upon hard, manual labour. Single men, often from non-English-speaking countries such as China and Italy, most often provided this unskilled labour. The crew of diggers photographed here may have been Italians, who because of their ethnicity and lifestyle were viewed by Vancouver's anglophone majority as 'foreigners.' (City of Vancouver Archives, ALBUM A-16 p. 19)

with non-White status but also with poverty. When arguing that over-crowding and unsanitary conditions were endemic 'among the foreign element,' Marrion identified as foreign some Asians (Chinese and Japanese), some Europeans (Italians), 'and the poor class of white people' in Vancouver.[15]

WHILE PROVIDING the most obvious source of outsider status in pre-war Vancouver, race and ethnicity also had a gendered quality. Many of Vancouver's 'foreigners' were working-age men, either married or single, who lived in the city for all or part of the year without families. As data for 1911 on the relationship between birthplace and sex reveal, the eight largest groups with the most unbalanced demographic structures – Greeks, Chinese, East Indians, Italians, Japanese, Austro-Hungarians, Scandinavians, and Russians – were 'immigrants' (see Table 8.2). But not all unattached men were culturally 'foreign,' as the gap between the total population of British-born males and females in the city – 19,281 versus 11,408 – indicates. The categories of race or ethnicity and masculinity overlapped but were not synonymous. While tending to reinforce one another as sources of marginalization, they functioned independently to place thousands of single men outside the realm of respectable men and women living in families.

Sociologists have argued that British Columbia's labour market was segmented by race, certain categories of semi- and unskilled work being designated for Asians at half to two-thirds the rates paid to Whites for similar employment.[16] By 1914, British Columbia's workforce included 19,000 Chinese, 8,000 Japanese, and 2,000 East Indian workers, the majority of whom laboured at low-status and often seasonal jobs. Forest industry mills in particular required large amounts of rough labour and looked increasingly to Asians to provide it. In 1901 'Japanese formed 25 per cent and Chinese 12 per cent of the total workforce in the principal lumber mills of the province,' a proportion that grew steadily to the end of the First World War. Japanese and East Indian workers concentrated in sawmills, the Chinese in shingle mills. In evidence presented to the BC Commission on Labour in 1913, two union spokesmen from Vancouver testified that Asians had practically driven White labour out of the province's mills. At the J. Hanbury and Company mill on False Creek, Japanese and 'Hindoos' made up half the sawmill labour force in 1912 but almost the whole of it four years later. The salmon fishing and coal mining industries also employed significant numbers of Asians, but unlike forest industry workers many lived in resource-based communities such as Steveston and Cumberland rather than in Vancouver. When they returned from fishing in the north, some Japanese labourers found jobs in sawmills and shingle bolt camps around Vancouver.[17]

Of these minority groups, the Chinese pursued the greatest range of employment. Best known is their work as butchers and general labourers in salmon canneries of the Fraser River and lower coastal region, from which many returned to Vancouver's Chinatown in the off-season. Some Chinese took up market gardening in the vicinities of Victoria and Vancouver, a business they monopolized by 1900. In a manner characteristic of minority groups of low status, other Chinese 'found petty commerce attractive, increasingly so after the turn of the century.' In 1902, for example, thirty-five Chinese laundries employed three-quarters of Vancouver's laundry workforce. These small and poorly capitalized businesses competed with four mechanized steam laundries owned by Whites. While some of the Chinese businesses 'provided services to the white community ... others dealt exclusively with a Chinese clientele.' The economic interests of Whites and Chinese intersected most fully in the homes of prosperous

Table 8.2

Vancouver's population by birthplace and sex, 1911

	Males	Females	Total	Males as % of total
Greece	211	15	226	97.7
China	3,241	123	3,364	96.3
India	634	47	681	93.1
Italy	1,681	241	1,922	87.5
Japan	1,415	426	1,841	76.9
Austria Hungary	366	134	500	73.2
Scandinavia	1,295	593	1,888	68.6
Russia	402	204	606	66.3
Britain	19,281	11,408	30,689	62.8
Canada	23,405	20,572	43,977	53.2
United States	5,509	4,892	10,401	53.0
Other	2,786	1,520	4,306	66.8
Total	60,226	40,175	100,401	60.1

Source: Fifth Census of Canada, 1911, vol. 2, table 16

White business and professional families, where Chinese men found work as cooks. A vibrant labour market allowed most White women to avoid the poorly paid and demanding field of domestic service, leaving the task to Chinese men like Yow, 'the ill-mannered and tyrannical cook' in *The Innocent Traveller*, Ethel Wilson's fictionalized account of West End life before the War.[18]

Historians and sociologists of British Columbia have tended to associate 'foreign' with Asian, but Table 8.2 reveals that the broader concept of ethnicity is more appropriate than the narrower one of race to a discussion of Vancouver's 'outsiders.' As suggested above, the language of race was applied to non-British Whites as well as to non-Whites, and Asians were joined as low-status workers by southern and eastern Europeans. Here again family status reinforced ethnicity, for the vast majority of Vancouver's Greek, Italian, Austro-Hungarian, and Russian workers had come as sojourning men without women. Most found employment at semi- and unskilled labouring jobs, though some Greeks and Italians were active as penny capitalists in confectionery and service businesses.[19]

Of these European 'foreigners,' the Italian population exceeded that of the largest Asian group, the Chinese, in the summer months of the prewar period. Highly transient, Italian labourers excelled as 'shovellers on the top of the Earth' and 'diggers and muckers' beneath it, departing from Vancouver when the winter rains arrived. With their ability to outwork 'the Englishmen and British subjects' on city street and drain construction projects, they competed directly and successfully with unskilled labourers from the dominant culture. By contrast, as F.H. McMillan of the Vancouver Trades and Labor Council noted in evidence presented to the BC Commission on Labour, 'The Orientals confine themselves to occupations in which there is no competition from white men.'[20]

Despite their strength in the labour market and their ability to command high wages, Vancouver's Italians remained outside the dominant anglophone community. Social thought of the period offers one explanation: being southern European, Roman Catholic, and poor, Italian men were perceived as different from and inferior to northern Europeans. But Italians themselves contributed in a more active way to their status as outsiders. Like Asian workers, they had come to make money and intended to leave when their stay was no longer profitable. Except for a small minority of Italians who had established families in Vancouver, the majority aspired to create a better life for their families in the old country and exhibited no desire to become established members of local society. Instead, they kept to themselves within the ethnic world of the immigrant sojourner. The rough ways of Italian labourers clashed dramatically with those of Vancouver's respectable majority on weekends when, having pooled their savings, they purchased liquor by the barrelful. For city police, responding to 'a row among the Italians' became a Saturday night ritual. In addition, Italians refused to have anything do with the labour movement and rejected 'all efforts to persuade them to organize with other city laborers in the Civic Employees' Union.' Respectable workers of Vancouver's middling stratum resented the Italians' willingness to live poorly in order to accumulate cash savings, scoffed at their rough demeanour, and disliked their standoffishness, their rejection of the established community's ways and institutions. As the *British Columbia Federationist* noted in a critical tone, the Italians were 'very clannish.'[21]

Other White males were less 'foreign' in cultural terms than were Italians but still found themselves outside the mainstream of respectable society. Loggers offer perhaps the best example of how lifestyle functioned as an additional determinant of marginal status. James Conley has shown that most loggers were single men. They were also 'racially, but not ethnically, homogeneous,' few Asians being employed in logging camps. Whereas loggers in the 1870s and 1880s had come predominantly from eastern North America, men of continental European origin had become more prominent by the twentieth century. As noted in Table 8.1, Scandinavians increased from 1.2 per cent of Vancouver's population in 1891 to 1.9 in 1911 as more Swedish and Norwegian loggers entered the coastal forests. By the end of the First World War, British Columbia's loggers were almost evenly divided between men of Canadian, British, or American origin and men of European origin, especially Scandinavians and Russians.[22]

When loggers finally quit the forest, driven out by fatigue, isolation, bad conditions, or the desire to celebrate Christmas, they usually headed by the next available boat for Vancouver's Gastown. The overwhelmingly masculine character of Gastown was captured superbly by Martin Allerdale Grainger in *Woodsmen of the West,* a fictionalized study of west coast loggers based on Grainger's own experiences as a forester in British Columbia. As you enter Vancouver's waterfront area along Cordova,

Carrall, and Powell Streets, Grainger wrote, 'you notice a gradual change in the appearance of the shop windows. The shoe stores, drug stores, clothing stores, phonograph stores cease to bother you with their blinding light ... You leave "high tone" behind you.' Shop windows now displayed 'faller's axes, swamper's axes – single-bitted, double-bitted; screw jacks and pump jacks, wedges, sledge-hammers, and great seven-foot saws with enormous shark teeth, and huge augers for boring boomsticks.' The people outside the shops were also different. 'You see few women. Men look into the windows; men drift up and down the street; men lounge in groups upon the curb. Your eye is struck at once by the unusual proportion of big men in the crowd, men that look powerful even in their town clothes ... You are among loggers.' Gastown's male residents remained, in the words of another contemporary observer, entirely 'ignorant of anything savoring of home life.'[23] As such, they challenged J.W. Wilkinson's ideal of a society of men and women living in families.

Upon arriving in Vancouver, some loggers chose to lodge in rooming houses where champagne and a 'certain society' guaranteed a high time and a fast dissipation of hard-earned savings. Others selected respectable hotels where friendly proprietors and sympathetic bartenders offered protection from 'shady characters' and the loggers' own indiscretions. Regardless of where they stayed, the first two days would be spent getting 'good-and-drunk.' Thereafter, most loggers moved in a geographically circumscribed area that centred on the waterfront and extended through a section of streets lined with saloons, hotels, employment agencies, and cheap recreational facilities such as movie houses, poolrooms, and shooting galleries. On the outer margin were the brothels of Chinatown and Shore Street (see Map 7.1).

The saloon, the hotel, and the street became home, the place where sociability occurred and information about employment was acquired. Seeing off the Union Steamship's boat, the *Cassiar*, each Tuesday and Thursday evening also served both a ritualistic social function – it made a 'pleasing break in the monotony of drifting up the street to the Eureka, and having a drink with the crowd in the Columbia bar, and standing drinks to the girls at number so-and-so Dupont Street' – and the practical role of generating useful information about jobs. Eventually, however, having drunk too much booze and spent too much money, loggers once again faced the harsh reality of making a living. After striking a deal with a boss logger, often within the friendly confines of a saloon, the logger would find himself heading north again, his stay in Vancouver almost entirely devoid of contact with respectable working- and middle-class families.[24]

Located a few blocks south of Gastown, the ethnic enclave of Chinatown was marked by a similarly dramatic imbalance between numbers of men and women. The role of family was somewhat more complex here than in Gastown, however, because a handful of Chinese merchants who commanded considerable wealth and exercised substantial authority within the community were able to differentiate themselves from the majority below by creating families in Vancouver. The history of Yip Sang illustrates the point. After working in California and British Columbia for more than twenty years before settling in Vancouver in 1888, the 'impoverished immigrant' established what was to become one of the city's largest Chinese trading enterprises, the Wing Sang Company. As Yip Sang's wealth grew, so did his capacity to keep a large family. Three of his four wives lived with him in the Wing Sang building on Dupont Street, as did many of their nineteen sons, four daughters, and sixty-seven grandchildren. A six-storey addition to the main company structure was required to house them. Guided by the Confucian values of filial piety, domestic harmony, and ancestor worship, Yip Sang exemplified the Chinese patriarch.[25]

The lifestyle of most local Chinese differed vastly, however. Faced with discriminatory legislation and a wage structure that accorded Chinese workers from half to two-thirds the income of Whites for comparable tasks, Vancouver's Chinese labourers and small businessmen lived 'in a predominantly married-bachelor society' while keeping families in China. Men found themselves 'crowded to suffocation' in Chinatown tenements constructed close to one another to maximize land use.[26] Yun Ho Chang, who arrived from China in 1908, remembered living and working in a small room into which four bunkbeds had been crammed and where food was cooked. Sometimes home was a back-alley shack or the cellar of a merchant's store. To save money at low wages Chinatown's sojourning men had to work desperately long hours, challenging notions held by respectable workers of a 'fair' day's work at a 'fair' wage. Faced with social isolation and the absence of family, men turned for recreation to prostitution, opium smoking, and gambling. For almost a generation, prostitutes worked out of Chinatown, and throughout the neighbourhood illegal gambling houses hid 'behind storefronts which sold cigarettes and pop or fruit as a cover.' As one elderly Chinese later explained, 'There was no family, everyone was single ... If you went to the gambling house, you could talk and laugh ... Where else could we go?'[27]

Although sojourning immigrants and seasonal resource industry workers defined the inner city, women were not entirely absent from this gendered space encompassing the waterfront, the Chinese, the Japanese, and the old business sections of Vancouver. Some were prostitutes but not all. As Table 8.2 reveals, women were proportionately more prevalent among northern European residents than among southern European or Asian ones. The high entry fee for Chinese immigrants – the head tax demanded of incoming Chinese increased from $50 in 1885 to $100 in 1900 and $500 in 1903 – precluded all but the richest Chinese merchants from bringing wives to Canada. Consequently, Vancouver's Chinese community had few women – twelve adult females compared to 812 adult males in 1891 – and of these more than half were the wives of merchants. The 123 Chinese females in Vancouver in 1911 included children, merchants' wives, and prostitutes.

Until 1907 almost all Japanese immigrants were male, but the demographic imbalance began to right itself with the inauguration in 1908 of a 'picture bride' scheme that brought Japanese women to British Columbia. Whereas sixty-four children had been born in Canada to Japanese parents by 1900, the number had increased to 4,000 by 1920.[28]

The Italian population also began to dig roots in the city in the decade after 1900, and a few families together established the institutional infrastructure of an ethnic community. Clustering on three streets east of Westminster Avenue (now Main Street) in Strathcona, they founded the Sons of Italy fraternal society, the Sacred Heart Catholic Church, and the Societa Veneta.[29]

Except for the wives of Chinese merchants, 'immigrant' women contributed to the family economy by generating income. Some did so by means of wage labour. Japanese women, for instance, found employment on the canning lines of salmon canneries. The 1911 census listed 241 Italian child and adult females in Vancouver, and many of the women worked at home by providing board and room to single men. One early resident, born in the city to Italian parents, recalls living in a house that had two kitchens: one for the family and one for boarders, most of whom were loggers. Another Italian resident of the prewar period asserts that 'in the home most of the women had boarders, in some cases as many as 18.'[30] It is unlikely, however, that the presence of a few women lessened the stigma accorded to residents of the inner city by Vancouver's respectable majority, who feared the area not only as a place inhabited by men without families but also as a centre of poor 'foreigners.'

In contrast to the Italians, and Chinese, Aboriginal people were almost entirely absent from civic discourse on identity and belonging. Urbanization had marginalized Burrard Inlet's Native and Mixed-Blood residents through a massive influx of Europeans. The Mission Reserve on the north shore remained the largest cluster of Natives on the Inlet, with 224 members at the end of 1913. By contrast, the 1891 census listed only 109 Aboriginal people in Vancouver, and the 1911 census 117.[31] Some Native men continued to work as longshoremen or millhands at city lumber mills, but the social and symbolic separation of Native from non-Native peoples that accompanied urbanization was a more significant phenomenon. Natives figured prominently in civic festivals and celebrations primarily as exotic 'others' rather than as members of the community.[32]

Their status as outsiders is revealed in the successful effort of civic and provincial government leaders to gain control of the Kitsilano Reserve at the entrance to False Creek. The 'people of Vancouver' had long viewed the property as important to the city's growth and the Native presence there as an impediment to urban development. At the end of 1911 the provincial government initiated a process to purchase the reserve and extinguish Aboriginal title. After negotiating for more than a year, the parties agreed in March 1913 that the band's twenty members would sell their rights for $218,750 and vacate the property. The government allocated a further $1,000 to facilitate the removal of ancestral remains. Native residents professed satisfaction with an agreement that accorded all but one of them a sum of $11,250 apiece, but critics argued that the land had been greatly undervalued. Whatever the merits of the terms, the agreement diminished even further an already negligible Native presence in Vancouver.[33]

THE ROLE THAT POVERTY played in constructing a social boundary between citizens and 'outsiders' is illustrated in the response of Vancouver's respectable majority to the plight of the economically disadvantaged. Constitutionally Canada's regional governments bore responsibility for the welfare of the poor, and in the British and Canadian traditions this

Native people encamped
along the shore of Burrard
Inlet, ca. 1900. As the photograph illustrates, Native people occupied a place at the
margin of urban society.
(Vancouver Public Library
9525)

responsibility in turn was derogated to the local, or municipal, governments. In 1887 the Vancouver City Council created a board of health to be under the general supervision of a medical health officer who was to provide for the 'immediate relief' of sick and destitute persons and families. Some years later this role was expanded to include the care of 'pauper patients where required by the Mayor and Chairman of the Health Committee.'[34] But municipal taxpayers also believed that, whatever the government's financial resources, it should help only the most desperate and helpless, the remainder to be looked after by families or private charities. As noted in Chapter 3, limited by its small financial resources and the belief, shared across Vancouver's three classes, that indiscriminate charity would erode the work ethic and thus undermine self-sufficiency, City Council provided only minimal assistance to the unemployed and the poor during the 1890s.

Vancouver's ratepaying citizens continued to deal with the underprivileged in their midst after 1900 much as they had before: through private charitable organizations that the civic government supported financially. But seasonal and cyclical unemployment severely tested the city government's ability to aid destitute residents, especially during the economic downturns of 1907-8 and 1913-15. Financial and moral concerns raised by government aid to able-bodied but unemployed men were exacerbated in turn by ethnocentric feelings among the city's ethnic majority against 'foreign' labourers seeking financial assistance from Canadian-, British-, and American-born taxpayers.

The city government's treatment of old and indigent men illustrates some of the assumptions that guided the process of providing assistance. Vancouver in 1891 was a new city of working-age migrants. Ninety-two per cent of the adult population was less than fifty years old, and only a handful were over sixty. No such statistics exist for the early 1900s, but logic suggests that as the city aged so did its population. The growing number of elderly men requiring assistance emerged as a political issue in 1904 when Alderman Edward Odlum noted that providing for old men had become a steady drain upon the treasury and urged that the city build a home to care for them. Francis Williams, another alderman and, like Odlum, a Methodist, lobbied hard over the next two years for a city-run home, arguing that it 'would be scandalous if the City did not make provision for the old and infirm people.' Most councillors disagreed. Reflecting concern about limited financial resources and fear that Vancouver might be inundated with paupers, they began in 1907 to place needy cases in an old building that had formerly housed the City Hospital. The rest were forced to cope on their own or leave town. Even Williams's political ally and fellow labourist John Morton feared that a city-funded home for men would make Vancouver 'the dumping ground for all the hoboes on the Coast.'[35]

The story of three old men offers a telling commentary on the assumptions that guided the social policy of Vancouver's respectable majority. Controversy erupted when the three old-timers 'objected to do[ing] work in return for ... assistance.' As a consequence, they were ordered to appear on 15 March 1905 before the Health Committee of City Council. One of the men, Mr. Crabb, stated forcefully that 'he had done enough work in his 81 years, and did not feel inclined to try to do any more. If the City would not give him something to eat, he would hunt up another place.' The Health Committee charged Crabb with 'being quarrelsome.' Its members agreed that 'giving relief to the large number of old and disabled men' who were applying was a 'serious problem,' but although their concern increased their response remained traditional. As Indiana Matters has argued, 'non-infirm elderly were expected to work and support themselves, just as others did.' The rest should be attended to by family and friends. 'If the city could link an aged indigent to anyone else, no matter how remote the connection, it limited its aid to providing a one-way ticket out of town.' Ratepayers finally agreed in 1912 to fund an old people's home for sixty-eight men and women. To be eligible, however, an applicant had to be over sixty and have resided in the city for at least ten years.[36]

Unemployment taxed community resources more severely than any other source of social need. Though regional, national, and international in origin, unemployment burdened local communities with its social costs. Vancouver's civic government responded in the same manner as other Canadian cities: by placing the onus for providing relief on the private sector. Leading the way were several charitable institutions that sought to aid homeless and transient men. In the post-1910 decade the three largest provided beds for more than 600 men per night; they also offered a healthy serving of gospel religion along with shelter and food. The city helped fund the Salvation Army's Metropole Hostel, the Vancouver City Rescue Mission, and the Central City Mission through municipal grants but otherwise sought to keep public involvement to a minimum.[37]

Yet at certain times high levels of joblessness threatened social order and required a more direct response from government. An ebb and flow of public and private leadership in managing the distribution of relief resulted. As early as February 1894 City Council had set up a scheme to employ 100 men for up to six weeks, the program to be managed by a special relief committee of Council. An experiment in linking voluntary associations and the civic government occurred at the end of 1895, when the Vancouver Friendly Help Society was formed at the behest of the Vancouver Council of Women and local clergy to administer public and private charitable funds efficiently. Drawing on the Charity Organization Movement of Britain and the United States, volunteers were to determine through interviews and visits the worthiness of applicants for assistance, thus sorting the worthy from the unworthy and limiting both the costs and the debilitating moral effect of charity.[38] The Society 'fade[d] into obscurity' but was reorganized at the end of 1906. Consisting of representatives from City Council, churches, and charitable organizations such as the Victorian Order of Nurses and the Women's Christian Temperance Union, it took over 'the entire charge of cases for relief' then being cared for by the city. Its goal remained the same as that of its predecessor: to distribute relief systematically.[39]

So great was the need among unemployed workers in the winter of 1907-8 that City Council reinstituted a program of direct relief. The magnitude of unemployment and the demand of out-of-work labourers for the right to gather on city streets and speak there without harassment led to another direct relief program in January 1912. A year later unemployment had become so severe that the city absorbed the organization and staff of the Associated Charities – the umbrella group of private charities that had succeeded the Friendly Help Society in 1908 – for the purpose of distributing relief and other forms of charity in a businesslike fashion. For the first time it also began to give 'public aid to able-bodied, non-resident single men.'

In 1914 Council tried once more to place all social assistance back into the hands of the private sector and worked with citizens' groups to establish the Employment and Relief Association. This organization failed either to provide additional efficiencies or to generate private charitable funds, and the city re-established its own relief department soon after. Further layoffs accompanied the outbreak of war and in November 1914 the city once again created work for single men, this time clearing land in return for board. The provincial government's continued refusal to help pay for these special works projects led the city to cut off all project funding for non-resident single men in April 1915. A riot ensued.[40]

The principles that guided assistance to the unemployed remained the same in the 1910s as in the 1890s. Aid was to be limited to the worthy, as proof of which work was required. But moral rectitude was only one of the necessary qualifications. Being married and from the local community also helped men secure relief. As the labour market became increasing glutted, James Findlay, Vancouver mayor in 1912, spoke of trying to hire for city construction gangs only married men and property owners, especially those with families and a 'permanent' stake in the community. One other assumption permeated charitable endeavours: assistance was to be given first to people whose ethnic identity was British. As Findlay put it, 'I am a proud Britisher, and the fact that Britishers are out of work in this fair Vancouver of ours touches me deeply'; employment on city work must favour as much as possible people born in Canada and Britain. He might have added, so must aid to the unemployed.[41]

During the prewar period, the Medical Health Officer's annual reports regularly featured concern over the housing condition of Vancouver's 'floating' and 'foreign' population. 'Foreigners,' the reports stated, could be found herded into lodging houses in the Water Street district and into 'hothouses of dirt, contagion and disease' on Powell and Hastings Streets.[42] To some extent such stories documented the reality of substandard housing in the inner city. Cabins were single-room dwellings opening off a porch running along one side of a building. Of sixty-two cabins examined by health officials in the waterfront-East End area, more than half were found to lack proper ventilation, lighting, and cleanliness. An obvious explanation is the 1,167 men, 198 women, and 126 children jammed into them.[43] Margaret Andrews has shown that while health conditions were better in Vancouver than in comparable Canadian cities of the period, such was not the case in the inner city, where the rate of death from disease was much higher than in Vancouver as a whole.[44]

Nevertheless, Health Department reports and ethnocentric comments in discourse about relief also represented something more general: a feeling among respectable families of British heritage that they were under siege from the transients, foreigners, and unattached men flooding into the area to look for work. Ethnocentrism was hardly new to the prewar period. As noted earlier, Joseph Franklin had argued in the mid-1890s against granting relief to unemployed Italian labourers, suggesting instead that assistance be given only to 'citizens.' What differed was the context. The prewar prosperity that heightened expectations of quick riches also created anxiety about Vancouver's character. This sense of unease explains why comments about legitimate and illegitimate recipients of relief were cast much more explicitly in ethnic terms from about 1911 than they had been earlier. Responding to the plight of the indigent and unemployed, it seems, was intricately tied to the broader process by which Vancouver's respectable majority established its collective identity.

VANCOUVER'S FLOATING POPULATION challenged the values and lifestyle of the respectable majority, especially on downtown streets. Lacking homes or roots in the community, transients and seasonal workers took to the streets for both recreational and practical purposes. The streets gained importance because of the lack of parks and public squares in Vancouver.[45] Streets in the zone between the waterfront and Chinatown were especially busy on Saturday nights. As one observer put it when reminiscing about the prewar years, the street corners were filled with music, on one corner the Industrial Workers of the World (IWW) singing 'Solidarity Forever,' on another a religious group singing 'There is honey in the rock for you my brother,' and on yet another the Salvation Army band booming out 'We will understand each other when the mists have rolled away.'[46] Businesses like Woodward department store on Hastings Street complained that crowds milling about in front of their premises hindered trade. Indeed, 'thousands of people [were said to be] wandering about the streets every Sunday evening with nowhere to go.'[47] The streets also fulfilled economic needs. For some, like Greek ice cream pedlars, they were a place of business. For others, such as transient labourers, streets were the equivalent of the union man's Labour Temple, where between seven and eight o'clock each morning the city's 'unorganized element' scanned the boards of employment offices in search of work.[48]

City streets were not just neutral places where people filled time and occasionally did business. All space is socially constructed, and its use reflects structures of power within the community.[49] The fact that respectability was defined in terms of families and homes located in outlying areas meant that suburban streets were generally quiet and uncontentious. In residential areas a significant portion of people's lives unfolded in the private domain of home and garden. Not so in the inner city, where the majority of residents controlled little private space and thus made public streets an integral part of their daily lives. In the core area, and especially in the neighbourhood filled with cheap hotels and crowded rooming houses and populated by transient males, the city streets became 'contested terrain.' Here they were a locus of conflict between groups representing different economic and social interests and articulating different visions of urban society.[50] The image of Salvation Army and IWW preachers competing for the hearts and minds of Vancouver's floating population certainly captures one aspect of this conflict. But the contest for influence in downtown streets could also reverberate out through the city as a whole, challenging the security of the upper and middling strata and evoking the use of police and government to control threatening behaviour. The free speech fights of 1909 and 1912 pitted agents of Vancouver's respectable and rough populations against one another in an explicit example of status conflict.

Three organizations of working people were involved: the IWW (or Wobblies), the Socialist Party of Canada (SPC), and the Vancouver Trades and Labor Council (VTLC). The 1909 conflict occurred when city officials and the Vancouver police decided to stop IWW meetings on downtown streets. As early as 1907 Mayor Bethune had expressed concern that 'hoboes were drifting into the City from the outside all the time,' and argued that they 'needed watching.' Anxiety over the number of hoboes and transients coming into the city increased as the labour market began to grow again following the 1907-8 recession, and a crackdown on left-leaning street speakers that started on 4 April 1909 reflected the fear that transient workers led by radical labour leaders posed a threat to Vancouver's social order. The IWW and SPC speakers were told to stop addressing crowds in the streets but the Salvation Army was not. Arrests were made, and the VTLC organized a protest rally at City Hall. The street battle culminated on 18 May with the intervention of police at a SPC-sponsored rally of almost 1,000 people. Police harassment then ended, but resumed again in January 1912 when James Findlay, who had just won election as mayor on a platform of defending the interests of unemployed family men and British citizens, 'called for an "iron hand" to deal with unrest in the streets.' On the Saturday after his Council had passed a motion forbidding all outdoor meetings, four men were arrested for leading an IWW-sponsored gathering at the corner of Cordova and Carrall. More arrests followed the next day. A week later, police waded into a crowd of several thousand at the Powell Street grounds on the edge of Japantown, a long line of them using their clubs 'with ferocious design and savage effect. Defenceless men were knocked senseless and bleeding to the ground.' Organized to test the anti-free speech by-law, the gathering generated a violent reaction and thirty arrests. Subsequent meetings were broken up, and arrests for vagrancy increased. Both the city and provincial governments assured representatives of the VTLC and SPC that free speech would be allowed in public squares but not in the streets. Labour spokesmen agreed, and an 18 February meeting took place without incident.[51]

Historian Mark Leier, who has studied Vancouver's free speech fights closely, demonstrates the existence of a sharp division between the Wobblies, who eschewed constitutional and parliamentary means of expression in favour of extraparliamentary methods such as direct action in the streets, and leaders of the labour movement and Socialist Party, who were willing to work within existing parliamentary institutions and sought to distance themselves from the Wobblies and their supporters. Thus, in 1909 when city authorities responded to street meetings with arrests and police harassment, trade union leaders offered little support to the Wobblies or the arrested men. The Vancouver Trades and Labor Council expressed only marginal interest in the free speech issue, focusing instead on its own reform agenda of supporting an eight-hour workday for civic employees and opposing the Laurier government's Naval Bill. VTLC executive James McVety, a Socialist, claimed that quiet diplomacy with the mayor 'was more important than the IWW's resistance in the streets and courtroom theatrics.' L.D. Taylor's pro-labour newspaper, the *Vancouver Daily World,* denounced speakers who blocked city streets. When the free speech movement erupted again in January 1912, the VTLC and SPC did 'little to organize the first protests among the unemployed' and worked to separate themselves from the street meetings. The *British Columbia Federationist* argued that 'street meetings ... have always been a nuisance,' and McVety opposed the use of force against 'constituted authorities.'[52]

When placed within the context of cultural and social tensions in pre-war Vancouver, differences between the VTLC and the Socialist Party on one side and the IWW on the other appear less a narrow conflict among labour and radical groups than a broadly based separation of respectable from not so respectable residents, of 'citizens' and 'immigrants.' Thus, when the VTLC newspaper noted that many Vancouverites believed licence fees for bars should be higher to keep out tramps and to 'protect local men who live in the city and have their homes and property here,' it spoke for more than just the labour elite.[53] It also articulated the views of a significant portion of the working class, men and women with families who shared few interests with the large floating and foreign populations of the downtown core. It probably also spoke for the longshoreman who, when harassed in April 1912 by a police constable for standing on a street corner in the waterfront area while waiting to go to work – 'Move or I'll put the boot to you,' the constable is said to have ordered – replied that he had lived in Vancouver for twenty-two years and was 'a stevedore of good standing.' Was a 'citizen' to expect such abuse?[54]

The social anxiety that led to this confrontation between a respectable working man and the police is also revealed in the Vancouver Police Department Prisoners' Record Books.[55] These records list the names of people charged with offences under the Criminal Code, the reason for arrest, date of arrest, and disposition. Arrest records often tell more about perceptions of law and order at any given point than they do about actual criminal behaviour. Thus, for example, North American cities experienced periodic outbursts of concern about moral issues such as prostitution that had little to do with the incidence of prostitution and much to do with the fears and insecurities of the dominant community. Increased arrests for order offences are, in these instances, better described as 'arrest waves' than 'crime waves.' As such they usefully illustrate social attitudes.[56]

Prewar Vancouver experienced such an arrest wave. A comparison of arrests for the years 1906 and 1913 indicates a much greater level of concern about issues of moral and social order at the height of the prewar boom than seven years earlier. As indicated in Table 8.3, the proportion of arrests made for crimes against order, such as vagrancy or keeping a 'disorderly house,' almost doubled. The proportion for crimes against property and of crimes against the person – mainly theft and assault, respectively – dropped. In particular, vagrancy charges jumped from 36 to 57 per cent of total arrests, a product of the anxiety created among Vancouver's respectable and stable population by the hordes of unattached men who filled inner-city streets at night and on weekends. Arrests for sex-related offences also increased, from 3 per cent of the total to 20 per cent. Indeed, the number of women among those arrested grew by a ratio of nine, roughly approximating the increased number of arrests for sex-related crimes.

The people arrested were marginal to mainstream society in a number of ways. They worked almost entirely at low-status jobs such as day labour or in some aspect of the sex trade, including prostitution, pimping, and providing musical entertainment in brothels. They also constituted a more diverse group ethnically and racially than the city as a whole. Only 21 per cent of those arrested in 1913 were Canadian-born, a slight drop from seven years earlier. By contrast, the number born on the European continent doubled, from 8 to 17 per cent. More significant is the racial character of the group. Overall, non-Whites made up an almost identical proportion in 1906 and 1913 (20 per cent), but within this group the proportion of Blacks jumped dramatically, from one-tenth to one-third of the American total and from 7 to 12 per cent of all people arrested. Mainly charged with sex offences, Black men and women added a highly visible face to the group of outsiders – sex trade workers – that most sharply challenged the mores of Vancouver's respectable majority.[57]

The arrest records illuminate the bottom rung of Vancouver's status hierarchy, revealing a group that, while part of the working class, lived a vastly different lifestyle from members of the respectable middling stratum. The free speech fights similarly illustrated stresses that divided Vancouver's working class against itself. The skilled and economically secure worker who was raising a family, belonged to a craft-organized trade union, took part in union picnics, baseball games, and balls, had joined the Odd Fellows Lodge, owned or rented a small cottage in Mount Pleasant, and voted in provincial and municipal elections lived in a very different social world from that of single loggers for whom cheap hotels, 'skidway

Table 8.3

Arrests in Vancouver, 1906 and 1913

	Crimes against order		Crimes against property		Crimes against the person		Other Crimes	
	(%)	Number	(%)	Number	(%)	Number	(%)	Number
1906	44.8	81	44.1	78	9.0	16	1.1	2
1913	85.1	662	10.8	84	3.2	25	0.9	7

Note: The data include cases that were discharged or dismissed.
Sources: CVA, Vancouver Police Department, Prisoners Record Books, 1898-1917, Series 2, 1906, pp. 70-157 (Loc. 76-C-2) and 1913, pp. 28-159 (Loc. 116-E-1)

saloons,' shooting galleries, prostitutes, and Sunday Wobblie meetings constituted Vancouver society. Ethnicity and race erected even larger barriers between Italian street labourers, Chinese cannery workers, and Black prostitutes on the one hand and the Canadian-, British-, and American-born majority on the other. Such evidence suggests that, at the bottom of the social hierarchy, as at the top, status played an important role in structuring Vancouver's social boundaries.

Conclusion

Throughout the early history of settlement on Burrard Inlet, Europeans organized their economic activity according to a capitalist mode of production, and the resulting wage system divided residents along class lines. The most obvious characteristic of the settlements that emerged on Burrard Inlet in the 1860s was their dependence on sawmills. Moodyville functioned much like a company town, its economy based almost entirely on the operation of a single, export-oriented sawmill. Despite an economic base somewhat broader than that of its cross-harbour neighbour, Granville also emerged in response to the needs of the lumber industry and continued into the 1880s to depend upon it.

Economic relations shaped the structure of lumber society on Burrard Inlet. Mill owners, managers, and their families stood at the pinnacle of power, their unequalled capacity to provide jobs reinforced by geographic isolation and the small scale of settlement communities. Social contact was personal, harkening back to a preindustrial era when patron-client relationships structured life in rural societies. A few families headed by machinists, engineers, independent stevedores, lesser mill officials, and south shore shopkeepers joined the mill managers to form an upper social clique. Through their roles as mothers, teachers, nurses, and moral leaders, the women in these families defined the management-centred group as respectable and thus served to distance themselves from the wage earners and Native people who constituted the bulk of the Inlet's population. Social coherence was much greater at the top of lumber society than at the bottom, a condition that enhanced the class authority of the mill managers. By contrast, the transient and ethnically diverse mill workers lacked the permanence to develop a class identity.

Beginning in the mid-1880s, rapid urbanization broadened the economic base and class structure of Burrard Inlet. Plans for the construction of a transcontinental railway terminus at Coal Harbour ignited a growth boom that drew thousands of people to the area and transformed the village of Granville into the city of Vancouver. Dramatic change occurred within the wage-earning population, where ethnic diversity and an important Native presence gave way to an overwhelmingly White working class of British heritage. An important strike of mill workers in the spring of 1886 and the formation of a city-wide trades and labour council at the end of the decade revealed the blossoming of class consciousness among elements of the working class. Commercial growth stimulated expansion of the small business sector, out of which emerged an identifiable middle class. At the upper end of the class system, the growth boom of the 1880s inflated a small cluster of sawmill owners and managers into a class of capitalists and corporate managers.

It was in the upper class that Vancouverites acted most purposefully in a class-conscious manner.[1] In the late 1880s, business leaders formed competitive factions that differed according to interests – the Canadian Pacific Railway on the west side, the Oppenheimer group on the east – and to their place within the structure of capitalism. The CPR was an example of monopoly capitalism; the sawmills, commercial houses, and real estate firms provide examples of personal or entrepreneurial capitalism. Yet the unity of the CPR and Oppenheimer factions at election time revealed their common understanding of the relationship between business and government and hence of class interests. Business leaders also acted aggressively and collectively to defend their property when prosperity gave way to depression in the 1890s. By contrast, the depression left Vancouver's fledgling trade union movement fragile and on the edge of collapse.

As the economy again grew at the end of the 1890s, the class tensions inherent in a capitalist mode of production gained more concrete expression. Population growth, renewed economic vigour, and the restructuring of resource industries – especially hard rock mining and salmon canning – from local and entrepreneurial forms of ownership to externally controlled and bureaucratic ones all created strains that exacerbated an already unstable provincial political climate. Outside observers now spoke of conflict between capital and labour as one of British Columbia's most pressing problems. The emergence of new trade unions, a labour newspaper, and a provincial labour party testified to the growth of a vibrant working-class culture in Vancouver. Within the upper class, the aggressive opposition of leading businessmen to unions reflected a heightened sense of shared interests. The bitter United Brotherhood of Railway Employees' strike of 1903 and subsequent open-shop movement among employers marked the culmination of a half decade of increasing antagonism between capital and labour and the emergence of class as an important form of social identity.

But how important? Several influences limited the extent to which class defined the identities of and relationships between Vancouverites. Rapid population growth kept social relations fluid. The speculative ethos that prevailed in British Columbia during the prewar years held out to working people the hope of material progress and the prospect of social advancement into the middle, or perhaps even upper, classes. Easy access to the bountiful resources of the province not only encouraged such aspirations but, for some, opened the door to prosperity. For many, the boom at least temporarily countered the centrifugal tendency towards class separation that had gained force around 1900.

In addition, the lack of a substantial industrial base precluded an important source of working-class solidarity characteristic of more heavily industrialized cities: shared economic interests reinforced by work-centred and community-centred patterns of association. Vancouver was not a factory city like those of central Canada or the American midwest, where thousands of workers could be found toiling for a single industry in the same city, in some cases many of them in the same building.[2] Nor did Vancouver have a large population of European workers who, being White, were able to vote, and whose family-based community life served as a potential source of class action against employers.[3]

The limited capacity of industrial production to stimulate class awareness is revealed by the history of Vancouver's leading industry: forestry. Lumber and shingle mills employed the city's greatest concentration of wage workers and offered rich potential for the creation of class-conscious industrial organization and action. In practice, however, skill and race intersected in ways that presented a formidable barrier to class mobilization among lumber workers. The minority of millhands who were skilled and White, including sawyers, saw filers, foremen, millwrights, and engineers, formed 'virtually a labour aristocracy.'[4] Loggers and most operatives in Vancouver's smaller sash and door factories enjoyed a similarly privi leged status. By contrast, the majority of mill jobs required little or no skill, and mill owners successfully manipulated popularly held attitudes about race to designate skilled positions as 'White' and unskilled ones as 'non-White.' When strikes among forest industry workers did take place, they usually involved employees who were not unionized and generally occurred along racially segmented lines. Consequently, in Vancouver's most important industry the working class was sharply divided against itself. In turn, industry-specific division diminished the potential for class mobilization among the wage-earning population as a whole.

Not surprisingly, given the city's economic structure, class leadership among Vancouver's working people came from the most privileged sector of the working class: White men of British heritage whose skills provided them with employment security, solid wages, and the ability to develop a sense of community with fellow workers off the job. Such privileged workers tended to see class interests in narrow terms and to limit their empathy for wage earners who were less skilled, less settled, and often not part of the ethnic and racial majority. The fact that many workers – most of whom were men without families in Vancouver considered themselves to be sojourners and had no desire to participate in local institutions such as trade unions intensified fragmentation.

The upper class, defined in this study as both those who owned or managed the means of production and those whose interests or outlook linked them to owners, had the advantage of ideological consensus and ethnic coherence. Firmly committed to a defence of capitalism – especially the rights of private property – and a faith in British institutions, the upper class faced fewer impediments when forced to defend its class interests. The salmon canners' successful use of state power in 1900 to break the Fraser River salmon fishermen's strike illustrates well how economic power, reinforced by social ties, allowed capitalists to mobilize quickly when their interests were threatened by an assertive working class. One has to consider, then, that another reason for limited class mobilization among working people was the sheer power of business to limit their development as a class. That power was sometimes exerted but often merely implicit in the relationship of capital and labour.

Yet to emphasize business power alone is to ignore the complexity of social relations and especially the ideological and structural conditions that characterized prewar Vancouver. The city remained to 1913 a new society where expectations of material betterment lessened awareness of class differences. Racial and occupational diversity also diminished the potential of wage-earning people to develop a common identity. By the 1900s, then, class had emerged for Vancouverites as an important but by no means predominant source of identity and behaviour.

THE HISTORIAN of early Vancouver faces an interpretive dilemma. Vancouver society was hardly egalitarian, and if class does not by itself explain the differences in attitudes and behaviour of Shaughnessy Heights lumber barons, Mount Pleasant tradesmen, and East End labourers, what does? This book has suggested that identities were not fixed by economic relations but rather reflected a host of influences, of which the system of production was only one. Equally important was European migrants' quest for status, a process of social definition based on mutual regard or prestige that structured relationships in a hierarchical manner from the very outset of settlement on Burrard Inlet. Status provided an obvious source of social differentiation, as the prominence of professional people among Society leaders, the shared lifestyle of respectable middle- and working-class families, and the lack of empathy by skilled workers for the unskilled all attest.

Two sources of prestige were particularly important in structuring social identities in Vancouver: ethnic and racial status, and family status. As early as the 1870s a British background carried prestige on Burrard Inlet. The mill-centred elite successfully cloaked itself in the mantle of respectability by linking economic power to British ethnicity. In so doing it differentiated itself from the ethnically and racially heterogeneous majority of residents on the Inlet. Urbanization dramatically redefined the ethnic character of the working class. When, in the mid-1880s, men looking for investment opportunities and work flooded into Granville/Vancouver, the workforce that emerged was overwhelmingly White, Protestant, and of British heritage. The Inlet's Native and Mixed-Blood population did not disappear from the south shore but declined rapidly as a proportion of the whole. A few hundred Native people remained on reserves in the Vancouver area, and the Moodyville mill continued to function much as it had in the past by employing Aboriginal and Chinese labourers. In the new city of Vancouver, however, to be of Native heritage or from a non-British background was to be marginalized, to be cast outside the mainstream.

Rather than divide the elite from the majority, as it did in the 1870s, British ethnicity now functioned as an instrument that linked the majority across class lines. The attack by White workers on Chinese labourers and the effort of government and police to clear away the Indian rancherie to the east of Hastings Mill, both in 1887, marked the apex of this early movement by the new anglophone majority to establish its cultural dominance.

The racial category of 'whiteness' illustrates as well the importance of status as an instrument of social differentiation. Vancouver must be seen as one small part of a larger Britannic world, the city's dominant culture influenced by the high tide of British imperialism. But 'whiteness' also proved useful as an instrument by which Vancouver's people of British heritage secured their status as respectable 'citizens' within the local community. The extent to which the city's British majority constructed a language of race to serve this status-defining function was revealed during the prewar boom, when an influx of Italian workers challenged the majority's cultural and social identity. In response, the latter defined Italians as 'non-White,' and thus as outsiders. In this sense, Vancouver's dominant ethnic group marginalized Italians as 'immigrants,' just as it had the Chinese, Japanese, and Sikhs.

These groups also stood apart from the anglophone majority for another reason: the members of each were mainly single men, and from the outset of settlement on Burrard Inlet being married and living in a family was associated with respectability. When, in the mid-1870s, Mrs. Alexander sang to a multitude of rough loggers and millhands on Dominion Day, she not only presented the voice of middle-class morality to a working-class audience but also symbolized the ideal of domesticity and family. Yet transiency and a disproportionately male population typified life on the industrial frontier, and this condition persisted during the early city-building years. The expulsion of shack dwellers from the city's shoreline in the mid-1890s marked an important stage in the establishment of social norms in Vancouver: respectability meant families and homes, and roughness meant the single sex and impermanent lifestyle of squatters and transients. By 1913 the city's single men, 'foreigners,' and poor occupied a distinct inner core of the city that gave geographic expression to their social identity as people outside the mainstream of civic discourse.

The mainstream majority was drawn from all three classes. Its members saw themselves as respectable 'citizens' entitled to participate fully in civic affairs. They were hardly a uniform group, divided as they were by differences of income, lifestyle, and outlook. Despite the highly complex hierarchy of status that had evolved within Vancouver's ethnic majority, however, two distinct strata are discernible: an upper group topped by a cluster of families that had established themselves early as the city's leaders in business; and a broad middling group that included members of the middle and upper working classes. Both groups looked down upon ethnic and racial minorities, transient men, and the poor as people lacking the 'essential' qualities required of 'citizens.' Residents of the upper and middling strata defined themselves in part through their rejection of people in the lower stratum, the two opposites bound together in 'a dialectic of representational inclusion and exclusion.'[5]

To argue that historians must consider the role of status as well as class when exploring the makeup of Canadian cities is not to question the relevance of class analysis; capitalist societies are intrinsically class societies. But the meaning of class was complex and contingent, a product of the particularizing influences of time and place. As Richard Oestreicher discovered when exploring the nature of class consciousness in late nineteenth-century Detroit, working people had multiple identities and loyalties, and they responded to concrete situations in ways that seemed appropriate to the occasion.[6] Thus, in Vancouver, a growth boom to 1913 softened class tensions and created a shared sense that material advancement was possible within the existing capitalist order. Within only a few years, however, economic distress caused by depression and war spawned a general strike that divided much of the city along class lines. What class meant to the people of Vancouver in 1912 differed substantially from what it meant to them in 1919, when the 'effervescent optimism' of the boom years had evaporated.

An examination of status identities allows for a fuller exploration of this complexity. In particular, by focusing on the economic, ethnic and racial, and family aspects of status this study has shown how perceptual and behavioural differences *within* classes were often as important to the way people lived their lives as differences *between* classes. High-status families spent much time and large amounts of money separating themselves from the masses below, including from members of the middle class. Yet upper- and middle-class 'citizens' shared with 'ordinary' but respectable folk of the working class a profound sense of social distance from the floaters and immigrants whom they viewed as outsiders, as people who were not and should not be Vancouverites. That boundary, which coursed through the heart of the working class, constituted a division that for much of the prewar boom period more fundamentally structured Vancouver society than the boundary separating capital from labour.

Notes

Abbreviations

BCARS	British Columbia Archives and Records Service
CPRC	Canadian Pacific Railway Correspondence
CPRCA	Canadian Pacific Railway Corporate Archives
CVA	City of Vancouver Archives
NAC	National Archives of Canada
UBCSCD	University of British Columbia Library, Special Collections Division
UTTFRBR	University of Toronto, Thomas Fisher Rare Book Room
VBPCP	Vancouver Board of Park Commissioners' Papers
VF	Vertical file

Introduction

1 Hugh Keenleyside, *Memoirs of Hugh L. Keenleyside* (Toronto: McClelland and Stewart 1981), vol. 1, *Hammer the Golden Day,* 40.

2 Computer-assisted community studies, often posing as their central question the nature of mobility (geographic and social) during the early stages of industrialization in North America, are generally categorized as 'the new urban history.' For example, see Stephen Thernstrom, *Poverty and Progress: Social Mobility in a Nineteenth-Century City* (Cambridge, MA: Harvard University Press 1964); Peter R. Knights, *The Plain People of Boston 1830-1860: A Study in City Growth* (New York: Oxford University Press 1971); Michael B. Katz, *The People of Hamilton, Canada West. Families and Class in a Mid-Nineteenth-Century City* (Cambridge, MA: Harvard University Press 1975); Clyde Griffen and Sally

Griffen, *Natives and Newcomers: The Ordering of Opportunity in Mid-Nineteenth-Century Poughkeepsie* (Cambridge, MA: Harvard University Press 1978); and Michael B. Katz, Michael J. Doucet, and Mark J. Stern, *The Social Organization of Early Industrial Capitalism* (Cambridge, MA: Harvard University Press 1982).

The 'new urban history' was, however, merely a subset of the much broader field of urban history. The themes explored by Canadian urban historians are surveyed in Alan F.J. Artibise and Gilbert A. Stelter, *Canada's Urban Past: A Bibliography to 1980 and Guide to Canadian Urban Studies* (Vancouver: University of British Columbia Press 1981), xiii-xxxii and Gilbert A. Stelter, 'The City-Building Process in Canada,' in *Shaping the Urban Landscape: Aspects of the Canadian City-Building Process,* ed. Gilbert A. Stelter and Alan F.J. Artibise (Ottawa: Carleton University Press 1982), 1-29

3 The first two censuses, which became available to researchers in the mid-1980s, have been coded, computerized, and analyzed; the 1901 census, which opened in 1993, has not been examined systematically. The 1911 manuscript census is not yet available to researchers.

4 Throughout the book I use the word 'businessmen' to refer to the upper stratum within Vancouver's business community. As noted later in the Introduction, I identified 322 top business people in Vancouver, of whom all but two were men. Since this group was overwhelmingly masculine, I have decided to refer to its members as 'businessmen.' To use a phrase such as 'business people' would imply a greater degree of gender equality than the evidence merits.

5 See Robert A.J. McDonald, 'Business Leaders in Early Vancouver, 1886-1914' (PhD dissertation, University of British Columbia 1977).

6 Michael Frisch, 'American Urban History as an Example of Recent Historiography,' *History and Theory* 18 (1979):371. Also see Bryan D. Palmer, 'Modernizing History,' and Michael Katz, 'Reply,' in Committee on Labour History *Bulletin* 2 (Autumn 1976):16-31.

7 The phrase 'milltown to metropolis' is from Alan Morley, *Vancouver: From Milltown to Metropolis* (Vancouver: Mitchell Press 1961).

8 A good example from the Canadian literature is Alan F.J. Artibise's *Winnipeg: A Social History of Urban Growth, 1874-1914* (Montreal and Kingston: McGill-Queen's University Press 1975), which led the way in establishing urban history as an important field of historical inquiry during the 1970s. Yet social groups are portrayed by Artibise in undifferentiated terms, especially the upper portion of Winnipeg society, which he sees as a monolithic 'commercial elite.' For a critical comment on this portrayal of Winnipeg's social organization, see Robert A.J. McDonald, 'The Business Elite and Municipal Politics in Vancouver 1886-1914,' *Urban History Review* 11, 3 (February 1983):12.

Exceptions to the argument that historians studying cities in the 1970s tended to ignore social relations and social conflict can be found in John Bodnar, *Immigration and Industrialization: Ethnicity in an American Mill Town, 1870-1940* (Pittsburgh: University of Pittsburgh Press 1977); Bryan D. Palmer, *A Culture in Conflict: Skilled Workers and Industrial Capitalism in Hamilton, Ontario, 1860-1914* (Montreal: McGill-Queen's University Press 1979); and Daniel J. Walkowitz, *Worker City, Company Town: Iron and Cotton-Worker Protest in Troy and Cohoes, New York, 1855-84* (Urbana: University of Illinois Press 1981). Interestingly, while these books focus on urban places, their authors wrote as social historians of immigrants and working people rather than as urban historians.

9 See Robin Fisher, 'Matters for Reflection: *BC Studies* and British Columbia History,' *BC Studies* 100 (Winter 1993-4):66-8 and 75; Martin Robin, *The Rush for Spoils: The Com-*

pany Province, 1871-1933 (Toronto: McClelland and Stewart 1972), *Pillars of Profit: The Company Province, 1934-1972* (Toronto: McClelland and Stewart 1973), and 'The Social Basis of Party Politics in British Columbia,' in *Party Politics in Canada*, 2nd ed., ed. Hugh Thornburn (Toronto: Prentice-Hall 1967), 201-12; W. Peter Ward, 'Class and Race in the Social Structure of British Columbia, 1870-1939,' *BC Studies* 45 (Spring 1980):17-35 (quotation from p. 35) and 'Race and Class in British Columbia: A Reply,' *BC Studies* 50 (Summer 1981):52; and Rennie Warburton, 'Race and Class in British Columbia: A Comment,' *BC Studies* 49 (Spring 1981):79-85.

10 For instance, Jeremy Mouat has questioned the argument that labour in British Columbia's mining districts was exceptionally militant or radical, a staple of earlier writing on the subject; Mark Leier has made a strong case for exploring intraclass as well as interclass conflict; James Conley has interpreted the collective action of salmon fishermen in terms of the capital structure of the industry, illustrating, for example, the different interests of wage-earning fishermen and commodity-producing fishermen; and Alicja Muszynski has suggested that the persistence of precapitalist relations of production among Native cannery workers – their ability to meet subsistence needs in part through customary, non-market methods such as hunting and gathering – allowed them to work seasonally in the canneries along the north coast for wages below what they would have required if fully dependent on wage labour. See Jeremy Mouat, 'The Genesis of Western Exceptionalism: British Columbia's Hard-Rock Miners, 1895-1903,' *Canadian Historical Review* 71 (September 1990):317-45; Mark Leier, 'Ethnicity, Urbanism, and Labour Aristocracy: Rethinking Vancouver Trade Unionism, 1889-1909,' *Canadian Historical Review* 74 (December 1993):510-34; James Conley, 'Relations of Production and Collective Action in the Salmon Fishery, 1900-1925,' in *Workers, Capital, and the State in British Columbia: Selected Papers*, ed. Rennie Warburton and David Coburn (Vancouver: UBC Press 1988), 86-116; and Alicja Muszynski, 'Race and Gender: Structural Determinants in the Formation of British Columbia's Salmon Cannery Labour Force,' in *Class, Gender, and Region: Essays in Canadian Historical Sociology*, ed. Gregory S. Kealey (St. John's: Committee on Canadian Labour History 1988), 103-20.

11 Joy Parr, *The Gender of Breadwinners: Women, Men, and Change in Two Industrial Towns, 1880-1950* (Toronto: University of Toronto Press 1990), 3-11 and 245 (quotations from pp. 8 and 9). I support Parr's call for flexible categories of analysis and agree with her conclusion that no categories 'either singly or in conjunction, map the whole of social existence' (p. 245). Our approaches do lead to somewhat different conclusions about the relationship between categories, however. Whereas Parr emphasizes the 'simultaneity of ... ways of being' (she explores gender and class), I argue that the particularizing influences of time and place can make some identities more important than others at given points in history.

12 David Cannadine, 'Cutting Classes,' *New York Review of Books*, 17 December 1992, pp. 52-7 (quotation from p. 57).

13 Mariana Valverde, *The Age of Light, Soap, and Water: Moral Reform in English Canada, 1885-1925* (Toronto: McClelland and Stewart 1991), 14 and 166 (quotation).

14 Carol Smart, 'Feminist Jurisprudence,' in *Dangerous Supplements: Resistance and Renewal in Jurisprudence*, ed. Peter Fitzpatrick (London: Pluto Press 1991), 138.

15 Theoretical literature interpreting the structure of capitalist society from a Marxist perspective includes Leonard Beeghley, *Social Stratification in America: A Critical Analysis of Theory and Research* (Santa Monica, CA: Goodyear Publishing 1978), chap. 1 and 2; Nicos Poulantzas, 'On Social Classes,' in *Classes, Power, and Conflict: Classical and Con-*

temporary Debates, ed. Anthony Giddens and David Held (Berkeley: University of California Press 1982), 101-11 and 112-29; Erik Olin Wright, *Class, Crisis, and the State* (London: NLB 1978), 30-97; Val Burris, 'The Neo-Marxist Synthesis of Marx and Weber on Class,' in *The Marx-Weber Debate*, ed. Norbert Wiley (Newbury Park, CA: Sage 1987), 67-90; and Warburton, 'Race and Class in British Columbia,' 79-85. E.P. Thompson's definition of class in humanistic and subjective rather than structural terms offered a very attractive alternative to the one I employ here, but his insistence that class expresses itself through conflict raised practical problems if applied to a whole city of more than 100,000 people, where conflicts were many and varied. For a useful discussion of Thompson's place in theoretical literature on class, see Christopher Kent, 'Presence and Absence: History, Theory, and the Working Class,' *Victorian Studies* 29 (Spring 1986):437-49.

16 Beeghley, *Social Stratification in America*, 27-41; Giddens and Held, eds., *Classes, Power, and Conflict*, 60-86; and Anthony Giddens, *The Class Structure of the Advanced Societies* (1973; reprint, London: Hutchison 1980), 41-52; Weber's words are cited in Beeghley, *Social Stratification in America*, 31.

17 Giddens, *Class Structure of the Advanced Societies*, 78.

18 Frank Parkin, 'Social Closure and Class Formation,' in Giddens and Held, *Classes, Power, and Conflict*, 175. Also see Burris, 'Neo-Marxist Synthesis of Marx and Weber on Class,' 67-90 and Reinhard Bendix, 'Inequality and Social Structure: A Comparison of Marx and Weber,' *American Sociological Review* 39 (April 1974):149-61.

19 Peter Burke, *History and Social Theory* (Cambridge: Polity Press 1992), 62-3 (quotation) and Giddens, *Class Structure of the Advanced Societies*, 50-2. Löic Wacquant writes of 'widening areas of overlap and convergence between Marxist and Weberian approaches ... New Class theorists, for instance, draw as much on Weber as they do on Marx ... The ritual opposition of these two traditions of class theory is no longer meaningful and profitable. One must now build on both of them to try to transcend their common interests' ('Making Class: The Middle Class(es) in Social Theory and Social Structure,' in *Bringing Class Back In: Contemporary and Historical Perspectives*, ed. Scott G. McNall, Rhonda F. Levine, and Rick Fantasia [Boulder, CO: Westview Press 1991], 50). Val Burris concludes her study, 'The Neo-Marxist Synthesis of Marx and Weber on Class,' with the following observation: 'In terms of the classical definitions, it is impossible to classify many contemporary theorists as either Marxist or Weberian in any unambiguous sense ... it is no longer possible to draw a sharp line between opposing theoretical schools' (p. 87).

20 Burris, 'Neo-Marxist Synthesis of Marx and Weber on Class,' 74-5.

21 Ibid., 75. Also see Wacquant, 'Making Class,' 51 and 57-8.

22 Giddens, *Class Structure of the Advanced Societies*, 20.

23 Beeghley, *Social Stratification in America*, 30 and Giddens, *Class Structure of the Advanced Societies*, 80.

24 Seymour Martin Lipset, 'Social Class,' in *Social Stratification: Canada*, ed. James E. Curtis and William G. Scott (Scarborough, ON: Prentice-Hall 1973), 25-6. Also see Gunther Roth and Claus Wittich, eds., *Economy and Society: An Outline of Interpretive Sociology* (New York: Bedminster Press 1968), 302-7 and 927-40 and Giddens, *Class Structure of the Advanced Societies*, 43-4.

25 Kurt B. Meyer and Walter Buckley, *Class and Society*, 3rd. ed. (New York: Random House 1970), 46.

26 Bendix, 'Inequality and Social Structure,' 152.
27 Frank Parkin, *Marxism and Class Theory: A Bourgeois Critique* (London: Tavistock Publishers 1979), 34.
28 Frank Parkin, 'Social Closure and Class Formation,' 176. Burris argues that 'Weberian theorists typically subsume racial divisions under the general category of *status* group formation, whereas Marxists tend to conceptualize racial oppression as a variant of *national* or colonial oppression' ('Neo-Marxist Synthesis of Marx and Weber on Class,' 77).
29 James S. Woodsworth, *On the Waterfront* (Ottawa: n.p. n.d.), UBCSCD, pamphlet, p. 4. For Woodsworth's social and political philosophy, see Kenneth McNaught, *A Prophet in Politics: A Biography of J.S. Woodsworth* (Toronto: University of Toronto Press 1959).
30 Through extensive research in city directories, biographical dictionaries, newspapers, and especially the provincial Registration of Companies records, I identified a total of 320 businessmen and 2 businesswomen as Vancouver's business leaders or subleaders. This total is divided between two periods as follows: 1890-3 leaders, 21, and subleaders, 45; 1910-13 leaders, 91, and subleaders, 185. All but two were men. Of the 322, 20 appeared in one of the leadership categories for both periods. The number included in the other leadership groups are: Society, 302; civic politicians, 150; and officers of the Vancouver Trades and Labor Council, 39. As will be noted in Chapter 6, Society members were defined through associational ties of both men and women, though for analytical purposes each Society family is identified through the name of the male head of the household. The 150 members of City Council from 1886-1914 included 136 who served as aldermen only, 8 who served as both aldermen and mayor, and 6 as mayor. All were men, as were the 39 executive members of the VTLC.
    I have identified in earlier publications my criteria for determining all but the VTLC officers. For top business people, see McDonald, 'The Business Elite and Municipal Politics in Vancouver,' 3, 6 (table 2), and 12-13 n. 11 and 'Vancouver's "Four Hundred": The Quest for Wealth and Status in Canada's Urban West, 1886-1914,' *Journal of Canadian Studies* 25 (Autumn 1990):56 and 70 nn. 10 and 12. Since the 1983 article, I have reassigned one member of the prewar subleadership group to the leaders (increasing the latter from 90 to 91 and decreasing the former from 186 to 185; I have also changed the name 'second level business leaders' to 'subleaders.' The labour elite is drawn from executive members of the Vancouver Trades and Labor Council. I devised a point system that assigned nine points for one term (each term was of six months duration) as president, three points for one term as vice-president or general-secretary, and one point for some other position (such as treasurer or trustee). Data were compiled from the list of officers registered in the Vancouver Trades and Labor Council Minutes. For 'Society', see 'Vancouver's "Four Hundred."' Social and economic information about members of the various leadership groups was drawn from city directories, various biographical sources, especially newspapers of the period, and the 1891 Nominal Census. Probate records were also searched and proved much more fruitful for economic and social leaders than for Labor Council executives.
31 Julius Gould and William L. Kolb, eds., *A Dictionary of the Social Sciences* (New York: Free Press 1964), 234 and Seymour Martin Lipset and Aldo Salari, eds., *Elites in Latin America* (New York: Oxford 1967), vii-viii.
32 Wacquant, 'Making Class,' 51.
33 Modern scholarship on the concept of citizenship flows from a seminal essay published in 1949 by British sociologist T.H. Marshall, 'Citizenship and Social Class.' Marshall posited

an evolutionary model of progress from the emergence of civil rights in the eighteenth century to political rights in the nineteenth and social in the twentieth. My use of the term departs from the main current of scholarship on the subject by emphasizing its social and cultural meaning in a local setting. I define 'citizenship' much as sociologist Bryan S. Turner does, as 'social membership within modern political collectivities.' In this sense, citizenship is taken as 'a genuinely sociological as distinct from a legal or political notion.' My approach is also informed by the argument of David Held that 'citizenship is about involvement of people in the community in which they live.' Exploration of this membership, Held suggests, must involve a 'variety of dimensions of social life which have been central to the struggle over citizenship.' See T.H. Marshall and Tom Bottomore, *Citizenship and Social Class* (London: Pluto Press 1992); Bryan S. Turner, 'Contemporary Problems in the Theory of Citizenship,' in *Citizenship and Social Theory,* ed. Turner (London: Sage 1993), 2-3; and David Held, 'Citizenship and Autonomy,' in *Social Theory and Modern Societies: Anthony Giddens and His Critics,* ed. David Held and John B. Thompson (Cambridge: Cambridge University Press 1989), 173.

Chapter 1: Crowded between Forest and Shore

1 Published work on Vancouver Island coal mining includes John Belshaw, 'The Standard of Living of British Miners on Vancouver Island, 1848-1900,' *BC Studies* 84 (Winter 1989-90):37-64; Jeremy Mouat, 'The Politics of Coal: A Study of the Wellington Miners' Strike of 1890-91,' *BC Studies* 77 (Spring 1988):3-29; and H. Keith Ralston, 'Miners and Managers: The Organization of Coal Production on Vancouver Island by the Hudson's Bay Company, 1848-1862,' in *The Company on the Coast,* ed. E. Blanche Norcross (Nanaimo: Nanaimo Historical Society 1983), 42-55.

For salmon canning, see Geoff Meggs, *Salmon: The Decline of the British Columbia Fishery* (Vancouver: Douglas and McIntyre 1991); Alicja Muszynski, 'Race and Gender: Structural Determinants in the Formation of British Columbia's Cannery Labour Force,' in *Class, Gender, and Region: Essays in Canadian Historical Sociology,* ed. Gregory S. Kealey (St. John's: Committee on Canadian Labour History 1988), 103-20; Dianne Newell, 'The Rationality of Mechanization in the Pacific Salmon Canning Industry before the Second World War,' *Business History Review* 62 (Winter 1988):626-55; and H. Keith Ralston, 'Patterns of Trade and Investment on the Pacific Coast, 1867-1892: The Case of the British Columbia Salmon Canning Industry,' *BC Studies* 1 (1968-9):37-45.

The best work on the social history of forestry along the northwest coast in the nineteenth century focuses on the American industry. See Norman Clark, *Mill Town: A Social History of Everett, Washington* (Seattle: University of Washington Press 1970); Richard A. Rajala, 'Bill and the Boss: Labor Protest, Technological Change, and the Transformation of the West Coast Logging Camp, 1890-1930,' *Journal of Forest History* 33 (October 1989):168-79; and William G. Robbins, *Hard Times in Paradise: Coos Bay, Oregon, 1850-1986* (Seattle: University of Washington Press 1988).

The best social history of a resource-extractive community in British Columbia before 1900 is Cole Harris, 'Industry and the Good Life around Idaho Peak,' *Canadian Historical Review* 66, 3 (September 1985):315-43.

2 The term 'frontier' is used in this chapter much as Don Harrison Doyle employed it in *The Social Order of a Frontier Community: Jacksonville, Illinois, 1825-1870* (Urbana: University of Illinois Press 1978), 3, to refer loosely to the period when settlement was beginning and the social order was relatively unfixed. It is not employed in the Turner-

ian sense as defined by Ray Allen Billington, *America's Frontier Heritage* (New York: Holt, Rinehart and Winston 1966).

3 *The British Columbia Directory for 1882-83* (Victoria: R.T. Williams 1882), 235.

4 Eric Nichol, *Vancouver* (Toronto: Doubleday 1970), 11-21; Kay Cronin, *Cross in the Wilderness* (Vancouver: Mitchell Press 1960), 122-4; Thomas A. Lascelles, O.M.I., *Mission on the Inlet* (Vancouver: St. Paul's Province, Order of the Oblates of Mary Immaculate 1984), 5-15; and CVA, Add. MSS 54, Matthews Collection (hereafter cited as Matthews Collection), files 00634 and 03345 re elk, and 00610 and 02051 re missionaries.

5 Charles Hill-Tout, *The Salish People*, ed. with introduction by Ralph Maud (Vancouver: Talonbooks 1978), 2:27-30 and 3:11-19.

6 Cole Harris, 'The Lower Mainland, 1821-81,' in *Vancouver and Its Region,* ed. Graeme Wynn and Timothy Oke (Vancouver: UBC Press 1992), 42.

7 In conversation with Major Matthews, August Jack Khatsahlano, who was born at Whoi-Whoi in 1877, claimed that Squamish people had lived there continuously before Europeans arrived. Anthropological evidence suggests, however, that the Squamish began to reside at Burrard Inlet year round only when the sawmills employed their labour. See Homer G. Barnett, *The Coast Salish of British Columbia* (1955; reprint, Westport, CT: Greenwood Press 1975), 9-10 and 31-4; Wilson Duff, *The Upper Stalo Indians* (Victoria: British Columbia Provincial Museum 1952), 27; Major J.S. Matthews, comp., *Conversations with Khatsahlano, 1932-1954* (Vancouver: City of Vancouver Archives 1955), 31, 35A, 213, and 246; Matthews Collection, file 06588; and Harris, 'Lower Mainland,' 301.

8 Figures derived from Canada, Nominal Census 1881, microfilm C-13284, British Columbia, Division 187 (New Westminster), Subsection D7 (Coast of Mainland), 35-44 and 50-62: Skuhuamish Indians on Burrard Inlet. The locations of Squamish villages are discussed in Matthews, *Conversations*, 31.

9 F.G.H. Brooks, 'Vancouver's Origins' (MA thesis, University of British Columbia 1952), 26-37; Kathleen Marjorie Woodward-Reynolds, 'A History of the City and District of North Vancouver' (MA thesis, University of British Columbia 1943), 11-20; Joseph C. Lawrence, 'Markets and Capital: A History of the Lumber Industry of British Columbia (1778-1952)' (MA thesis, University of British Columbia 1957), 9-20; and F.W. Howay, 'Early Shipping in Burrard Inlet, 1863-1870,' *British Columbia Historical Quarterly* 1 (1937):3-20 (quotation from p. 4).

10 Brooks, 'Vancouver's Origins,' 26-37; Howay, 'Early Shipping,' 3-20 and Lawrence, 'Markets and Capital,' 20-7.

11 Thomas R. Cox, *Mills and Markets: A History of the Pacific Coast Lumber Industry to 1900* (Seattle: University of Washington Press 1974), 21-137; Lawrence, 'Markets and Capital,' 4-15; and Brooks, 'Vancouver's Origins,' 55.

12 Newton H. Chittenden, *Travels in British Columbia* (1882; reprint, Vancouver: G. Soules 1984), 66-7; *Illustrated History of British Columbia* (Victoria: [?] 1884), 301-2; *British Columbia Directory for 1882-83,* 234; and the Rev. Stott, 'The Mills of Moodyville,' Matthews Collection, file 04420.

13 Quotations from Lawrence, 'Markets and Capital,' 35-6. For an excellent description of a New Westminster mill in the 1880s, see Morley Roberts, *The Prey of the Strongest* (London: T. Fisher Unwin 1906), 1-21.

14 R.H. Alexander, 'Reminiscences of the Early Days of British Columbia,' CVA, Vancouver Art, Historical, and Scientific Society Records, Add. MSS 336, p. 113; also see Matthews Collection, files 02473 and 03307.

15 Matthews, *Conversations*, 253; Matthews Collection, files 00596, 02473, 03307, 04420, 04479, 06260, and 06588; Canada, *Sessional Papers*, 1879, vol. 6, Department of the Interior, Indian Affairs Branch, 'Annual Report, 1878,' no. 7, pp. 72-3; and ibid., 1885, vol. 3, Department of Indian Affairs, 'Annual Report 1884,' no. 3, p. 104. For a general discussion of the role that Native people played in the industrial economy of late nineteenth-century British Columbia, see Rolf Knight, *Indians at Work: An Informal History of Native Indian Labour in British Columbia* (Vancouver: New Star Books 1978) and John Lutz, 'After the Fur Trade: The Aboriginal Labouring Class of British Columbia 1849-1890,' *Journal of the Canadian Historical Association* n.s. 3 (1992):69-94.

16 Canada, *Sessional Papers*, 1878, vol. 8, Department of the Interior, Indian Affairs Branch, 'Special Appendix D,' no. 10, p. lii. My thanks to John Lutz for this reference.

17 Douglas Cole and Bradley Lockner, eds., *The Journals of George M. Dawson* (Vancouver: UBC Press 1990), vol. 1, *British Columbia, 1875-1878,* 115.

18 Morley Roberts, *The Western Avernus: or, Toil and Travel in Further North America*, new ed. (Westminster: A. Constable 1896), 162; Lawrence, 'Markets and Capital,' 35-6; Matthews Collection, file 01835; George M. Grant, *Ocean to Ocean: Sandford Fleming's Expedition through Canada in 1872* (Rutland, VT: C.E. Tuttle 1967), 323; and Edward M. Towler, 'Old-Timers Interviewed,' *Pacific Coast Lumberman* 4, 4 (April 1920):39.

19 Cole and Lockner, eds., *Journals of George M. Dawson*, 115. Excellent descriptions of Moodyville are to be found in the Matthews Collection, files 04420 (Rev. Stott) and 03270 (Muriel Crackanthorp), and in BCARS, VF: Moodyville, microfilm #0436-0439 (Patrick Allen); and Burrard Inlet, microfilm #0452-0455 (Ruby Bower).

20 James C. McCulley to his parents, 5 September 1875, BCARS, E/C/M13, McCulley Correspondence.

21 Brooks, 'Vancouver's Origins,' 39-40; Nichol, *Vancouver*, 32-6 and 40-3; and John Deighton to his brother, 28 June 1870, BCARS, E/B/D36, Deighton Correspondence, Outward.

22 Matthews Collection, files 01836, 02605, and 04179 (quotation from file 02605) and *Nanaimo Free Press*, 5 July 1876.

23 John Warren Bell, Memoirs, CVA, Add. MSS 144, p. 79A; also see Matthews Collection, file 01835 (quotation from file 06260 [the Rev. C.M. Tate]).

24 *British Columbia Directory for 1882-83*, 235. Also see Cole and Lockner, eds., *Dawson*, 117-18 and Matthews Collection, file 02051 (Calvert Simson).

25 Brooks, 'Vancouver's Origins,' 42-6; F.W. Howay, 'Early Settlement on Burrard Inlet,' *British Columbia Historical Quarterly* 1 (April 1937):103-4, 106-9; and Matthews Collection, file 01835 (George Black). Quotation from Matthews.

26 Refers to men and women of European and Native descent, the latter mainly Mixed-Blood, but not to Native people living on reserves outside the lumber villages.

27 In the words of Arthur Austin Langley, 'When I came here in 1882 there were few families on Burrard Inlet' (Matthews Collection, file 01835). Also see (Mrs.) C.E. Cordiner to John Jessop, 5 June 1876, BCARS, British Columbia, Superintendent of Education Correspondence, 1872-17, microfilm reel 1. My thanks to Clint Evans for references re education on Burrard Inlet and to Jean Barman, for whom Clint's research was carried out.

28 In addition, Burrard Inlet ferry boat operator Captain James Van Bramer, Hastings Sawmill foremen Leon Nahu and Charles Coldwell, and Moodyville millhand Secundo Caresco, among others, also created families with women indigenous to the area. See Matthews Collection, files 00312, 00313, 01460, 01835, 01838, 02473, 05089, and 06612 (quotation from file 01835) and Bell, Memoirs, 176.

29 See Table 1.2 for a description of the method used to identify from the 1881 Nominal Census people of Native descent who lived in the lumber villages of Burrard Inlet. The Gonzaleses are listed in both the 1891 and 1901 censuses as Gonzales, but in 1881 as Onsalez. The 1901 census also identifies Emma Gonzales as 'Indian Other Breed.' My thanks to Roderick Barman and Jean Barman for the 1901 information.

30 By 1891, the number at Moodyville had increased to nine, with four women working as longshore workers, three as general labourers, and two as cooks. Of these, six were Native, one Mixed-Blood, one Chinese, and one Swedish. See Canada, Nominal Census 1891, microfilm T-6290, British Columbia, District 2 (New Westminster), Subdistrict A (Burrard Inlet), and Division 2a, pp. 20-42.

31 For casual labour by Native women, see Matthews, *Conversations*, 248 and Matthews Collection, file 06596; for school teachers, see Matthews Collection, file 02052. While virtually nothing is known about prostitutes, novelist Daphne Marlatt identifies Birdie Stewart as Vancouver's first madam (*Ana Historic: A Novel* [Toronto: Coach House Press 1988], 47). For Emily Susan Patterson and John Patterson, who came to Hastings Sawmill from the Columbia River in 1873 before moving to Moodyville in 1874, see Major J.S. Matthews, 'Early Vancouver: Narratives of Pioneers of Vancouver, B.C.,' CVA, typescript, vol. 4, 147-9 and 185 and Nora M. Duncan, *The Heroine of Moodyville: An Epic of Burrard Inlet, 1883,* CVA, Pamphlet 1936-52. My thanks to Helen Shore for alerting me to Emily Patterson's role as midwife and lay nurse at Burrard Inlet in the 1870s and 1880s.

32 Cole and Lockner, eds., *Journals of George M. Dawson*, 115.

33 'Bygone Days in Vancouver: ... A Talk with R.H. Alexander,' BCARS, VF (R.H. Alexander), microfilm #1622.

34 For Kanakas in general see Matthews Collection, files 02424, 04420, 05089, 06596, and 06612; for Frisadie, file 03345. For a comment on the relationship between Kanakas and Natives on the west coast during the fur trade, see E. Momilani Naughton, 'Hawaiians in the Fur Trade: Cultural Influence on the North West Coast, 1811-1875' (MA thesis, Western Washington University 1983), 28-40.

35 The functions of 'Society' on Burrard Inlet are described in the Matthews Collection, files 01263, 02051, 02052, 03090, 03270, and 04420 (quotation from file 02052), and Bell, Memoirs, 82; for the role of visiting ships, see the Matthews Collection, file 03270 and the *Mainland Guardian*, 18 July 1883, p. 3 and 11 August 1883, p. 3 (quotation from 11 August); and for St. James Church, see Matthews Collection, files 02052 and 06236 and Jessie Parnes, 'History of St. James,' CVA, St. James Anglican Church Records, Add. MSS 570, p. 4.

36 J.K. Johnson, *Becoming Prominent: Regional Leadership in Upper Canada, 1791-1841* (Kingston and Montreal: McGill-Queen's University Press 1989), 88; Peter Bailey, '"Will the Real Bill Banks Please Stand Up?" Towards a Role Analysis of Mid-Victorian Working Class Respectability,' *Journal of Social History* 12 (Spring 1979):338; and Geoffrey Best, *Mid-Victorian Britain, 1851-1875* (London: Weidenfeld and Nicolson 1971), 257.

37 W. Wymond Walkem, 'Christmas Thirty-Eight Years Ago,' in *Stories of Early British Columbia* (Vancouver: 1914), 91 and 'Bygone Days in Vancouver,' BCARS, VF (R.H. Alexander), microfilm #1622. The extent to which loggers of British birth or background saw themselves, and were viewed by others, as 'respectable' remains unclear. Their position was ambiguous, and probably varied according to context. Farther south, a Union soldier stationed in Oregon during the American Civil War depicted

lumbermen there as 'Roughs'; the close association of these woodsmen with Native women appears to have contributed significantly to the observer's perception of their low status. See Gunter Barth, ed., *All Quiet on the Yamhill: The Civil War in Oregon. The Journal of Corporal Royal A. Bensell* (Eugene, OR: 1959), 145-7.

38 James C. McCulley to his parents, 5 September 1875, BCARS, E/C/M13, McCulley Correspondence; and 'Petition of 18 February 1888 to H.B. Raycroft, Sup't. of Provincial Police, Victoria, B.C.,' BCARS, GR 429, British Columbia, Attorney-General, Correspondence, box 2, file 1:1888, doc. 149/88.

39 Quotation from Matthews, *Conversations*, 253-4; also see Bell, Memoirs, 28 and 'Bygone Days in Vancouver,' BCARS, VF (R.H. Alexander), microfilm #1622.

40 Matthews, *Conversations*, 94; and Matthews Collection, file 06612, vol. 1, M237.

41 Canada, *Sessional Papers*, 1879, vol. 6, Department of Interior, Indian Affairs Branch, 'Annual Report, 1878,' no. 7, pp. 73 and ibid., 1885, vol. 3, Department of Indian Affairs, 'Annual Report, 1884,' no. 3, p. 104; and Roberts, *Prey of the Strongest*, passim.

42 T.H. Mathers to John Jessop, 13 April 1876, BCARS, British Columbia, Superintendent of Education Correspondence 1872-97, GR 1445, microfilm reel 1. Also see Henry W. Hughes to John Jessop, 16 February 1877, ibid., microfilm reel 1; (Miss) A.I. Goring to C.C. McKenzie, 24 March 1879 and A.I. Colbeck to C.C. McKenzie, 19 April 1880, ibid., microfilm reel 2; and A.I. Colbeck to C.C. McKenzie, 27 October 1882, ibid., microfilm reel 3.

43 The definition of 'paternalism' employed here is drawn from Bryan D. Palmer, *Working-Class Experience: Rethinking the History of Canadian Labour, 1800-1991*, 2nd ed. (Toronto: McClelland and Stewart 1992), 41-8. Also see John Kleinig, *Paternalism* (Totowa, NJ: Rowman and Allanheld 1984), 4-7. For an excellent study of paternalism in an industrial setting in mid-to-late Victorian England, see Patrick Joyce, *Work, Society and Politics: The Culture of the Factory in Later Victorian England* (London: Methuen 1982), xxi, 53, 79, 92-9, 110, 124, 134-57, and 186. For a Canadian example of paternalism in an early industrial setting, see Christian Norman, 'A Company Community: Garden Island, Upper Canada at Mid-Century,' *Canadian Papers in Rural History* 2 (1980):113-34.

44 Mechanic's Institute of Burrard Inlet, Minutes, 1869-84, CVA, Vancouver Art, Historical and Scientific Society Records, vol. 26, file 253; Mount Hermon Lodge Membership Lists, 1869-85, and Correspondence, especially letters of 30 September 1879 and 31 January 1882, BCARS, Freemasons Records, Add. MSS 002, box 4, files 1-2 and 4; Matthews Collection, files 00671 and 04306; and Brooks, 'Vancouver's Origins,' 73-7.

45 In 1882-3 the owner and manager of the Moodyville sawmill sat as two of Moodyville's four school trustees, while on the south shore the mill manager functioned as secretary of the Granville board. On both sides of the Inlet school buildings were provided by the sawmill companies. See Matthews Collection, files 02052 and 00903 and Helen Boutilier, 'Vancouver's Earliest Days,' *British Columbia Historical Quarterly* 10 (1946):157.

46 For the close connection between justices of the peace and local communities in the colonies of British North America before Confederation, see Allan Greer, 'The Birth of the Police in Canada,' in *Colonial Leviathan: State Formation in Mid-Nineteenth-Century Canada*, ed. Allan Greer and Ian Radforth (Toronto: University of Toronto Press 1992), 18-19.

47 *British Columbia Gazette* 13, 14 (April 1873):1 and 14, 28 (July 1876):165; and Boutilier, 'Vancouver's Earliest Days,' 157 n. 10.

48 Walkem, 'Christmas Thirty-Eight Years Ago,' 189; also see H.B. Roycroft to the Attorney-General, 23 February 1888, BCARS, British Columbia, Attorney-General, Correspondence, GR 429, box 2, doc. 149/88.

49 BCARS, VF (Burrard Inlet), microfilm #0455-0456.

50 Quotations from *Mainland Guardian*, 1 July 1876 and 2 July 1873; also see ibid., 4 July 1874 and 3 July 1880; Matthews Collection, files 01213, 02050, 02051, 02403, and 04420; and BCARS, VF (Moodyville), microfilm #0436-0439.

51 *Vancouver News*, 20 October 1886, p. 1. The reference here is to the club when reconstituted in 1886 after being formed seven years earlier.

52 *Mainland Guardian*, 4 July 1874, 3 and Matthews Collection, file 00030 (Hedley W. Otton).

53 Matthews Collection, file 03270 (Muriel Crackanthorp).

54 'Pioneer Judges Wife – Memoirs of Life in B.C., 1864-1906,' NAC, MG29 C54, vol. 1, file 1, pp. 19-24.

55 Diary, 1 July 1876, BCARS, Rev. Charles Montgomery Tate Papers, Add. MSS 303, vol. 1, folder 5.

56 Alexander, 'Reminiscences,' 13.

57 Potlatches occurred at the Hastings Mill rancherie in 1884 and 1885, Whoi-Whoi in 1885, and Seymour Creek in 1889. See Matthews, *Conversations*, 23, 199, 240, 268, 278, and 284 and Matthews Collection, file 01263. Quotations from Grant, *Ocean to Ocean*, 323.

58 BCARS, British Columbia, Attorney-General, Depositions, GR 419, vol. 878, box 14, files 1876/7 and 1876/8.

59 Matthews Collection, file 04191 and Walkem, 'Christmas Thirty-Eight Years Ago,' 92-4.

60 This point is suggested in Palmer, *Working-Class Experience*, 42.

61 The strike took place in early April and significantly influenced the subsequent civic election. Knights of Labor organizers who had accompanied navvies down to the coast from Interior railway construction camps appear to have been actively involved in the strike. See the reminiscences of W.H Gallagher and Hedley W. Otton in the Matthews Collection, files 01835 and 00030. Also see ibid., files 01749 and 02052.

Chapter 2: City Builders

1 The Dominion Day celebrations of 1889 and 1890 are documented in *Vancouver Daily World* (hereafter *World*), 2 July 1889, pp. 1 and 2 and 2 July 1890, p. 1; *Daily News-Advertiser* (hereafter *News-Advertiser*), 29 June, 1889, p. 1, 30 June 1889, p. 1, 2 July 1889, p. 1, and 2 July 1890, pp. 1 and 8; and *Daily Colonist* (hereafter *Colonist*), 1 July 1890, p. 5.

2 *World*, 2 July 1889, 1.

3 Mary Ryan, 'The American Parade: Representations of the Nineteenth-Century Social Order,' in *The New Cultural History*, ed. Lynn Hunt (Berkeley: University of California Press 1989), 133.

4 The values symbolized by nineteenth-century cities in Britain are explored in Asa Briggs, *Victorian Cities* (Harmondsworth: Penguin Books 1963).

5 Correspondence between the BC government and the CPR concerning the Vancouver land grant is published in British Columbia, Legislative Assembly, *Sessional Papers,* 1885, pp. 129-36 and 385-6. See also Norbert MacDonald, 'The Canadian Pacific Railway and Vancouver's Development to 1900,' *BC Studies* 35 (Autumn 1977):9 and 11.

6 G.W.S. Brooks, 'Edgar Crow Baker: An Entrepreneur in Early British Columbia,' *BC Studies* 31 (Autumn 1976):31-4 and Patricia E. Roy, *Vancouver: An Illustrated History*

(Toronto: James Lorimer and Company 1980), 14 and 16. Quotations from MacDonald, 'Canadian Pacific Railway,' 16.

7 Quotations from CVA, Matthews Collection (hereafter Matthews Collection), file 00030 and Eric Nichol, *Vancouver* (Toronto: Doubleday 1970), 56. Also see 'The Petition of the Residents of Vancouver in the District of New Westminster,' 15 February 1886, CVA, Add. MSS 651.

8 John A. Eagle, *The Canadian Pacific Railway and the Development of Western Canada, 1896-1914* (Kingston: McGill-Queen's University Press 1989), 173-231. Quotation from James B. Hedges, *Building the Canadian West: The Land and Colonization Policies of the Canadian Pacific Railway* (1939; reprint, New York: Macmillan 1971), 86-7.

9 H. Abbott to W.C. Van Horne, 2 June 1886, CPRCA, Van Horne Papers, file 13087.

10 Robert A.J. McDonald, 'City-Building in the Canadian West: A Case Study of Economic Growth in Early Vancouver, 1886-1893,' *BC Studies* 43 (Autumn 1979):11; L.A. Hamilton to W.C. Van Horne, 19 May 1886 (telegram), CPRCA, Van Horne Papers, file 13240; and W.C. Van Horne to J.M. Browning, 17 December 1890, NAC, CPRC, Letterbook 36, microfilm M2274.

11 Mrs. Algeron St. Maur, *Impressions of a Tenderfoot during a Journey in the Far West* (London: J. Murray 1890), 35.

12 J.M. Browning to W.C. Van Horne, 7 February 1889 and H. Abbott to W.C. Van Horne, 17 September 1894 (enclosed memo from O.G. Evan Thomas), CPRCA, Van Horne Papers, files 23329 and 77949. Quotation from Thomas's memo.

13 The business affiliations of Vancouver's most powerful entrepreneurs and managers are discussed in Robert A.J. McDonald, 'Business Leaders in Early Vancouver, 1886-1914' (PhD dissertation, University of British Columbia 1977), 52-74, 118-32, and appendix A.

14 R.E. Gosnell, *A History of British Columbia* (together with *Sixty Years of Progress*) part 2 by R.E. Gosnell (Vancouver and Victoria: British Columbia Historical Association 1913), 194 n. 3; M. Picken, comp., *City of Vancouver. Terminus of the Canadian Pacific Railway; British Columbia Handbook* (Vancouver: Vancouver Daily News 1887), 29; *News-Advertiser*, 5 March 1890, p. 2, 9 October 1890, p. 8, 20 January 1892, p. 8, 7 February 1892, p. 8, 10 February 1892, p. 1, 5 April 1892, p. 5, and 1 January 1898, p. 5; and *World*, 30 June 1890, p. 1 and 11 April 1891, p. 15.

15 J.B. Kerr, *Biographical Dictionary of Well-Known British Columbians* (Vancouver: Kerr and Begg 1890), 271; and *World*, 11 April 1891, pp. 11 and 15.

16 British Columbia, Attorney-General, Companies Office, Company Registration Files, file 29 (1878), microfilm reel 1; *British Columbia Gazette* 30 (3 January 1890):14 and 30 (3 April 1890):312; Jessie M. Van der Burg, 'A History of the Union Steamship Company of British Columbia, 1889-1943,' manuscript, University of British Columbia [1943?], 7; and *News-Advertiser*, 26 November 1890, p. 8, 16 September 1892, p. 1, and 29 March 1893, p. 7. Charles Rand was chosen by the *San Francisco Call* as its source for a story on Vancouver; see the *News-Advertiser*, 8 December 1888, p. 3.

17 *World*, 11 April 1891, pp. 5 and 11; *News-Advertiser*, 12 October 1888, p. 8 and 24 July 1890, p. 8; and E.O.S. Scholefield and F.W. Howay, *British Columbia from the Earliest Times to the Present* (Vancouver: S.J. Clarke 1914), 4:844.

18 Kerr, *Biographical Dictionary*, 197; *World*, 3 March 1890, p. 1, 11 April 1891, pp. 4 and 19, and 20 June 1896, p. 27; *News-Advertiser*, 3 September 1890, p. 1, 1 January 1891, p. 1, 5 April 1892, p. 5, and 23 June 1892, p. 8; B.C. Reg. of Cos., file 9 (1890), microfilm reel 1; and Victor Ross, 'The Bank of British Columbia,' *A History of the Canadian Bank of*

Commerce (Toronto: Oxford University Press 1920), 1:334.

19 McDonald, 'City-Building,' 24-7.

20 British Columbia, Legislative Assembly, *Sessional Papers*, 1892, 'Timber Inspector's Report,' 344-5; *Williams' Illustrated Official British Columbia Directory 1892* (Victoria: R.T. Williams 1892), 780; and *World*, 11 April 1891, p. 9.

21 *Williams' Illustrated Official British Columbia Directory 1892*, 780-2; and *World*, 11 April 1892, pp. 9-10.

22 W.K. Lamb, 'The Trans-Pacific Service, 1887-1891,' *British Columbia Historical Quarterly* 1 (1937):143-64 and 4 (1940):29-47 and 76-106.; and *News-Advertiser*, 1 January 1889, p. 2 and 11 October 1898, p. 5.

23 The method used to identify Vancouver's business leaders and subleaders for the period 1890-3 is discussed in the Introduction. Also see Robert A.J. McDonald, 'The Business Elite and Municipal Politics in Vancouver 1886-1914,' *Urban History Review* 11 (February 1983):1-14.

24 Changes in the franchise section of the Vancouver Charter are documented in the *Statutes of British Columbia*, 49 Victoria 1886, c.32, pp. 152-65; 50 Victoria 1887, c.37, pp. 143-4; 52 Victoria 1889, c.40, pp. 281-2; and 54 Victoria 1891, c.72, pp. 549-50. Women and men were granted the civic franchise on equal terms in 1886 but used it unequally because of property requirements – most property was held by men – and social attitudes. In 1917 women gained the right to run for civic office. See Gillian Weiss, '"As Women and as Citizens": Clubwomen in Vancouver 1910-1928' (PhD dissertation, University of British Columbia 1983), 87 and 90.

25 *Colonist*, 17 March 1887, pp. 1 and 4 and 5 April 1887, p. 1; and *News-Advertiser*, 13 December 1887, p. 4, 4 March 1888, p. 4, 7 March 1888, p. 2, and 4 December 1889, p. 8.

26 Patricia E. Roy, 'The Preservation of the Peace in Vancouver: The Aftermath of the Anti-Chinese Riot of 1887,' *BC Studies* 31 (Autumn 1976):44-59 and Kay J. Anderson, *Vancouver's Chinatown: Racial Discourse in Canada, 1875-1980* (Montreal and Kingston: McGill-Queen's University Press 1991), 76-68.

27 *Vancouver News*, 5 January 1887, p. 4, 22 February 1887, p. 1, 23 February 1887, p. 2, and 30 March 1887, p. 1; and *News-Advertiser*, 27 March 1888, pp. 1 and 4, 24 May 1888, p. 6, and 9 April 1889, p. 8.

28 *Vancouver News*, 1 March 1887, p. 1; and *News-Advertiser*, 9 August 1887, pp. 1 and 2, 16 August 1887, pp. 1 and 4, 30 August 1887, p. 2, 25 September 1887, p. 4, and 20 March 1888, p. 4.

29 The early history of Vancouver's water system is outlined in *Vancouver News*, 7 September 1886, p. 1 and 30 January 1887 to 25 March 1887, passim; *Vancouver Daily Advertiser*, 22 January 1887, p. 1; *News-Advertiser*, 14 April 1887 to 27 May 1887, passim, 1 June 1887, p. 2, 3 June 1887, p. 1, 5 June 1887, p. 1, and 1 January 1889, pp. 1-2; and Louis P. Cain, 'Water and Sanitation Services in Vancouver: A Historical Perspective,' *BC Studies* 30 (Summer 1976):27-33.

30 *Vancouver News*, 11 December 1886, p. 1; *News-Advertiser*, 9 December 1889, p. 4 and 12 January 1893, p. 1.

31 *Vancouver News*, 23 February 1887, p. 2; *News-Advertiser*, 4 June 1889, p. 1, 25 July 1889, p. 4, 14 August 1889, p. 2, 16 August 1889, p. 4, and 30 September 1894, p. 4; and CVA, City Clerk's Correspondence, vol. 2 (1889), #1642 (microfilm).

32 Vancouver, By-Law #94, CVA, City Clerk's Department Records, *By-Laws*, vol. 1 (microfilm), pp. 561-8; Vancouver, 3 and 10 February and 14 April 1890, CVA, City Clerk's Department Records, City Council Minutes, vol. 3 (microfilm).

33 *News-Advertiser*, 19 March 1890, p. 8. At least one other city, Calgary, was similarly

divided; see Max Foran, 'Early Calgary 1875-1895: The Controversies Surrounding the Townsite Location and the Direction of Town Expansion,' in *Cities in the West,* ed. A.R. McCormack and Ian Macpherson (Ottawa: National Museum of Man 1975), 26-45.

34 *News-Advertiser*, 19 February 1889, p. 8.

35 Ibid., 19 July 1887, p. 4. David Oppenheimer's attempt to sell his company's wharf to the City exemplifies his tendency to use political power for personal advantage; see *Vancouver News,* 29 July 1886 to 18 January 1887 and *News-Advertiser,* 4 June 1889 to 5 October 1889.

36 Quotation from A.W. Ross to W.C. Van Horne, 30 August 1886, CPRCA, Van Horne Papers, file 13087; also see J.S. Matthews, 'Early Vancouver: Narrative of Pioneers in Vancouver, B.C.,' CVA, typescript, 2:235.

37 *British Columbia Federationist* (hereafter *Federationist*), 6 May 1912, p. 3.

38 Quotation from W.C. Van Horne to H. Abbott, 22 March 1888, NAC, CPRC, Letterbook 25, microfilm M2266. Also see A.W. Ross to W.C. Van Horne, 21 March 1888 and H. Abbott to W.C. Van Horne, 29 March 1888, CPRCA, Van Horne Papers, file 19918; and *News-Advertiser*, 10 September 1887, p. 1, 23 October 1888, p. 1, 8 November 1888, p. 8, and 7 March 1890, p. 4.

39 H. Abbott to W.C. Van Horne, 29 February 1890 and 19 March 1890, CPRCA, Van Horne Papers, file 27608.

40 W.C. Van Horne to J.M. Browning, 11 October 1889 and 8 November 1889, NAC, CPRC, Letterbook 32, microfilm M2271; F.S. Barnard to W.C. Van Horne, 6 March 1890, CPRCA, Van Horne Papers, file 27608.

41 *News-Advertiser*, 8 November 1888, p. 8.

42 Max Foran reaches a similar conclusion about municipal politics in frontier Calgary; see Foran, 'The Calgary Town Council, 1854-1895: A Study of Local Government in a Frontier Environment' (MA thesis, University of Calgary 1970), iii-iv and passim.

43 *News-Advertiser*, 8 November 1888, p. 8, 4 December 1888, p. 5, 24 November 1889, p. 8, 21 December 1889, p. 8, and 24 December 1889, p. 8.

44 Quotation from *News-Advertiser*, 19 March 1890, p. 8. Also see ibid., 6 December 1889, p. 8 and 10 December 1889, p. 4; W.C. Van Horne to J.M. Browning, 11 October 1889, NAC, CPRC, Letterbook 32, microfilm M2271; and F.S. Barnard to W.C. Van Horne, 6 March 1890, CPRCA, Van Horne Papers, file 27608.

45 Reminiscences of W.H. Gallagher and Hedley W. Otton in the Matthews Collection, files 01835 and 00030 and *Vancouver Daily Province* (hereafter *Province*), 6 December 1924, p. 22, reminiscence by Harry Cotton. Also see Roy, *Vancouver*, 16.

46 Bryan D. Palmer, *Working-Class Experience: Rethinking the History of Canadian Labour, 1800-1991,* 2nd ed. (Toronto: McClelland and Stewart 1992), 124.

47 For the relationship between the 1886 civic election and the 1886 mill strike, see Matthews Collection, file 01835 (W.H. Gallagher), file 00030 (Hedley W. Otton), and files 01749 and 02052. For the 1887 strike, see *Colonist,* 19 April 1885, p. 2 and 10 June 1887, p. 1; *News-Advertiser,* 9 June 1887, pp. 1 and 2; and BCARS, VF (Moodyville), microfilm #0436-0439. The four mills that struck in June 1887 included the large Moodyville and Hastings sawmills.

48 The carpenters' strike can be traced in the *News-Advertiser* and *World,* 5 to 17 July 1889; the longshoremen's strike in the same papers from 3 September to 4 October 1889; and the printers' strike in Eugene Forsey, *Trade Unions in Canada 1812-1902* (Toronto: University of Toronto Press 1982), 220.

49 *News-Advertiser*, 4 September 1889, p. 8 and 18 September 1889, p. 4; *World*, 27 September 1889, p. 2, 28 September 1889, p. 4, 4 October 1889, p. 4, and 8 October 1889, p. 4. Quotation from Forsey, *Trade Unions*, 220-1.

50 Quotation from Elizabeth Bloomfield, 'Boards of Trade and Canadian Urban Development,' *Urban History Review* 8, 2 (October 1983):83. For the founding of the Board see *News-Advertiser*, 1 to 24 September 1887. For the Board's role in civic debate, see John Devine to T.F. McGuigan, 26 March 1888, CVA, City Clerk's Correspondence, vol. 2, MCR-3, #1646 (microfilm) and *News-Advertiser*, 27 December 1890, p. 1.

51 *Federationist*, 27 December 1912, p. 24; *News-Advertiser*, 6 December 1889, p. 1; Vancouver Trades and Labor Council, CVA, Add. MSS 307, Minutes, vol. 1 (1889-97), pp. 1-164; and Paul Phillips, *No Power Greater: A Century of Power in British Columbia* (Vancouver: BC Federation of Labour 1967), 19-20. Quotation from *World*, 20 June 1896, p. 6.

52 For a discussion of these business structures, see McDonald, 'Business Leaders in Early Vancouver,' 14-152 and appendices A and B and Angus Everett Robertson, 'The Pursuit of Power, Profit, and Privacy: A Study of Vancouver's West End Elite, 1886-1914' (MA thesis, University of British Columbia 1977), 168-261.

53 Forsey, *Trade Unions*, 220. Quotation from *Federationist*, 6 May 1912, p. 3.

54 Carl Abbott, *Boosters and Businessmen: Popular Economic Thought and Urban Growth in the Antebellum Middle West* (Westport, CT: Greenwood Press 1981), 198.

55 *Vancouver News*, 29 March 1887, p. 1 and Dominion Day Celebrations, Minutes, CVA, Add. MSS 47, file 1.

56 *News-Advertiser*, 5 April 1891, p. 1.

57 Anderson, *Vancouver's Chinatown*, 66-7 (quotations) and Roy, 'The Preservation of Peace in Vancouver,' 44-59.

58 *News-Advertiser*, 5 April 1889, p. 1. This description is of the rancherie two years after its Native residents had been expelled in 1887. Clearly, then, it continued to function, though the 1889 story suggests that it may have become less a centre for Native people and more the place to which Vancouver's most marginal residents gravitated. The 1889 story says that the rancherie was 'composed of nearly every nationality under heaven, including Siwashes and Negroes,' and was 'often a refuge of criminals.'

59 Quotations from ibid., 13 July 1889, p. 4 and *News-Advertiser*, 10 May 1887, p. 4. Also see *Vancouver News*, 8 March 1887, p. 4, 15 March 1887, p. 4, 5 April 1887, p. 4, and *News-Advertiser*, 2 May 1887, p.4 and 9 July 1887, p. 4. My thanks to Duncan Stacey for these references.

60 Anderson, *Vancouver's Chinatown*, 46. Also see 16, 24-7, and 104.

61 *Vancouver News*, 26 July 1886, p. 1 and 14 September 1886, p. 4; Minutes of Meeting at Presbyterian Hall, 18 February 1888, CVA, City Clerk's Correspondence, 10-A-1, vol. 1, file 16, series 20, p. 957; and Petition of Women's Christian Temperance Union to City Council, 8 January 1890, ibid., 10-A-3, vol. 3, file 4, series 20, p. 2,394.

62 *News-Advertiser*, 3 May 1890, p. 8. For Pollay's advocacy of the single tax, see Vancouver Trades and Labor Council, 26 February 1892 and 4 November 1892, CVA, Add. MSS 307, Minutes, vol. 1 (1889-97), p. 179 and 260.

63 *News-Advertiser*, 9 July 1887, p. 4.

64 William Pleming, 'Memories of Early Vancouver,' CVA, William Pleming Papers, Add. MSS 132, pp. 19, 19a. Also see *Province*, 1 April 1952, p. 2 and the Matthews Collection, file 03681.

65 'Preliminary Inventory,' CVA, Add. MSS 760, Knights of Pythias, Mount Pleasant Lodge #11, Papers.

Chapter 3: Monopolists and Plain People

1 For quotations, see *Daily News-Advertiser* (hereafter *News-Advertiser*), 1 December 1889, p. 4 and 9 December 1889, p. 4. Also see ibid., 5-9 December 1889, p. 4 and 24 December 1889, p. 8.

2 Alfred D. Chandler, Jr., *The Visible Hand. The Managerial Revolution in American Business* (Cambridge, MA: Harvard University Press 1977), 9-10.

3 British Columbia, Attorney-General, Companies Office, Company Registration Files, file 133 (1890), microfilm reel 1 and file 33 (1897), microfilm reel 2; M.I. Rogers, *B.C. Sugar* (Vancouver: British Columbia Sugar Refining Company 1958), passim; and B.T. Rogers, Private Letter Book, BC Sugar Company Archives, passim.

4 J.M. Browning to W.C. Van Horne, 20 March 1890, CPRCA, Van Horne Papers, file 27608.

5 J.M. Browning to W.C. Van Horne, 29 August 1894 and Harry Abbott to W.C. Van Horne, 17 September 1894, CPRCA, Van Horne Papers, file 27608; W.C. Van Horne to R.B. Angus, 22 August 1894 and W.C. Van Horne to Harry Abbott, 2 and 7 September 1894, NAC, CPRC, Letterbook 47, microfilm M2283.

6 E.H. Rogers, ed., *Jonathan Rogers* (Vancouver: n.p. 1948). The problems faced by local business during the 1890s are suggested in the Sweeny Diary, CVA, Campbell Sweeny Papers, typescript prepared by Major J.S. Matthews, passim.

7 *News-Advertiser*, 19 May 1897, p. 8, 11 February 1898, p. 8, and 26 July 1899, p. 8.

8 *News-Advertiser*, 25 June 1891, p. 1.

9 *News-Advertiser*, 28 March 1896, p. 6.

10 John T. Saywell, ed. and intro., *The Canadian Journal of Lady Aberdeen 1893-1898* (Toronto: Champlain Society 1960), 144.

11 Quotation from J. Buntzen to [?] Bennett, 27 October 1897, UBCSCD, British Columbia Electric Railway Company Papers (hereafter BCER Papers), General Managers' Letter Books, AXB 3-2 (1897), p. 83. For the formation of BC Electric, see George Green, 'Some Pioneers of Light and Power,' *British Columbia Historical Quarterly* 2 (1938):153-60.

12 Major J.S. Matthews, comp., *Conversations with Khatsahlano, 1932-1954* (Vancouver: City of Vancouver Archives 1955), 288.

13 Vancouver, 12 January and 12 February 1891, CVA, City Clerk's Department Records, City Council Minutes, vol. 4 (microfilm)

14 H. Abbott to T.F. McGuigan, 9 February 1891, CVA, City Clerk's Correspondence, vol. 4 (1891), #3364-3367 (microfilm). For the early history of railway regulation in Canada, see Ken Cruikshank, *Close Ties: Railways, Government, and the Board of Railway Commissioners, 1851-1933* (Montreal and Kingston: McGill-Queen's University Press 1991), 56-60.

15 'The Application of the City of Vancouver to the Board of Railway Commissioners re: the Matter of the Railway Act of 1903 and the Crossing of Certain Streets by the Canadian Pacific Railway in the City of Vancouver, 4 July 1904,' CVA, City Clerk's Correspondence, vol. 19 (1903-4), #15045 (microfilm).

16 'Shorthand Notes of Hearing on July 14, 1894 in the Judicial Committee of the Privy Council' and Harry Abbott to T.F. McGuigan, 27 July 1894, CVA, City Clerk's Correspondence, vol. 6 (1893-4), #5530-5557 and #5572 (microfilm). The CPR's arbitrary control of street ends was also a problem at this time in Calgary; see Maxwell L. Foran, 'The

Calgary Town Council, 1884-1895: A Study of Local Government in a Frontier Environment' (MA thesis, University of Calgary 1970), 10-11.

17 R. Marpole to T.F. McGuigan, 31 May 1899, CVA, City Clerk's Correspondence, vol. 14 (1899), #11044 (microfilm) and A. St. George Hammersley to T.F. McGuigan, 28 January 1901, ibid., vol. 17 (1901), #13028 (microfilm).

18 *News-Advertiser*, 15 June 1898, p. 3.

19 Prominent examples include engineers H.J. Cambie and H.O. Bell-Irving, contractors D.B. Charleson and A.G. Ferguson, and medical doctor J.M. Lefevre.

20 H. Abbott to W.C. Van Horne, 2 April 1889 and [?] Abbott to W.C. Van Horne, 18 April [1891], CPRCA, Van Horne Papers, file 23709.

21 *News-Advertiser*, 3 May 1888, p. 4, 11 August 1888, p. 8, and 13 December 1892, p. 5; Marjorie Allan, *Christ Church Cathedral, 1889-1939: A Short History* (Vancouver: University Press 1939), 4-18.

22 Vancouver Club, *Historical Notes, Constitution and House Rules, List of Members amended to 31st May 1936* (Vancouver: n.p. n.d.), 7-11 and ibid., *Constitution: Rules and Regulations and Lists of Members of the Vancouver Club, Adopted 25 March 1893* (Vancouver: n.p. 1896), 3-4, CVA, Vancouver Club Papers, Add. MSS 306. For the Brockton Point Athletic Association see *News-Advertiser*, 10 May 1888, p. 6, 15 May 1888, p. 1, 3 June 1888, p. 1, and 31 December 1889, p. 1.

23 *Vancouver Daily World* (hereafter *World*), 11 April 1891, p. 6 and Harry T. Logan, *Tuum Est: A History of the University of British Columbia* (Vancouver: University of British Columbia Press 1958), 13.

24 J.B. Kerr, *Biographical Dictionary of Well-Known British Columbians* (Vancouver: Kerr and Begg 1890), 77; E.O.S. Scholefield and F.W. Howay, *A History of British Columbia* (together with *Sixty Years of Progress*), part 2 by R.E. Gosnell (Vancouver and Victoria: British Columbia Historical Association 1913), 106; and *Vancouver Daily Province* (hereafter *Province*), 16 February 1903, p. 1.

25 The Abbotts' social role is documented in Robert A.J. McDonald, 'Business Leaders in Early Vancouver, 1886-1914' (PhD dissertation, University of British Columbia 1977), 237-8 and *Province*, 6 February 1975, p. 37. Quotation from Hunt, 'Mutual Enlightenment in Early Vancouver, 1886-1916' (PhD dissertation, University of British Columbia 1986), 39.

26 H. Heywood, from the *Boston Transcript*, noted in Norbert MacDonald, *Distant Neighbors: A Comparative History of Seattle and Vancouver* (Lincoln: University of Nebraska Press 1987), 42.

27 On the withdrawal of business leaders from an active role in city government, see Robert A.J. McDonald, 'The Business Elite and Municipal Politics in Vancouver 1886-1914,' *Urban History Review* 11, 3 (1983):1-14.

28 Useful introductions to the subject of populism are provided by Lawrence Goodwyn, *Democratic Promise: The Populist Movement in America* (New York: Oxford University Press 1976) and essays by Peter Wiles, 'A Syndrome, Not a Doctrine,' and Peter Worsley, 'The Concept of Populism,' in *Populism: Its Meaning and National Characteristics*, ed. Ghita Ionescu and Ernest Gellner (London: Weidenfeld and Nicolson 1969), 166-79 and 212-50.

29 The concept of a 'producers' ideology' is discussed in David Montgomery, *Beyond Equality: Labor and the Radical Republicans 1862-1872* (New York: A. Knopf 1967), 14-16; Eric Foner, *Free Soil, Free Labor, Free Men: The Ideology of the Republican Party Before the Civil*

War (New York: Oxford University Press 1970), 11-39; John S. Gilkeson, Jr., *Middle-Class Providence, 1820-1940* (Princeton: Princeton University Press 1986), 106 (quotation), 121-3, 128, and 350; Bryan D. Palmer, *A Culture in Conflict: Skilled Workers and Industrial Capitalism in Hamilton, Ontario, 1860-1914* (Montreal: McGill-Queen's University Press 1979), 101-22; and Craig Heron, 'Labourism and the Canadian Working Class,' *Labour/Le Travail* 13 (Spring 1984):59-60.

30 Quotations from Ramsay Cook, 'Tillers and Toilers: The Rise and Fall of Populism in Canada in the 1890s,' Canadian Historical Association *Historical Papers* (1984):11 and Peter Love, *Labour and the Money Power: Australian Labour Populism 1890-1950* (Melbourne: Melbourne University Press 1984), 31. For California, see Michael Kazin, 'The Great Exception Revisited: Organized Labor and Politics in San Francisco and Los Angeles, 1870-1940,' *Pacific Historical Review* 55 (August 1986):381.

31 Patrick Joyce, *Visions of the People: Industrial England and the Question of Class 1848-1914* (New York: Cambridge University Press 1991), 78 and 87-90; Heron, 'Labourism,' 55-60; Bryan D. Palmer, 'Most Uncommon Common Men: Craft and Culture in Historical Perspective,' *Labour/Le Travailleur* 1 (1976):6-31; and the *Independent*, 22 February 1901, p. 1. On charity, also see Vancouver Trades and Labor Council, 5 November 1895, CVA, Add. MSS 307, Minutes, vol. 1 (1889-97), p. 466.

32 On the negative connotations of the term 'class,' see Joyce, *Visions of the People*, 65. Concerning 'classes' and 'masses' see ibid., 309; the *Golden Era*, 21 July 1899, cited in Jeremy Mouat, 'Mining in the Settler Dominions: A Comparative Study of the Industry in Three Communities from the 1880s to the First World War' (PhD dissertation, University of British Columbia 1988), 61-2; and *Independent*, 7 July 1900, p. 1. The term 'plain people' was coined by George Bartley at the end of the decade; see *Independent*, 31 March 1900, p. 2. In *The Populist Moment: A Short History of the Agrarian Revolt In America* (New York: Oxford University Press 1978), Lawrence Goodwyn documents the importance of such terms as 'plain people,' 'producing classes,' 'monopolists,' 'the people,' 'the masses,' and 'the classes' to the discourse of agrarian revolt in late-nineteenth-century America. Quotation from Gilkeson, *Middle-Class Providence*, 53-4.

33 UBCSCD, Harry Cowan Papers, Scrapbook no. 1, quotation from Gene Howard Homel, '"Fading Beams of the Nineteenth Century:" Radicalism and Early Socialism in Canada's 1890s,' *Labour/Le Travailleur* 5 (1980):9. Peter Love portrays Australian reform thought of the 1890s as being similarly eclectic (*Labour and the Money Power*, 14-20 and 28-36). Single tax was particularly popular at the beginning of the decade in Vancouver; see *News-Advertiser*, 26 September 1889, p. 8, 11 January 1891, p. 8, 13 January 1891, p. 8, 6 December 1891, p. 8, 18 February 1892, p. 4, and 2 November 1897, p. 6. On the eclectic nature of reform in California in the 1890s, see Kazin, 'The Great Exception Revisited.'

34 Quotations from *World*, 19 May 1890, pp. 1 and 3 and *News-Advertiser*, 9 January 1898, p. 5; also see *World*, 14 June 1890, p. 4 and 15 December 1891, p. 5 and *News-Advertiser*, 1 June 1890, p. 8, 19 October 1890, p. 4, 9 December 1890, p. 4, and 13 January 1891, p. 4.

35 For the Vancouver Trades and Labor Council's policy statements, see *World*, 10 May 1890, p. 1; *News-Advertiser*, 14 January 1892, p. 8, 17 January 1893, p. 3, 25 March 1894, p. 3, 8 December 1894, p. 8, 19 December 1896, p. 5, 29 January 1897, p. 3, and 11 June 1898, p. 3; and Vancouver Trades and Labor Council, 10 February 1893, 29 January 1897, CVA, Add. MSS 307, Minutes, vol. 1 (1889-97), p. 295 and p. 537.

36 Quotations from *Vancouver Ledger*, 24 November 1902, located in UBCSCD, Harry

Cowan Papers, Scrapbook no. 1, p. 114 and *Province*, 29 November 1900, p. 3. For his early years and self-image, see *World*, 28 August 1893, p. 2, 17 November 1902, p. 1, and 20 November 1902, p. 4 and *Daily Colonist*, 5 September 1900, p. 6.

37 *News-Advertiser*, 17 January 1892, p. 8 and 12 July 1892, p. 5.

38 Quotations from *World*, 9 June 1896, p. 6 and *Province*, 22 September 1900, p. 3.

39 Maxwell's political rise is documented in Thomas Robert Loosemore, 'The British Columbia Labor Movement and Political Action, 1879-1906' (MA thesis, University of British Columbia 1954), 64-84; *News-Advertiser*, 16 April 1893, p. 1, 21 April 1894, p. 5, 10 May 1894, p. 1, 17 April 1896, p. 6, 29 April 1896, p. 6, and 15 November 1896, p. 3; Vancouver Trades and Labor Council, 1 March 1895, 10 April 1896, CVA, Add. MSS 307, Minutes, vol. 1 (1889-97), p. 433 and p. 495; and *Province*, 18 November 1902, p. 1.

40 Quotation from *News-Advertiser*, 26 September 1897, p. 3. The 1894 provincial election is covered in numerous newspaper stories of April and May 1894.

41 Margaret A. Ormsby, *British Columbia: A History*, rev. ed. (Toronto: Macmillan 1971), 304-18 (quotation from p. 307); Scholefield and Howay, *A History of British Columbia*, 131-9; Martin Robin, *The Rush for Spoils: The Company Province 1871-1933* (Toronto: McClelland and Stewart 1972), 23, 41, and 59-60; and Robert E. Cail, *Land, Man, and the Law: The Disposal of Crown Lands in British Columbia, 1871-1913* (Vancouver: University of British Columbia Press 1974), 14, 141-4, and 152-8. The Esquimalt and Nanaimo Railway bonus came from the federal government, which had received it from the provincial.

42 Quotations from *News-Advertiser*, 19 June 1890, p. 8 and 10 May 1894, p. 1, and Canada, Royal Commission on Chinese Immigration, *Report* (Ottawa: Queen's Printer 1885), 157.

43 *World*, 19 May 1890, p. 1 and *News-Advertiser*, 19 June 1890, p. 8.

44 Christopher Armstrong and H.V. Nelles, *Monopoly's Moment: The Organization and Regulation of Canadian Utilities, 1830-1930* (Philadelphia: Temple University Press 1986), 141-42 and 146. Also see Christopher Armstrong and H.V. Nelles, 'The Rise of Civic Populism in Toronto 1870-1920,' in *Forging a Consensus: Historical Essays on Toronto*, ed. Victor L. Russell (Toronto: University of Toronto Press 1984), 192-237.

45 Quotations in order of presentation from *News-Advertiser*, 15 December 1891, p. 3, 28 June 1891, p. 4, and 23 June 1891, pp. 1 and 8; and J. Buntzen to R.M. Horne-Payne, 17 May 1898, UBCSCD, BCER Papers, Confidential Correspondence Outward, box 41, p. 62.

46 By-law votes are recorded in *News-Advertiser*, 9 May 1893, p. 1, 28 June 1894, p. 8, and 4 October 1894, p. 1. The newspaper also records extensive debate before each of these votes.

47 Quotations from ibid., 20 November 1894, p. 3 and 12 September 1894, p. 4. Also see ibid., 20 April 1894, p. 5 and 13 March 1895, p. 8.

48 Armstrong and Nelles, *Monopoly's Moment*, 97-100, 132, 144-5, and 157-8; J. Buntzen to F. Hope, 27 February 1901, UBCSCD, BCER Papers, General Managers' Letter Books, AXB 3-3 (1901), pp. 59-62 and J. Buntzen to R.M. Horne-Payne, 22 October 1901, ibid., Confidential Correspondence Outward, box 41, pp. 191-3; *News-Advertiser*, 29 January 1895, p. 3; *Independent*, 2 February 1901, p. 1; and British Columbia, Legislative Assembly, *Journals*, 1894-5 (Victoria: Queen's Printer 1895), appendices.

49 See *News-Advertiser*, August-November 1894, November 1895, 7 January 1896, p. 3, and 17 March 1896, p. 3; J. Buntzen to F. Hope, 23 April 1901, UBCSCD, BCER Papers, General Managers' Letter Books, AXB 3-3 (1901), pp. 125-30.

50 *News-Advertiser*, 5 December 1893, p. 1, 15 December 1893, p. 3, 21 December 1893, p. 3, 23 December 1893, p. 4; 23 January 1894, p. 5, 28 January 1894, p. 4, 30 January 1894, p.

5, and 20 February 1894, p. 5.

51 Ibid., 20 March 1894, p. 5, 15 August 1894, p. 5, 5 September 1894, p. 5, 27 September 1894, p. 1, and 3 October 1894, p. 5.

52 Marianna Valverde, *The Age of Light, Soap, and Water: Moral Reform in English Canada, 1885-1925* (Toronto: McClelland and Stewart 1991), 10-11.

53 David Frank, 'Of Pride, Parades and Picnics: Labour Days Past,' *New Maritimes* 8, 1 (October 1989):5-7 and Palmer, *A Culture in Conflict,* 57-9. For the United States, see Michael Kazin and Steven J. Ross, 'America's Labor Day: The Dilemma of a Workers' Celebration,' *Journal of American History* 78, 4 (March 1992):1,299-1,302.

54 *British Columbia Federationist,* 27 December 1912, p. 24; *Western Wage-Earner,* September 1909, p. 12; *World,* 8 September 1903, pp. 1 and 5, 2 September 1905, pp. 6 and 10, and 5 September 1908, p. 6; *News-Advertiser,* 18 July 1905, p. 2; and Patrick Burden, 'Labour Day,' in Working Lives Collective, *Working Lives: Vancouver 1886-1986* (Vancouver: New Star Books 1985), 141.

55 *News-Advertiser,* 4 July 1891, p. 5, 1 July 1892, p. 1, 3 July 1895, p. 3, 3 July 1896, pp. 1 and 5, 27 June 1897, p. 8, and 2 July 1897, p. 3; *World,* 2 July 1892, p. 4, 3 July 1893, p. 2, 2 July 1898, p. 8, and 3 July 1900, pp. 2 and 5; and Dominion Day Celebrations, CVA, Add. MSS 47, files 1, 3, and 6.

56 Bryan D. Palmer, *Working-Class Experience: The Rise and Reconstitution of Canadian Labour, 1800-1980* (Toronto: Butterworth 1983), 32-3 and 75 and *World,* 6 September 1898, pp. 5 and 7. Co-operative schemes are discussed in Eugene Forsey, *Trade Unions in Canada 1812-1902* (Toronto: University of Toronto Press 1982), 221. Vancouver printers, while on strike, created their own newspaper, *The New World.* Vancouver Trades and Labor Council, 15 September 1893, CVA, Add. MSS 307, Minutes, vol. 1 (1889-97), p. 347 (a plan by tailors to create a co-op shop); ibid., 5 June 1896, p. 504, 12 April 1895, p. 439, and 4 December 1896, p. 532 (the VTLC endorses the idea of a co-op store); and *News-Advertiser,* 5 September 1896, p. 2 (discussion of the Fraser Valley Industrial Society, an operating co-operative fish cannery on the Fraser River near New Westminster, and of two other co-op schemes, one for a cannery, the other a lumber mill).

57 *World,* 28 August 1893, p. 2. Also see Susan Davis, *Parades and Power: Street Theatre in Nineteenth-Century Philadelphia* (Philadelphia: Temple University Press 1986), 137, 142, and 157-8.

58 Quotations from *World,* 8 September 1890, pp. 2 and 8. Also see Davis, *Parades and Power,* 164; *World,* 6 September 1898, pp. 5 and 71; and *Province,* 5 September 1899, p. 2.

59 Alex S. Black et al. to Mayor of Vancouver, 29 January 1893, CVA, City Clerk's Correspondence, 10-A-6, vol. 6, file 8, series 20; *News-Advertiser,* 18 August 1896, p. 6; and 6 December 1900, CVA, Police Court Records, 37-C-7, series 188, p. 65.

60 Quotations from Vancouver Trades and Labor Council, 6 December 1895, CVA, City Clerk's Correspondence, 10-A-6, Minutes, vol. 9, file 7, series 20 and *News-Advertiser,* 5 December 1895, p. 6. Also see ibid., 7 February 1894, p. 5, 5 December 1895, p. 6, 10 December 1895, p. 3, and 6 November 1906, p. 2. For a good discussion of the intellectual foundations of these attitudes, see Stephen A. Speisman, 'Munificent Parsons and Municipal Parsimony: Voluntary vs. Public Poor Relief in Nineteenth Century Toronto,' *Ontario History* 65 (1973):32-49.

61 Jill Wade, '"Shaughnessy" or "Slum"? Home or Homelessness? Marginal Housing in Vancouver, 1886-1950' (manuscript 1993) and *News-Advertiser,* 25 September 1894, p. 3 and 27 September 1894, p. 7.

62 Vancouver Board of Trade to Mayor, 14 May 1891, CVA, City Clerk's Correspondence, 10-A-4, vol. 4, file 3, series 20, p. 3,241; J.M. Browning to W.C. Van Horne, 16 December 1891, CPRCA, Van Horne Papers, file 70243; and *News-Advertiser*, 19 August 1894, p. 1 and 27 September 1894, p. 7 (quotation).

63 Quotations from *News-Advertiser*, 19 August 1894, p. 1 and 18 September 1894, p. 3. The petition to City Council is in the CVA, City Clerk's Correspondence, vol. 6 (1893), #5212 ff, 3 September 1893 (microfilm).

64 *News-Advertiser*, 14 August 1894, p. 1; A. St. George Hammersley to Chief of Police, 22 September 1894, CVA, City Clerk's Correspondence, 10-A-3, vol. 7, file 1, series 20, p. 5,921 (microfilm); and *World*, 22 August 1894, p. 5.

65 Kay J. Anderson, *Vancouver's Chinatown: Racial Discourse in Canada, 1875-1980* (Montreal and Kingston: McGill-Queen's University Press 1991), 81-8 (quotation from p. 85); *News-Advertiser*, 16 May 1893, p. 3, 4 February 1896, p. 3, 25 August 1896, p. 3, and 22 December 1896, p. 6; and Court Testimony (Jun Kee vs. Vancouver), 20 August 1897, CVA, City Clerk's Correspondence, vol. 11 (1896-7), #9120 (microfilm).

66 I defined labour leaders as executive members of the Vancouver Trades and Labor Council. I devised a point system that assigned nine points for one (six-month) term as president, three points for one term as vice-president or general secretary, and one point for some other position, such as treasurer or trustee. Those who acquired nine points were identified as leaders and their social characteristics examined. Social data were derived from various biographical sources and from the 1891 Nominal Census. For business leaders see Robert A.J. McDonald, 'Vancouver's "Four Hundred": The Quest for Wealth and Status in Canada's Urban West, 1886-1914,' *Journal of Canadian Studies* 25, 3 (Fall 1990):55-73.

67 Homel, '"Fading Beams of the Nineteenth Century,"' 32.

Chapter 4: Capital and Labour

1 S.P. Mosher, 'The Social Gospel in British Columbia: Social Reform as a Dimension of Religion, 1900-1920' (MA thesis, University of Victoria 1974), 64.

2 J.A. Hobson, *Canada To-day* (London: T.F. Unwin 1906), 32.

3 Henry Bell-Irving to John [Bell-Irving], 20 October 1897 and 24 November 1897, CVA, Bell-Irving Family Papers, vol. 83, Correspondence Out.

4 Quotation from *Daily News-Advertiser* (hereafter *News-Advertiser*) 22 March 1895, p. 7. Also see Robert A.J.McDonald, 'Victoria, Vancouver, and the Economic Development of British Columbia, 1886-1914,' in *British Columbia: Historical Readings,* ed. W. Peter Ward and Robert A.J. McDonald (Vancouver: Douglas and McIntyre 1981), 369-72 and 377-83.

5 Norbert MacDonald, *Distant Neighbors: A Comparative History of Seattle and Vancouver* (Lincoln: University of Nebraska Press 1987), 47.

6 Canadian Bank of Commerce, *Charter and Annual Reports 1867-1907* (Toronto: [?]), 387, 415, and 457; B.E. Walker to W.C. Ward, 3 November 1899, UTTFRBR, Walker Papers, box 19, Correspondence Out; *News-Advertiser*, 16 September 1897, p. 6 and 30 July 1899, p. 4; and Robert A.J. McDonald, 'Business Leaders in Early Vancouver, 1886-1914' (PhD dissertation, University of British Columbia 1977), 81-2.

7 Quotations from G.R. Parkin, *The Great Dominion* (London: Macmillan 1895), 169 and R.E. Gosnell, *The Year Book of British Columbia, 1897* (Victoria: n.p. 1897), 200. Also see *Vancouver Daily World* (hereafter *World*), 11 April 1897, p. 17 and McDonald 'Business

Leaders in Early Vancouver,' 82-8.

8 McDonald, 'Victoria, Vancouver, and the Economic Development of British Colum-bia,' 377-83. Quotation from *The A-Y-P Book of Vancouver, B.C.: 1909* (Vancouver: Daily World 1909), 45.

9 Production and royalty statistics are drawn from British Columbia, Legislative Assem-bly, *Sessional Papers*, 1901, 'Timber Inspectors' Report,' pp. 520-5, 1908, pp. H46-H54, and 1911, pp. H75-H81; the number of mills from James Robert Conley, 'Class Conflict and Collective Action in the Working Class of Vancouver, British Columbia, 1900-1919' (PhD dissertation, Carleton University 1986), 199; the industry labour force from the *Fifth Census of Canada, 1911*, vol. 3, table 9, p. 214; and data on corporate wealth from McDonald, 'Business Leaders in Early Vancouver,' 365 n. 15 and appendix B.

10 H. Keith Ralston, 'The 1900 Strike of Fraser River Sockeye Salmon Fishermen' (MA thesis, University of British Columbia 1965), 25 and 35-8 and Dianne Newell, ed. and intro., *The Development of the Pacific Salmon Canning Industry: A Grown Man's Game* (Montreal and Kingston: McGill-Queen's University Press 1989), 20-8 and 205-6.

11 The structure of Vancouver capitalism is discussed more fully in Robert A.J. McDon-ald, 'West Coast Capitalism: The Structure of Business Leadership in Vancouver, British Columbia, 1890-1913' (paper presented to the BC Studies Conference, Simon Fraser University, November 1988).

12 B.E. Walker to Lord Grey, 5 November 1906, UTTFRBR, Walker Papers, box 20, Cor-respondence Out.

13 *Vancouver Daily Province* (hereafter *Province*), 25 April 1901, p. 1; *News-Advertiser*, 10 October 1906, p. 2; and R.H.H. Alexander to Sir T.G. Shaughnessy, 20 November 1906, CPRCA, Shaughnessy Papers, file 82481. Quotation from May Fitz-Gibbon to Sir T.G. Shaughnessy, 21 November 1907, ibid., file 85132.

14 *News-Advertiser*, 12 February 1890, p. 3.

15 W.C. Van Horne to [Francis Carter-] Cotton, 6 October 1896, NAC, CPRC, Letter-book 51, microfilm #M2287.

16 *World*, 12 April 1899, p. 4 and NAC, Canada, Department of Labour Strikes and Lock-outs Files (hereafter Strikes and Lockouts), RG 27 microfilm reel 3, file 3159A. These files were later revised; the revised files are hereafter cited as Strikes and Lockouts, RG 27 (revised).

17 Strikes and Lockouts, RG 27, microfilm reel 3, file 3235.

18 Quotations from British Columbia, Commission on Labour, 1912-14, Transcripts of Evidence (hereafter BCCL, Evidence), 7 March 1913 (J.W. Wilkinson), BCARS, RG 684, vol. 3, file 8, p. 180.

19 *Independent*, 31 March 1900, p. 3 and 12 April 1902, p. 2 (quotation).

20 *News-Advertiser*, 10 May 1894, p. 1 and 16 January 1897, pp. 4-5.

21 Quotation from Conley, 'Class Conflict and Collective Action,' 483. Evidence gleaned from throughout Conley's dissertation indicates the following number of union locals formed in Vancouver: 1898, 8; 1899, 5; 1900, 8; 1901, 3; 1902, 10; 1903, 8. For the province as a whole, see Paul A. Phillips, *No Power Greater: A Century of Labour in British Columbia* (Vancouver: BC Federation of Labour 1967), 37.

22 *Independent*, 3 May 1902, p. 8.

23 *Labour Gazette* 3 (January 1903):517.

24 Canada, Department of Labour, *Wages and Hours of Labour in Canada, 1901-1921* (Ottawa: King's Printer 1921), 5 and 8 and Patricia E. Roy, 'The B.C.E.R. and Its Street

Railway Employees,' *BC Studies* 16 (Winter 1972-3):3-24.

25 *Labour Gazette* 3 (January 1903):517 and *News-Advertiser*, 4 June 1892, p. 8. Quotation from BCCL, Evidence, 17 January 1913 (J.A. Key), BCARS, RG 684, vol. 1, file 1, p. 69.

26 Quotation from Craig Heron, 'Labourism and the Canadian Working Class,' *Labour/ Le Travail* 13 (Spring 1984):59. An example of how economic privilege blunted enthusiasm for organizing the unskilled is J. Hugh Tuck, 'The United Brotherhood of Railway Employees in Western Canada, 1898-1905,' *Labour/Le Travailleur* 11 (Spring 1983):82-3.

27 W. Peter Ward, *White Canada Forever* (Montreal: McGill-Queen's University Press 1978), 16-17, 81, and 112; Conley, 'Class Conflict and Collective Action,' 212-13; *Province*, 25 April 1901, p. 1; and Gillian Creese, 'Class, Ethnicity, and Conflict: The Case of Chinese and Japanese Immigrants, 1880-1923,' in *Workers, Capital, and the State in British Columbia: Selected Papers,* ed. Rennie Warburton and David Coburn (Vancouver: UBC Press 1988), 55-85.

28 W. Peter Ward, 'Population Growth in Western Canada, 1901-1971,' in *The Developing West*, ed. John E. Foster (Edmonton: University of Alberta Press 1983), 163-72; G.W. Bertram, 'Historical Statistics on Growth and Structure of Manufacturing in Canada, 1870-1957,' in *Conference on Statistics, 1962 and 1963*, ed. H. Henripin and A. Asimakopulous (Toronto: Canadian Political Science Association and University of Toronto Press 1964), 119 and table 6; and John Lutz, 'Losing Steam: The Boiler and Engine Industry as an Index of British Columbia's Deindustrialization, 1880-1915,' Canadian Historical Association *Historical Papers* (1988):180-5 and passim.

29 Quotation from Veronica Strong-Boag, 'The Girl of the New Day: Canadian Working Women in the 1920s,' *Labour/Le Travailleur* 4 (1979):135 and 137. Also see Paul Phillips and Erin Phillips, *Women and Work: Inequality in the Labour Market* (Toronto: James Lorimer and Company 1983), chap. 1 and James Conley, 'Class Conflict and Collective Action,' 461 and 652.

30 Quotations from *Independent*, 3 November 1900, p. 2. Also see Conley, 'Class Conflict and Collective Action,' 629, 646, and 656-60.

31 Quotation from Eleanor A. Bartlett, 'Real Wages and the Standard of Living in Vancouver, 1901-1929,' *BC Studies* 51 (Autumn 1981):8 and Patricia E. Roy, 'Vancouver: "The Mecca of the Unemployed," 1907-1929,' in *Town and City*, ed. Alan F.J. Artibise (Regina: Canadian Plains Research Center 1981), 31-55. Also see *Province*, 6 August 1912, p. 1 and *News-Advertiser*, 6 September 1911, p. 1.

32 Conley, 'Class Conflict and Collective Action,' 685 and Robert A.J. McDonald, 'Working Class Vancouver, 1886-1914: Urbanism and Class in British Columbia,' *BC Studies*, 69-70 (Spring-Summer 1986):43.

33 Doug Cruikshank, 'The Last of the Old-Time Smokers,' 8-9 (quotation) and 'Why May 1929? The Real Story of How It All Began,' 18-21, in United Brotherhood of Carpenters and Joiners of America, Local 452, *The First Hundred Years* (Vancouver: United Brotherhood of Carpenters and Joiners of America Local 452 1990); *News-Advertiser*, 1 December 1897, p. 4; *Independent*, 21 April 1900, p. 1, 24 November 1900, p. 1, 24 August 1901, p. 1, 23 November 1901, p. 2, 30 November 1901, p. 1, and 28 December 1901, p. 1; *Labour Gazette* 6 (May 1906):1,002; and *Western Wage-Earner*, August 1910, p. 8.

34 The method employed to determine the identities of Vancouver Trades and Labor Council leaders is explained in Chapter 3, n. 66. The four semi- and unskilled workers who became leaders in the 1898-1903 period are John Peary (union of street railway-

men), T.H. Cross (postal employees), W.J. Lamrick (retail clerks), and F.J. Russell (freight handlers). The other seven are George Bartley, Harry Cowan, and George Wilby (printers), John Crowe (cigar makers), Joseph Dixon (carpenters), James Jeffries (bricklayers), and J.H. Watson (boilermakers).

35 Quotation from Phillips, *No Power Greater*, 39. Strike issues are discussed more fully in McDonald, 'Working Class Vancouver,' 55-7.

36 Andrew Yarmie, 'The Right to Manage: Vancouver Employers' Associations, 1900-1923,' *BC Studies* 90 (Summer 1990):42.

37 H.O. Bell-Irving to Fred Williams, 12 July 1899, CVA, Bell-Irving Family Papers, vol. 83, Correspondence Out; Edmund B. Kirby to George Gooderham, 6 February 1900, cited in Jeremy Mouat, 'Mining in the Settler Dominions: A Comparative Study of the Industry in Three Communities from the 1880s to the First World War' (PhD dissertation, University of British Columbia 1988), 61. Information for this paragraph was derived from ibid., 33-126.

38 Mouat, 'Mining in the Settler Dominions,' 59.

39 Ralston, 'The 1900 Strike of Fraser River Sockeye Salmon Fishermen,' passim (quotation from 94-5).

40 Geoff Meggs, *Salmon: The Decline of the British Columbia Fishery* (Vancouver: Douglas and McIntyre 1991), 39; Ralston, 'The 1900 Strike of Fraser River Sockeye Salmon Fishermen,' 45, 129-30, 148, and 158; and *News-Advertiser*, 27 April 1898, p. 3 and 12 April 1899, p. 2.

41 Quotation from Ralston, 'The 1900 Strike of Fraser River Sockeye Salmon Fishermen,' 129. For the militia, see ibid., 129-41 and Meggs, *Salmon*, 65. For the Vancouver Board of Trade's reaction to the eight-hour day legislation, see *News-Advertiser*, 14 February 1900, p. 5.

42 Christine Mullins and Arthur F. Harvey, *Russell & DuMoulin: The First Century 1889-1989* (Vancouver: Russell and DuMoulin 1990), 24-6.

43 See Conley, 'Class Conflict and Collective Action,' chap. 5.

44 Quotation from J. Buntzen to Employees, 1 August 1902, UBCSCD, British Columbia Electric Railway Company Papers (hereafter BCER Papers), box 41, Correspondence Inward. Also see R.M. Horne-Payne to J. Buntzen, 21 March 1900, ibid; *Independent*, 11 May 1901, p. 3; and Roy, 'The B.C.E.R and Its Employees,' 3-24.

45 For the CPR, see Tuck, 'The United Brotherhood of Railway Employees,' 77-8 and 88 and Conley, 'Class Conflict and Collective Action,' 464-72, 482-96, and 517. For strike-breakers, see *World*, 27 September 1889, p. 2, 12 April 1899, p. 4, and 3 May 1899, p. 7; Eugene Forsey, *Trade Unions in Canada 1812-1902* (Toronto: University of Toronto Press 1982), 263, 340, and 342; and Strikes and Lockouts, RG 27, microfilm reel 2, file 3123 and microfilm reel 3, file 3152.

46 Conley, 'Class Conflict and Collective Action,' 320-7 and 334-43.

47 Quotation from *Province*, 6 March 1903, p. 1. For the United Brotherhood of Railway Employees strike, see Strikes and Lockouts, RG 27 (revised), vol. 2333; Tuck, 'United Brotherhood of Railway Employees,' 63-88; and Conley, 'Class Conflict and Collective Action,' 483-92.

48 Yarmie, 'The Right to Manage,' 47 and Paul Craven, *'An Impartial Umpire': Industrial Relations and the Canadian State 1900-1911* (Toronto: University of Toronto Press 1980), 246-52. Quotation from the *British Columbia Federationist*, August 1917, cited in Conley, 'Class Conflict and Collective Action,' 563.

49 Quotation from R.H. Sperling to Hiram Williams, 12 April 1911, UBCSCD, BCER Papers, General Managers' Letter Books, AXB 3-4 (January-June 1911); also see Yarmie, 'The Right to Manage,' 42-57; Vancouver, 19 May 1904, CVA, City Clerk's Department Records, City Council Minutes, vol. 3 (microfilm); and *Independent*, 9 July 1904, p. 1.

50 *Labour Gazette* 3 (December 1902):430, 4 (April 1904):1,002, and 4 (May 1904):1,140-1; *Independent*, 9 July 1904, p. 2; and Conley, 'Class Conflict and Collective Action,' 344-7.

51 See three essays in Carol Wilton, ed., *Beyond the Law: Lawyers and Business in Canada, 1830 to 1930,* Essays in the History of Canadian Law Series, vol. 4 (Toronto: Osgoode Society 1990): Carol Wilton, 'Introduction: Beyond the Law – Lawyers and Business in Canada, 1830 to 1930,' 3-44; Jonathan S. Swainger, 'Ideology, Social Capital, and Entrepreneurship: Lawyers and Business in Red Deer, Alberta, 1900 to 1920,' 377-402 (quotation from p. 392); and Elizabeth Bloomfield, 'Lawyers as Members of Urban Business Elites in Southern Ontario, 1860 to 1920,' 123-6.

52 Of 276 top businessmen of the 1910-13 period, twenty-five identified themselves as professional men. All were part of the second rank (or subleaders). Consisting of sixteen lawyers, six doctors, a teacher, an architect, and an engineer, they constituted 9 per cent of the leadership group, up three times from the early 1890s. They moved easily between the worlds of business and the professions, exposing a shared foundation of class-based goals and aspirations. Three lawyers held directorships in specific groups of companies, while two others defined themselves as specialists in company law. Of the latter, W.E. Burns headed a speculative oil company, acting 'as counsel for a number of mining companies,' and James H. Lawson, Jr., provided expertise in the field of timber land law. Some lawyers specialized as company promoters. For instance, J.A. Harvey promoted the Bank of Vancouver and the Dominion Stock and Bond Company, both speculative ventures typical of the period, while Robert S. Lennie, noted for his promotional skills in the mining industry, became the largest mine owner in the Slocan region after organizing the $2.5 million Slocan Star Mine in 1911 and the Silver King Mines a year later. Two doctors appear to have given up medicine for business and four others participated in both. See McDonald, 'Business Leaders in Early Vancouver,' 161-4 and appendix B.

53 *Independent*, 2 November 1901, p. 1.

54 Aulay Morrison to Sir Wilfrid Laurier, 7 September 1901, cited in Mouat, 'Mining in the Settler Dominions,' 58. Also see Thomas Robert Loosemore, 'The British Columbia Labor Movement and Political Action, 1879-1906' (MA thesis, University of British Columbia 1954), 104-10, 115-22, 126-30, 136-9, 149-51, and 186-94 and *Electoral History of British Columbia 1871-1986* (Victoria: Elections British Columbia and the Legislative Library 1988), 82-3 and 95-6.

55 Quotations from *Independent,* 31 March 1900, p. 2 and 23 June 1900, p. 4. Also see ibid., 12 May 1900, p. 2, 7 July 1900, p. 1, 29 September 1900, p. 1, 6 October 1900, p. 2, 23 November 1901, p. 1, and 21 December 1901, p. 1.

56 *News-Advertiser*, 6 January 1894, p. 4 and 3 August 1897, p. 3; for Brown, also see Vancouver Trades and Labor Council, 6 November 1902, CVA, Add. MSS 307, Minutes, vol. 3 (1902-8), p. 91.

57 Quotations in order of presentation from *Independent*, 12 May 1900, p. 6, 7 July 1900, p. 1, and 26 September 1903, p. 1; *Province*, 22 October 1900, p. 2; and *Independent*, 24 November 1900, p. 1.

58 One Conservative Party supporter in 1904 proposed buying George Bartley's *Independent* and using it to shift 'the Labour vote from the ranks of the Liberal party where it

is largely to be found' (Unacknowledged memo re: buying the *Independent*, 22 July 1904, UBCSCD, G.H. Cowan Papers, box 1, file 2). In a letter of 27 November 1909, F.C. Wade told Sir Wilfrid Laurier that Vancouver's 'Board of Trade consists of about four hundred members, most of whom are Conservatives' (Laurier Papers re: British Columbia, microfilm, #162816-162824). Also see McDonald, 'Business Leaders in Early Vancouver,' 308-14.

59 *Independent*, 28 April 1900, p. 1 (quotation) and 16 June 1900, p. 1.

60 Quotations from Diary, 16 April 1902, CVA, Bell-Irving Family Papers, vol. 25 and H.O. B[ell]-I[rving] to John [Bell-Irving], 14 May 1899, ibid., vol. 83, Correspondence Out. Also see *Independent*, 24 November 1900, p. 1 and 1 December 1900, p. 2 and *Province*, 30 May 1901, p. 2.

61 Canada, House of Commons, *Debates (Hansard)*, vol. 8, 25 June 1900, 8,179 (George Maxwell) and Meggs, *Salmon*, 39 and 43.

62 Quotation from Loosemore, 'British Columbia Labor Movement and Political Action,' 183. For the socialist movement in British Columbia, see A. Ross McCormack, *Reformers, Rebels, and Revolutionaries: The Western Canadian Radical Movement 1899-1919* (Toronto: University of Toronto Press 1977), chaps. 2-4 and 6; Ross Alfred Johnson, 'No Compromise – No Trading: The Marxist Socialist Tradition in British Columbia' (PhD dissertation, University of British Columbia 1975); and Ronald Grantham, 'Some Aspects of the Socialist Movement in British Columbia' (MA thesis, University of British Columbia 1942).

63 T.R.E. McInnes to Sir Wilfrid Laurier, 25 October 1909, Laurier Papers re: British Columbia, microfilm reel 5, #161311-161318.

Chapter 5: Incorrigible Optimists

1 See Robert A.J. McDonald, 'Victoria, Vancouver, and the Economic Development of British Columbia, 1886-1914,' in *British Columbia: Historical Readings*, ed. W. Peter Ward and Robert A.J. McDonald (Vancouver: Douglas and McIntyre 1981), 377-8 and 381-2.

2 Patricia E. Roy, *Vancouver: An Illustrated History* (Toronto: James Lorimer and Company 1980), 168; Norbert MacDonald, *Distant Neighbors: A Comparative History of Seattle and Vancouver* (Lincoln: University of Nebraska Press 1987), 156; and CVA, Vancouver, Health Department, series 1, Medical Health Officer's Records, *Annual Reports*, PDS 11, 1911, p. 17, 1912, p. 30, 1913, p. 12, 1916, p. 12, and 1919, p. 12.

3 A large number of 'sailors and seamen' are included as part of Victoria's 'Transportation' sector (52 per cent), which may explain why 'Transportation' constituted a disproportionately high proportion of its workforce.

4 McDonald, 'Victoria, Vancouver, and the Economic Development of British Columbia,' 385 and John Lutz, 'Losing Steam: The Boiler and Engine Industry as an Index of British Columbia's Deindustrialization, 1880-1915,' Canadian Historical Association *Historical Papers* (1988):180-5.

5 The commercial workforce was calculated from data in the 'Trade and Merchandising' category of *Fifth Census of Canada, 1911*, vol. 6, table 6, p. 294-5. Data for financial business, including banks, insurance companies, and loan and trust enterprises, were deleted from the census table to more closely approximate commercial employment alone. Also see Robert A.J. McDonald, 'Business Leaders in Early Vancouver, 1886-1914' (PhD dissertation, University of British Columbia 1977), 83-6 and 135. Quotations from *Western Lumberman* 8, 4 (May 1911):47 and Henry J. Boam, *British Columbia: Its His-*

tory, People, Commerce, Industry and Resources (London: Sells 1912), 177.

6 Calculated from the *Fifth Census of Canada, 1911*, vol. 6, table 6 and Michael Piva, *The Condition of the Working Class in Toronto, 1900-1921* (Ottawa: University of Ottawa Press 1979), 15-25.

7 For building permits, see 'Report of the Building Inspector,' CVA, Vancouver, *Financial Statements and Annual Reports*, PDS 1.3, 1936, p. 91; James Conley, '"Open Shop' Means Closed to Union Men": Carpenters and the 1911 Vancouver Building Trades General Strike,' *BC Studies* 91-2 (Autumn-Winter 1991-2):128-9 (quotation); McDonald, 'Business Leaders in Early Vancouver,' 106-7; and Robin Ward, *Robin Ward's Vancouver* (Madiera Park: Harbour Publishing 1990), 22-5 and 64-71.

8 Canada, Nominal Census, 1891, microfilm T-6290, British Columbia, District 2 (New Westminster), Subdistrict C1 (Vancouver City); and *Fifth Census of Canada, 1911*, vol. 6, table 6, 292-5. The number of barristers and solicitors listed for 1891 are 28 (plus 1 judge), while doctors, physicians, and surgeons equalled 29; for 1911 the census lists 254 lawyers and notaries and 185 physicians and surgeons.

9 This definition of metropolitanism – as the centralization of services in a 'mother city,' and the extension of these services to its satellites – is developed by Wilbur R. Thompson in *A Preface to Urban Economics* (Baltimore: Johns Hopkins Press 1965), 14.

10 W.K. Lamb, 'Robie L. Reid (1866-1945): A Memoir,' *British Columbia Historical Quarterly* 9 (1945):84; David R. Verchère, *A Progression of Judges: A History of the Supreme Court of British Columbia* (Vancouver: UBC Press 1988), 117-20 and 148-9; and Vancouver Law Association, Law Society of British Columbia Archives, Minutes (1892-1902), passim. Quotations from Chief Justice Hunter to Sir Wilfrid Laurier, 15 September 1909, Laurier Papers re: British Columbia, microfilm reel 5, #159803-159807.

11 L.G. McPhillips to Richard McBride, 3 March 1909, BCARS, British Columbia, Premiers' Papers, 1909, Private Correspondence, #214/1909; *Daily News-Advertiser* (hereafter *News-Advertiser*), 22 August 1908, p. 3 and 19 December 1908, p. 7; Harry T. Logan, *Tuum Est: A History of the University of British Columbia* (Vancouver: University of British Columbia 1958), 7-11 and passim; Principal J.G. Brown, 'Methodist Colleges' and Rev. J.A. Logan, 'Westminster Hall,' in *Commemorative Review of the Methodist, Presbyterian and Congregational Churches in British Columbia*, ed. Rev. E.A. Davis (Vancouver: Wrigley Printing 1925), 243-9 and 251-9; and Frank Alexander Peake, *The Anglican Church in British Columbia* (Vancouver: Mitchell Press 1959), 149-60. Quotation from Lower Mainland University Committee, *University Location in British Columbia: A Summary of the Arguments* ... ([Vancouver?]: n.p. 1910), 17.

12 *Fifth Census of Canada, 1911*, vol. 3, table 9, p. 214.

13 For a fuller discussion of the size of secondary manufacturing firms in Vancouver to 1911, see McDonald, 'Business Leaders in Early Vancouver,' 90-4.

14 Quotations from *British Columbia Federationist* (hereafter *Federationist*), 28 March 1913, p. 2 and the Rev. R.J. Wilson, 'British Columbia – Her Opportunity and Responsibility,' *Westminster Hall Magazine* 1, 6 (November 1911):24.

15 For railways and the wheat economy, see Canada, Royal Commission on Dominion-Provincial Relations, *Report*, Book 1, *Canada, 1867-1939* (1940; reprint, Ottawa: Queen's Printer 1954), 66-79; and Kenneth A. Buckley, *Capital Formation in Canada, 1896-1930*, rev. ed. (Toronto: University of Toronto Press 1974), 2 and 46; and W.T. Easterbrook and H.G.J. Aitken, *Canadian Economic History* (Toronto: University of Toronto Press 1956), 381-440. For the role of the Grand Trunk Pacific Railway in opening northern

British Columbia, see Frank Leonard, "A Thousand Blunders': The Grand Trunk Pacific Railway Company and Northern British Columbia, 1902-1919' (PhD dissertation, York University 1989).

16 *British Columbia Financial Times* 1, 1 (16 May 1914):3.

17 W.A. Carrothers, 'Forest Industries of British Columbia,' in A.R.M. Lower, *The North American Assault on the Canadian Forest* (Toronto: Ryerson Press 1938), 237; Robert E. Cail, *Land, Man, and the Law: The Dispersal of Crown Land in British Columbia, 1871-1913* (Vancouver: University of British Columbia Press 1974), 103; Stephen Gray, 'Forest Policy and Administration in British Columbia, 1912-1928' (MA thesis, Simon Fraser University 1981), 17-22; and Joseph C. Lawrence, 'Markets and Capital: A History of the Lumber Industry in British Columbia (1778-1952)' (MA thesis, University of British Columbia 1957), 11-15.

18 Patricia E. Roy, 'Progress, Prosperity and Politics: The Railway Policies of Richard McBride,' *BC Studies* 47 (Autumn 1980):3-28 and Cail, *Land, Man and the Law*, 54. Quotation from the Montreal *Journal of Commerce,* 15 December 1914, in Bank of Vancouver Papers, NAC, RG 19, vol. 228, file 616-2.

19 Vancouver loan and trust companies are discussed in McDonald, 'Business Leaders in Early Vancouver,' 110-14. For British investment in prewar British Columbia, see Jacob Viner, *Canada's Balance of International Indebtedness 1900-1913* (Cambridge, MA: Harvard University Press 1924); D.G. Paterson, *Direct British Investment in Canada, 1890-1914* (Toronto: University of Toronto Press 1976), passim; and Matthew Simon, 'New British Investment in Canada, 1865-1914,' *Canadian Journal of Economics* 3 (1970):240-6 and 249.

20 *Vancouver Daily Province* (hereafter *Province*), 9 November 1910, p. 1 and 27 September 1911, p. 1, *Monetary Times,* 28 August 1909, p. 950; and *Western Lumberman* 8, 6 (July 1911):26. For lumber investment, see McDonald, 'Victoria, Vancouver, and the Economic Development of British Columbia,' 386-7.

21 L.D. McCann, 'Urban Growth in a Staple Economy: The Emergence of Vancouver as a Regional Metropolis, 1886-1914,' in *Vancouver: Western Metropolis,* ed. L.J. Evenden (Victoria: Department of Geography, University of Victoria 1978), 33 and *Fifth Census of Canada, 1911,* vol. 6, table 6. Quotations from Fred W. Field, *Capital Investments in Canada,* 3rd ed. (Montreal: Monetary Times of Canada 1914), 251 and R.E. Vernède, *The Fair Dominion: A Record of Canadian Impressions* (London: K. Paul, Trench, Trubner and Company 1911), 259.

22 Information for this paragraph drawn from an undated letter sent by George H. Salmon to the Provincial Archives of British Columbia, found in BCARS, VF (George H. Salmon).

23 Bertrand W. Sinclair, *The Inverted Pyramid* (Toronto: Frederick D. Goodchild 1924), 69.

24 Victor Ross, 'The Bank of British Columbia,' *A History of the Canadian Bank of Commerce* (Toronto: Oxford University Press 1920), 1:334; *News-Advertiser*, 16 September 1892, p. 8; and BCARS, British Columbia, Attorney-General, Estate Records, BC Supreme Court, Vancouver Probates, GR 1415, microfilm B7261, file 1914/3430.

25 E.O.S. Scholefield and F.W. Howay, *British Columbia from the Earliest Times to the Present* (Vancouver: S.J. Clarke 1914), 4:833; *Daily Colonist* (hereafter *Colonist*), 21 November 1919, pp. 1 and 13; and BCARS, British Columbia, Attorney-General, Estate Records, BC Supreme Court, Vancouver Probates, GR 1415, file 1919/6572.

26 Michael Bliss, *Northern Enterprise: Five Centuries of Canadian Business* (Toronto:

McClelland and Stewart 1987), 268; E.P. Neufeld, *The Financial System of Canada: Its Growth and Development* (Toronto: Macmillan 1972), 111, 178, and 289; and Trust Companies Regulation Act, *Revised Statutes of British Columbia,* 1911, vol. 1, 509-10.

27 Garnett Weston, 'Vancouver's Trust and Insurance Companies,' *British Columbia Magazine* 7, 6 (1911):636 and 638. Also see The Editor, 'Trust and Loan Companies,' *Westward Ho! Magazine* 1, 6 (September 1907), 45.

28 Sinclair, *Inverted Pyramid,* 61 and 69. For a more general condemnation of the moral climate of prewar British Columbia and of the role of trust companies in creating that climate, see Ministerial Union of the Lower Mainland of B.C., *The Crisis in B.C.: An Appeal for Investigation* (Vancouver: Saturday Sunset Press 1916).

29 *Henderson's Greater Vancouver City Directory for 1914* (Vancouver: Henderson Publishing Company 1914), 785; *Westward Ho! Magazine* 4, 1 (January 1909):77-8; *British Columbia Magazine* 7, 11 (1911):1,196; and *News-Advertiser,* 16 January 1909, p. 7.

30 W.E. Hodges, 'Dominion Trust Company: Special Report as at October 10th, 1914,' BCARS, British Columbia, Attorney-General, Dominion Trust, Part 8, p. 187-94.

31 Quotation from NAC, CPRC, Correspondence Outward, Letterbook 107, microfilm M3065, file 562, p. 596. Also see BCARS, British Columbia, Attorney-General, Dominion Trust, Part 3, pp. 210-12; Scholefield and Howay, *British Columbia,* 3:1,113; and Martin Nordegg, *The Possibilities of Canada are Truly Great: Memoirs, 1906-1924,* ed. and intro. T.D. Regehr (Toronto: Macmillan 1971), 18-20. Von Alvensleben is said to have directed up to $7 million of German capital into British Columbia land, timber, fish canning, and coal mining firms.

32 *Province,* 7 November 1914, p. 2, 11 November 1914, p. 16, 12 December 1914, p. 6, 8 February 1915, p. 1, 15 March 1915, p. 15, 3 September 1915, p. 7, and 27 March 1916, p. 10. Also see BCARS, British Columbia, Attorney-General, Dominion Trust, Part 1, p. 34, Part 2, pp. 11-15, Part 3, p. 147, and Part 8, p. 193. Quotation from *Province,* 22 February 1916, p. 1.

33 BCARS, British Columbia, Attorney-General, Coroners' Inquests, GR 431, file 1914/411.

34 British Columbia, Attorney-General, Dominion Trust, Part 1, p. 5; Part 2, pp. 15-16; Part 5, pp. 26-8; Part 8, pp. 138ff and 187-90; and Part 9, pp. 8, 17, 24, 28, and 39. Also see Arnold's obituary in *Vancouver Sun,* 13 October 1914, p. 4.

35 For a discussion of the value for social historians of studying wealth held by elites, see W.D. Rubinstein's 'Introduction' to *Wealth and the Wealthy in the Modern World,* ed. Rubinstein (London: Croom Helm 1980), 11-18 and 'Modern Britain,' ibid., 46-53. Gustavus Meyers's *A History of Canadian Wealth* is a study of political economy rather than of privately held wealth in Canada.

36 Analyzing probate records poses an obvious problem for a study of wealth created before 1914, since most prominent Vancouver businessmen continued thereafter to make, spend, and lose money. To limit this distortion the estate records of leading businessmen were read only to 1939, thus generating a reasonable sample of wealth holding by early Vancouver's top businessmen but avoiding the further misrepresentation of new wealth created by sustained prosperity starting in the early 1940s. Increasingly sophisticated mechanisms for transferring one's wealth to tax shelters or family members also undoubtedly limited the net value of estates through the interwar years. Despite these limitations, however, estate records do offer very useful suggestions about the scale and character of wealth created by a society. For legislation governing probate records in British Columbia, see the Succession Duty Act of 1894 in *Revised Statutes of British Columbia,* 1897, vol. 2, 1,953-8; Succession Duty Act of 1897 in *Statutes of the*

Province of British Columbia, 1907, 155-7; and Administration Act, *Revised Statutes of British Columbia,* 1911, vol. 1, 31-67.

37 Quotations from W.G. Cameron and Thos. Kidd, 'First Report of the Board of Taxation,' 5 April 1918, in Robert Murray Haig, *Reports of the Board of Taxation, with a Report on Taxation in the Province of British Columbia by Robert Murray Haig* (Victoria: Wm. H. Cullin 1919), Q6. For Hendry, see Scholefield and Howay, *British Columbia,* 4:720; *Western Canada Lumberman* 5, 10 (October 1908):[?] and 7, 2 (December 1910):17; *Canadian Forestry Journal* 12 (August 1910):671-2; BCARS, British Columbia, Attorney-General, Estate Records, BC Supreme Court, Vancouver Probates, GR 1415, file 1916/ 4158.

38 For Rogers, see BCARS, British Columbia, Attorney-General, Estate Records, BC Supreme Court, Vancouver Probates, file 1918/5079, Michael Kluckner, ed , *M.I. Rogers 1869-1965* (Vancouver: [Private] 1987), 97-8; and John Schreiner, *The Refiners: A Century of BC Sugar* (Vancouver: Douglas and McIntyre 1989), 70-3.

39 Peter C. Newman, *The Canadian Establishment* (Toronto: McClelland and Stewart 1981), 2:45. The story of British Columbia's first attempt to create a locally based chartered bank also reveals the limited financial strength of Vancouver capitalists. Chartered in 1908, the Bank of Vancouver collapsed in 1914. It did so despite having among its Vancouver shareholders three leading lumbermen and three prominent wholesalers. See NAC, Bank of Vancouver Papers, RG 19, vol. 228, file 616-2, vol. 1 and vol. 231, file 616-2, vol. 2-3; J. Castell Hopkins, *Canadian Annual Review of Public Affairs, 1907-1914* (Toronto: Canadian Review Company 1907), 41; *Monetary Times,* 14 March 1908, p. 1550 and 18 April 1908, p. 1770; and W.R. Houston, ed , *The Annual Financial Review, Canadian* (Toronto: W. Briggs 1912), 12:137, (1913), 13:37, and (1914), 14:134.

40 Quotations in order of presentation are from *Federationist,* 5 April 1912, p. 1; British Columbia, Commission on Labour, 1912-14, Transcripts of Evidence (hereafter BCCL, Evidence), 20 January 1913 (Charles Cassidy), BCARS, RG 684, vol. 1, file 2, p. 149; Sinclair, *Inverted Pyramid,* 69, Alfred H. Lewis, *South Vancouver, Past and Present* (Vancouver: Western Publishing 1920), 14, 16, 18, and 20; and Cameron and Kidd, 'First Report of the Board of Taxation,' Q6-Q7. For other, less class-specific, comments on the real estate boom in Vancouver, see *News-Advertiser,* 11 April 1909, p. 19 and 21 August 1909, p. 9, and Interview with H.H. Stevens by Colleen Toppings (1964), part 4, in UBCSCD, Colleen Toppings Bourke Collection, box 1-2.

41 Geographic distribution was determined from a survey of applications in the original source; see *British Columbia Gazette* 52 (September-October 1912):9,074-168.

42 Ibid., p. 9,091 and *Economist,* 21 February 1914, p. 392 (quotation).

43 Henry Bell-Irving to his sons at Loretto School, Scotland, [14-25 November 1907?], CVA, Bell-Irving Family Papers, Add. MSS 1, vol. 86, Correspondence Out; Scholefield and Howay, *British Columbia,* 3:950-5; *Vancouver Sun,* 13 October 1959, p. 13; and *British Columbia Magazine* 10, 5 (1914):248.

44 For studies of American elites see Reinhard Bendix, 'Social Mobility and the American Business Elite,' in Seymour Martin Lipset and Reinhard Bendix, *Social Mobility in Industrial Society* (Berkeley and Los Angeles: University of California Press 1959), 114-43; Jocelyn Maynard Ghent and Frederic Cople Jaher, 'The Chicago Business Elite: 1830-1930. A Collective Biography,' *Business History Review* 50 (Autumn 1976):288-328; John N. Ingham, *The Iron Barons: A Social Analysis of an American Urban Elite, 1874-1965* (Westport, CT: Greenwood Press 1978); Norbert MacDonald, 'The Business Leaders of Seattle, 1880-1910,' *Pacific Northwest Quarterly* 50 (January 1959):1-13; three essays by

William Miller, 'The Business Elite in Business Bureaucracies: Careers of Top Executives in the Early Twentieth Century,' 'American Historians and the Business Elite,' and 'The Recruitment of the American Business Elite' in *Men in Business*, ed. William Miller (1952; reprint, New York: Harper Torchbooks 1962), 286-305, 309-28, and 329-37; C. Wright Mills, 'The American Business Elite: A Collective Portrait,' *Journal of Economic History* 6 (1946):20-44; and Mabel Newcomer, *The Big Business Executive: The Factors That Made Him, 1900-1950* (New York: Columbia University Press 1955).

Canadian studies include T.W. Acheson, 'Changing Social Origins of the Canadian Industrial Elite, 1880-1910,' *Business History Review* 47 (1973):189-217; Wallace Clement, *The Canadian Corporate Elite: An Analysis of Economic Power* (Toronto: McClelland and Stewart 1975); Norbert MacDonald, *Distant Neighbours: A Comparative History of Seattle and Vancouver* (Lincoln: University of Nebraska Press 1987), chap. 5, 78-101; and John Porter, *The Vertical Mosaic: An Analysis of Class and Power in Canada* (Toronto: University of Toronto Press 1965).

45 *Colonist*, 21 February 1931, p. 4; *Province*, 19 February 1931, pp. 1 and 2; and Henry Doyle, 'Rise and Decline of the Pacific Salmon Fisheries,' UBCSCD, manuscript, vol. 1, pp. 191-2.

46 Acheson, 'Changing Social Origins,' 216.

47 Gunter Barth, *Instant Cities: Urbanization and the Rise of San Francisco and Denver* (New York: Oxford University Press 1975), 168 and 170 and Paul Voisey, 'In Search of Wealth and Status: An Economic and Social Study of Entrepreneurs in Early Calgary,' in *Frontier Calgary: Town, City, and Region 1875-1914*, ed. Anthony W. Rasporich and Henry C. Klassen (Calgary: University of Calgary Press, McClelland and Stewart West 1975), 232 and passim.

48 Of 322 people who met the criteria I used to define business leaders or subleaders for the 1890-3 and 1910-13 periods – the criteria are defined in appendix A of McDonald, 'Business Leaders in Early Vancouver' – only two were women. One, Alice Berry, was instrumental in forming the World Printing and Publishing Company in 1905, which bought the *Vancouver Daily World* newspaper. She first became the managing director and remained vice-president in 1911. Tina Cuthbertson, about whom little is known, headed Thos. B. Cuthbertson and Company, a men's clothing business that at one time owned five stores in Vancouver and Victoria. For Alice Berry, see Scholefield and Howay, *British Columbia*, 4:928. For Tina Cuthbertson, see *Province*, 4 February 1913, p. 1 and 13 October 1950, p. 15. Top business leaders and their companies are listed in McDonald, 'Business Leaders,' 501.

49 In other words, social mobility is defined here as movement from a wage labour to a wage employer position; occupations were traced through city directories. Also see Mark Leier, *Where the Fraser River Flows. The Industrial Workers of the World in British Columbia* (Vancouver: New Star Books 1990), 101-2.

50 *News-Advertiser*, 13 February 1917, pp. 1 and 7; British Columbia, Attorney-General, Companies Office, Company Registration Files, file 2854/1897, microfilm reel 19; and Elizabeth Norcross, 'Mary Ellen Smith: The Right Woman in the Right Place at the Right Time,' in *Not Just Pin Money: Selected Essays on the History of Women's Work in British Columbia*, ed. Barbara Latham and Roberta Pardzo (Victoria: Camosun College 1984), 357-64.

51 Scholefield and Howay, *British Columbia*, 3:1002-5 and *Province*, 17 October 1964, p. 23.

52 The criteria for defining 'leaders' of the Vancouver Trades and Labor Council are described in Chapter 3, n. 66. Occupations were traced through city directories.

53 Canada, Department of Labour, Strikes and Lockouts Files, NAC, RG 27, microfilm reel 4, file 3378. Also see Henry Bell-Irving to C.A. Richards, 15 June 1911, CVA, Bell-Irving Family Papers, vol. 87, Correspondence Out.

54 For high prices, see *News-Advertiser*, 25 April 1912, p. 4; *Federationist*, 29 August 1913, p. 5; BCCL, Evidence, 12 March 1913 (J.G. Davidson), BCARS, RG 684, vol. 4, file 1, p. 44; *Province*, 5 September 1914, p. 15; and Eleanor A. Bartlett, 'Real Wages and the Standard of Living in Vancouver, 1901-1929,' *BC Studies* 51 (Autumn 1981):51-2. Labour sources estimated that unemployed in Vancouver had reached 10,000 by February 1914 and 15,000 by October; see *Federationist*, 21 November 1913, p. 1, 6 February 1914, p. 25, and 13 April 1914, p. 1 and *Labour Gazette* 15 (October 1914):460.

55 Ruben Bellan, *Winnipeg First Century: An Economic History* (Winnipeg: Queenston House Publishing 1978), 118-19 and 123; Kenneth Norrie and Douglas Owram, *A History of the Canadian Economy* (Toronto: Harcourt Brace Jovanovich 1991), 411-15; and 'Report of the Building Inspector,' CVA, Vancouver, *Financial Statements and Annual Reports*, PDS 1.3, 1936, p. 91.

56 The Norrie and Owram textbook, *A History of the Canadian Economy,* offers an example of the general failure of historians to distinguish British Columbia's history from that of the prairie region. The British Columbia perspective is presented in Jean Barman, *The West beyond the West: A History of British Columbia* (Toronto: University of Toronto Press 1991).

57 Bellan, *Winnipeg*, 121 and 123 and Cameron and Kidd, 'First Report of the Board of Taxation,' Q6. For provincial tax revenues, see Haig, 'A Preliminary Report to the Taxation Board,' in *Reports of the Board of Taxation, with a Report on Taxation in the Province of British Columbia by Robert Murray Haig* (Victoria: Wm. H. Cullin 1919), table 1, Q82-Q83 and Q120.

58 Bellan, *Winnipeg*, 127.

59 For rents and vacancy rates see *Federationist*, 9 July 1915, p. 2. For trust companies see McDonald, 'Business Leaders in Early Vancouver,' 116; for unemployment see *Labour Gazette* 15 (September 1914):367 and 16 (September 1915):280 and *Federationist*, 12 February 1915, p. 1, 5 March 1915, p. 2, and 6 March 1915, p. 2.

60 *Federationist*, 16 October 1914, p. 2, 29 January 1915, p. 2, 25 June 1915, p. 1, and 16 April 1915, p. 1 and *Labour Gazette* 15 (November 1914) to 16 (August 1916):passim. The *Labour Gazette* 16 (April 1916): 1,090 quoted a government source stating that 100,000 people had departed from British Columbia. For Vancouver's changing population see CVA, Vancouver, Health Department, series 1, Medical Health Officer's Records, *Annual Reports*, PDS 11, 1912, p. 30, 1913, p. 12, and 1916, p. 12.

Chapter 6: The Wealthy Business and Professional Class

1 Board of Temperance and Moral Reform of the Methodist Church and the Board of Social Service and Evangelism of the Presbyterian Church, *Vancouver, British Columbia: The Report of ... an Intensive Social Survey ...* (1913), United Church B.C. Conference Archives, Dobson Papers, box A2, file C, p. 11.

2 Drawing from Max Weber's differentiation of class and status, Anthony Giddens concludes that 'Whereas class expresses relationships involved in production, status groups express those involved in consumption, in the form of specific "styles of life."' See Giddens, *The Class Structure of the Advanced Societies*, 2nd ed. (London: Unwin Hyman 1981), 43-4.

3 The marriages and school attendance patterns of prominent business families are discussed in Robert A.J. McDonald, 'Business Leaders in Early Vancouver, 1886-1914' (PhD dissertation, University of British Columbia 1977), 245-6. The private schools that B.T. Rogers's children attended are documented in Michael Kluckner, comp. and ed., *M.I. Rogers, 1869-1895* (Victoria: J. Gudewill 1987), 58, 83, 101, 106, 123, 116, 119-20, and 122. The private schools in British Columbia that children of local business and social leaders attended are discussed in Elizabeth Bell-Irving, *Crofton House School: The First Ninety Years, 1898-1988* (Vancouver: Crofton House School 1988) and Jean Barman, *Growing up British in British Columbia: Boys in Private Schools* (Vancouver: University of British Columbia Press 1984).

4 BTR[ogers] to A.R.I. Heward, 18 June 1900, BC Sugar Company Archives, B.T. Rogers Private Papers and Kluckner, *M.I. Rogers*, 54.

5 For Davis, see the *Vancouver Daily Province* (hereafter *Province*), 2 March 1940, p. 10; for Senkler, see E.O.S. Scholefield and F.W. Howay, *British Columbia from the Earliest Times to the Present* (Vancouver: S.J. Clarke 1914), 4:1,100-3 and *Vancouver Sun*, 29 March 1926, p. 13.

6 A.G. Bradley, *Canada in the Twentieth Century* (London: Archibald Constable 1905), 382. My thanks to Jean Barman for this reference.

7 Information about the Tupper family is drawn from George MacLean Rose, ed., *A Cyclopaedia of Canadian Biography: Being Chiefly Men of the Time* (Toronto: Rose Publishing 1888), 712-13; H.J. Morgan, ed., *The Canadian Men and Women of the Time*, 2nd ed. (Toronto: W. Briggs 1912), 1,113; and *Victoria Daily Times*, 31 March 1927, p. 15.

8 The social pages of the *Province* and the *Vancouver Daily World* (hereafter *World*) reveal that the Tuppers were part of a clique of the city's most prestigious families. The organizations that either Sir Charles or Lady Tupper served in some honorary or executive capacity included the Vancouver General Hospital, the women's auxiliaries of the Vancouver General Hospital and St. Paul's Hospitals, the Children's Aid Society, the Red Cross, the Society for the Prevention of Cruelty of Animals, the Daughters of the Empire (municipal chapter), the Canadian Handicrafts Guild, the British Columbia Society of Fine Arts, the Vancouver Council of Women, the Women's Exchange, the Vancouver Club, the University Club, and the Connaught Skating Club.

9 Western emulation of eastern social practices is suggested in Paul Voisey, 'In Search of Wealth and Status: An Economic and Social Study of Entrepreneurs in Early Calgary,' in *Frontier Calgary: Town, City, and Region 1875-1914*, ed. Anthony W. Rasporich and Henry C. Klassen (Calgary: Calgary University Press, McClelland and Stewart West 1975), 236; J.M.S. Careless, 'Aspects of Urban Life in the West, 1870-1914,' in *Prairie Perspectives 2*, ed. Anthony W. Rasporich and Henry C. Klassen (Toronto: Holt, Rinehart and Winston 1973), 73; and Lawrence H. Larsen, *The Urban West at the End of the Frontier* (Lawrence: Regents Press of Kansas 1978), xi and 2.

10 The best British study of how fundamental economic and social changes in the nineteenth century produced new methods of defining social prestige is Leonore Davidoff, *The Best Circles: Society Etiquette and the Season* (London: Croom Helm 1973). For the United States, see E. Digby Baltzell, *Philadelphia Gentlemen: The Making of a National Upper Class* (1958; reprint, Chicago: Quandrangle Books 1971), 15-30 and 46-69 and Frederick Cople Jaher, *The Urban Establishment: Upper Strata in Boston, New York, Charleston, Chicago, and Los Angeles* (Urbana: University of Illinois Press 1982), 1-14.

11 *Province*, 16 June 1900, p. 13.

12 Angus Everett Robertson, 'The Pursuit of Power, Profit and Privacy: A Study of Vancouver's West End, 1886-1914' (MA thesis, University of British Columbia 1977), 47 and Bell-Irving, *Crofton House School*.

13 Barman, *Growing up British in British Columbia*, 27-8.

14 Davidoff, *The Best Circles*, 41-9 and Robertson, 'Pursuit of Power,' 37-45.

15 Robertson, 'Pursuit of Power,' 16 and passim. Also see Isabel Marion Tupper, *The History of the Georgian Club* (Vancouver: Georgian Club 1961), 1 and Irene Howard, 'Shockable and Unshockable Methodists in *The Innocent Traveller*,' *Essays on Canadian Writing* 23 (Spring 1982):107-34.

16 The *Province* instituted its 'women's department' in February 1900; its first Society column appeared on 17 February.

17 On the social role of the *World* newspaper and the importance of naming, see Marjory Lang and Linda Hale, 'Women of *The World* and Other Dailies: The Lives and Times of Vancouver Newspaperwomen in the First Quarter of the Twentieth Century,' *BC Studies* 85 (Spring 1990):3-23 and *World*, 21 October 1901, p. 2. For Julia Henshaw, see *Province*, 19 November 1937, p. 12; and *The Canadian Magazine* 18 (1901-2):220-1.

18 Angus Robertson has shown that members of Society organized their 'at home' schedules by area in order 'to facilitate social interaction in a rational manner' across the entire west end neighbourhood; see 'Pursuit of Power,' 41-5.

19 *Province*, 10 November 1900, p. 6.

20 *World*, 12 October 1901, p. 2 and *Province*, 19 October 1901, p. 4.

21 Quotation from Stephen Leacock, *Arcadian Adventures with the Idle Rich*, New Canadian Library no. 10 (1914; reprint, Toronto: McClelland and Stewart 1969), 17. Also see Thorstein Veblen, 'The Theory of the Leisure Class,' in *Class, Status and Power: A Reader in Social Stratification*, ed. Reinhard Bendix and Seymour Martin Lipset (Glencoe, IL: The Free Press 1953), 37.

22 Elite ownership of automobiles and yachts is discussed in McDonald, 'Business Leaders in Early Vancouver,' 274-5. Quotation from *Province*, 29 January 1912, p. 24.

23 *Province*, 25 April 1913, p. 8. The high status of horse shows is suggested in Baltzell, *Philadelphia Gentlemen*, 206 and 362.

24 McDonald, 'Business Leaders in Early Vancouver,' 275-6. Quotation from *Province*, 21 January 1911, p. 5.

25 For the Davis family see *Province*, 13 January 1913, p. 6, 26 June 1936, p. 8 (quotation), and 2 March 1940, p. 10; also see H.R. Bell-Irving to Mr. Sprott, 19 July 1910, CVA, Bell Irving Family Papers, vol. 87, Correspondence Out and Kluckner, *M.I. Rogers*, 54.

26 E.M.W. Gibson, 'The Impact of Social Belief on Landscape Change: A Geographical Study of Vancouver' (PhD dissertation, University of British Columbia 1972), 95-6 and 107 and Harold Kalman, Ron Phillips, and Robin Ward, *Exploring Vancouver: The Essential Architectural Guide* (Vancouver: UBC Press 1993), 147-9. Quotations from J.S. Matthews, 'Early Vancouver: Narrative of Pioneers in Vancouver, B.C.,' CVA, typescript, vol. 1, p. 104 and Gibson, 'Impact of Social Belief,' 95

27 Hugh Keenleyside, *Memoirs of Hugh L. Keenleyside* (Toronto: McClelland and Stewart 1981), vol. 1, *Hammer the Golden Day*, 44.

28 McDonald, 'Business Leaders in Early Vancouver,' 260, table 35 and 'Vancouver's "Four Hundred": The Quest for Wealth and Status in Canada's Urban West, 1886-1914,' *Journal of Canadian Studies* 25, 3 (Autumn 1990):60. The phrase 'leading business families' refers here to business leaders and subleaders for the 1910-13 period; 'social leaders'

refers to members of 'Society' as defined in Chapter 1 and discussed later in this chapter.

29 Deryk W. Holdsworth, 'House and Home in Vancouver: The Emergence of a West Coast Landscape 1886-1929' (PhD dissertation, University of British Columbia 1981), chap. 6 and 'House and Home in Vancouver: Images of West Coast Urbanism, 1886-1929,' in *The Canadian City: Essays in Urban History*, ed. Gilbert A. Stelter and Alan F.J. Artibise (Toronto: McClelland and Stewart 1977), 201-3; Janet Bingham, *Samuel Maclure, Architect* (Ganges, BC: Horsdal and Schubart 1985), 73-89; and *Province*, 31 August 1912, p. 23.

30 *Province*, 27 August 1913, p. 3.

31 Barman, *Growing up British in British Columbia*, 17, 23, 29 (quotation), 55-6, and 62.

32 Keenleyside, *Memoirs*, 15-69 (quotations from pp. 57 and 42).

33 Ibid., 76-7 and Barman, *Growing up British in British Columbia*, 28-31 (quotation from p. 28). At least three of Henry Bell-Irving's sons were educated at Loretto in Scotland (ibid., 119); Campbell Sweeny's two sons attended Haileybury College, England (*Province*, 23 November 1940, p. 5 and 15 February 1966, p. 22).

34 The data upon which this paragraph and the one that follows are based are located in McDonald, 'Vancouver's "Four Hundred,"' 66-8.

35 J.A. Hobson, *Canada To-day* (London: T.F. Unwin 1906), 27.

36 Among the group of prewar business leaders from which all Society members have been excluded, only 15.4 per cent were Anglican, whereas 33.4 per cent belonged to one of three lower-status denominations: Methodist, Baptist, or Roman Catholic. By contrast, among the group of social leaders from which business leaders have been excluded, 67.5 per cent were Anglicans and only 7.8 per cent Methodists, Baptists, or Roman Catholics.

37 The reference to 'invented' is from Voisey, 'In Search of Wealth and Status': 'the only real difference between pioneer classes [in Calgary] was money. Other distinctions had to be invented' (p. 236). Also see Barman, *Growing up British in British Columbia*, 17 and 55.

38 For Campbell, see Scholefield and Howay, *British Columbia*, 3:476-80 and BCARS, British Columbia, Attorney-General, Estate Records, BC Supreme Court, Vancouver Probates, GR 1415, file 1933/18,406. For Ward, see Scholefield and Howay, *British Columbia*, 4:269 and BCARS, British Columbia, Attorney-General, Estate Records, BC Supreme Court, Vancouver Probates, GR 1415, file 1931/16,266. City directories and social registers were also used.

39 Baltzell, *Philadelphia Gentlemen*, 336 and 343; John Gilkeson, *Middle-Class Providence, 1820-1940* (Princeton: Princeton University Press 1986), 143; John Ingham, *The Iron Barons: A Social Analysis of an American Urban Elite, 1874-1965* (Westport, CT: Greenwood Press 1978), 84, 96, and 223; and T.W. Acheson, 'Changing Social Origins of the Canadian Industrial Elite, 1880-1910,' *Business History Review* 47 (1973):214.

40 The Terminal City Club began as the Metropolitan Club but was reorganized as the Terminal City Club in 1899. See F.C. Cotton, J.C. Keith, Rt. G. Tatlow, and Joseph Whetham to W.C. Van Horne, 27 October 1890, CVA, CPR Papers, Add. MSS 42, and Terminal City Club, *A Narrative History of the Terminal City Club, Limited: Constitution and House Rules, Roster of Membership*, pp. 10, 12, and 13, CVA, Terminal City Club Papers, Add. MSS 309.

41 These figures actually overestimate the difference, because the businesses analyzed include only BC companies for which assets are known, and exclude national corporations such as banks and the CPR; their chief executives were likely candidates for membership in the Vancouver Club.

42 The social and occupational characteristics of business leaders and subleaders who belonged to the Vancouver and Terminal City clubs are compared in McDonald, 'Business Leaders in Early Vancouver,' 250-6.

43 See Baltzell, *Philadelphia Gentlemen* and Jaher, *The Urban Establishment*, and John N. Ingham, 'The American Urban Upper Class: Cosmopolitans or Locals?' *Journal of Urban History* 2, 1 (November 1975):69 and 85.

44 Of the two directories, the *Elite Directory of Vancouver* (Vancouver: Thomson Stationery Company 1908) and the *Vancouver Social Register and Club Directory* (Vancouver: Welch and Gibbs 1914), the latter is the most complete. Its social index lists 2,491 registrants (pp. 11-75), of which 2,270 were couples, 89 single men (an unknown number of them widowers), 96 widows, and 36 single women. Some couples listed their children while others did not; I have not included these children in my calculation; I reached a round number of 8,000 by assuming that each of the 2,270 couples had an average of 1.5 children or other family members (such as parents or unmarried sisters) still living in the city but not included in the *Social Register* in their own right.

45 Vancouver's club hierarchy is defined in McDonald, 'Business Leaders in Early Vancouver,' 225-6 and 247-59 and 'Vancouver's "Four Hundred,"' 56 and 70 n. 10. Also see Frederic Cople Jaher, 'Style and Status: High Society in Late Nineteenth-Century New York,' in *The Rich, the Well Born, and the Powerful: Elites and Upper Classes in History*, ed. Jaher (Urbana: University of Illinois Press 1973), 263 and 281.

46 See Leonore Davidoff and Catherine Hall, *Family Fortunes: Men and Women of the English Middle Class, 1780-1850* (Chicago: University of Chicago Press 1987), 74, 185, 227, and 275.

47 See Scholefield and Howay, *British Columbia*, 3:149 (Stewart quotation) and Keenleyside, *Memoirs*, 35.

48 For a discussion of the ideology of separate spheres and of maternal feminism in Canada before the First World War, see Alison Prentice et al., *Canadian Women: A History* (Toronto: Harcourt Brace Jovanovich 1988), 142-68.

49 Quotation from Petition of Women's Christian Temperance Union to Mayor and Aldermen, 15 May 1891, CVA, City Clerk's Correspondence, 10-A-5, file 11, series 20; also see Petition of Women's Christian Temperance Union to Mayor and Council, 8 January 1890, ibid., file 4, series 20.

50 For the role of Lady Reid see Gillian Weiss, '"As Women and as Citizens": Clubwomen in Vancouver 1910-1928' (PhD dissertation, University of British Columbia 1983), 38, and *Daily News-Advertiser* (hereafter *News-Advertiser*), 1 February 1896, p. 1. For Anna Beecher, see *News-Advertiser*, 18 November 1896, p. 3 and 30 January 1897, p. 5 and *Province*, 12 January 1911, p. 8. Two other organizational leaders were Mrs. Mellon and Sarah McLagan. For Mrs. Mellon see Alfred Ian Hunt, 'Mutual Enlightenment in Early Vancouver, 1886-1916' (PhD dissertation, University of British Columbia 1987), 48-50, 115-17, and 132 and *News-Advertiser*, 29 January 1898, p. 5. For Sarah McLagan, see *World*, 6 February 1900, p. 6 and Lang and Hale, 'Women of the *World* and Other Dailies,' 3-6. Lady Reid served as Vancouver's first female school trustee (in 1898-9) and was the only woman to be elected to the school board until 1912.

51 For the Vancouver General Hospital, see *Vancouver News*, 21 November 1886, p. 4; *News-Advertiser*, 19 April 1891, p. 8 and 1 May 1891, p. 5; and *Province*, 8 January 1910, p. 17. For the Royal Margarete Club of St. Paul's Hospital, see *Province*, 27 September 1912, p. 8 and 5 October 1912, p. 5. For the Seamen's Institute, see *Province*, 6 January 1913, p. 8. For the Society for the Prevention of Cruelty to Animals, see *Province*, 9 January 1913,

p. 8 and 22 November 1913, p. 8. Socially prominent women joined elite men in other charities, including the Victorian Order of Nurses (VON), the Red Cross, and the Children's Aid Society. For the VON, see _News-Advertiser_, 30 April 1898, p. 10 and 9 December 1911, p. 13 and _Province_, 5 February 1909, p. 9; for the Red Cross, _Province_, 22 March 1900, p. 3 and _World_, 22 March 1902, p. 8; and for the Children's Aid Society, Anne Margaret Angus, _Children's Aid Society of Vancouver, B.C., 1901-1951_, CVA, Pamphlet 1951-71, pp. 6-13. For the Alexandra Orphanage, see _Province_, 14 February 1908, p. 2.

52 Hunt, 'Mutual Enlightenment,' 97-101 (quotations from p. 101).

53 For the Georgian Club, see Tupper, _The History of the Georgian Club_, 2-3 and _Province_, 17 December 1910, p. 5 and 6 February 1912, p. 8; and for the Athenaeum Club, see Blanche E. Holt, 'Women of the West in Clubland: The Athenaeum Club, Vancouver, B.C.,' _British Columbia Magazine_ 7, 3 (1911):188-90 and _Province_, 2 May 1911, p. 5. For the Women's Canadian Club, see _World_, 25 March 1909, p. 6 and _Province_, 30 September 1910, p. 5. The Vancouver Local Council of Women is discussed later in this chapter.

54 The only comprehensive study of high culture in early Vancouver is Hunt, 'Mutual Enlightenment.' Quotation from a statement uttered in 1919 by Judge F.W. Howay, president of the Art, Historical and Scientific Association (p. 88).

55 Pierre Bourdieu, _Distinction: A Social Critique of the Judgement of Taste_ (Cambridge, MA: Harvard University Press 1984), xiii-xiv, 1-7, 13-16, 32, and 40-4 (quotations from pp. 7 and xiv). British-born architect R. MacKay Fripp associated taste with 'cultivated leisure' when speaking about Vancouver in 1899. 'This is the west,' he wrote, 'and ... there has not been sufficient time to evolve a standard in the matters of taste. There are no old established interests, no cultivated leisure class ... Every man is fully occupied in making a way for himself' ('British Columbia Letter, II,' _The Canadian Architect and Builder_ 12 (July 1899):138, cited in Hunt, 'Mutual Enlightenment,' 78).

56 Quotations from Hunt, 'Mutual Enlightenment,' 48 and _News-Advertiser_, 14 October 1890, p. 8. Also see _News-Advertiser_, 5 October 1890, p. 1 and 27 February 1892, p. 8 and William Wylie Thom, 'The Fine Arts in Vancouver, 1886-1930: An Historical Survey' (MA thesis, University of British Columbia 1969), 3-9.

57 Thom, 'Fine Arts in Vancouver,' 28-36; Hunt, 'Mutual Enlightenment,' 97-102; _Province_, 21 May 1910, p. 7 (mag. sec.), 17 October 1911, p. 1, and 12 April 1912, p. 8; and Emily Carr, _Growing Pains: The Autobiography of Emily Carr_ (Toronto: Oxford University Press 1946), 205-7 (quotation).

58 Quotations from Hunt, 'Mutual Enlightenment,' 90 (taken from the unpublished preamble of a 1912 guide to the AHSA-sponsored Museum and Art Gallery) and 51 (from a speech by the Rev. Tucker to Governor-General Aberdeen in 1894). For the British orientation of the AHSA, see ibid., 62, 83, and 130-6.

59 For the City Beautiful movement see Walter Van Nus, 'The Fate of City Beautiful Thought in Canada, 1893-1930,' Canadian Historical Association, _Historical Papers_ (1975):191-210; Paul Boyer, _Urban Masses and Moral Order in America, 1820-1920_ (Cambridge, MA, and London: Harvard University Press 1978), chap. 8; Diane B. Hinds, 'The Evolution of Urban Public Design in Europe and America: Vancouver Adaptation to 1913' (MA thesis, University of British Columbia 1979), chap. 4; and Graeme Wynn, 'The Rise of Vancouver,' in _Vancouver and Its Region_, ed. Graeme Wynn and Timothy Oke (Vancouver: UBC Press 1992), 116-21.

60 Boyer, _Urban Masses_, 263-4 and 272-6 and William H. Wilson, 'J. Horace McFarland and the City Beautiful Movement,' _Journal of Urban History_ 7 (May 1981):320-30.

61 For the Vancouver Tourist Association, see McDonald, 'Business Leaders in Early Vancouver,' 320-30 and *News-Advertiser*, 26 June 1902, p. 1 and 28 June 1902, p. 2. For the early stages of the movement to beautify the city, see *News-Advertiser*, 10 July 1901, p. 4, 10 July 1903, p. 4, 23 May 1905, p. 1, 27 May 1906, p. 4, 1 June 1906, p. 2, 8 August 1906, p. 2, and 10 April 1910, p. 2. The comment on architecture is from *Province*, 1 April 1912, p. 6.

62 'Description of Proposed Foreshore Railway, Stanley Park, Vancouver, B.C.,' August 1910, and G.J. Ashworth to Board of Park Commissioners, 27 September 1910, 4 May 1911, and 10 June 1911, CVA, VBPCP, series 81, 48-C-3, file 1; and CVA, City Clerk's Department, Nominations and Elections, vol. 1 (1886-1924), 1912 Election Returns, MCR-4, p. 294.

63 George F. Chadwick, *The Park and the Town: Public Landscape in the 19th and 20th Centuries* (London: Architectural Press 1966), 221-5; 'Proposed Plan for the Improvement of Coal Harbour ... suggested by Jonathan Rogers and Geo. H. Webster, C.E.,' 8 September 1909, CVA, Matthews Collection, Add. MSS 54, Stanley Park Correspondence; R.A. Pope to Mayor of Vancouver, 4 October 1911, CVA, VBPCP, series 81, 48-E-1, file 10; and Thomas H. Mawson to Chairmen and Members, Vancouver Board of Park Commissioners, 17 April and 20 June 1912, ibid., file 7 and 16 October 1912, ibid., file 10.

64 Evidence for paragraph detailed in Robert A.J. McDonald, '"Holy Retreat" or "Practical Breathing Spot"?: Class Perceptions of Vancouver's Stanley Park, 1910-1913,' *Canadian Historical Review* 65 (June 1984):146.

65 The Park Board's intellectual orientation and social character are explored in McDonald, '"Holy Retreat" or "Practical Breathing Spot"?' 135-45 and 153. On the ethos of Progressivism see Robert H. Wiebe, *The Search for Order, 1877-1920* (New York: Hill and Wang 1967) and Carolyn Strange, 'From Modern Babylon to a City upon a Hill: The Toronto Social Survey Commission of 1915 and the Search for Sexual Order in the City,' in *Patterns of the Past: Interpreting Ontario's History*, ed. Roger Hall, William Westfall, and Laurel Sefton MacDowell (Toronto and Oxford: Dundurn Press 1988), 255-77. For the identity of park commissioners, see William C. McKee, 'The History of the Vancouver Park System, 1886-1929' (MA thesis, University of Victoria 1976), appendix 2.

66 *News-Advertiser*, 30 January 1897, p. 5.

67 H.B. Perry to Mr. Rawlings, Secretary, Board of Park Commissioners, 17 February 1912, CVA, VBPCP, series 81, 48-C-7, vol. 9, file 10 and *News-Advertiser*, 21 January 1912, p. 26 and 23 February 1912, p. 2.

68 Quotations from *News-Advertiser*, 23 February 1912, p. 2 and 16 May, 1912, p. 7. Also see *News-Advertiser*, 2 April 1912, p. 11, 9 May 1912, p. 4, and 12 March 1912, p. 11. I determined the social status of the Local Council of Women executive by comparing the names of LCW officers elected for the year 1912-13 with the names of Society families and entrants in the social index section of *The Vancouver Social Register and Club Directory*. Of the ten LCW officers, none belonged to Society but eight were listed in the *Social Register* (see *Province*, 7 February 1911, p. 7).

69 Evidence for this paragraph is presented in McDonald, '"Holy Retreat" or "Practical Breathing Spot"?' 133-5 and 144.

70 For Tupper, see Geoff Meggs, *Salmon: The Decline of the British Columbia Fishery* (Vancouver: Douglas and McIntyre 1991), 43 and Cicely Lyons, *Salmon: Our Heritage. The Story of a Province and an Industry* (Vancouver: BC Packers 1969), 216. For Davis, see G. McL. Brown to Sir T.G. Shaughnessy, 21 January 1902, CVA, Shaughnessy Papers, file 66287.

Chapter 7: The Artisan or Moderately Well-To-Do Class

1 Quotation from *Vancouver Sun,* 5 June 1946, p. 9. For Taylor's background, see *Who's Who in British Columbia, 1933-1934* (Victoria: S.M. Carter 1934), 167; the *Vancouver Daily Province* (hereafter *Province*), 5 June 1946, pp. 1, 2, 4, and 7; and *Vancouver Sun,* 5 June 1946, pp. 1, 4, and 9. For his role as a booster, see Percy F. Godenrath, 'Advertising a City,' *Westward Ho! Magazine* 5, 3 (September 1909):556 and *Vancouver Sun,* 5 June 1946, p. 9.

2 For Stevens's background, see *Who's Who in Western Canada,* ed. C.W. Parker (Vancouver: Canadian Press Association 1911), 1:350; *Vancouver Sun,* 3 May 1967, p. 3 and 5 May 1967, p. 6; and Henry J. Boam, comp., *British Columbia: Its History, People, Commerce, Industries and Resources* (London: Sells 1912), 180. For his role as trust company director, see *Who's Who and Why,* ed. C.W. Parker (Vancouver: International Press 1914), 5:875 and British Columbia, Attorney-General, Companies Office, Company Registration Files, file 2516 (1897), microfilm reel 15 (Western Canada Trust Company, Ltd.). For club associations, see the *Vancouver Social Register and Club Directory* (Vancouver: Welch and Gibbs 1914), 98, 104, 112, and 122 and *Vancouver Sun,* 6 May 1967, p. 8.

3 *Independent,* 24 November 1900, p. 1 and S.J. Gothard to Richard McBride, 20 October 1909, BCARS, British Columbia Premiers' Papers (1909), Private Correspondence (McBride), doc. 892/1909. Working-class support for Taylor is indicated in *Province,* 14 January 1910, pp. 1 and 3, *Daily News-Advertiser* (hereafter *News-Advertiser*), 21 December 1910, p. 7, and *Vancouver Daily World* (hereafter *World*), 11 January 1910, p. 1, 12 January 1910, p. 1, 6 January 1911, pp. 1 and 5, and 7 January 1911, p. 7. For the Vancouver Trades and Labor Council's endorsement of Taylor in 1911, see *News-Advertiser,* 7 January 1911, p. 4 and *World,* 6 January 1911, pp. 1 and 5, and 3 February 1911, p. 20.

4 Final quotation in *World,* 11 January 1910, p. 1. For Douglas's policies, see *News-Advertiser,* 4 January 1910, p. 11 and *Province,* 9 January 1909, p. 13, 10 January 1910, p. 13, and 13 January 1910, p. 5. For Taylor's policies, see *News-Advertiser,* 30 December 1908, p. 2, 13 January 1909, pp. 1 and 2, and 8 January 1910, p. 6.

5 *Province,* 14 January 1910, p. 3 and *Western Wage-Earner,* February 1910, p. 12. In its 14 January story, the *Province* claimed that Taylor's win had come from 'the solid Socialist vote of perhaps 1500,' which he had received; the Local Option League had given some additional support. Taylor's own newspaper, the *World,* stressed the importance of votes from the hill districts of Fairview and Mount Pleasant, and from the East End.

6 *Vancouver Sun,* 6 May 1967, p. 8 and Richard Wilbur, *H.H. Stevens 1878-1973* (Toronto: University of Toronto Press 1977), 12-14.

7 Quotations from *Vancouver Sun,* 5 May 1967, p. 6.

8 *News-Advertiser,* 7 January 1912, p. 2 and *Vancouver Sun,* 5 June 1946, p. 1.

9 *Vancouver Sun,* 4 May 1967, p. 6; interview with H.H. Stevens by Colleen Toppings (1964), part 2, in UBCSCD, Colleen Toppings Bourke Collection, box 1-2; and *News-Advertiser,* 6 August 1910, p. 10.

10 Quotations from Wilbur, *H.H. Stevens,* 109 and 16.

11 On Stevens's policies, see ibid., 16, 82, and 109ff; *News-Advertiser,* 1 February 1910, p. 1 and 6 August 1910, p. 10; *Province,* 12 January 1910, p. 8; and *Vancouver Sun,* 8 May 1967, p. 10. My interpretation of the history of Stevens's populism differs from that of his biographer, who describes him as a 'latter-day Populist.' See Wilbur, *H.H. Stevens,* 145.

12 *News-Advertiser,* 3 January 1894, p. 8 and 6 January 1894, p. 4 and Vancouver Trades and Labor Council, 6 November 1902, CVA, Add. MSS 307, Minutes, vol. 3 (1902-8), p. 91.

13 British Columbia, Commission on Labour, 1912-14, Transcripts of Evidence (hereafter BCCL, Evidence), 17 January 1913 (J.A. Key), BCARS, RG 684, vol. 1, file 1, p. 69.

14 Canada, Department of Labour, Strikes and Lockouts Files, NAC (hereafter Strikes and Lockouts), RG 27, microfilm reel 3, file 3159A, p. L269; Strikes and Lockouts, RG 27, (revised), vol. 2334, file 3159.5.

15 The relationship between economic and non-economic issues in Vancouver labour disputes is discussed in Robert A.J. McDonald, 'Working Class Vancouver, 1886-1914: Urbanism and Class in British Columbia,' *BC Studies* 69-70 (Spring-Summer 1986):55-6, especially table 5.

16 James Conley, ""Open Shop' Means Closed to Union Men": Carpenters and the 1911 Vancouver Building Trades General Strike,' *BC Studies* 91-2 (Autumn-Winter 1991-2):142. Information on the 1911 building trades strike is drawn from ibid., 127-51; Andrew Yarmie, 'The Right to Manage: Vancouver Employers' Associations, 1900-1923,' *BC Studies* 90 (Summer 1991):58-61; Strikes and Lockouts, RG 27 (revised), vol. 2335, files 3335, 3356, 3365, 3365a, and 3378; Strikes and Lockouts, RG 27, microfilm reel 4, files 3335, 3356, 3365, and 3378; BCCL, Evidence, 20 January 1913 (Charles Cassidy), BCARS, RG 684, vol. 1, file 2, p. 143; 7 March 1913 (J.W. Wilkinson), ibid., vol. 3, file 8, p. 165; 10 March 1913 (J.W. Wilkinson), ibid., vol. 3, file 9, pp. 222-4; and *News-Advertiser*, 26 May 1911, p. 12, 2 June 1911, p. 1, 4 June 1911, pp. 1 and 2, and 27 June 1911, p. 1

17 Quotations from Conley, ""Open Shop' Means Closed to Union Men,"" 139 and 136 and Yarmie, 'Right to Manage,' 58 and 59.

18 In 'Working Class Vancouver' I argued that 15 per cent of Vancouver's 'workforce' was unionized; but I defined 'workforce,' as does the published census, to include business people and professionals as well as wage workers. The 22 per cent figure used here is based on James Conley's figure of 7,277 union members in Vancouver locals in 1911, and is calculated for wage earners only. As in 'Working Class Vancouver,' I continue to assume that about two-thirds of the workforce was working class. See McDonald, 'Working Class Vancouver,' 36 and 45 and James R. Conley, 'Frontier Labourers, Crafts in Crisis, and the Western Labour Revolt: The Case of Vancouver, 1900-1919,' *Labour/Le Travail* 23 (Spring 1989):30.

For the most complete examination of the trade union movement in early Vancouver, see Conley, 'Class Conflict and Collective Action in the Working Class of Vancouver, British Columbia' (PhD dissertation, Carleton University 1986). For women in trade unions, see Star Rosenthal, 'Union Maids: Organized Women Workers in Vancouver 1900-1915,' *BC Studies* 41 (Spring 1979):36-55; Elaine Bernard, *The Long Distance Feeling* (Vancouver: New Star Books 1982); Irene Howard, *The Struggle for Social Justice in British Columbia: Helena Gutteridge, the Unknown Reformer* (Vancouver: UBC Press 1992), chap. 6; and Marie Campbell, 'Sexism in British Columbia Trade Unions, 1900-1920,' in *In Her Own Right: Selected Essays on Women's History in B.C.*, ed. Barbara Latham and Cathy Kess (Victoria: Camosun College 1980), 167-86. For the IWW, see Mark Leier, *Where the Fraser River Flows: The Industrial Workers of the World in British Columbia* (Vancouver: New Star Press 1990); Strikes and Lockouts, RG 27 (revised), vol. 2334, file 3282; *Western Wage-Earner*, August 1910, pp. 14 and 15; and *News-Advertiser*, 21 July 1910, p. 1, 22 July 1910, p. 1, 23 July 1910, p. 14, and 23 July 1910, p. 15. Quotation from A. Ross McCormack, *Reformers, Rebels, and Revolutionaries: The Western Canadian Radical Movement 1899-1919* (Toronto: University of Toronto Press 1977), 102.

19 For labourism, see Craig Heron, 'Labourism and the Canadian Working Class,'

Labour/Le Travail 13 (Spring 1984):45-76.

20 MacMillan was elected for Ward 6 in 1906, 1908, and 1909; Morton for Ward 5 in 1903-6 and 1908-9; Macpherson for Ward 4 in 1903-4 and 1910-11; and Williams for Ward 6 in 1904-6.

21 *News-Advertiser*, 21 February 1908, p. 3, 16 February 1909, p. 8, 11 April 1909, p. 8, 1 February 1910, p. 1, and 11 May 1911, p. 2; *Western Wage-Earner,* July 1910, p. 4; and *World,* 3 February 1911, p. 20.

22 *News-Advertiser*, 26 March 1905, p. 2, 13 February 1906, p. 2, 8 December 1908, p. 2, and 16 December 1909, pp. 1 and 11 and *Western Wage-Earner*, May 1910, p. 5.

23 *News-Advertiser*, 9 February 1909, p. 5; R.H. Sperling to Secretary, London, 20 January 1908, UBCSCD, British Columbia Electric Railway Company Papers, General Managers' Letter Books, AXB 3-3 (January-June 1908), 2565 (quotation); and R.H. Sperling to George Kidd, 20 January 1910, ibid., 3-3 (January-June 1910), 3544.

24 The views of Labourists are expressed in *Independent*, 14 February 1903, p. 3 and *News-Advertiser*, 25 January 1906, p. 2, 10 July 1906, p. 2, 23 October 1908, p. 3, 30 November 1908, p. 2, 12 December 1908, p. 2, 27 April 1909, p. 3, 25 August 1909, p. 2, and 31 December 1909, p. 4. For the federal government's role in alienating water lots to private corporations, see Cicely Lyons, *Salmon: Our Heritage. The Story of a Province and an Industry* (Vancouver: BC Packers 1969), 174-7 and S. McClay to A.E. Blount, 26 June 1916, University of British Columbia Library, Borden Papers re: British Columbia (microfilm), Marine #28,146.

25 For attitudes re: the hospital, see *Independent*, 21 December 1901, p. 4 and 1 February 1902, p. 1. For the city exhibition, see *World*, 6 January 1911, p. 2. For recreation space, see *News-Advertiser*, 24 November 1891, p. 1, 11 October 1893, p. 5, 6 August 1895, p. 3, 31 August 1895, p. 8, 10 December 1895, p. 3, 16 January 1897, p. 5, and 7 September 1898, p. 8; *Independent*, 31 March 1900, p. 4, 5 January 1901, p. 2, and 12 October 1901, p. 2; and Robert A.J. McDonald, '"Holy Retreat" or "Practical Breathing Spot"?: Class Perceptions of Vancouver's Stanley Park, 1910-1913,' *Canadian Historical Review* 65 (June 1984):127-53.

26 Paragraph drawn from McDonald, 'Working Class Vancouver,' 60-1.

27 *News-Advertiser*, 2 September 1910, p. 4, 7 September 1910, p. 4, 20 September 1910, p. 1, 18 January 1911, p. 8 (quotation), 31 May 1911, p. 11, 28 June 1911, p. 2, 19 January 1912, p. 3, and 16 April 1912, p. 9; *Western Wage-Earner*, October 1910, pp. 12-13; *British Columbia Federationist* (hereafter *Federationist*), 20 February 1912, p. 2 and 5 December 1913, p. 8; BCCL, Evidence, 10 March 1913 (F.C. Wade), BCARS, RG 684, vol. 3, file 9, p. 220 and 10 March 1913 (J.W. Wilkinson), ibid., p. 222; and Executive Committee, Vancouver Branch, Industrial Peace Association, to Richard McBride, n.d., BCARS, British Columbia, Premiers' Papers, 1911, Correspondence In, #201/1911.

28 Robert H. Wiebe, *The Search for Order, 1877-1920* (New York: Hill and Wang 1967), 129.

29 *News-Advertiser*, 2 June 1899, p. 4 and 29 July 1900, p. 8; Eugene Forsey, *Trade Unions in Canada 1812-1902* (Toronto: University of Toronto Press 1982), 276.

30 *News-Advertiser*, 4 April 1895, p. 5.

31 Vancouver's booster organizations are examined in Robert A.J. McDonald, 'Business Leaders in Early Vancouver, 1886-1914' (PhD dissertation, University of British Columbia 1977), 320-3.

32 Quotations from *News-Advertiser*, 16 November 1897, p. 5 and 24 November 1897, p. 6. For the plebiscite votes, see *News-Advertiser*, 6 March 1898, p. 7 and 7 July 1901, p. 6.

Debate can be traced in the paper during September 1896, March-April 1897, and October 1897-March 1898.

33 *Independent*, 25 January 1902, p. 1 and 3 May 1902, p. 5; Board of Temperance and Moral Reform of the Methodist Church and the Board of Social Service and Evangelism of the Presbyterian Church, *Vancouver, British Columbia: The Report of ... an Intensive Social Survey ...* (1913) (hereafter cited as Vancouver, *Report of ... Social Survey*), United Church B.C. Conference Archives, Dobson Papers, box A2, file C, pp. 11-12 and 14-15; Petition to the Mayor and Council, n.d., CVA, City Clerk's Correspondence, vol. 13 (1897-8), #10236 (microfilm); and W.H. Callicott to City Clerk, 27 December 1907, CVA, Board of Police Commissioners' Papers, 75-A-4.

34 Quotations from *Independent*, 4 January 1902, p. 4 and *Federationist*, 4 November 1912, p. 2. For Williams, see the CVA, Matthews Collection, Add. MSS 54, file 04940.

35 Quotations from *Independent*, 26 April 1902, p. 3 and BCCL, Evidence, 7 March 1913 (J.W. Wilkinson), BCARS, RG 684, vol. 3, file 8, p. 168.

36 See Mark Leier, 'Which Side Are They On? Bureaucracy, Class, and Ideology in the Vancouver Trades and Labor Council, 1889-1910,' manuscript, 1993, chap. 6.

37 Petition from Women's Christian Temperance Union to the Mayor and Council, 31 July 1891, CVA, City Clerk's Correspondence, 10-A-5, vol. 5, file 4, series 1 (Petitions 1891); BCCL, Evidence, 18 January 1913 (C.F Burkhart), BCARS, RG 684, vol. 1, file 2, p. 104; and 12 March 1913 (C.E. Herritt), ibid., vol. 4, file 1, p. 35.

38 *News-Advertiser*, 9 March 1912, p. 7.

39 Quotation from J. Bird, attorney for the Western Canada Amusement Corporation, to the Mayor, Chairman of the Board of Licence Commissioners, 12 April 1911, CVA, Board of Police Commissioners' Correspondence, 75-A-6, vol. 3, file 4, series 2.

40 East End Improvement and Protective Association to Mayor and Council [Petition], 15 June 1906, CVA, Board of Police Commissioners' Correspondence, 75-A-4, file 13, series 2. Police tolerance of red light districts in Vancouver is explored in Deborah Nilsen, 'The "Social Evil": Prostitution in Vancouver, 1900-1920,' in *In Her Own Right*, ed. Latham and Kess, 205-28.

41 Neil Larry Shumsky, 'Tacit Acceptance: Respectable Americans and Segregated Prostitution, 1870-1910,' *Journal of Social History* 4 (Summer 1986):672 and passim.

42 Deryck W. Holdsworth, 'Cottages and Castles for Vancouver Home Seekers,' *BC Studies* 69-70 (Spring-Summer 1986):11-32 (quotation from p. 31) and Jill Wade, *Houses for All: The Struggle for Social Housing in Vancouver, 1915-50* (Vancouver: UBC Press 1994), 10-11 (quotation). In Chapter 1 of *Houses for All*, Wade provides a critical evaluation of Holdsworth's interpretation of Vancouver housing to 1929.

43 Wade, *Houses for All*, 24-6 and Holdsworth, 'House and Home in Vancouver: Images of West Coast Urbanism, 1886-1929,' in *The Canadian City: Essays in Urban History*, ed. Gilbert A. Stelter and Alan F.J. Artibise (Toronto: McClelland and Stewart 1977), 186.

44 Graeme Wynn, 'The Rise of Vancouver,' in *Vancouver and Its Region*, ed. Graeme Wynn and Timothy Oke (Vancouver: UBC Press 1992), 89-105; Jean Barman, 'Neighbourhood and Community in Interwar Vancouver: Residential Differentiation and Civic Voting Behaviour,' *BC Studies* 69-70 (Spring-Summer 1986): 99-101; Donna McCririck, 'Opportunity and the Workingman: A Study of Land Accessibility and the Growth of Blue Collar Suburbs in Early Vancouver' (MA thesis, University of British Columbia 1981); and Holdsworth, 'House and Home in Vancouver,' 186-211.

45 Quotations from Boam, *British Columbia*, 175 and Holdsworth, 'Cottages and Castles

for Vancouver Home-Seekers,' 29

46 Wynn, 'The Rise of Vancouver,' 144.

47 Wade, *Houses for All*, chap. 1 and Vancouver, *Report of ... Social Survey*, 8 (quotations).

48 The economic function of fraternal societies is discussed in John Charles Herbert Emery, 'The Rise and Fall of Fraternal Methods of Social Insurance: A Case Study of the Independent Order of Oddfellows of British Columbia Sickness Insurance 1874-1951' (PhD dissertation, University of British Columbia 1993). Emery estimates that, before 1930, 'as much as 13% of the province's total population' secured insurance through fraternal organizations (p. 34).

49 Mary Ann Clawson, *Constructing Brotherhood: Class, Gender, and Fraternalism* (Princeton: Princeton University Press 1989), 15, 78, and 253-5.

50 *Henderson's Greater Vancouver, New Westminster and Fraser Valley Directory 1911* (Vancouver: Henderson's Publishing Company 1911), 264. The associational ties of social leaders and civic politicians were determined from a variety of biographical and newspaper sources; I have discussed the elites in two publications, 'Vancouver's "Four Hundred": The Quest for Wealth and Status in Canada's Urban West, 1886-1914,' *Journal of Canadian Studies* 25, 3 (Autumn 1990):55-73 and 'The Business Elite and Municipal Politics in Vancouver 1886-1914,' *Urban History Review* 11, 3 (February 1983):1-14. A variety of new fraternal societies joined the Inlet's first lodge, Mount Hermon Lodge, starting in 1886; see *Vancouver News*, 3 October 1886, p. 1 and 11 December 1886, p. 6; *Vancouver Daily Advertiser*, 10 June 1886, p. 4, and *News-Advertiser*, 21 June 1894, p. 5.

51 Influenced by the work of Mary Ann Clawson, Bryan Palmer is less categorical in more recent work than he had been earlier in asserting that fraternal and benevolent societies were class institutions. See Bryan D. Palmer, *Culture in Conflict: Skilled Workers and Industrial Capitalism in Hamilton, Ontario, 1860-1914* (Montreal: McGill-Queen's University Press 1979), 39-46 and *Working-Class Experience: Rethinking the History of Canadian Labour, 1800-1991*, 2nd ed. (Toronto: McClelland and Stewart 1992), 96. Greg Kealey demonstrates that the Orange Lodge in late-nineteenth-century Toronto was primarily a working-class institution; see 'The Orange Order in Toronto: Religious Riot and the Working Class,' in *Essays in Canadian Working Class History*, ed. Gregory S. Kealey and Peter Warrian (Toronto: McClelland and Stewart 1976), 20. For Cascade Lodge officers, see *News-Advertiser*, 21 November 1888, p. 8. The importance to skilled workers of fraternal society participation in the early 1890s is suggested in the following comment from the Vancouver Trades and Labor Council, 20 May 1892, CVA, Add. MSS 307, Minutes, vol. 1 (1889-97), p. 205: 'Mr. Amos asked if the Trades were going to take part in the 1st July celebration. It was stated in reply that owing to many Union Men belonging [to] Friendly Societies that were taking part it would make our ranks look too small.'

52 John Gilkeson, *Middle-Class Providence 1820-1940* (Princeton: Princeton University Press 1986), 151-60 (quotation from p. 155) and Clawson, *Constructing Brotherhood*, 95-104.

53 For example, see Richard Jules Oestreicher, *Solidarity and Fragmentation: Working People and Class Consciousness in Detroit, 1875-1900* (Urbana and Chicago: University of Illinois Press 1989), 36-8; Jon C. Teaford, *Cities of the Heartland: The Rise and Fall of the Industrial Midwest* (Bloomington and Indianapolis: Indiana University Press 1993), chap. 2; Michael B. Katz, Michael J. Doucet, and Mark J. Stern, *The Social Organization of Early Industrial Capitalism* (Cambridge, MA: Harvard University Press 1982), 27 and 77-9; and Roy Rosenzweig, *Eight Hours for What We Will: Workers and Leisure in an Industrial City, 1870-1920* (Cambridge, MA: Cambridge University Press 1983), 82, 87-9,

106-117, and 225.

54 The notion that citizenship is a socially constructed status is suggested in Bruce Curtis, 'Preconditions of the Canadian State: Educational Reform and the Construction of a Public in Upper Canada, 1837-1846,' in *The 'Benevolent' State: The Growth of Welfare in Canada*, ed. Allan Moscovitch and Jim Albert (Toronto: Garamond Press 1987), 47-67; Lykke De La Cour, Cecilia Morgan, and Mariana Valverde, 'Gender Regulation and State Formation in Nineteenth-Century Canada,' in *Colonial Leviathan: State Formation in Mid-Nineteenth-Century Canada*, ed. Allan Greer and Ian Radforth (Toronto: University of Toronto Press 1992), 163-91; Mariana Valverde, *The Age of Light, Soap, and Water: Moral Reform in English Canada, 1885-1925* (Toronto: McClelland and Stewart 1991), 26; Gillian Creese, 'Class, Ethnicity, and Conflict. The Case of Chinese and Japanese Immigrants, 1880-1923,' in *Workers, Capital, and the State in British Columbia: Selected Papers*, ed. Rennie Warburton and David Coburn (Vancouver: UBC Press 1988), 55-85; and Peter S. Li, *The Chinese in Canada* (Toronto: Oxford University Press 1988), 23-40.

55 The probate records of the nine can be found in BCARS, British Columbia, Attorney-General, Estate Records, BC Supreme Court, Vancouver Probates, GR 1415: file 1917/5146 (Mark A. Beach); file 1935/21,685 (John Crow); file 1926/11,517 (Joseph Dixon); file 1920/6919 (John Adam Fulton); file 1924/9654 (William George); file 1940/26,728 (Walter Hepburn); file 1930/15,960 (Daniel McCormick O'Dwyer); and file 1917/4688 (William Towler); and ibid., New Westminster Probates, GR 1422, file 1935/4805 (Charles Boardman).

56 Mark Beach worked as a street railwayman; the other eight were for a period of their lives in Vancouver skilled artisans. The eight are Charles Boardman (machinist); John Crow (cigar maker, and later cigar manufacturer); Joseph Dixon (carpenter, and later store fixtures manufacturer); John Fulton (typographer); William George (shoemaker, and later city construction foreman); Walter Hepburn (carpenter, and later contractor); D.M. O'Dwyer (painter); and William Towler (bricklayer, and later 'poultry fancier'). Six of the nine belonged to fraternal or ethnic societies such as the Odd Fellows and Sons of England, but none to elite clubs.

57 E.O.S. Scholefield and F.W. Howay, *British Columbia from the Earliest Times to the Present* (Vancouver: S.J. Clarke 1914), 4:1,123-4 (quotation).

Chapter 8: The Immigrant Section

1 Kay J. Anderson, *Vancouver's Chinatown. Racial Discourse in Canada, 1875-1980* (Montreal and Kingston: McGill-Queen's University Press 1991), 17. Also see Robert Miles, *Racism* (London and New York: Routledge 1989), 38-9.

2 Miles, *Racism*, 46.

3 Patricia E. Roy, *Vancouver: An Illustrated History* (Toronto: James Lorimer and Company 1980), 169, tables 7 and 8.

4 This literature includes W. Peter Ward, *White Canada Forever: Popular Attitudes and Public Policy toward Orientals in British Columbia* (Montreal: McGill-Queen's University Press 1978); Patricia E. Roy, *A White Man's Province: British Columbia's Politicians and Chinese and Japanese Immigrants, 1858-1914* (Vancouver: University of British Columbia Press 1989) and 'British Columbia's Fear of Asians, 1900-1950,' in *British Columbia: Historical Readings*, ed. W. Peter Ward and Robert A.J. McDonald (Vancouver: Douglas and McIntyre 1981), 657-70; Gillian Creese, 'Class, Ethnicity, and Conflict: The Case of the Chinese and Japanese Immigrants, 1880-1923,' in *Workers, Capital, and the State in*

British Columbia: Selected Papers, ed. Rennie Warburton and David Coburn (Vancouver: UBC Press 1988), 55-85; and Anderson, *Vancouver's Chinatown*, 3-33.

5 Paragraph drawn from Anderson, *Vancouver's Chinatown*, 20-3, 39-47, 61 (quotation), and 72-3. I am indebted to Anderson for the central idea of this chapter: viz., that social boundaries between groups are negotiated, and not fixed by cultural or physical differences (p. 16); thus, she suggests, the idea of 'race,' while rooted in the broad currents of nineteenth-century European thought, took on new meaning in the context of a recently formed and still fluid settler society in British Columbia. I am much less convinced by the overall argument of *Vancouver's Chinatown*. While the argument – that an analysis of Anglo-European discourse on the category 'Chinese' in Canada reveals Vancouver's Chinatown to have been a European rather than a Chinese construction, symbolizing the 'counter-idea' of what settler society should be – is original and provocative, it becomes much less persuasive as we move across time to the late twentieth century. For a fuller assessment of the book see reviews by Robert McDonald in *Labour/Le Travail* 30 (Fall 1992):279-82; Tina Loo in *Queen's Quarterly* 99, 3 (Fall 1992):705-9; and Timothy J. Stanley in *BC Studies* 97 (Spring 1993):84-7.

6 Anderson, *Vancouver's Chinatown*, 46.

7 Peter S. Li, *The Chinese in Canada* (Toronto: Oxford University Press 1988), 28 and H.F. Angus, 'The Legal Status in British Columbia of Residents of Oriental Race and Their Descendants,' in *The Legal Status of Aliens in Pacific Countries,* ed. Norman MacKenzie (London: Oxford University Press 1937), 77-88. The term 'region of recent settlement' is from John P. Fogerty, 'The Comparative Method and the Nineteenth Century Regions of Recent Settlement,' *Historical Studies* 19 (1981):412-29.

8 Ward, *White Canada Forever*, 65, 80, and 108-9 and Hugh Johnston, *The East Indians in Canada*, Canada's Ethnic Groups Series, Booklet no. 5 (Ottawa: Canadian Historical Association 1984), 6

9 Quotations from Ward, *White Canada Forever*, 82-3; Report of Robert Marrion to Dr. Underhill, 15 January 1912, CVA, Vancouver, Health Department, series 1, Medical Health Officer's Records, *Annual Reports*, PDS 11, 1911; and Johnston, *The East Indians in Canada*, 9. Also see ibid., 6-9; Ward, *White Canada Forever*, 88-93; and Hugh Johnston, *The Voyage of the Komagata Maru: The Challenge to Canada's Colour Bar* (Vancouver: UBC Press 1989).

10 Ward, *White Canada Forever*, 3-117 (quotation from p. 83).

11 Vancouver, Board of Police Commissioners' Minutes, 5 June 1912, CVA, 75-A-7, vol. 3, file 2, series 2; ibid., 14 August 1913, CVA, 75-A-1, Minutes, vol. 3, file 3, series 1; and *Daily News-Advertiser* (hereafter *News-Advertiser*), 23 September 1911, p. 6.

12 Quotation from British Columbia, Commission on Labour, 1912-14, Transcripts of Evidence (hereafter BCCL, Evidence), 7 March 1913 (H. Paper), BCARS, RG 684, vol. 3, file 8. Two newspaper stories placed the city's Italian population in the fall of 1911 at between 5,000 and 6,000; see *News-Advertiser*, 6 September 1911, p. 1 and 14 October 1911, p. 9.

13 The idea and quotations are from Miles, *Racism*, 71-6, as well as 38 and 79. The relationship between colour as a socially constructed identity and class is explored in David R. Roediger, *The Wages of Whiteness: Race and the Making of the American Working Class* (London: Verso 1991).

14 *News-Advertiser*, 28 December 1911, p. 4 and 11 December 1913, p. 7. In another instance – the walkouts by Italian street construction workers in the summer of 1910 – a story in the

News-Advertiser (23 July 1910, p. 15) described the skilled steam shovel operators who stayed at work as 'white men'; by implication, the striking Italian labourers were not 'white.'

15 Report of Robert Marrion to Dr. Underhill, 9 January 1912, CVA, Vancouver, Health Department, series 1, Medical Health Officer's Records, *Annual Reports,* PDS 11, 1911.

16 Creese, 'Class, Ethnicity, and Conflict,' 59-60 and Alicja Muszynski, 'The Creation and Organization of Cheap Wage Labour in the British Columbia Fishing Industry' (PhD dissertation, University of British Columbia 1986), 10-19.

17 For the lumber industry, see Creese, 'Class, Ethnicity, and Conflict,' 71; James Robert Conley, 'Class Conflict and Collective Action in the Working Class of Vancouver, British Columbia, 1900-1919' (PhD dissertation, Carleton University 1986), 213-14 and 217-18; *British Columbia Federationist* (hereafter *Federationist*), 18 July 1913, p. 1; and Roy, *A White Man's Province,* 177. The Japanese were especially prominent as fishermen on the Fraser River, holding 42 per cent of the salmon fishing licences issued in 1900 and almost 50 per cent in 1920; see Ken Adachi, *The Enemy That Never Was: A History of the Japanese Canadians* (Toronto: McClelland and Stewart 1976), 47 and 105. The comment on Japanese worker-fishermen is from James Conley, 'Relations of Production and Collective Action in the Salmon Fishery, 1900-1925,' in Warburton and Coburn, *Workers, Capital, and the State in British Columbia,* 96. For Cumberland, see Lynne Bowen, *Boss Whistle: The Coal Miners of Vancouver Island Remembered* (Lantzville, BC: Oolichan Books 1982), 68, 77-8, and 89.

18 Quotations from Ward, *White Canada Forever,* 16 and Irene Howard, 'Shockable and Unshockable Methodists in *The Innocent Traveller,*' in *Essays on Canadian Writing* 23 (Spring 1982):123.

19 The latter observation is mainly impressionistic. For instance, two East End residents of Strathcona in the early twentieth century, Nora Hendrix and Myer Freedman, recalled Italian shoeshine stands, Italian taxis, and Jewish pedlars in the area; see Daphne Marlatt and Carole Itter, comps. and eds., *Opening Doors: Vancouver's East End* (Victoria: Ministry of Provincial Secretary and Government Services 1979), 63. The term 'penny capitalism' is drawn from John Benson, 'Working-Class Capitalism in Great Britain and Canada, 1867-1914,' *Labour/Le Travail* 12 (Autumn 1983):145-54.

20 Quotations from BCCL, Evidence, 11 March 1913 (J.H. McVety), BCARS, RG 684, vol. 3, file 10 and 7 January 1913 (F.H. McMillan), ibid., vol. 1, file 1.

21 First quotation from *News-Advertiser,* 6 September 1911, p. 1; next two from *Federationist,* 13 November 1914, p. 2.

22 Conley, 'Class Conflict and Collective Action,' 6. The city's Swedes and Norwegians are described as 'lumberjacks' in Vancouver, *Report of ... Social Survey,* 7. The institutional development of Vancouver Swedes is discussed in Irene Howard, *Vancouver's Svenskar: A History of the Swedish Community in Vancouver* (Vancouver: Vancouver Historical Society 1970).

23 Quotations from Martin Allerdale Grainger, *Woodsmen of the West,* New Canadian Library no. 42 (1908; reprint, Toronto: McClelland and Stewart 1964), 13 and *Federationist,* 4 November 1911, p. 2.

24 Paragraph written from Grainger, *Woodsmen of the West,* 13-17. Also see Conley, 'Class Conflict and Collective Action' and *Federationist,* 26 October 1912, p. 2.

25 Pete McMartin, 'Portrait of a Patriarch: Yip Sang 1845-1927,' *Vancouver Sun,* 2 December 1993, p. 1; Paul Yee, *Saltwater City: An Illustrated History of the Chinese in Vancouver* (Vancouver: Douglas and McIntyre 1988), 31-2; and Li, *The Chinese in Canada,* 57.

26 Quotations from Li, *The Chinese in Canada,* 56 and David Chuenyan Lai, *Chinatowns: Towns within Cities in Canada* (Vancouver: UBC Press 1988), 81.
27 Quotations from Marlatt and Itter, *Opening Doors,* 41 and Li, *The Chinese in Canada,* 81.
28 Paul Yee, 'Chinese Business in Vancouver, 1886-1914' (MA thesis, University of British Columbia 1983), 49; and Li, *The Chinese in Canada,* 58-68. Based on evidence presented to the Royal Commission on Chinese and Japanese Immigration, Li asserts that of twenty-seven Chinese women in Vancouver in 1902, sixteen were married to merchants (p. 58). Also see Adachi, *The Enemy That Never Was,* 87-108.
29 For the Japanese, see Adachi, *The Enemy That Never Was,* 50-1, 112, 123, and 131; for the Sikhs, see Johnston, *The East Indians in Canada,* 8-9; and for Italians, see Marlatt and Itter, *Opening Doors,* 29, 41, 70, and 73 and Board of Temperance and Moral Reform of the Methodist Church and the Board of Social Service and Evangelism of the Presbyterian Church, *Vancouver, British Columbia: The Report of ... an Intensive Social Survey* (1913), United Church B.C. Conference Archives, Dobson Papers, box A2, file C, p. 8. The three streets listed in the *Report* were Harris, Union, and Keefer.
30 Quotations from Marlatt and Itter, *Opening Doors,* 33 and 42.
31 Canada, *Sessional Papers,* 1912-13, vol. 21, Department of Indian Affairs, 'Annual Report 1913,' no. 27, pp. 14-15; Canada, Nominal Census 1891, microfilm T-6290, British Columbia, District 2 (New Westminster), Subdistrict C1 (Vancouver City); and *Fifth Census of Canada, 1911,* vol. 2, table 7, pp. 170-1.
32 For employment by Native men as longshoremen, see Rolf Knight, *Indians at Work: An Informal History of Native Indian Labour in British Columbia* (Vancouver: New Star Books 1978), 115 and 123-8. In an interview with Major Matthews on 23 November 1936, August Jack Khahtsahlano stated, 'I had lots of money then [forty years ago]. I work for old Tait [W.L. Tait, sawmill, at Third Avenue and Granville St., afterwards Rat Portage Lumber Co. Mill]; work for him nine years, and then for Jenkins, the logger. [Note: The Tait and Rat Portage sawmills employed many Indians from nearby reserve]'; see Major J.S. Matthews, comp., *Conversations with Khatsahlano, 1932-1954* (Vancouver: City of Vancouver Archives 1955), 55. For examples of Native participation in celebratory events such as carnivals and expositions, see *News-Advertiser,* 25 August 1896, p. 8 and *World,* 7 September 1909, p. 1.
33 The negotiations that led Kitsilano Indian Band members to sell their reserve are outlined in BCARS, British Columbia, Attorney-General, Kitsilano Indian Reserve, 1912-16, GR 1323, file 457-8-12, pp. 21, 29, 33, 44, 71-8, and 83-6.
34 John Taylor, 'The Urban West, Public Welfare, and a Theory of Urban Development,' in *Cities in the West,* ed. A.R. McCormack and I. Macpherson (Ottawa: National Museum of Man 1975), 294.
35 Quotations from *News-Advertiser,* 28 April 1906, p. 22. Also see *News-Advertiser,* 7 June 1904, p. 5, 7 February 1905, p. 2, 22 December 1905, p. 4, and 18 August 1906, p. 2.
36 Quotations from ibid., 16 March 1905, p. 5 and Diane L. [now Indiana] Matters, 'Public Welfare Vancouver Style, 1910-1920,' *Journal of Canadian Studies* 14, 1 (Spring 1979):11.
37 Matters, 'Public Welfare,' 4-6; Jill Wade, *Houses for All: The Struggle for Social Housing in Vancouver, 1919-50* (Vancouver: UBC Press 1994), 22-3; Central City Mission, *Central City Mission, 1908-1958: 50 Years of Service,* CVA, Pamphlet 1958-86; and CVA, City Clerk's Correspondence, vol. 43 (1912) #33124 and #33150 and vol. 45 (1913) #34208 (microfilm).
38 For the history of relief policy in the mid-1890s, see *News-Advertiser,* 6 February 1894, p. 5, 7 February 1894, p. 5, 5 December 1895, p. 6, and 14 December 1895, p. 8 and Tay-

lor, 'The Urban West,' 298-9; for the Charity Organization Movement, see James Pitsula, 'The Emergence of Social Work in Toronto,' *Journal of Canadian Studies* 14, 1 (Spring 1979):35-42 and Paul Boyer, *Urban Masses and Moral Order in America, 1820-1920* (Cambridge, MA: Harvard University Press 1978), 143-61.

39 Quotations from *News-Advertiser*, 6 November 1906, p. 2 and 8 December 1906, p. 1. Also see CVA, Vancouver, Health Department, series 1, Medical Health Officer's Records, *Annual Reports*, PDS 11, 1906, p. 14, 1907, p. 14, and 1908, p. 75.

40 *News-Advertiser*, 11 September 1908, p. 7 and 22 December 1911, p. 7; *World*, 18 March 1909, p. 6; Taylor, 'The Urban West,' 298-9 and 302-3; and Matters, 'Public Welfare,' 5-6 (quotation).

41 Quotations from *News-Advertiser*, 30 December 1911, p. 2 and the *Vancouver Daily Province*, 15 August 1912, p. 26. Also see *News-Advertiser*, 11 December 1907, p. 3, 18 December 1909, p. 2, 30 December 1911, p. 2, and 11 December 1913, p. 7.

42 Quotation from *News-Advertiser*, 26 May 1912, p. 1. Also see the CVA, Vancouver, Health Department, series 1, Medical Health Officer's Records, *Annual Reports*, PDS 11, 1906-13. An example of the anxiety that 'foreign' immigrants were causing local health officials is suggested in the April 1911 statement of Dr. F.T. Underhill, Vancouver's MHO, that the city was 'on the verge of a serious situation through the rapid influx of an indigent population, for which there is no adequate means of caring' (*News-Advertiser*, 28 April 1911, p. 1).

43 CVA, Vancouver, Health Department, series 1, Medical Health Officer's Records, *Annual Reports*, PDS 11, 1912, p. 21; Wade, *Houses for All*, 17-23; and *News-Advertiser*, 23 September 1911, p. 6.

44 Margaret W. Andrews, 'Medical Services in Vancouver, 1886-1920: A Study of the Interplay of Attitudes, Medical Knowledge and Administrative Structures' (PhD dissertation, University of British Columbia 1979), 1, 3-7, 17-18, 20-2, and 33; *News-Advertiser*, 14 October 1911, p. 9 and 26 May 1912, p. 1; and Roy, *Vancouver: An Illustrated History*, 176 n. 43. For comparative purposes, see Terry Copp, *The Anatomy of Poverty: The Condition of the Working Class in Montreal, 1897-1929* (Toronto: McClelland and Stewart 1974), 100 and Alan F.J. Artibise, *Winnipeg: A Social History of Urban Growth, 1874-1914* (Montreal: McGill Queen's University Press 1975), 31. Medical health officials and others often commented on Vancouver's plentiful supply of fresh water; see *News-Advertiser*, 21 August 1891, p. 12 and 31 October 1912, p. 2.

45 The lack of accessible and usable public space in Vancouver is noted in *News-Advertiser*, 11 October 1893, p. 5; *Independent*, 20 October 1900, p. 3, 2 February 1901, p. 2, and 12 October 1901, p. 2; *Federationist*, 6 July 1912, p. 2; and George Feaver, '"Self-Respect and Hopefulness": The Webbs in the Canadian West,' *BC Studies* 43 (Autumn 1979):59.

46 *Mount Pleasant Early Days: Memoirs of Reuben Hamilton, Pioneer 1890* (Vancouver: City Hall 1957), 14, in CVA, Pamphlet 1957-60.

47 Quotation from *News-Advertiser*, 12 September 1911, p. 1. For business concern about crowded streets, see Dickson's Importing Company to the Mayor, Chairman of the Board of Licence Commissioners, 21 July 1911, CVA, Board of Police Commissioners' Correspondence, 75-A-1, vol. 2, file 2, series 1 and Woodward's Department Store to Mayor, Chairman of the Board of Licence Commissioners, 15 October 1912, ibid., 75-A-7, vol. 4, file 14, series 2 and 18 October 1912, ibid., 75-A-1, vol. 3, file 3, series 1.

48 BCCL, Evidence, 11 March 1913 (J.H. McVety), BCARS, RG 684, vol. 3, file 10, p. 324.

49 Susan G. Davis, *Parades and Power: Street Theatre in Nineteenth-Century Philadelphia*

(Philadelphia: Temple University Press 1986), 13-14.

50 The phrase 'contested terrain' is used by Davis in *Parades and Power,* 14 and Judith R. Walkowitz, *City of Dreadful Delight: Narratives of Sexual Danger in Late-Victorian London* (Chicago: University of Chicago Press 1992), 41-80.

51 This and subsequent paragraphs are drawn from Mark Leier's thorough study of the free speech conflicts in Vancouver; see 'Solidarity on Occasion: The Free Speech Fights of 1909 and 1912,' *Labour/Le Travail* 23 (Spring 1989):39-64 and *Where the Fraser River Flows: The Industrial Workers of the World in British Columbia* (Vancouver: New Star Books 1990), 64-85. The three quotations, in order of appearance, are from: *News-Advertiser,* 11 September 1907, p. 1; Leier, 'Solidarity on Occasion,' 48; and *Federationist,* 8 June 1912, in UBCSCD, Colleen Toppings Bourke Collection, box 1-3.

52 Quotations from Leier, 'Solidarity on Occasion,' 39 and *Where the Fraser River Flows,* 71, 76, and 83. 'Street meetings' quotation originally from *Federationist.*

53 *Western Wage-Earner,* February 1910, cited in Leier, 'Solidarity on Occasion,' 62-3.

54 Letter from a longshoreman to the Mayor, Chairman of the Board of Licence Commissioners, 22 April 1912, CVA, Board of Police Commissioners' Correspondence, 75-A-7, vol. 4, file 14, series 2.

55 CVA, Vancouver, Police Department, Prisoners' Record Books, 1898-1917, series 2, 1906, pp. 70-157, Loc.76-C-2 and ibid., 1913, pp. 28-159, Loc.116-E-1.

56 The phrase 'arrest waves' is taken from Eric H. Monkkonen, *Police in Urban America 1860-1920* (Cambridge: Cambridge University Press 1981), 74-5. Also see James P. Huzel, 'The Incidence of Crime in Vancouver during the Great Depression,' in *Vancouver Past: Essays in Social History,* ed. Robert A.J. McDonald and Jean Barman (Vancouver: University of British Columbia Press 1986), 227; John C. Weaver, *Crimes, Constables, and Courts: Order and Transgression in a Canadian City, 1816-1970* (Montreal and Kingston: McGill-Queen's University Press 1995), 108-18 and 131-9; and Deborah Nilsen, '"The Social Evil": Prostitution in Vancouver, 1900-1920,' in *In Her Own Right: Selected Essays on Women's History in B.C.,* ed. Barbara Latham and Cathy Kess (Victoria: Camosun College 1980), 205-28.

57 The birthplaces of those arrested in 1906 and 1913 were: USA, 27.1 per cent and 32.5 per cent; Britain, 28.2 per cent and 22.4 per cent; Canada, 24.1 per cent and 20.6 per cent; Europe, 8.2 per cent and 16.5 per cent; Asia, 11.8 per cent and 7.3 per cent; and other, 0.6 per cent and 0.6 per cent. The breakdown by sex is: 1906, male 97.1 per cent and female 2.9 per cent; and 1913, male 74.0 per cent and female 26.0 per cent. The non-White portion of those arrested equalled 20.1 per cent of the total in 1906 and 20.2 per cent in 1913. When sorted by racial group the percentages are, for 1906 and 1913: Asian, 11.8 per cent and 7.3 per cent; Black, 6.5 per cent and 12.0 per cent; and Native or Mixed-Blood, 1.8 per cent and 0.9 per cent. Among Americans, Blacks in 1906 constituted 10.9 per cent of the total; this percentage was made up of 8 Black men and 2 Black women. By 1913, the percentage of Blacks among the Americans arrested had increased to 32.3 per cent; of these, 47 were women (18.5 per cent of the American total) and 35 were men (13.8 per cent).

Conclusion

1 The idea that class consciousness is likely to emerge first at the top of the social spectrum is far from novel. See, for instance, Jean Barman, 'Ethnicity in the Pursuit of Status: British Middle and Upper-Class Emigration to British Columbia in the Late

Nineteenth and Early Twentieth Centuries,' *Canadian Ethnic Studies* 18, 1 (1986):45; Robert Galois and Cole Harris, 'Recalibrating Society: The Population Geography of British Columbia in 1881,' *The Canadian Geographer* 38, 1 (1994):51; C. Wright Mills, *The Power Elite* (New York: Oxford University Press 1956), 30; and John N. Ingham, *The Iron Barons: A Social Analysis of an American Urban Elite, 1874-1965* (Westport, CT: Greenwood Press 1978), 227.

2 The point is illustrated well by a comparison of Vancouver's economic structure with that of American midwestern cities described in Jon C. Teaford, *Cities of the Heartland: The Rise and Fall of the Industrial Midwest* (Bloomington and Indianapolis: Indiana University Press 1993), 48-71 and 102-11.

3 American historians have discovered that ethnicity functioned both as a foundation of class identity and as a source of division among working people. For a sampling of the extensive American literature on this subject, see James R. Barrett, 'Unity and Fragmentation: Class, Race, and Ethnicity on Chicago's South Side, 1900-1920,' in '*Struggle a Hard Battle': Essays on Working-Class Immigrants*, ed. D. Hoerder (DeKalb, IL: Northern Illinois University Press 1986), 229-53 and Richard Jules Oestreicher, *Solidarity and Fragmentation: Working People and Class Consciousness in Detroit, 1875-1900* (Urbana and Chicago: University of Illinois Press 1989).

4 James Robert Conley, 'Class Conflict and Collective Action in the Working Class of Vancouver, British Columbia, 1900-1919' (PhD dissertation, Carleton University 1986), 255.

5 Robert Miles, *Racism* (London: Routledge 1989), 38.

6 Oestreicher, *Solidarity and Fragmentation*, 222-3 and 230-3.

Select Bibliography

Archival Sources, Collections, and Government Sources

Alexander, R.H. 'Reminiscences of the Early Days of British Columbia.' Vancouver Art, Historical, and Scientific Society Records. Add. MSS 336. City of Vancouver Archives

Allan, Marjorie. *Christ Church Cathedral, 1889-1939: A Short History.* Pamphlet. Vancouver: University Press 1939. Special Collections Division. University of British Columbia Library.

Angus, Anne Margaret. *Children's Aid Society of Vancouver, B.C., 1901-1951.* Pamphlet 1951-71. City of Vancouver Archives

Bank of Vancouver. Papers. RG 19. National Archives of Canada

Bell, John Warren. Memoirs. Add. MSS 144. City of Vancouver Archives

Bell-Irving Family. Papers. Add. MSS 001 and 592. City of Vancouver Archives

Board of Temperance and Moral Reform of the Methodist Church and the Board of Social Service and Evangelism of the Presbyterian Church. *Vancouver, British Columbia: The Report of ... an Intensive Social Survey ...* 1913. Hugh Dobson Papers. United Church B.C. Conference Archives. University of British Columbia

Borden, Sir Robert. Borden Papers re: British Columbia. University of British Columbia Library. Microfilm

Bourke, Colleen Toppings. Collection. Special Collections Division. University of British Columbia Library

British Columbia. Attorney-General. Company Registration Files. Companies Office, Victoria

–. Attorney-General. Coroners' Inquests. GR 431. British Columbia Archives and Records Service

–. Attorney-General. Correspondence In, 1872-1910, 1911-14. GR 429, GR 1323, and GR 1324. British Columbia Archives and Records Service. Microfilm

–. Attorney-General. Estate Records. BC Supreme Court. Vancouver Probates, GR 1415 and GR 1416. New Westminster Probates, GR 1422. Victoria Probates, GR 1304. British Columbia Archives and Records Service

–. Commission on Labour, 1912-14. Transcripts of Evidence. RG 684. British Columbia Archives and Records Service

–. Legislative Assembly. 'Timber Inspector's Reports.' *Sessional Papers,* 1892-1911

–. Legislative Assembly. 'Tabulated List of Companies Incorporated, Licensed and Registered in the Province of British Columbia Made up to 31 October 1912.' *Sessional Papers,* 1913

–. Superintendent of Education Correspondence, 1872-1897. University of British Columbia Library. Microfilm

British Columbia Electric Railway Company. Papers. Special Collections Division. University of British Columbia Library

Canada. *Census of Canada,* 1881, 1891, 1901, 1911, 1921

–. Department of Labour. *Labour Gazette,* 1901-15

–. Department of Labour, Strikes and Lockouts Files. RG 27 original and revised. National Archives of Canada. Microfilm

–. Department of Labour. *Wages and Hours of Labour in Canada, 1901-1921.* Ottawa: King's Printer 1921

–. Nominal Census 1881. British Columbia, Division 187 (New Westminster), Subsection B (S.D. North), pp. 86-114 and Subsection D7 (Coast of Mainland), pp. 35-44 and 50 62. Microfilm C-13284

–. Nominal Census 1891. British Columbia, District 2 (New Westminster), Subdistrict A (Burrard Inlet), Division 2a, pp. 20-42, and Subdistrict C1-C11 (Vancouver City). Microfilm T-6290

–. Royal Commission on Chinese Immigration. *Report.* Ottawa: Queen's Printer 1885

. Royal Commission on Dominion-Provincial Relations *Report.* Book 1, *Canada, 1867-1939.* 1940. Reprint, Ottawa: Queen's Printer 1954

–. *Sessional Papers,* 1878, Vol. 8 and 1879, Vol. 6. Department of the Interior, Indian Affairs Branch Annual Reports

–. *Sessional Papers,* 1885. Vol. 18. Department of Indian Affairs Annual Reports

Canadian Pacific Railway Company. Correspondence Outward. Letterbooks of Sir William Van Horne and Sir Thomas G. Shaughnessy. MG28 III 20. National Archives of Canada. Microfilm

–. Papers. Add. MSS 54. City of Vancouver Archives

Central City Mission. *Central City Mission, 1908-1958: 50 Years of Service.* Pamphlet 1958-96. City of Vancouver Archives

Cowan, Harry. Papers. Special Collections Division. University of British Columbia Library

Deighton, John. Correspondence Outward, 1870. E/B/D36. British Columbia Archives and Record Service

Doyle, Henry. 'Rise and Decline of the Pacific Salmon Fisheries.' Special Collections Division. University of British Columbia Library. Manuscript

Duncan, Nora. *The Heroine of Moodyville: An Epic of Burrard Inlet, 1883.* Pamphlet 1936-52. City of Vancouver Archives

Electoral History of British Columbia. Victoria: Elections British Columbia and the Legislative Library 1988

Hamilton, Reuben. *Mount Pleasant Early Days: Memoirs of Reuben Hamilton, Pioneer 1890.* Pamphlet 1957-60. City of Vancouver Archives

Knights of Pythias. Papers. Add. MSS 760. City of Vancouver Archives

–. Royal Lodge No. 6. *25th Anniversary Roll Call, 8 June 1914.* Pamphlet 14-1. City of Vancouver Archives

Laurier, Sir Wilfrid. Laurier Papers re: British Columbia. University of British Columbia Library. Microfilm

McBride, Sir Richard. Private Correspondence. British Columbia Premiers' Papers. GR 441. British Columbia Archives and Records Service

McCulley, James. Correspondence Outward, 1875. E/C/M13. British Columbia Archives and Records Service

Matthews, Major J.S. Collection. Add. MSS 54. City of Vancouver Archives

–. 'Early Vancouver: Narratives of Pioneers of Vancouver, B.C.' 1932-56. 7 vols. City of Vancouver Archives. Typescript

Mechanics' Institute of British Columbia. Minutes. Vancouver Art, Historical and Scientific Society Records. Add. MSS 336. City of Vancouver Archives

Ministerial Union of the Lower Mainland of B.C. *The Crisis in B.C.: An Appeal for Investigation.* Pamphlet. Vancouver: Saturday Sunset Press 1916. Special Collections Division. University of British Columbia

Mount Hermon Lodge. Membership Lists, 1869-85. Freemasons Records. Add. MSS 002. British Columbia Archives and Records Service

Parnes, Jessie. 'History of St. James.' Add. MSS 570. City of Vancouver Archives

Pleming, William. Papers. Add. MSS 132. City of Vancouver Archives

Rogers, Benjamin T. Private Letter Book. BC Sugar Company Archives

Shaughnessy, Sir Thomas G. Correspondence Inward (cited as Shaughnessy Papers). Canadian Pacific Railway Corporate Archives

Sweeny, Campbell. Papers. Add. MSS 022. City of Vancouver Archives

Tate, Rev. Charles Montgomery. Papers. Add. MSS 303. British Columbia Archives and Records Service

Terminal City Club, Papers. Add. MSS 309. City of Vancouver Archives

Vancouver. Board of Trade, *Annual Reports,* 1887-1914. Add. MSS 300. City of Vancouver Archives

–. City Clerk's Department Records [By-laws, Correspondence Inward, Correspondence Outward, City Council Minutes, Nomination Papers, Record of Elections, and Voters' Lists]. City of Vancouver Archives

–. *Financial Statements and Annual Reports.* PDS 1.3. City of Vancouver Archives

–. Health Department. Medical Health Officer's Records. PDS 11. City of Vancouver Archives

–. Park Board Records [Correspondence, Minutes, Journals, Newsclippings, and Photographs]. City of Vancouver Archives

–. Police Board and Police Department Records [General Files, Minutes, Photographs, Prisoners' Record Books, and Scrapbook. City of Vancouver Archives

–. Police Court Records. City of Vancouver Archives

Vancouver Club. Papers. Add. MSS 306. City of Vancouver Archives

Vancouver Law Association. Minutes, 1892-1902. Law Society of British Columbia Archives

Vancouver Trades and Labor Council. Minutes, 1889-1914. Add. MSS 307. City of Vancouver Archives. Microfilm

Van der Burg, Jessie M. 'A History of the Union Steamship Company of British Columbia, 1889-1943.' [1943?] Special Collections Division. University of British Columbia Library. Manuscript

Van Horne, Sir William. Correspondence Inward (cited as Van Horne Papers). RG 1. Canadian Pacific Railway Corporate Archives

Walker, Edmund. Papers. Thomas Fisher Rare Book Room. University of Toronto Library

Selected Periodicals

British Columbia Federationist, Vancouver, 1911-15

British Columbia Financial Times, Vancouver, 1914-15

British Columbia Gazette, 1873-1913

Daily Colonist, Victoria, 1887-1914 (Title varies: *Daily British Colonist,* 1872-86)

Daily News-Advertiser, Vancouver, 1887-1917 (Title varies)

Independent, Vancouver, 1900-4

Mainland Guardian, New Westminster, 1873-83

Monetary Times, Montreal, 1890-1914

Saturday Sunset, Vancouver, 1912-15

Vancouver Daily Advertiser, 1886-7

Vancouver Daily Province, 1900-52 (Title varies: *Province,* 1898-1900)

Vancouver Daily World, 1888-1914

Vancouver News, 1886-7

Vancouver Sun, 1912-14

Victoria Daily Times, 1884-1914

Western Clarion, Vancouver, 1903-14

Western Wage-Earner, Vancouver, 1909-11

Westminster Hall Magazine (1909-16)

Westward Ho! Magazine (1907-10). (Title varies: *Man-to-Man Magazine,* 1910-11, and *British Columbia Magazine,* 1911-15)

Books and Articles

Abbott, Carl. *Boosters and Businessmen: Popular Economic Thought and Urban Growth in the Antebellum Middle West.* Westport, CT: Greenwood Press 1981

Acheson, T.W. 'Changing Social Origins of the Canadian Industrial Elite, 1880-1910.' *Business History Review* 47 (1973):189-217

Adachi, Ken. *The Enemy That Never Was: A History of the Japanese Canadians.* Toronto: McClelland and Stewart 1976

Anderson, Kay J. *Vancouver's Chinatown: Racial Discourse in Canada, 1875-1980.* Montreal and Kingston: McGill-Queen's University Press 1991

Armstrong, Christopher, and H.V. Nelles. *Monopoly's Moment: The Organization and Regulation of Canadian Utilities, 1830-1930.* Philadelphia: Temple University Press 1986

Artibise, Alan F.J. *Winnipeg: A Social History of Urban Growth, 1874-1914.* Montreal and

Kingston: McGill-Queen's University Press 1975

–, ed. *Town and City.* Regina: Canadian Plains Research Center, University of Regina 1981

Artibise, Alan F.J., and Gilbert A. Stelter. *Canada's Urban Past: A Bibliography to 1980 and Guide to Canadian Urban Studies.* Vancouver: University of British Columbia Press 1981

Bailey, Peter. 'Will the Real Bill Banks Please Stand Up?: Towards a Role Analysis of Mid-Victorian Working Class Respectability.' *Journal of Social History* 12 (Spring 1979):336-53

Baltzell, Digby E. *Philadelphia Gentlemen: The Making of a National Upper Class.* Chicago: Quandrangle Books 1971

Barman, Jean. *Growing up British in British Columbia: Boys in Private Schools.* Vancouver: University of British Columbia Press 1984

–. 'Ethnicity in the Pursuit of Status: British Middle and Upper-Class Emigration to British Columbia in the Late Nineteenth and Early Twentieth Centuries.' *Canadian Ethnic Studies* 18, 1 (1986):32-52

–. 'Neighbourhood and Community in Interwar Vancouver: Residential Differentiation and Civic Voting Behaviour.' *BC Studies* 69-70 (Spring-Summer 1986):97-142

–. *The West beyond the West: A History of British Columbia.* Toronto: University of Toronto Press 1991

Barnett, Homer G. *The Coast Salish of British Columbia.* Westport, CT: Greenwood Press 1975

Barth, Gunter, ed. *All Quiet on the Yamhill: The Civil War in Oregon. The Journal of Corporal A. Bensell.* Eugene: University of Oregon 1959

–. *Instant Cities: Urbanization and the Rise of San Francisco and Denver.* New York: Oxford University Press 1975

Bartlett, Eleanor A. 'Real Wages and the Standard of Living in Vancouver, 1901-1929.' *BC Studies* 51 (Autumn 1981):3-63

Beeghley, Leonard. *Social Stratification in America: A Critical Analysis of Theory and Research.* Santa Monica, CA: Goodyear Publishing 1978

Bellan, Ruben. *Winnipeg First Century: An Economic History.* Winnipeg: Queenston House Publishing 1978

Bell-Irving, Elizabeth. *Crofton House School: The First Ninety Years, 1898-1988.* Vancouver: Crofton House School 1988

Belshaw, John. 'The Standard of Living of British Miners on Vancouver Island, 1848-1900.' *BC Studies* 84 (Winter 1989-90):37-64

Bender, Thomas. *Community and Social Change in America.* New Brunswick, NY: Rutgers University Press 1978

Bendix, Reinhard. 'Inequality and Social Structure: A Comparison of Marx and Weber.' *American Sociological Review* 39 (April 1974):149-61

Bendix, Reinhard, and Seymour Martin Lipset, eds. *Class, Status and Power: A Reader in Social Stratification.* Glencoe, IL: The Free Press 1953

Benson, John. 'Working-Class Capitalism in Great Britain and Canada, 1867-1914.' *Labour/Le Travail* 12 (Autumn 1983):145-54

Bernard, Elaine. *The Long Distance Feeling.* Vancouver: New Star Books 1982

Bertram, G.W. 'Historical Statistics on Growth and Structure of Manufacturing in Canada, 1870-1957.' In Canadian Political Science Association, *Conference on Statistics, 1962 and 1963,* edited by H. Henripin and A. Asimakopulous. Toronto: Canadian Political Science Association and University of Toronto Press 1964

Best, Geoffrey. *Mid-Victorian Britain, 1851-1875*. London: Weidenfeld and Nicolson 1971

Billington, Ray Allen. *America's Frontier Heritage*. New York: Holt, Rinehart and Winston 1966

Bingham, Janet. *Samuel Maclure, Architect*. Ganges, BC: Horsdal and Schubart 1985

Bliss, Michael. *Northern Enterprise: Five Centuries of Canadian Business*. Toronto: McClelland and Stewart 1987

Bloomfield, Elizabeth. 'Boards of Trade and Canadian Urban Environment.' *Urban History Review* 8, 2 (October 1983):77-99

Boam, Henry J. *British Columbia: Its History, People, Commerce, Industry and Resources*. London: Sells 1912

Bodnar, John. *Immigration and Industrialization: Ethnicity in an American Mill Town, 1870-1940*. Pittsburgh: University of Pittsburgh Press 1977

Bourdieu, Pierre. *Distinction: A Social Critique of the Judgement of Taste*. Cambridge, MA: Harvard University Press 1984

Boutilier, Helen. 'Vancouver's Earlier Days.' *British Columbia Historical Quarterly* 10 (1946):151-71

Bowen, Lynne. *Boss Whistle: The Coal Miners of Vancouver Island Remembered*. Lantzville, BC: Oolichan Books 1982

Boyer, Paul. *Urban Masses and Moral Orders in America, 1820-1920*. Cambridge, MA and London: Harvard University Press 1978

Bradley, A.G. *Canada in the Twentieth Century*. London: Archibald Constable 1905

Bradstreet's Book of Commercial Ratings: Dominion of Canada. Vol. 174. New York: Bradstreet Company 1911

Briggs, Asa. *Victorian Cities*. Harmondsworth: Penguin Books 1968

The British Columbia Directory for 1882-83. Victoria: R.T. Williams 1882

Brooks, G.W.S. 'Edgar Crow Baker: An Entrepreneur in Early British Columbia.' *BC Studies* 31 (Autumn 1976):23-34

Buckley, Kenneth A. *Capital Formation in Canada, 1896-1930*. rev. ed. Toronto: University of Toronto Press 1974

Burke, Peter. *History and Social Theory*. Cambridge: Polity Press 1992

Cail, Robert E. *Land, Man and the Law: The Disposal of Crown Lands in British Columbia, 1871-1913*. Vancouver: University of British Columbia Press 1974

Cannadine, David. 'Cutting Classes.' *New York Review of Books* 17 (December 1992):52-7

Carr, Emily. *Growing Pains: The Autobiography of Emily Carr*. Toronto: Oxford University Press 1946

Chadwick, George F. *The Park and the Town: Public Landscape in the 19th and 20th Centuries*. London: Architectural Press 1966

Chandler, Alfred D., Jr. *The Visible Hand. The Managerial Revolution in American Business*. Cambridge, MA: Harvard University Press 1977

Chittenden, Newton H. *Travels in British Columbia*. 1882. Reprint, Vancouver: G. Soules 1984

Clark, Norman. *Mill Town: A Social History of Everett, Washington*. Seattle: University of Washington Press 1970

Clawson, Mary Ann. *Constructing Brotherhood: Class, Gender and Fraternalism*. Princeton: Princeton University Press 1989

Clement, Wallace. *The Canadian Corporate Elite: An Analysis of Economic Power*. Toronto:

McClelland and Stewart 1975

Cole, Douglas, and Bradley Lockner, eds. *The Journals of George M. Dawson*. Vol. 1, *British Columbia, 1875-1878*. Vancouver: UBC Press 1990

Conley, James Robert. 'Frontier Labourers, Crafts in Crisis, and the Western Labour Revolt: The Case of Vancouver, 1900-1919.' *Labour/Le Travail* 23 (Spring 1989):9-37

–. '"Open Shop' Means Closed to Union Men": Carpenters and the 1911 Vancouver Building Trades General Strike.' *BC Studies* 91-2 (Autumn-Winter 1991-2):127-52

Cook, Ramsay. 'Tillers and Toilers: The Rise and Fall of Populism in Canada in the 1890s.' Canadian Historical Association *Historical Papers* (1984):1-21

Copp, Terry. *The Anatomy of Poverty: The Condition of the Working Class in Montreal, 1897-1929*. Toronto: McClelland and Stewart 1974

Cox, Thomas R. *Mills and Markets: A History of the Pacific Coast Lumber Industry to 1900*. Seattle: University of Washington Press 1974

Craven, Paul. '*An Impartial Umpire': Industrial Relations and the Canadian State 1900-1911*. Toronto: University of Toronto Press 1980

Cronin, Kay. *Cross in the Wilderness*. Vancouver: Mitchell Press 1960

Cruikshank, Ken. *Close Ties: Railways, Government, and the Board of Railway Commissioners, 1851-1933*. Montreal and Kingston: McGill-Queen's University Press 1991

Curtis, James, E., and William G. Scott, eds. *Social Stratification: Canada*. Scarborough, ON: Prentice-Hall 1973

Davidoff, Leonore. *The Best Circles: Society Etiquette and the Season*. London: Croom Helm 1973

Davidoff, Leonore, and Catherine Hall. *Family Fortunes: Men and Women of the English Middle Class, 1780-1850*. Chicago: University of Chicago Press 1987

Davis, E.A., ed. *Commemorative Review of the Methodist, Presbyterian and Congregational Churches in British Columbia*. Vancouver: Wrigley Printing 1925

Davis, Susan. *Parades and Power: Street Theatre in Nineteenth-Century Philadelphia*. Philadelphia: Temple University Press 1986

Doyle, Don Harrison. *The Social Order of a Frontier Community: Jacksonville, Illinois, 1825-1870*. Urbana: University of Illinois Press 1978

Duff, Wilson. *The Upper Stalo Indians*. Victoria: British Columbia Provincial Museum 1952

Eagle, John A. *The Canadian Pacific Railway and the Development of Western Canada, 1896-1914*. Kingston: McGill-Queen's University Press 1989

Easterbrook, W.T. and H.G.J. Aitken. *Canadian Economic History*. Toronto: University of Toronto Press 1956

Elite Directory of Vancouver. Vancouver: Thomson Stationery Company 1908

Evenden, L.J., ed. *Vancouver: Western Metropolis*. Victoria: University of Victoria 1978

Fairburn, Miles. *The Ideal Society and Its Enemies: The Foundations of Modern New Zealand Society 1850-1900*. Auckland, NZ: Auckland University Press 1989

Feaver, George. '"Self-Respect and Hopefulness": The Webbs in the Canadian West.' *BC Studies* 43 (Autumn 1979):45-65

Field, Fred W. *Capital Investments in Canada*. 3rd ed. Montreal: Monetary Times of Canada 1914

Fisher, Robin. '*BC Studies* and British Columbia History.' *BC Studies* 100 (Winter 1993-4):59-77

Fitzpatrick, Peter, ed. *Dangerous Supplements: Resistance and Renewal in Jurisprudence*.

London: Pluto Press 1991

Fogerty, John P. 'The Comparative Method and the Nineteenth Century Regions of Recent Settlement.' *Historical Studies* 19 (1981):412-29

Foner, Eric. *Free Soil, Free Labor, Free Men: The Ideology of the Republican Party before the Civil War.* New York: Oxford University Press 1970

Forsey, Eugene. *Trade Unions in Canada 1812-1902.* Toronto: University of Toronto Press 1982

Foster, John F., ed. *The Developing West.* Edmonton: University of Alberta Press 1983

Frank, David. 'Of Pride, Parades and Picnics: Labour Days Past.' *New Maritimes* 8, 1 (October 1989):5-7

Frisch, Michael. 'American Urban History as an Example of Recent Historiography.' *History and Theory* 18 (1979):350-77

Galois, Robert, and Cole Harris. 'Recalibrating Society: The Population Geography of British Columbia in 1881.' *The Canadian Geographer* 38, 1 (1994):37-54

Ghent, Maynard, and Frederick Cople Jaher. 'The Chicago Business Elite: 1830-1930. A Collective Biography.' *Business History Review* 50 (Autumn 1976):288-328

Giddens, Anthony. *The Class Structure of the Advanced Societies.* London: Hutchison 1980

Giddens, Anthony, and David Held, eds. *Classes, Power and Conflict: Classical and Contemporary Debates.* Berkeley: University of California Press 1982

Gilkeson, John S., Jr. *Middle-Class Providence, 1820-1940.* Princeton: Princeton University Press 1986

Goodwyn, Lawrence. *Democratic Promise: The Populist Movement in America.* New York: Oxford University Press 1976

Gosnell, R. Edward. *The Year Book of British Columbia.* Victoria: n.p. 1897

–. *A History of British Columbia.* Vancouver and Victoria: British Columbia Historical Association 1913

Gould, Julius, and William L. Kolb, eds. *A Dictionary of the Social Sciences.* New York: Free Press 1964

Grainger, Martin Allerdale. *Woodsmen of the West.* New Canadian Library no. 42. 1908. Reprint, Toronto: McClelland and Stewart 1964

Grant, George M. *Ocean to Ocean: Sandford Fleming's Expedition through Canada in 1872.* Rutland, VT: C.F. Tuttle 1967

Green, George. 'Some Pioneers of Light and Power.' *British Columbia Historical Quarterly* 2 (1938):153-60

Greer, Allan, and Ian Radforth, eds. *Colonial Leviathan: State Formation in Mid-Nineteenth Century Canada.* Toronto: University of Toronto Press 1992

Griffen, Clyde, and Sally Griffen. *Natives and Newcomers: The Ordering of Opportunity in Mid-Nineteenth Century Poughkeepsie.* Cambridge, MA: Harvard University Press 1978

Haig, Robert Murray. *Reports of the Board of Taxation, with a Report on Taxation in the Province of British Columbia by Robert Murray Haig.* Victoria: Wm. H. Cullin 1919

Hall, Roger, William Westfall, and Laurel Sefton MacDowell, eds. *Patterns of the Past: Interpreting Ontario's History.* Toronto and Oxford: Dundurn Press 1988

Harris, Cole. 'Industry and the Good Life around Idaho Peak.' *Canadian Historical Review* 66, 3 (September 1985):315-43

Hedges, James B. *Building the Canadian West: The Land and Colonization Policies of the Canadian Pacific Railway.* New York: Macmillan 1971

Held, David, and John B. Thompson, eds. *Social Theory of Modern Societies: Anthony Gid-*

dens and His Critics. Cambridge: Cambridge University Press 1989

Henderson's Greater Vancouver City Directory for 1914. Vancouver: Henderson Publishing Company 1914

Henderson's Greater Vancouver, New Westminster and Fraser Valley Directory 1911. Vancouver: Henderson Publishing Company 1911

Heron, Craig. 'Labourism and the Canadian Working Class.' *Labour/Le Travail* 13 (Spring 1984):45-76

Hobson, J.A. *Canada To-day*. London: T.F. Unwin 1906

Hoerder, D., ed. *'Struggle a Hard Battle': Essays on Working-Class Immigrants*. DeKalb, IL: Northern Illinois University Press 1986

Holdsworth, Deryk W. 'Cottages and Castles for Vancouver Homeseekers.' *BC Studies* 69-70 (Spring-Summer 1986):11-32

Holt, Blanche E. 'Women of the West in Clubland: The Athenaeum Club, Vancouver, B.C.' *British Columbia Magazine* 7 (1911):188-90

Homel, Gene Howard. 'Fading Beams of the Nineteenth Century: Radicalism and Early Socialism in Canada's 1890s.' *Labour/Le Travailleur* 5 (1980):7-33

Hopkins, Castell J. *Canadian Annual Review of Public Affairs, 1907-1914*. Toronto: Canadian Review Company 1907

Houston, W.R., ed. *The Annual Financial Review, Canadian*. Toronto: W. Briggs 1912-14

Howard, Irene. *Vancouver's Svenskar: A History of the Swedish Community in Vancouver*. Vancouver: Vancouver Historical Society 1970

–. 'Shockable and Unshockable Methodists in *The Innocent Traveller*.' *Essays on Canadian Writing* 23 (Spring 1982):107-34

–. *The Struggle for Social Justice in British Columbia: Helena Gutteridge, the Unknown Reformer*. Vancouver: UBC Press 1992

Howay, F.W. 'Early Settlement on Burrard Inlet.' *British Columbia Historical Quarterly* 1 (April 1937):101-43

–. 'Early Shipping in Burrard Inlet, 1863-1870.' *British Columbia Historical Quarterly* 1 (April 1937):3-20

Hunt, Lynn, ed. *The New Cultural History*. Berkeley: University of California Press 1989

Ingham, John N. 'The American Urban Upper Class: Cosmopolitans or Locals?' *Journal of Urban History* 2, 1 (November 1975):67-87

–. *The Iron Barons: A Social Analysis of an American Urban Elite, 1874-1965*. Westport, CT: Greenwood Press 1978

Ionescu, Ghita, and Ernest Gellner, eds. *Populism: Its Meaning and National Characteristics*. London: Weidenfeld and Nicolson 1969

Jaher, Frederick Cople, ed. *The Rich, The Well Born, and the Powerful: Elites and Upper Classes in History*. Urbana: University of Illinois Press 1973

–. *The Urban Establishment: Upper Strata in Boston, New York, Charleston, Chicago, and Los Angeles*. Urbana: University of Illinois Press 1982

Johnson, J.K. *Becoming Prominent: Regional Leadership in Upper Canada, 1791-1841*. Kingston and Montreal: McGill-Queen's University Press 1989

Johnston, Hugh. *The East Indians in Canada*. Canada's Ethnic Groups Series, booklet no. 5. Ottawa: Canadian Historical Association 1984

–. *The Voyage of the Komagata Maru: The Challenge to Canada's Colour Bar*. Vancouver: UBC Press 1989

Joyce, Patrick. *Work, Society and Politics: The Culture of the Factory in Later Victorian Eng-*

land. London: Methuen 1982

–. *Visions of the People: Industrial England and the Question of Class 1848-1914.* New York: Cambridge University Press 1991

Kalman, Harold, Ron Phillips, and Robin Ward. *Exploring Vancouver: The Essential Architectural Guide.* Vancouver: UBC Press 1993

Katz, Michael B. *The People of Hamilton, Canada West: Families and Class in a Mid-Nineteenth Century City.* Cambridge, MA: Harvard University Press 1975

Katz, Michael B., Michael J. Doucet, and Mark J. Stern. *The Social Organization of Early Industrial Capitalism.* Cambridge, MA: Harvard University Press 1982

Kazin, Michael. 'The Great Exception Revisited: Organized Labor and Politics in San Francisco and Los Angeles, 1870-1940.' *Pacific Historical Review* 55 (August 1986):371-403

Kazin, Michael, and Steven J. Ross. 'America's Labor Day: The Dilemma of a Workers' Celebration.' *Journal of American History* 78 (March 1992):1,294-1,323

Kealey, Gregory S., ed. *Class, Gender and Region: Essays in Canadian Historical Sociology.* St. John's: Committee on Canadian Labour History 1988

Kealey, Gregory S., and Peter Warrian, eds. *Essays in Canadian Working Class History.* Toronto: McClelland and Stewart 1976

Keenleyside, Hugh. *Memoirs of Hugh L. Keenleyside.* Vol. 1, *Hammer the Golden Day.* Toronto: McClelland and Stewart 1981

Kent, Christopher. 'Presence and Absence: History, Theory, and the Working Class.' *Victorian Studies* 29 (Spring 1986):437-49

Kerr, J.B. *Biographical Dictionary of Well-Known British Columbians.* Vancouver: Kerr and Begg 1890

Kleinig, John. *Paternalism.* Totowa, NJ: Rowman and Allanheld 1984

Kluckner, Michael, ed. *M.I. Rogers 1869-1965.* Vancouver: privately printed 1987

Knight, Rolf. *Indians at Work: An Informal History of Native Indian Labour in British Columbia.* Vancouver: New Star Books 1978

Knights, Peter R. *The Plain People of Boston 1830-1860: A Study in City Growth.* New York: Oxford University Press 1971

Lai, David Chuenyan. *Chinatowns: Towns within Cities in Canada.* Vancouver: UBC Press 1988

Lamb, W.K. 'The Trans-Pacific Service, 1887-1891.' *British Columbia Historical Quarterly* 1 (1937):143-64

–. 'Robie L. Reid (1866-1945): A Memoir.' *British Columbia Historical Quarterly* 9 (1945):79-89

Lang, Marjory, and Linda Hale. 'Women of *The World* and Other Dailies: The Lives and Times of Vancouver Newspaperwomen in the First Quarter of the Twentieth Century.' *BC Studies* 85 (Spring 1990):3-33

Larsen, Lawrence H. *The Urban West at the End of the Frontier.* Lawrence: Regents Press of Kansas 1978

Lascelles, Thomas A., O.M.I. *Mission on the Inlet.* Vancouver: St. Paul's Province, Order of the Oblates of Mary Immaculate 1984

Latham, Barbara, and Cathy Kess, eds. *In Her Own Right: Selected Essays on Women's History in B.C.* Victoria: Camosun College 1980

Latham, Barbara, and Roberta Pardzo, eds. *Not Just Pin Money: Selected Essays on the History of Women's Work in British Columbia.* Victoria: Camosun College 1984

Lawrence, Joseph C. 'Markets and Capital: A History of the Lumber Industry of British Columbia, 1778-1952.' *British Columbia Historical Quarterly* 1 (1937):9-20

Leacock, Stephen. *Arcadian Adventures with the Idle Rich*. New Canadian Library no. 10. 1914. Reprint, Toronto: McClelland and Stewart 1969

Leier, Mark. 'Solidarity on Occasion: The Free Speech Fights of 1909 and 1912.' *Labour/Le Travail* 23 (Spring 1989):39-64

–. *Where the Fraser River Flows: The Industrial Workers of the World in British Columbia*. Vancouver: New Star Books 1990

–. 'Ethnicity, Urbanism, and Labour Aristocracy: Rethinking Vancouver Trade Unionism, 1889-1909.' *Canadian Historical Review* 74 (December 1993):510-34

Lewis, Alfred H. *South Vancouver Past and Present*. Vancouver: Western Publishing 1920

Li, Peter S. *The Chinese in Canada*. Toronto: Oxford University Press 1988

Lipset, Seymour Martin, and Reinhard Bendix. *Social Mobility in Industrial Society*. Berkeley and Los Angeles: University of California Press 1959

Lipset, Seymour Martin, and Aldo Salari, eds. *Elites in Latin America*. New York: Oxford University Press 1967

Logan, Harry T. *Tuum Est: A History of the University of British Columbia*. Vancouver: University of British Columbia Press 1958

Love, Peter. *Labour and the Money Power: Australian Labour Populism 1890-1950*. Melbourne: Melbourne University Press 1984

Lower, A.R.M. *The North American Assault of the Canadian Forest*. Toronto: Ryerson Press 1938

Lower Mainland University Committee. *University Location in British Columbia: A Summary of the Arguments* ... n.p.: 1910

Lutz, John. 'Losing Steam: The Boiler and Engine Industry as an Index of British Columbia's Deindustrialization 1880-1915.' Canadian Historical Association *Historical Papers* (1988):168-209

–. 'After the Fur Trade: The Aboriginal Labouring Class of British Columbia 1849-1890.' *Journal of the Canadian Historical Association* n.s. 3 (1992):69-94

Lyons, Cicely. *Salmon: Our Heritage. The Story of a Province and an Industry*. Vancouver: BC Packers 1969

McCormack, A. Ross. *Reformers, Rebels and Revolutionaries: The Western Canadian Radical Movement 1899-1919*. Toronto: University of Toronto Press 1977

McCormack, A.R., and Ian Macpherson, eds. *Cities in the West*. Ottawa: National Museum of Man 1975

MacDonald, Norbert. 'The Business Leaders of Seattle, 1880-1910.' *Pacific Northwest Quarterly* 50 (January 1959):1-13

–. 'Population Growth and Change in Seattle and Vancouver, 1880-1960.' *Pacific Historical Review* 39 (1970):297-320

–. 'The Canadian Pacific Railway and Vancouver's Development to 1900.' *BC Studies* 35 (Autumn 1977):3-36

–. *Distant Neighbors: A Comparative History of Seattle and Vancouver*. Lincoln: University of Nebraska Press 1987

McDonald, Robert A.J. 'City-Building in the Canadian West: A Case Study of Economic Growth in Early Vancouver, 1886-1893.' *BC Studies* 43 (Autumn 1979):3-29

–. 'The Business Elite and Municipal Politics in Vancouver 1886-1914.' *Urban History Review* 11 (February 1983):1-14

–. '"Holy Retreat" or "Practical Breathing Spot"?: Class Perceptions of Vancouver's Stanley Park, 1910-1913.' *Canadian Historical Review* 65 (June 1984):127-53

–. 'Working Class Vancouver, 1886-1914: Urbanism and Class in British Columbia.' *BC Studies* 69-70 (Spring-Summer 1986):33-70

–. 'Vancouver's "Four Hundred": The Quest for Wealth and Status in Canada's Urban West, 1886-1914.' *Journal of Canadian Studies* 25 (Autumn 1990):55-73

MacKenzie, Norman, ed. *The Legal Status of Aliens in Pacific Countries.* London: Oxford University Press 1937

McNall, Scott G., Rhonda F. Levine, and Rick Fantasia, eds. *Bringing Class Back In: Contemporary and Historical Perspectives.* Boulder, CO: Westview Press 1991

McNaught, Kenneth. *A Prophet in Politics: A Biography of J.S. Woodsworth.* Toronto: University of Toronto Press 1959

Marlatt, Daphne. *Ana Historic: A Novel.* Toronto: Coach House Press 1988

Marlatt, Daphne, and Carole Itter, comps. and eds. *Opening Doors: Vancouver's East End.* Victoria: Ministry of Provincial Secretary and Government Services 1979

Marshall, T.H., and Tom Bottomore. *Citizenship and Social Class.* London: Pluto Press 1991

Matters, Diane L. [now Indiana]. 'Public Welfare Vancouver Style, 1910-1921.' *Journal of Canadian Studies* 14, 1 (Spring 1979):3-15

Matthews, Major J.S. *Conversations with Khatsahlano, 1932-1954.* Vancouver: City of Vancouver Archives 1955

Maud, Ralph, ed. *The Salish People.* Vancouver: Talonbooks 1978

Meggs, Geoff. *Salmon: The Decline of the British Columbia Fishery.* Vancouver: Douglas and McIntyre 1991

Meyer, Kurt B., and Walter Buckley. *Class and Society.* 3rd ed. New York: Random House 1970

Meyers, Gustavus. *A History of Canadian Wealth.* New York: Argosy-Antiquarian 1968

Miles, Robert. *Racism.* London and New York: Routledge 1989

Miller, William, ed. *Men in Business.* New York: Harper Torchbooks, 1962

Mills, Wright C. 'The American Business Elite: A Collective Portrait.' *Journal of Economic History* 6 (1945):20-44

–. *The Power Elite.* New York: Oxford University Press 1956

Monkkonen, Eric H. *Police in Urban America 1860-1920.* Cambridge: Cambridge University Press 1981

Montgomery, David. *Beyond Equality: Labor and the Radical Republicans 1862-1872.* New York: A. Knopf 1967

Morgan, H.J., ed. *The Canadian Men and Women of the Time.* 2nd ed. Toronto: W. Briggs 1912

Morley, Alan. *Vancouver: From Milltown to Metropolis.* Vancouver: Mitchell Press 1961

Moscovitch, Allan, and Jim Albert, eds. *The 'Benevolent' State: The Growth of Welfare in Canada.* Toronto: Garamond Press 1987

Mouat, Jeremy. 'The Politics of Coal: A Study of the Wellington Miner's Strike of 1890-91.' *BC Studies* 77 (Spring 1988):3-29

–. 'The Genesis of Western Exceptionalism: British Columbia's Hard Rock Miners, 1895-1903.' *Canadian Historical Review* 71 (September 1990):317-45

–. *Roaring Days: Rossland's Mines and the History of British Columbia.* Vancouver: UBC Press 1995

Mullins, Christine, and Arthur E. Harvey. *Russell & DuMoulin: The First Century 1889-

1989. Vancouver: Russell and DuMoulin 1990

Neufeld, E.P. *The Financial System of Canada: Its Growth and Development.* Toronto: Macmillan 1972

Newcomer, Mabel. *The Big Business Executive: The Factors That Made Him.* New York: Columbia University Press 1955

Newell, Dianne. 'The Rationality of Mechanization in the Pacific Salmon Canning Industry before the Second World War.' *Business History Review* 62 (Winter 1988):626-55

–. *The Development of the Pacific Salmon Industry: A Grown Man's Game.* Montreal and Kingston: McGill-Queen's University Press 1989

Newman, Peter C. *The Canadian Establishment.* Vol. 2. Toronto: McClelland and Stewart 1981

Nicol, Eric. *Vancouver.* Toronto: Doubleday 1970

Norcross, Blanche. *The Company on the Coast.* Nanaimo: Nanaimo Historical Society 1983

Norrie, Kenneth, and Douglas Owram. *A History of the Canadian Economy.* Toronto: Harcourt Brace Jovanovich 1991

Oestreicher, Richard Jules. *Solidarity and Fragmentation: Working People and Class Consciousness in Detroit, 1875-1900.* Urbana and Chicago: University of Illinois Press 1989

Ormsby, Margaret A. *British Columbia: A History.* rev. ed. Toronto: Macmillan 1971

Palmer, Bryan D. 'Modernizing History,' and Michael Katz, 'Reply.' Committee on Labour History, *Bulletin* 2 (Autumn 1976):16-31

–. 'Most Uncommon Common Men: Craft and Culture in Historical Perspective.' *Labour/Le Travailleur* 1 (1976):6-31

–. *A Culture in Conflict: Skilled Workers and Industrial Capitalism in Hamilton, Ontario, 1860-1914.* Montreal: McGill-Queen's University Press 1979

–. *Working-Class Experience: The Rise and Reconstitution of Canadian Labour, 1880-1980.* Toronto: Butterworth 1983

–. *Working-Class Experience: Rethinking the History of Canadian Labour, 1880-1991.* 2nd ed. Toronto: McClelland and Stewart 1992

Parker, C.W. *Who's Who in Western Canada.* Vancouver: Canadian Press Association 1911

–. *Who's Who and Why.* Vancouver: International Press 1914

Parkin, Frank. *Marxism and Class Theory: A Bourgeois Critique.* London: Tavistock 1979

Parkin, G.R. *The Great Dominion.* London: Macmillan 1895

Parr, Joy. *The Gender of Breadwinners: Women, Men and Change in Two Industrial Towns, 1880-1950.* Toronto: University of Toronto Press 1990

Paterson, D.G. *Direct British Investment in Canada, 1890-1914.* Toronto: University of Toronto Press 1976

Peake, Frank Alexander. *The Anglican Church in British Columbia.* Vancouver: Mitchell Press 1959

Phillips, Paul. *No Power Greater: A Century of Power in British Columbia.* Vancouver: BC Federation of Labour 1967

Picken, M., comp. *City of Vancouver. Terminus of the Canadian Pacific Railway; British Columbia Handbook.* Vancouver: Vancouver Daily News 1887

Pitsula, James. 'The Emergence of Social Work in Toronto.' *Journal of Canadian Studies* 14, 1 (Spring 1979):35-42

Piva, Michael. *The Condition of the Working Class in Toronto, 1900-1921.* Ottawa: University of Ottawa Press 1979

Porter, John. *The Vertical Mosaic: An Analysis of Class and Power in Canada.* Toronto:

University of Toronto Press 1965

Prentice, Alison, Paula Bourne, Gail Cuthbert Brandt, Beth Light, Wendy Mitchinson, and Naomi Black. *Canadian Women: A History.* Toronto: Harcourt Brace Jovanovich 1988

Rajala, Richard A. 'Bill and the Boss: Labor Protest, Technological Change, and the Transformation of the West Coast Logging Camp, 1890-1930.' *Journal of Forest History* 33 (October 1989):168-79

Ralston, H. Keith. 'Patterns of Trade and Investment on the Pacific Coast, 1867-1892.' *BC Studies* 1 (1968-9):37-45

Rasporich, Anthony W., and Henry C. Klassen, eds. *Prairie Perspectives 2.* Toronto: Holt, Rinehart and Winston 1973

–. *Frontier Calgary: Town, City and Region 1875-1914.* Calgary: University of Calgary Press, McClelland and Stewart West 1975

Regehr, T.D., ed. *The Possibilities of Canada are Truly Great: Memoirs, 1906-1924.* Toronto: Macmillan 1971

Robbins, William G. *Hard Times in Paradise: Coos Bay, Oregon, 1850-1986.* Seattle: University of Washington Press 1988

Roberts, Morley. *The Western Avernus: or, Toil and Travel in Further North America.* New Westminster: A. Constable 1896

–. *The Prey of the Strongest.* London: T. Fisher Unwin 1906

Robin, Martin. *The Rush for Spoils: The Company Province, 1871-1933.* Toronto: McClelland and Stewart 1972

Roediger, David R. *The Wages of Whiteness: Race and the Making of the American Working Class.* London: Verso 1991

Rogers, E.H., ed. *Jonathan Rogers.* Vancouver: 1948

Rogers, M.I. *B.C. Sugar.* Vancouver: British Columbia Sugar Refining Company 1958

Rose, George MacLean, ed. *A Cyclopaedia of Canadian Biography; Being Chiefly Men of the Time.* Toronto: Rose Publishing 1888

Rosenthal, Star. 'Union Maids: Organized Women Workers in Vancouver 1900-1915.' *BC Studies* 41 (Spring 1979):36-55

Rosenzweig, Roy. *Eight Hours for What We Will: Workers and Leisure in an Industrial City, 1870-1920.* Cambridge: Cambridge University Press 1983

Ross, Victor. *A History of the Canadian Bank of Commerce.* Toronto. Oxford University Press 1920

Roth, Gunther, and Claus Wittich, eds. *Economy and Society: An Outline of Interpretive Sociology.* New York: Bedminster Press 1968

Roy, Patricia E. 'The B.C.E.R. and Its Street Railway Employees.' *BC Studies* 16 (Winter 1972-3):3-24

–. 'The Preservation of the Peace in Vancouver: The Aftermath of the Anti-Chinese Riot of 1887.' *BC Studies* 31 (Autumn 1976):44-59

–. 'British Columbia's Fear of Asians, 1900-1950.' *Histoire sociale/Social History* 13, 25 (May 1980):161-72

–. 'Progress, Prosperity and Politics: The Railway Policies of Richard McBride.' *BC Studies* 47 (Autumn 1980):3-28

–. *Vancouver: An Illustrated History.* Toronto: James Lorimer 1980

–. *A White Man's Province: British Columbia's Politicians and Chinese and Japanese Immigrants, 1858-1914.* Vancouver: UBC Press 1989

Rubinstein, W.D. *Wealth and the Wealthy in the Modern World.* London: Croom Helm 1980

Russell, L., ed. *Forging a Consensus: Historical Essays on Toronto.* Toronto: University of Toronto Press 1984

Saywell, John T., ed. *The Canadian Journal of Lady Aberdeen 1893-1898.* Toronto: Champlain Society 1960

Scholefield, E.O.S., and F.W. Howay. *British Columbia from the Earliest Times to the Present.* Vols. 3 and 4. Vancouver: S.J. Clarke 1914

Schreiner, John. *The Refiners: A Century of BC Sugar.* Vancouver: Douglas and McIntyre 1989

Shumsky, Neil Larry. 'Tacit Acceptance: Respectable Americans and Segregated Prostitution, 1870-1910.' *Journal of Social History* 4 (Summer 1986):205-28

Simon, Matthew. 'New British Investment in Canada, 1865-1914.' *Canadian Journal of Economics* 3 (1970):238-54

Sinclair, Bertrand W. *The Inverted Pyramid.* Toronto: Frederick D. Goodchild 1924

Speisman, Stephen A. 'Munificent Parsons and Municipal Parsimony: Voluntary vs Public Poor Relief in Nineteenth Century Toronto.' *Ontario History* 65 (1973):32-49

Stelter, Gilbert A., and Alan F.J. Artibise, eds. *The Canadian City: Essays in Urban History.* Toronto: McClelland and Stewart 1977

–. *Shaping the Urban Landscape: Aspects of the Canadian City-Building Process.* Ottawa: Carleton University Press 1982

St. Maur, Mrs. Algeron. *Impressions of a Tenderfoot during a Journey in the Far West.* London: J. Murray 1890

Strong-Boag, Veronica. 'The Girl of the New Day: Canadian Working Women in the 1920s.' *Labour/Le Travailleur* 4 (1979):131-65

Teaford, Jon C. *Cities of the Heartland: The Rise and Fall of the Industrial Midwest.* Bloomington and Indianapolis: Indiana University Press 1993

Thernstrom, Stephen. *Poverty and Progress: Social Mobility in a Nineteenth-Century City.* Cambridge, MA: Harvard University Press 1964

Thompson, Wilbur R. *A Preface to Urban Economics.* Baltimore: Johns Hopkins Press 1965

Thornburn, Hugh, ed. *Party Politics in Canada.* 2nd ed. Toronto: Prentice-Hall 1967

Towler, Edward M. 'Old-Timers Interviewed.' *Pacific Coast Lumberman* 4 (April 1920):39

Tuck, Hugh J. 'The United Brotherhood of Railway Employees in Western Canada, 1898-1995.' *Labour/Le Travailleur* 11 (Spring 1983):63-89

Turner, Bryan S., ed. *Citizenship and Social Theory.* London: Sage 1993

Tupper, Isabel Marion. *The History of the Georgian Club.* Vancouver: Georgian Club 1961

United Brotherhood of Carpenters and Joiners of America, Local 452. *The First Hundred Years.* Vancouver: United Brotherhood, Local 452 1990

Valverde, Mariana. *The Age of Light, Soap and Water: Moral Reform in English Canada, 1885-1925.* Toronto: McClelland and Stewart 1991

Vancouver Social Register and Club Directory. Vancouver: Welch and Gibbs 1914

Van Nus, Walter. 'The Fate of City Beautiful Thought in Canada, 1893-1930.' Canadian Historical Association *Historical Papers* (1975):191-210

Verchère, David R. *A Progression of Judges: A History of the Supreme Court of British Columbia.* Vancouver: UBC Press 1988

Vernède, R.E. *The Fair Dominion: A Record of Canadian Impressions.* London: K. Paul,

Trench, Trubner 1911

Viner, Jacob. *Canada's Balance of International Indebtedness 1900-1913*. Cambridge, MA: Harvard University Press 1924

Wade, Jill. *Houses for All: The Struggle for Social Housing in Vancouver, 1915-50*. Vancouver: UBC Press 1994

Walkem, W. Wymond. *Stories of Early British Columbia*. Vancouver: News-Advertiser 1914

Walkowitz, Daniel J. *Worker City, Company Town: Iron and Cotton-Worker Protest in Troy and Cohoes, New York, 1855-84*. Urbana: University of Illinois Press 1981

Walkowitz, Judith R. *City of Dreadful Delight: Narratives of Sexual Danger in Late-Victorian London*. Chicago: University of Chicago Press 1992

Warburton, Rennie. 'Race and Class in British Columbia: A Comment.' *BC Studies* 49 (Spring 1981):79-85

Warburton, Rennie, and David Coburn, eds. *Workers, Capital and the State in British Columbia: Selected Papers*. Vancouver: UBC Press 1988

Ward, Robin. *Robin Ward's Vancouver*. Madeira Park: Harbour Publishing 1990

Ward, W. Peter. *White Canada Forever: Popular Attitudes and Public Policy toward Orientals in British Columbia*. Montreal: McGill-Queen's University Press 1978

-. 'Class and Race in the Social Structure of British Columbia, 1870-1939.' *BC Studies* 45 (Spring 1980):17-35

-. 'Race and Class in British Columbia: A Reply.' *BC Studies* 50 (Summer 1981):52

Ward, W. Peter, and Robert A.J. McDonald, eds. *British Columbia: Historical Readings*. Vancouver: Douglas and McIntyre 1981

Weaver, John C. *Crimes, Constables, and Courts: Order and Transgression in a Canadian City, 1816-1970*. Montreal and Kingston: McGill-Queen's University Press 1995

Weston, Garnett. 'Vancouver's Trust and Insurance Companies.' *British Columbia Magazine* 7 (1911).19 25

Wiebe, Robert H. *The Search for Order, 1877-1920*. New York: Hill and Wang 1967

Wilbur, Richard. *H.H. Stevens 1878-1973*. Toronto: University of Toronto Press 1977

Wiley, Norbert, ed. *The Marx-Weber Debate*. Newbury Park, CA: Sage 1987

Williams' Illustrated Official British Columbia Directory 1892. Victoria: R.T. Williams 1892

Wilson, William H. 'J. Horace McFarland and the City Beautiful Movement.' *Journal of Urban History* 7 (May 1981):320-39

Wilton, Carol, ed. *Beyond the Law: Lawyers and Business in Canada, 1830 to 1930*. Essays in the History of Canadian Law Series vol. 4. Toronto: Osgoode Society 1990

Working Lives Collective. *Working Lives: Vancouver 1886-1986*. Vancouver: New Star Books 1985

Wright, Eric Olin. *Class, Crisis, and the State*. London: NLB 1978

Wynn, Graeme, and Timothy Oke, eds. *Vancouver and Its Regions*. Vancouver: UBC Press 1992

Yarmie, Andrew. 'The Right to Manage: Vancouver Employer's Associations, 1900-1923.' *BC Studies* 91 (Summer 1991):40-75

Yee, Paul. *Saltwater City: An Illustrated History of the Chinese in Vancouver*. Vancouver: Douglas and McIntyre 1988

Theses, Dissertations, and Papers

Andrews, Margaret W. 'Medical Services in Vancouver, 1886-1920: A Study of the Interplay of Attitudes, Medical Knowledge and Administrative Structures.' PhD dissertation, University of British Columbia 1979

Brooks, F.G.H. 'Vancouver's Origins.' MA thesis, University of British Columbia 1952

Conley, James Robert. 'Class Conflict and Collective Action in the Working Class of Vancouver, British Columbia, 1900-1919.' PhD dissertation, Carleton University 1986

Emery, John Charles Herbert. 'The Rise and Fall of Fraternal Methods of Social Insurance: A Case Study of the Independent Order of Oddfellows of British Columbia Sickness Insurance 1874-1951.' PhD dissertation, University of British Columbia 1993

Foran, Max. 'The Calgary Town Council, 1854-1895: A Study of Local Government in a Frontier Environment.' MA thesis, University of Calgary 1970

Gibson, E.M.W. 'The Impact of Social Belief on Landscape Change: A Geographical Study of Vancouver.' PhD dissertation, University of British Columbia 1972

Grantham, Ronald. 'Some Aspects of the Socialist Movement in British Columbia.' MA thesis, University of British Columbia 1942

Gray, Stephen. 'Forest Policy and Administration in British Columbia, 1912-1928.' MA thesis, Simon Fraser University 1981

Hinds, Diane B. 'The Evolution of Urban Public Design in Europe and America: Vancouver Adaptation to 1913.' MA thesis, University of British Columbia 1979

Holdsworth, Deryk W. 'House and Home in Vancouver: The Emergence of a West Coast Landscape 1886-1929.' PhD dissertation, University of British Columbia 1981

Hunt, Ian. 'Mutual Enlightenment in Early Vancouver, 1886-1916.' PhD dissertation, University of British Columbia 1986

Johnson, Ross Alfred. 'No Compromise – No Trading: The Marxist Socialist Tradition in British Columbia.' PhD dissertation, University of British Columbia 1975

Leier, Mark. 'Which Side Are They On? Bureaucracy, Class and Ideology in the Vancouver Trades and Labour Council, 1889-1910.' Typescript 1993

Leonard, Frank. '"A Thousand Blunders": The Grand Trunk Pacific Railway and Northern British Columbia, 1902-1919.' PhD dissertation, York University, 1989

Loosemore, Thomas Robert. 'The British Columbia Labor Movement and Political Action, 1879-1906.' MA thesis, University of British Columbia 1954

McCririck, Donna. 'Opportunity and the Workingman: A Study of Land Accessibility and the Growth of Blue Collar Suburbs in Early Vancouver.' MA thesis, University of British Columbia 1981

McDonald, Robert A.J. 'Business Leaders in Early Vancouver, 1886-1914.' PhD dissertation, University of British Columbia 1977

–. 'West Coast Capitalism: The Structure of Business Leadership in Vancouver, British Columbia, 1890-1913.' Paper presented to the BC Studies Conference, Simon Fraser University 1988

McKee, William C. 'The History of the Vancouver Park System 1886-1929.' MA thesis, University of Victoria, 1976

Mosher, S.P. 'The Social Gospel in British Columbia: Social Reform as a Dimension of Religion, 1900-1920.' MA thesis, University of British Columbia 1974

Mouat, Jeremy. 'Mining in the Settler Dominions: A Comparative Study of the Industry in Three Communities from the 1880s to the First World War.' PhD dissertation, University of British Columbia 1988

Muszynski, Alicja. 'The Creation and Organization of Cheap Wage Labour in the British Columbia Fishing Industry.' PhD dissertation, University of British Columbia 1986

Naughton, E. Momilani. 'Hawaiians in the Fur Trade: Cultural Influence on the North West Coast, 1811-1875.' MA thesis, Western Washington University 1983

Ralston, H. Keith. 'The 1900 Strike of Fraser River Sockeye Salmon Fishermen.' MA thesis, University of British Columbia 1965

Robertson, Angus Everett. 'The Pursuit of Power, Profit, and Privacy: A Study of Vancouver's West End Elite, 1886-1914.' MA thesis, University of British Columbia 1977

Roy, Patricia E. 'Railways, Politicians and the Development of the City of Vancouver as a Metropolitan Centre 1886-1929.' MA thesis, University of Toronto 1963

–. 'The British Columbia Electric Railway Company, 1897-1928.' PhD dissertation, University of British Columbia 1970

Thom, William Wylie. 'The Fine Arts in Vancouver, 1886-1930: An Historical Survey.' MA thesis, University of British Columbia 1969

Wade, Jill. '"Shaughnessy" or "Slum"? Home or Homelessness? Marginal Housing in Vancouver, 1886-1950.' Typescript 1993

Weiss, Gillian. '"As Women and as Citizens": Clubwomen in Vancouver 1910-1928.' PhD dissertation, University of British Columbia 1983

Woodward-Reynolds, Kathleen Marjorie. 'A History of the City and District of North Vancouver.' MA thesis, University of British Columbia 1943

Yee, Paul. 'Chinese Business in Vancouver, 1886-1914.' MA thesis, University of British Columbia 1983

Index